D1246941

The First Book of The Bible

GENESIS

The First Book of The Bible

GENESIS

interpreted by

B. JACOB

His Commentary abridged, edited, and translated

by

Ernest I. Jacob and Walter Jacob

KTAV PUBLISHING HOUSE, INC.

NEW YORK

FERNALD LIBRARY
COLBY WOMEN'S COLLEGE
NEW LONDON, N.H. 03257

BS
1230
J2721/3
1974

3/21/25 Eastern 11.25

© COPYRIGHT 1974
ERNEST I. JACOB AND WALTER JACOB

Library of Congress Cataloging in Publication Data

Jacob, Benno, 1862-1945.
  The first book of the Bible: Genesis.

  Abridged translation of Das erste Buch der Tora:
Genesis.
  Bibliography: p.
  1. Bible. O.T. Genesis—Commentaries. I. Jacob, Ernest
I., ed. II. Jacob, Walter, 1930- ed. III. Bible. O.T.
Genesis. English. 1974. IV. Title.
BS1235.J2713 1974   222'11'077   74-1007
ISBN 0-87068-246-6

66287

MANUFACTURED IN THE UNITED STATES OF AMERICA

TABLE OF CONTENTS

Foreword

Exactly forty years—the traditional term in the Bible for a generation —have elapsed since Benno Jacob's great commentary on *Genesis* appeared. But it is a generation that has probably not seen its equal in all history for the variety and significance of the events that it produced. The *Genesis* volume was one of the victims of these events. No sooner had it appeared than the Nazis came to power and, as part of their master plan to destroy everything and everyone associated with civilization, the Jewish especially, put an end to its circulation. Copies of the original German edition, just like individual Jews in Germany and elsewhere in Europe, escaped the destruction; but not nearly enough.

When I began to prepare the draft of the new translation of the Torah for the Jewish Publication Society, I naturally consulted Jacob's *Genesis*. There weren't many commentaries, Jewish or non-Jewish, that I did not consult; it was nevertheless most rewarding to have Jacob's commentary before me, not only when a problem in interpretation and translation arose but even when the Hebrew text was clear, or at least seemed clear enough. For it was Jacob's approach to get to the heart of the passage, to determine in context what the preserved Hebrew text was meant to convey to the reader.

Jacob could not accept the Documentary Theory as understood and applied by biblical scholarship in the first two–three decades of the twentieth century, i.e., in pre-archaeology days. To the vast majority of Christian scholars, the Hebrew Bible came to an end when the New Testament came into being, whereas to Jacob, as to any Jew who knew Jewish-history, the Hebrew Bible did not come to an end; indeed, as a Jewish scholar looking back upon the panorama of biblical interpretation that covered the nearly two thousand years of the Common Era, Jacob saw the Bible as a reality that had become increasingly vital and meaningful in the mishnaic and later rabbinic periods.

Thus, to Jacob, the biblical text spoke as a unit, regardless of any composite origin; and when it spoke, he heard it say something not merely to the society of long ago in which it originated but also to all Jewish societies ever since, and to his own especially.

For example, scholars generally agree that the "light" that God created on the first day derives ultimately from an older Near Eastern belief according to which the chaos (=darkness) of the universe gave way to order (=light)—but only after a mighty contest between the two cosmic forces. On the other hand, Jacob has noted correctly, in commenting on the Hebrew text of the verse in the form that it finally acquired (1:3), "Here there is no trace of a struggle between light and darkness" and "Even light, the most sublime element, is only the creation of God."

Again, in the Introduction to "The Story of the Fathers" (chapters 12 ff.), Jacob asserts:

> If the narrative of the patriarchs of the people of Israel is to be understood according to the original intent, it must be viewed with the eyes of a son of this people for whom it was first written. The following main ideas must be remembered while reading it . . ."

So that Jacob's commentary becomes indispensable for the fuller understanding of what the Bible had said and has continued to say from its inception to our own days. Such commentaries on Genesis as those of S.R. Driver (1904; often reprinted) and G. von Rad (3rd edition, 1972) are of course of prime importance; but it is Jacob's commentary that gives their data and approach the perspective that makes for a whole view.

Dr. Ernest I. Jacob and Dr. Walter Jacob, respectively the son and grandson of the author, have done exceedingly well by their ancestor, without resorting to ancestor worship. The original, rather massive volume has been reduced by the elimination of the technical philological material and the argumentation against the Documentary Theory and what used to be called "higher" textual criticism; the specialist will readily consult the German original (now reprinted for the first time) for these discussions. The core of the commentary, however, has been turned into a forthright and lucid English, along the lines of "The First and Second Commandments' an Excerpt from the 'Commentary on Exodus'" by Benno Jacob (*Judaism*, 13 [Winter, 1964], 3–18), likewise prepared by Rabbi Walter Jacob (in consultation with his father, Rabbi Ernest I. Jacob).

It is with great satisfaction that this highly useful version is sent forth to serious students of the Bible; and it may be hoped that a similar version of Benno Jacob's *Exodus* will also see the light of day in the not too distant future.

January, 1974   Harry M. Orlinsky
                                 Effie Wise Ochs Professor of Bible
                                 Hebrew Union College—Jewish Institute
                                 of Religion, New York

Preface

This book seeks to present an English version of Benno Jacob's commentary on Genesis, originally written in German. We have abridged the German version to a third of the author's original work, "Das Erste Buch der Tora Genesis uebersetzt und erklaert" (Schocken Verlag, Berlin, 1934). The commentary is the result of a lifetime of Biblical studies; it appeared when Jewish publications in Germany could no longer reach a broader public, and therefore remained largely unknown.

The editors hope that nothing of interest to a serious reader and student has been omitted in this edition. However, the scholar interested in the linguistic and other arguments must turn to the original German edition. There he will also find a refutation of diverging opinions, and a great wealth of material which throws new light on the language, the religion, and history of the entire Bible.

This edition is intended for those who wish to understand the meaning of the Bible and thereby enrich their religious and ethical thinking. This reader will probably not be interested in modern controversies or the abundance of untenable opinions given about the book of Genesis through thousands of years; all this is more completely provided in B. Jacob's original work than anywhere else. That material, along with the contentions of the so-called Higher Criticism, has been omitted. They are important for the scholar, but not for the readers who wish to understand the present day text. Only comments by Jews and Gentiles which B. Jacob accepted, especially by interpreters not well known to the general public such as the great medieval Jewish commentators, have been retained. We hope that our readers will study the book and will feel rewarded by many new insights. We encourage them to note the numerous Biblical quotations which will provide a deeper insight into many matters.

Benno Jacob was a German rabbi, born at Breslau on September 8, 1862. He received his rabbinical training at the Jewish Theological Seminary and the degree of doctor of philosophy in classical languages at the University of Breslau. He occupied pulpits in Goettingen

(1891-1906), and Dortmund (1906-1929), ministering successfully to the spiritual needs of numerous congregants. Throughout his life he was a leader of German Jewry in religious education and organization and fought for the civil rights of the German Jews. He was active in establishing the professional position of the modern rabbi. However, his deeper love was Biblical research. He literally gave every free minute of his busy life to that avocation. Beginning in 1890 he has published many Biblical studies and books aside from articles in scholarly journals, political writings, sermons and textbooks. He started his commentary to Genesis in 1923, worked on it for ten years, and devoted all his time after retiring from the active rabbinate to it. Following the publication of this work he turned to the second book of Moses and left a complete and voluminous commentary to Exodus, which has thus far only been available on microfilm. Emigration from Germany under the Nazis hardly interrupted his studies. Thanks to the efforts of the late Chief Rabbi of England, Dr. J. H. Hertz, he found refuge and the possibility of continuing his work in that hospitable land. He died with his beloved Bible in his hand, at age of eighty-three on January 25, 1945 in London, after having survived the bombardments of that city and still seeing the tide of the Second World War turn toward victory. The aim of B. Jacob's Biblical research was to find the meaning of Scripture as intended by the writers or editors of the Bible, independent of old and new authorities, and mainly through the intensive study of the Hebrew language. His approach was philological and exegetical.

Benno Jacob dedicated the original version of this book to the memory of Franz Rosenzweig, the Jewish philosopher who persuaded him to undertake the commentary, and to the memory of his wife Helene Jacob, nee Stein; he was deeply grateful to his publisher, Salmon Schocken. The editors of this abridged verson are his son, Dr. Ernest I. Jacob, Rabbi Emeritus, and his grandson, Dr. Walter Jacob, Rabbi of the Rodef Shalom Congregation in Pittsburgh, Pennsylvania.

Chapter 1

In the beginning God created the heavens and the earth.

The story of creation leads up to man the subject of all history. The earth is prepared for him so that he may live, work and rest upon it. All this is placed into the frame of 'six days', not to write a historical account in the sequence of time, but to construct before our eyes the universe as a meaningful cosmos. It shall be concluded with God's resting at the beginning of the seventh day. The story is not intended to present scientific speculation or definitions; it is to serve practical religious interests, namely to assign man his place on earth.

It is the first great achievement of the Bible to present a divine creation from nothing in contrast to evolution or formation from a material already in existence. Israel's religious genius expresses this idea with monumental brevity. In all other creation epics the world originates from a primeval matter which existed before. No other religion or philosophy dared to take this last step. Through it God is not simply the architect, but the absolute master of the universe. No sentence could be better fitted for the opening of the Book of Books. Only an all pervading conviction of God's absolute power could have produced it.

The six days in which God's action builds man's house, furnishes it and places him at a well decked table begin only in the third verse. In these six days, God did not *create* the world, but *made* heaven and earth. The Bible wants to distinguish clearly between these two words; "to make" is also ascribed to man and plants in Hebrew; yet "to create" is only said of God. This word implies the conception of something totally new. Thus the commandment of the Sabbath is based upon "God *made* heaven and earth in six days", not that he created them (Ex. 20, 11; 31, 17). Only his making can serve as a model for human work. Divine creation and human actions are incompatible; divine creation is never described in detail as it is beyond description. Nor may it be introduced by God spoke, resolved, or willed as that would divide it into separate actions; for this reason it also remains timeless. It did not

1

require any, even the smallest unit of time, but stands outside of time.
That is the meaning of the opening word *in the beginning.* It expresses
the preliminary condition for all which happens in time; everything
else presupposes other events. The characteristic Biblical style begins a
narrative with the word "and". Only the creation could not start in this
manner. The Hebrew word for beginning signifies the first link in a
chain; after it similar links follow. They rank lower in value and in
sequence of time.

The Hebrew word for *God* is a grammatical plural form, but it is
always used in conjunction with singular verbs. The monotheistic
conception of the Bible is thus clearly demonstrated.

Heaven and earth are the universe, but the Hebrew language prefers
to show totalities divided into two parts.

Verse 2. *The earth was without form and void, and darkness was
upon the face of the deep; and the wind of God was fluttering over
the face of the waters.*

The Bible in accordance with its intention of describing the world of
man, dwells no longer on the heavens (compare Psalm 115,16) but
turns to the earth. *Without form and void* in Hebrew a pair of rhyming
words, reflecting by their sound the awful desolation of such a scene.
And the wind of God was fluttering over the face of the waters like the
vibrating, trembling wing movements of a bird over its nest without
forward motion. *The wind of God* comes from him and is at his service.

The First Day.

³*And God said, "Let there be light"; and there was light.* ⁴*And
God saw the light that it was good; and God separated between
light and darkness.* ⁵*God designated the light for the day, and the
darkness he designated for the night. And there was evening and
there was morning, one day.*

Every work of creation is introduced in this way (verses 3; 6; 9; 11;
14; 19; 23; 25) and all of them originate through God's word (see Psalm
33,6-9). It is a challenge to discover an intention and thought of God in
every work and creature. Out of this derives the Talmudic appellation
for God: "He who spoke and the world came into being."

At the first work of God the prompt effectiveness of a divine
commandment and the immediate, joyful and unconditional obedience
of the creation shall be exemplified; Let there be—and there was. Here
is no trace of a struggle between light and darkness.

Even light, the most sublime element, is only a creation of God. This is the second great idea of the Bible after the first that the heavens and earth were created out of nothing.

Verse 4. Not that God discovers the goodness of light upon further examination; for could it have been otherwise? (Rashbam) Rather he looked at the goodness of the light. His glance rested on it with pleasure; he enjoyed his creation (Psalm 104,31) which was benevolently presented to the lower world. The light reflects God's splendor and love which fill the earth (Psalm 33,5).

Creation in its particulars as in its totality (verse 30) is perfect and serves its purpose; it is beautiful and good. Everything that God has created is equipped with all capacities for its task and expresses the master's idea in the most perfect way.

Light is most congruous with God's own nature, a simile for absolute clarity and purity, for the highest happiness (Is. 2,5; 60,19 and many other times); it is life and joy. Biblical enthusiasm for light is well shown as it is a special creation and as the whole first day is devoted to it. The superior value of light becomes clear only when contrasted with darkness which for this reason is not abolished. Darkness is merely restricted to a section of time; God separated between light and darkness—they shall have nothing in common. A word indicating separation or division into species is not missing in any part of the narrative (day and night, heaven and earth, plants and animals). Following the creation of heaven and earth, God's work consists in organizing the world which means separating. It is a priestly and aristocratic spirit which emphasizes barriers; it abhors intermixing and neglect of distinctions. The Jewish ceremony of habdala "separation", the benediction over the light at the end of the Sabbath, is derived from this initial separation.

Verse 5. This verse does not give names to light and darkness, but assigns spheres to them (Rashi and others); similarly in verse 8 and 10. The primary orders of time and space are determined by God himself. For in them, at some time and at some place, everything in the world happens and lives. It does so either during the day or during the night, in heaven or on earth, on the solid ground or in the sea.

This assignment of time and space as a special act of God binds him to approve them as eternal and inviolable and to allow no change. It is the covenant made by God with them of which Jeremiah (33,20-25) speaks: "My covenant with day and night." Day and night shall never cease; the sky will always arch over the earth and the sea will never overstep its boundaries. The chaos of verse 2 will never return.

And there was evening and there was morning one day. After the light had been created, the first "day" of twelve hours took its course, as well as the first night; beginning in the evening and terminating in the morning one day was completed (Rashbam). Among an agricultural people as Israel of old, which could only farm by daylight, the day without question took precedence over the night. The Hebrew Bible and Judaism reflect a conception of life in which the day, light, and work have precedence.

One day, not meaning the first day, but a complete day containing day and night, evening and morning, so that now the second day and its work could follow.

This verse does not contradict the beginning of the Jewish Sabbath and festivals in the evening. The Sabbath shall be the day of rest, of non-performance of work. As there can be nothing but work or rest, the rest must begin where the work stops, namely in the evening. God began to rest at the moment when the sixth day was at an end; therefore the seventh day started in the evening, and consequently every succeeding day.

The creation of light, and only light, on the first day indicates clearly the meaning of the "days" in the story of creation. Indeed all efforts to understand these "days" as world periods of indefinite length are vain; this has been claimed in order to achieve conformity with the millions of years assumed by modern science for the origin of the universe. The Bible means by the word "day" only a day like ours. This is established for all six days as the seventh as a day of rest naturally means a period of 24 hours.

If it is possible to speak of God only allegorically, the "day" of creation is also but a metaphor. Creation consists in establishing limits; the measure of time limits is the day. The "days' ' of creation are an expression for the demarkation of the works of creation, it is the first order out of chaos. Therefore the light has a day to itself, although its creation consisted only in a single word and was completed at once.

The Second Day

⁶*And God said, "Let there be a firmament in the midst of the waters, and let it separate the waters from the waters."* ⁷*And God made the firmament, and it separated the waters which were under the firmament from the waters which were above the firmament. And it was so.* ⁸*And God designated the firmament for the*

heavens. And there was evening and there was morning, a second
day.

In other biblical passages the blue of the sky which seems to arch
over the earth is described as thin, but solid (Ex. 24,10) like the roof of a
tent (Is. 40,22; Psalm 104,2) or like a mirror of metal (Job 37,18); beyond
are the treasure houses of snow, dew, frost, and rain. This "heaven" has
gates and sluices through which the rain pours down on the earth (Gen.
7,11 etc). These mythical conceptions must not be taken for the
"science" of the Hebrews (Tuch); see Job 36,27. Nothing of this is told
in our verse, only that preceeding the emergence of the earth from the
waters one more preparation is necessary, namely the creation of a
firmament. It shall originate in the midst of the waters and divide them.

Verse 7. God made. "Making" said of God, is different from
"creating" as the substance from which God makes a request is already
in existence. Otherwise it is as incomprehensible a miracle as the
creation from nothing.

And it separated; the firmament produced the division by coming
into existence. Its function started simultaneously with its existence.

And it was so permanently; otherwise it could have been assumed
that the division was only temporary.

Verse 8. We do not hear of the further destiny nor of the purpose of
the waters above, nor any details of the nature and the substance of the
so-called heavens. We are only told that the watery chaos ceased as part
of the waters were separated for the above. Statements in other Biblical
passages are poetical amplifications and must not influence the
interpretation of the verse, nor must the temptation to reach some
reconciliation with modern science. The Bible cannot possibly contradict science as it only describes things according to appearances and
these never change. It will always appear as if there is a heaven just as
in spite of Copernicus the sun still rises and sets. Only the creation and
first origin are a miracle and always will be.

The Third Day

⁹And God said, "Let the waters be gathered together under the
heavens into one place, and let the dry land appear." And it was
so. ¹⁰God designated the dry land for the earth, and the waters
that were gathered together He designated for the seas. And God
saw that it was good. ¹¹And God said, "Let the earth put forth
vegetation, grasses yielding seed, and fruit trees bearing fruit in

*which is their seed, each according to its kinds, upon the earth."
And it was so.* [12]*The earth brought forth vegetation, grasses yielding seed, according to its kind, and trees bearing fruit in which is
their seed, according to its kind. And God saw that it was good.*
[13]*And there was evening and there was morning, a third day.*

It does not mean that all the waters are now together; but that they are
irrevocably tamed and limited by the sea shores (Jer. 5,22; Job 38,8ff)
and also by one sea level while on land heights and depths alternate. In
these respects their "place" is "one". With the receding of the waters
the dry land automatically becomes visible. In Hebrew the word for
"dry land" indicates that it was once covered with water. *And it was
so.* Wind and water obediently follow the command; biblical poetry has
often amplified on this.

Verse 10. The earth is mentioned first; the sea is less familiar to man
and more remote, as the night compared to the day in verse 5. The dry
land is the habitation of men who in poetical Biblical language may be
called "the inhabitants of the dry land" (Dan. 2,10).
And God saw that it was good because now the three parts of the
universe have been readied: heaven, earth, and sea. That this phrase
occurs two times on the third day has been interpreted as meaning that
God's works are also counted and that there were two works of creation
on this day. Yet the Bible counts only days of creation. God's works
cannot be counted.

Verse 11. This verse offers no scientific botany. The division of plants
would be insufficient for even the most primitive botanical system. Its
conceptions and distinctions are determined by a practical point of
view which is made to serve religious education. The earth's production of food for man and beast is ascribed to a divine word of creation.
Thus it was God who set the table for all beings. This had to be done
only in the beginning; he provided the earth with the capacity for
producing and the plants with a way to renew themselves constantly
by seed. Man shall respect the order set by God and not efface it.
Fruit trees The Hebrew word emphasizes the miracle which brings
nutritious fruit out of the hard and indigestible wood.

Verse 12. God's command (verse 11) and the execution (verse 12)
show a number of differences. The Haggada explains in its unscientific,
but charming way: The grasses took the trees as a model ("each according to its kind") and God commended them for it (Psalm 104,31), but

the trees did not quite obey; they were supposed to be "fruit trees" meaning trees all fruit; even the wood would have tasted like the fruit, but what a pity! Only trees, bearing fruit, appeared.

The Fourth Day

¹⁴And God said, "Let there be lights on the firmament of the heavens to separate the day from the night; and let them be for signs and for seasons and for days and years, ¹⁵and let them be lights on the firmament of the heavens to give light upon the earth." And it was so. ¹⁶And God made the two great lights, the greater light to rule the day, and the lesser light to rule the night; and the stars. ¹⁷And God set them on the firmament of the heavens to give light upon the earth, ¹⁸to rule over the day and over the night, and to separate the light from the darkness. And God saw that it was good. ¹⁹And there was evening and there was morning, a fourth day.

The creation of the heavenly bodies and their function is described by words which already appeared in the creation of the light on the first day and of the firmament on the second day; it is the continuation and conclusion of those creations. Light and the lightgiving bodies are intentionally treated separately. The heavenly bodies, while deified by other peoples, are purposely degraded; they are only functionaries of God for the service of the earth and its inhabitants. For this reason the heavenly lights are kindled only a little before living beings with eyes are created, beings which are awake and asleep, work and rest and need a computation of time; for to live means "to see the light." Only in connection with the heavenly bodies among all works is their function mentioned. They rule, but it is a reign exercised by two rivals alternately in the same territory. This presupposes a higher ruler from whom instructions are received. The Bible understands the admiration for these heavenly lights (Deut. 4,19 "And beware lest you lift up your eyes to heaven" etc.). They are indeed rulers in their time spheres, but only by the grace of God and within limits set for them.

Finally, they have their power of giving light not of themselves, but are places and bearers of light. The Hebrew word for them indicates this by a slight difference from the word for the "light" of verse 3. The "light" offers no danger of being worshipped in place of God; although it lends form to all things, in itself it is unformed. It too is a creation. The bearers of light, the heavenly bodies, are only derived from it. As an indication of their subordinate nature these servants are not called by names. The sun is "the greater light," the moon "the lesser light."

On the firmament of the heavens means on this side of the heavens. Separation of day and night exists only below the firmament of the heavens. God in his Heaven does not need it.

Verse 16. *The stars* are the great host of servants of second or third rank, as they (Psalm 136,9) belong to the moon and assist it in lighting the night. Basically this is the image of the heavenly king and the hosts of his brilliant servants.

The Fifth Day

²⁰*And God said, "Let the waters swarm of living creatures, and let birds be able to fly above the earth across the firmament of the heavens." ²¹So God created the great sea monsters and every living creature that moves, with which the waters swarm, according to their kinds, and every winged bird, according to its kind. And God saw that it was good. ²²And God blessed them, saying, "Be fruitful and multiply and fill the waters in the seas, and let birds multiply on the earth." ²³And there was evening and there was morning, a fifth day.*

With the fourth day the house of the world is ready for its inhabitants. Now life shall appear, first fish and birds. They are treated together because for both the land is not their only home, and for this reason they are more remote and stranger to man.

Let birds be able to fly above the earth across the firmament of the heavens. The verse describes in brief, but vivid words the happy freedom of the bird balancing in the air with the sky above and the earth beneath. By God's creative word even the elements foreign to man are populated with living beings; all three realms are mentioned in one verse: the heavens, earth, and sea.

Verse 22. Here the first blessing appears. For procreation two animals must join spontaneously whereas the plants produce seed and fruit unconsciously. *Let birds multiply on the earth.* Although the air is the sphere of the birds, their food is from the earth; there they build nests, lay eggs and hatch them. No beings live only in the air; this may be the reason why Biblical Hebrew has no word for air.

The Sixth Day

²⁴*And God said, "Let the earth bring forth living creatures according to their kinds: cattle and creeping things and beasts of the earth according to their kinds." And it was so. ²⁵And God made*

> *the beasts of the earth according to their kinds and the cattle*
> *according to their kinds, and everything that creeps on the ground*
> *according to its kind. And God saw that it was good.*

The earth shall bring forth animals as it had produced plants in verse
12. They shall be "living creatures" as in verse 20 the fish of the waters.
Thus the creation of the land animals is linked with both. Land and sea,
the two halves of the earth, are provided with organic life. In the
execution (verse 24) the earth is no longer the subject; God "makes" the
animals. Again a paradox of divine creation—on God's order matter
produces something apparently heterogeneous. For the animals are not
earth, but flesh and bone, skin and sinews, blood and fat. The earth
nourishes them and the earth becomes their grave; therefore it must be
their source. *Cattle* means all domesticated animals; *beasts* are the wild
and predaceous animals. The Hebrew here shows great creative vigor
which cannot be imitated in the translation.

Everything that creeps on the ground are the little animals which are
hardly higher than the ground and seem to cling to it.

The land animals do not receive a blessing. Their unlimited increase
would be unfortunate for man. However, fish and birds are not his
rivals on earth and not in his way.

Otherwise the author shows a universal and unprejudiced pleasure
in all creatures. God saw in regard to the animal world *that it was good.*
Nothing is despised due to its kind or is unclean of itself.

> ²⁶*Then God said, "Let us make a man! In our image, after our*
> *likeness; and let them have dominion over the fish of the sea, and*
> *over the birds of the heavens, and over all cattle, and over the*
> *whole earth, and over every creeping thing that creeps upon the*
> *earth." *²⁷*So God created man, in his own image, in the image of*
> *God he created him; male and female he created them.*

Man is created on the same day as the land animals as the earth is his
home too and as the structure of his body is like theirs. In these ways he
is their associate. Yet God's first word about him indicates that man is
the highest earthly being, both different and superior.

The "we" of God's speech refers to his heavenly court (Rashi and
many others). This shall show appreciation of man, the representative
of God on earth, as the most precious creature. The Bible also speaks of
such a heavenly court in 3,22 and in I Kings 22,19 and Is. 6,8; even in
our chapter the heavenly bodies are conceived as God's servants. It
does not indicate any active co-operation; polytheism is unthinkable in

view of the whole attitude of the chapter. It is also refuted by the singular of "he said" and "he created". The expression avoids the necessity of God's continuing "in *my* image."

Image of God is not meant physically as man is not markedly differ-ent from the higher mammals in his bodily organization. Nothing is said about the bodily structure of either the animals or man. There can be no doubt that through the entire Bible whenever its leading minds speak, God is a purely spiritual being without body or form. Expres-sions like God's eye, ear, mouth, hand, and similar ones are inevitable if anything comprehensible shall be stated about God's living activity. "God said" represents him as much in a human manner as "God's hand". This is the unanimous conviction of all authoritative teachers of Judaism. Those writers and prophets who proclaim God's incompara-ble majesty and absolute spirituality, for example Isaiah and Job, speak of him in a most human form. It may even be claimed that the more spiritual the conception, the more human the expression. The popular leaders of Israel were not as concerned about expressing themselves in a philosophically correct way as to speak of the living God.

In our image, after our likeness. In this passage man is chosen to dominate the animals; he possesses this superiority as an image of God. Thus only intellectual capacities and an innate talent for ruling can be meant. The daring comparison is made innocuous by adding that he is created and made by God. (Compare Psalm 8).

Let them have dominion the plural in anticipation of their future propagation and in contrast to the multitude of those to be dominated by him.

Verse 27. The verse is inspired by gratitude to the creator who so richly endowed and so highly ennobled man, as Rabbi Akiba expressed it (Abot III:18): "What sign of God's love that man was created in his image! What still greater love that he was told of being created in his image!"

In connection with man any expression as "according to their kind" is missing; no disparate and incompatible kinds of men exist; there are only the two sexes, male and female, which join each other in equality to produce men again. The Bible teaches unambiguously that only one human couple was formed in the beginning and that all men are descended from it. This is the opposite of racism and emphasizes the unity of mankind.

[28]*And God blessed them, and God said to them, "Be fruitful and multiply, and fill the earth and subdue it; and have dominion*

*over the fish of the sea and over the birds of the heavens and over
every living thing that moves upon the earth." ²⁹And God said,
"Behold, I have given you every plant yielding seed which is
upon the face of all the earth, and every tree with seed in its fruit;
you shall have them for food. ³⁰And to every animal of the earth,
and to every bird of the heavens, and to everything that creeps on
the earth that has the breath of life, I have given every green plant
for food." And it was so.³¹ And God saw everything that he had
made, and behold, it was very good. And there was evening and
there was morning, the sixth day.*

The blessing consists in the establishment and sanction of matrimo-
ny within the uniform species of man. After God has created man and
woman, he joins them together and consecrates their union as such;
following this he wishes them fertility.

Subdue it Man is given unlimited power over the earth. No human
work on it can be called a violation of God's will.

Verse 29. In his fatherly care God at once assigns to man the vegetation of the earth for his maintenance. Does this allot man only plants as
food and prohibits his partaking of meat until the descendants of Noah
(9,3)? Shall this teach an original state in which all life was respected, a
time when general peace prevailed on earth, not only between man and
animal, but also among the animals? The prophets proclaim it for the
end of days (Hos. 2,20; Is. 11,6ff; 65,25); thus the Messianic age would
be merely the regaining of a lost ideal condition of the first age.

Verse 31. As perfect as the works of God are separately, their harmony as a totality is the highest perfection.

The sixth day with the definite article, is entirely distinct from the
other days.

Chapter 2

The first three verses are obviously a part of chapter 1.

Thus the heavens and the earth were finished, and all the host of them. ²And God held a finishing of his work which he had made on the seventh day, and he desisted on the seventh day from all his work which he had made. ³So God blessed the seventh day and hallowed it, because on it he desisted from all his work which God had created to make.

Nothing is lacking nor will anything ever be added. The host of the heavens are the heavenly bodies which surround the throne of the Almighty; the host of earth are all the organic beings of the earth over which man has been installed as ruler and which he may use.

Verse 2. The Hebrew word for *work* is related to the word for messenger and indicates the realization of a thought, desire, and intention. The creator gave something of himself into his work as a man puts a part of himself into his messenger; the work represents him and speaks of him. Thus the creation speaks of God. The conception of "labor", either hard or easy, is not contained in the Hebrew word.

God held a finishing: this is the meaning of the Hebrew word, see II Chron. 29,17 and not that God finished his work on the seventh day which would contradict verse 1. It declares the work finished or that one stands opposite the finished work. It is a positive and formal expression for that which is mentioned negatively in *he desisted on the seventh day from all of his work.*

Verse 3. It is only a partial truth that God set a pattern for the Sabbath of man by ceasing from work. The Ten Commandments (Ex. 20,11) and Ex. 31,17 motivate the Sabbath by stating that God made the heavens and the earth in six days and "rested" on the seventh day. But this rest is as different from man's resting as divine "making" is from human making. Following the seventh day man will work again, but not God. After God has created the world completely and perfectly it runs its prescribed course automatically by the laws he has provided for it. The days and seasons change, vegetation continues, and animals and men propagate themselves without divine interference. It is remarkable that the word Sabbath is missing in these verses; it cannot reasonably be applied to God. Only man's work is composed of a rhythm of work and rest, but God did his work once in six days; after he had completed it he desisted from it forever.

God blessed the seventh day and hallowed it. The hallowing is the content of the blessing. Human blessing means "To wish well"; God's blessing means "To do good" (see Num 6,23ff.). If God has blessed the seventh day, he has equipped it with the power to do good as his blessing over beast and man equipped them with fertility. Not as if the day possessed this power in itself, because as a period of time it does not differ from all other days, but only for and through man who observes it. A day is "hallowed" by man conducting himself as holy for its duration (compare Lev. 11,44) by keeping away from everything profane.

The Sabbath is a symbol of freedom which more than in working and creating consists in resting and the power to command oneself to stop. Aside from God only the man who is not a slave of another man possesses this freedom. Therefore the Sabbath is given Israel after the redemption from Egyptian slavery as a gift which had been ready since the creation (Ex. 16,29).

Which God had created to make. The two terms "create" and "make" of chapter 1 are repeated. God had created *all*—by one act—and he had made *all* that is, he had given to everything its definite form, nature, and mode of action. He had created it in order to make it. It can also be said of man that he "makes" something, but that he creates and makes can be said only of God. Thus in this last phrase "create" and "make" are combined.

Of foreign creation myths only the Babylonian one is suitable for comparison. It is a poem named "Enuma elish" according to its opening words. The Biblical story of creation is vastly superior. In the Babylonian myth the creation is only a side theme; its interest is not in the earth, but in the heavens and in the gods. Man is created to serve the gods and as the sacrifices naturally go to the priests, this means serving the priests. In the first chapter of Genesis the story of creation does not lead up to Jerusalem, the Temple, and the sacrificial service, but to man as such and his dignity and all creation is encompassed with love.

The Descendants Of The Heavens And The Earth

⁴These are the descendants of the heavens and the earth after their creation, after the Lord God made the earth and the heavens.

The first human couple is described as descendants of the heavens and the earth; this metaphor organically joins nature and history. The book of Genesis later speaks of descendants of Adam (5,1), of Noah (6,9) etc, (altogether 10 times). It does not think in periods of time, but in descendants, fathers and sons, beginning with the heavens and the earth which God had created. All is a chain of descendants. Heaven and earth are from the outset created in view of man and his descendants. The meaning of creation lies in man and history.

The origin of the world is described fully by using both of the verbs "create" and "make"—to call into existence and to form purposefully. Once the heavens are mentioned first, and once the earth; this is done in order to prevent the misunderstanding that "heavens and earth" indicate a sequence in time. They have been created simultaneously; therefore often "the heavens and the earth", but once "the earth and the heavens"; compare Ex. 6,26f.: Aaron and Moses, then Moses and Aaron.

The combination of the two names for God, *The Lord God*, appears only in chapters 2 and 3 (and in Ex. 9,30). Everywhere else the Bible says either "God" or "the Lord". This must not necessarily indicate different authors with different usages as the so-called Higher Criticism of the Pentateuch assumes. One and the same author may not only use both names, but even alternate them with intention and art; under certain circumstances they may be combined as I believe to have shown for many passages.

The Hebrew term for "God" is a generic word whereas the Hebrew word for "The Lord" is a proper name. Its pronunciation is no longer known with certainty; many scholars assume it to have been Jahve. Its meaning is explained in Ex. 3,6–15 and 6,2–8 as: HE WILL BE THERE, he who can be expected with certainty to be there.

We know from chapter 1 that "God" is the creator of heaven and earth including man. Now the story of a commandment shall follow, namely the prohibition against eating from the tree of knowledge. This tests man's obedience and educates him in the fear of the Lord and the avoidance of sin. For man alone exists a "you shall" or "you shall not". Only regarding him may we speak of sin and guilt. Nature obeys God, because that is the law of its existence and action; it cannot act otherwise. It knows no will, only necessity. Man shall be impressed thoroughly by the force of the commandment, so he who gives it faces

man in his full majesty; that is the Lord God. The full name continues
through the whole story.

It has been claimed that the following chapter contains a second
story of creation. This is not conclusive as it would be a story of
creation in which nothing is created—neither the heavens nor the
earth, neither the sea nor the fish, nor as assumed birds, animals or
man. They are "formed" and a garden is planted at a certain spot on the
earth which therefore must already have existed.

In order to understand the chapter it is necessary to inquire into its
purpose. Man, created on the sixth day, shall propagate himself, shall
dominate all other living things, and live on the produce of the earth
(1,25–29). This will be the life of mankind. First man shall by his own
actions testify that no other kind of life would be possible for him. God
lets him try life in paradise. Man does not stand the test and so the
matter rests with the original intention of the creator. It is further the
nature of man that he must die, not only because he is a creature, but
also because he is organized in such a way that he propagates and
multiplies. A dream of immortality on this limited earth would have
had to abandon this. As man shall begin in a paradise, no food is yet
necessary on the rest of the earth; this is expressed as an introduction
by verses 5 and 6. Then follow verses 7–15 which speak of man in a
paradise; the two are related to each other like a container and its
contents. Therefore the story must first speak of man; the container
exists for the contents. Every important element must be properly
mentioned. The Hebrew language does this in sentences connected by
"and"; this does not always indicate sequence in time: he formed man
and he breathed into him the spirit of life and he planted a garden and
he placed man into it etc. Would it not be absurd if this were to indicate
the following sequence: first man is formed, then he must exist
nowhere until the garden is planted, and when finally placed into the
garden he must wait until trees and fruit grow. What a confused tale
this would be!

> 5When no plant of the field existed on the earth and no herb of the
> field had yet sprung up—for the Lord God had not caused it to
> rain upon the earth, and there was no man to till the ground, but a
> mist went up from the earth and watered the whole face of the
> ground—7then the Lord God formed man of dust from the ground
> and breathed into his nostrils the breath of life; and man became
> a living being.

Even if it had rained, no hand would have been present to till the
ground. Man already exists, but the forlorn condition of the soil now to

be changed is depicted. Here begins not only the story of paradise, but of all earliest history until the end of the great flood. Its theme deals with the relation of man and soil, two related words in Hebrew: adam—man and adama—soil. It will be man's destiny to cultivate the soil. This shall be described separately according to its importance and has intentionally not been touched upon in the first chapter. Man's relation to the soil has two aspects: he may rule it, (1,26–28) but he must also serve it in order to gain his living. This will be spoken of now. The hypothesis of a second story of creation is untenable because it would destroy this unity of the narrative. *No plant of the field was yet on the ground:* It existed, but had not yet reached the desired state (Compare Jer 14,5). Chapter 1 is here taken for granted. Vegetation and man have only not found each other. The same impression of desolation is created as in 1,2. The soil lacking rain and untilled by the hand of man is a chaos as the earth before God said, let there be light.

Verse 6. Would the plants not whither without rain? This verse is the answer; it proves once more that the creation of vegetation on the third day is assumed.

Verse 7. *The Lord God formed man of dust from the ground.* The ⌐⌐terial had to be mentioned to indicate that it is man's (Adam's) stiny to serve the soil (adama) and in the end to return to it as it ⌐orresponds to his origin. The soil is his cradle, his home, and his grave. The Hebrew expresses the relation of man and soil in this linguistically unique fashion: adam-adama, the one supplements the other. The underlying feeling is one of humility and realism. What is man?—dust, and what will be his end must have been his origin. Fancy and pride would have imagined a more sublime substance for man. *And he breathed into his nostrils the breath of life.* The Hebrew verb is one used for breathing upon the fire in forge and fireplace (Is. 54,16 and often). Breath is the sign of life, compare Psalm 104,29f. Even with this he only *became a living being* like (1,20 etc) the animals; a being which needs and desires to support its life through food. Man's spiritual nature lies in his being "an image of God" (1,26f.); yet here his earthly nature shall be emphasized. The phrase implies the tragic destiny of man—the rivalry between his sensual and his divine nature. This is not childlike and naive as these are deep and eternally true ideas about the nature of man, expressed in miraculously simple language.

> *⁸And the Lord God planted a garden in Eden in the East; and there he put the man whom he had formed. ⁹And out of the*

ground the Lord God made grow every tree that is pleasant to the sight and good for food, the tree of life also in the midst of the garden, and the tree of knowledge of good and evil.

In the East indicates the point of view of the Semite who orients himself eastward. Mankind's beginnings were in the East from where it moved westward. The Hebrew word *Eden* means delight. The word *paradise* is of Persian origin and may be found only in later books of the Bible.

There he put the man whom he had formed Garden and man suited each other, because both were related creations of God; he had planted the one and formed the other.

Verse 9 *And out of the ground* (adama). In paradise everything shall have the same origin and be related to each other: man, animals, and trees. The two trees will be discussed later.

¹⁰A river flowed out of Eden to water the garden, and from there it divided and became four rivers. ¹¹The name of one is Pishon; it is the one which flows around the whole land of Havilah, where there is gold; ¹²and the gold of that land is good; bdellium and onyx stone are there. ¹³The name of the second river is Gihon; it is the one which flows around the whole land of Cush. ¹⁴And the name of the third river is Hiddekel, which flows east of Assyria. And the fourth river is the Euphrates.

The garden is favored by a river; therefore rain was not needed. Nor is rain mentioned later whenever a blessing reminiscent of paradise is pronounced (27,28; Deut. 33,13). *From there*—after having left the garden.

Verse 11. Bdellium is a transparent resin of strong scent, bitter taste, and waxlike. Others take the Hebrew word for the name of a precious stone.

The numerous attempts to identify all four rivers and so to determine "the location of Paradise" have been in vain. The fourth river is definitely the Euphrates which was familiar to the Hebrews because it was near their own country; it needed no description and is mentioned last. The third river is certainly the Tigris, but can Euphrates and Tigris be named branches of one stream? As Cush is the Biblical term for Ethiopia, Jewish and Christian antiquity agreed that the second river must be the Nile. There is complete uncertainty about the first river although it is described most extensively. What is the purpose of these statements? If they should make the location of paradise conceivable, one must object that the verses rather describe the nature of the river after it had left the garden and became divided.

The whole passage is a product of fancy and nothing else; it is designed, not without irony, to disenchant us about the "paradise". It does not contain fairy tale treasures as in Ezek. 28,13f. Precious things like gold, bdellium, and onyx stone come from lands outside it although surrounded by a river from Eden. The garden of Adam is no "Paradise" and is indeed never called so in our story. Its whole delight consists in its trees with good-looking, edible fruit; it need not be tilled through toil, and can be easily watered from the river which flows through it. This garden is a very modest ideal. That cannot be ascribed to lack of phantasy. No people lacks phantasy if it intends to picture a paradise or a utopia. In the mind of Israel man is not destined for a life of enjoyment without duties; only the wicked desire such a life. The garden of Adam is intentionally reduced to a minimum.

> [15]The Lord God took the man and put him into the peace of the garden of Eden to till it and to keep it. [16]And the Lord God commanded the man, saying, "You may freely eat of every tree of the garden; [17]but of the tree of knowledge of good and evil you shall not eat, for the day that you eat of it you shall die."

Adam is put into the garden to work it and to care for it. Production and preservation are the two complementary sides of all human activity. Man's duty to care for the garden indicates that it is not his property. The garden belongs to God, not man.

It is remarkable that in this story God does not teach agriculture to man as in pagan mythologies. Adam learns it as he himself is a part of the soil; his own nature guides him much as a baby immediately reaches for his mother's breast. Nowhere in the Bible is man taught a mere technique by God.

The peace of the garden. Man shall work in the garden, but God has taught him by his own example that all work shall end in peaceful repose.

Verse 16. The way in which the garden will provide for man is discussed. Out of duties come rights; and this duty is of such a nature that it literally produces the right and enjoyment. "He who tends the fig tree will eat its fruit" (Prov. 27,18); however rights and enjoyment are immediately restricted. *The tree of knowledge of evil and good.* What is this knowledge? Why is the tree forbidden and the consequence death? The meaning of "good and evil" should be understood according to Deut 30,15f. "See, I have set before you this day life and good, death and evil . . . I command you this day, to love the Lord your God, to walk in his ways, and to keep his commandments . . . I have set before you life and death, blessing and curse, therefore choose life." The good is love of God shown by obedience to his commandments and it brings life and blessing; the evil is disobedience and it brings curse and death.

The first man reaches this knowledge by his experience with the prohibition. As he trespasses, he will afterwards know that he has chosen "the evil" and will recognize the difference from "the good" which obedience would have preserved for him. The tree is a touchstone for the distinction between the prohibited and the permitted, between good and evil, life and death. This is quite independent of the contents of the prohibition. The will to obey shows itself even more clearly if uninfluenced by any consideration of practical profit or loss, it only submits to the lawgiver.

Man is given a prohibition that he may know he is not God and has a master. The fruit of this tree was neither injurious nor poisonous; otherwise no penalty needed to be threatened; on the contrary it was "good for food". Merely the prohibition makes the fruit harmful. As object for the prohibition the fruit of a tree is chosen as it refers to the most elementary and central desire of man, his urge to eat. The tree stands in the center of the garden and the first command is a dietary law.

The rationalism of the story is admirable. No mystery exists to which man shall not penetrate. All the treasures belong to Adam because there is as yet no other owner. Nor is there a place in the garden which Adam must not enter. It is merely a borderline in his own conscience which he shall not cross.

Verse 17. *The day that you eat of it you shall die,* does not mean that he will die within twenty-four hours; Adam is still to live almost a thousand years. Whenever death comes, it will have to be regarded as penalty for this sin. The sentence is spoken in the day of the deed; the time until its execution is regarded as non-existent or only as a reprieve. Ideally deed and penalty are simultaneous as they stand in an inner relationship; this is the meaning of "the day", compare I Kings 2,37–42.

> *18Then the Lord God said, "It is not good that the man should be alone; I will make him a helper as it were corresponding to him."*
> *19So out of the ground the Lord God formed every beast of the field*

and every bird of the heavens, and brought them to the man to see what he would call them; and whatever the man called every living creature, that was its name. ²⁰The man gave names to all cattle, and to the birds of the heavens, and to every beast of the field; but for Adam there was not found a helper as it were corresponding to him.

Man is created for companionship and finds no happiness without it.

As it were corresponding to him, in bodily structure. The fact that God first forms the animals and brings them before man is not an unsuccessful experiment. Man shall not possess the excuse that, had he chosen his life partner, he would not have been incited to sin.

Verse 19. Man names the animals and God declares his approval in advance; this is another expression for his dominion over them (1,26–28). Man himself receives his name from God (5,2). By giving a name man expresses the relation of a thing to him, or what it shall or may mean to him. It so happens that man does not designate any animal with the feminine form of his own name, as later isha (woman) from ish (man): he recognizes none as his equal. Man observes the characteristics of *every living creature,* and names each according to the differences of bodily structure, manner of action, or way of life.

Verse 20. "All" cattle and "every" beast; but not "all" birds, perhaps because of their boundless multitude.

Animal belongs to animal and man cannot have a life and sex partnership with it. Man testifies thus to his own higher nature and acknowledges that it is a defection on his part later to keep company with the serpent.

²¹So the Lord God caused a deep sleep to fall upon the man, and while he slept took one of his ribs and closed up its place with flesh; ²²and the rib which the Lord God had taken from the man he built into a woman and brought her to the man. ²³Then the man said, "This at last is bone of my bones and flesh of my flesh; she shall be called woman, because she was taken out of man." ²⁴Therefore a man leaves his father and his mother and cleaves to his wife, and they become one flesh. ²⁵And the man and his wife were both naked and did not make each other ashamed.

The deep sleep shall make Adam insensible.

Verse 22. The story is a lofty and tender expression of the relation of man and woman. As man did not find a companion among the animals, only a new creation of God can help him. He shall not remain alone. In order to preserve the unity of mankind no second human being is created, but the wife is produced out of the already existing man. Woman, in this concept, is only another aspect of the species man. She shall be a helper to him, but weaker than he as she has to suffer, to conceive and bear children; she is the other half which needs protection. The closest analogy to this unique relationship is the child. It is formed in the deep darkness of its mother's womb until it comes out of her and is greeted by her as a part of herself which it will remain forever. The formation of the first woman is described according to this analogy. Therefore the unconsciousness of deep sleep comes over man; her formation takes place in the mystery of a darkness which only the eye of God penetrates (Psalm 139,11–16). The Hebrew word for "built" is suggestive of the word for son or child.

And he brought her to the man; God acts, so to speak, as best man for the first human couple (Midrash).

Verse 23. This verse is an exclamation of delight. Bone and flesh are the main parts of the body. From their physical relationship follows that man and woman belong together and are obliged to help each other (compare 29,14). Adam confirms God's work and intention. The derivation of the word woman (isha) from the word man (ish) is a popular etymology which for practical purposes rests on the similarity of sound. Ish and isha are related to each other as adam and adama.

Verse 24. This verse is a statement of the Bible, not of Adam. Father and mother are the natural roots of the child; with its brothers and sisters it has grown on the same stem. Husband and wife are from different families. Yet man forsakes father and mother for his wife and thus dissolves the strongest ties of body and soul. Can that be justified? The Biblical answer is that man finds in his wife a supplement to his own self. The first man could choose among other beings, but he was happy only when God created the wife, his wife, and brought her to him. The difference between the sexes is of God, an order of creation. The love between man and wife originates within themselves. The Bible approves of it by letting the two be regarded as one flesh.

Verse 25. They did not point to each other's nakedness as a disgrace.

Chapter 3

Now the serpent was more subtle than any other beast of the field that the Lord God had made. He said to the woman, "What? Did God say "You shall not eat of all the trees of the garden?" ²And the woman said to the serpent, "We may eat of the fruit of the trees of the garden, ³but God said, 'You shall not eat of the fruit of the tree which is in the midst of the garden, neither shall you touch it, lest you die.'"

The serpent is expressly called "made by God." It is not the personification of evil, neither the devil nor his disguise as in the old Persian myth. Philo saw in the serpent an allegory of the evil inclination, of sensual lust, which incites man to trespass the divine prohibition. No more suitable animal could have been found. It approaches imperceptibly, tortuously, twistingly and is the image of crookedness; it is apparently harmless and yet equipped with a terrible hidden weapon, slow and yet of lightning speed, secretive and yet familiar; the serpent is an image of crafty seduction. Its ability to speak has a parallel in Balaam's ass (Num. 22, 28) where it is without doubt irony. This chapter too is full of subtle divine irony.

It is not even necessary to assume an ethical allegory; the serpent may be taken concretely. Man had taken woman, an image of God, for his life partner. The animals attempt to pull him down to their level through the serpent, their slyest representative, and even use the woman for this. The fact that the serpent speaks, only puts the seduction into words. The greedy thoughts of man are put into the mouth of an animal as they come from the beast in man. The Hebrew plays on a word which means subtle, but also naked. It had been used in the second sense in the last verse of the preceeding chapter. It is the slyness of the serpent not to turn to Adam. The woman is more readily fooled because she is made to be courted; she is more credulous, easily moved and seduced.

Of all the trees of the garden. The serpent wants to hear the reply: indeed not of all, but of a certain tree. Thus it imperceptibly causes Eve to speak of the prohibited tree and leads her to the desired answer. The serpent, as if stammering, seems to seek for the right word and apologizes that it dares ask. It has heard of a prohibition, but does not quite understand it. Well—then men are to be pitied; you men are really worse off than we. It is an exclamation, half questioning, half reflecting as if the serpent had thought about this strange thing for a long time and had reached an unpleasant conclusion.

Verse 2. The serpent has aimed well. Everything now looks paltry to the woman. She speaks slightingly of the other trees as if they were of no value. She only dwells on the prohibited one. *The fruit,* a word which the serpent had not used, had already caught her eye. The tree seems to stand in the midst of the garden merely to spite her. She does not mention that God has called it the tree of knowledge of good and evil, for this would be embarrassing. By adding that they must not even touch it she shows her exasperation. The woman is not without guile. Similar thoughts had stirred within her; this had been noticed by the seducer with his delicate instincts.

Verse 4. Woman and serpent understand each other immediately. Both do not use God's full name, "the Lord God", but only "God". The animal does not know of a personal God. For this reason an animal is made the speaker for lust and rebellion. The seducer must first diminish the strict conception of a command and prohibition. "God" only "said" something. The woman at once repeats this weaker word, also the mere "God"; it is the echo of her own desire.

God's command is also changed: *Neither shall you touch it.* In order to be certain that a prohibition is observed a precautionary warning may be pronounced against actions which would lead to an infringement; it does not have the same force as the prohibition. The woman gives equal importance to both, as if touching the tree had been forbidden for its own sake and would bring death as an automatic consequence. She changes the moral relationship between prohibition and the threat of punishment into a mechanical one of cause and effect. This must provoke opposition and even derision as expressed in the Midrash which tells that the serpent suddenly pushed the woman against the tree, so that she touched it; then it triumphantly exclaimed: Now, did you die of it? A person who does not want to obey the law hides his disobedience behind arguments against the protective measures. As if he would obey when confronted by the law in all its bluntness and nakedness. He neither knows nor recognizes that the "hedge around the law" has been erected for his sake, not for the law's sake. The woman did not lie in adding this; God had really said so, but these words had been deferred until her speech. She only quotes the phrase so as to distort its meaning.

⁴But the serpent said to the woman, "Die? Oh no! ⁵But God knows that when you eat of it your eyes will be opened, and you will be like God, knowing good and evil."

The Hebrew in verse 4 has a unique form. The serpent's speech is of refined ambiguity. Her denial sounds absolute—you will never die. Or it may only refer to the last words of the woman and would then contain no contradiction against God's warning; see the commentary to 2, 17 (For in the day that you eat of it you shall die).

Verse 5. This is the utmost refinement. Every word is "true"; their eyes are later opened (verse 7); they gain knowledge of good and evil as only God knows it so far, hence they will be like God. Yet every word is a diabolic lie.

After the words *Die? Oh no!* it would be expected of the serpent to continue: on the contrary, you will live forever. The woman shall assume this, but the serpent does not say it. The seducer will not lie under any circumstances. Rather the serpent casts suspicion on God's motives; it suggests that God must have given this command in his own interest due to envy and jealousy. It had indeed been the intention of the divine prohibition that man should not presume to be God. A God is one who is not restricted by any prohibition.

The reply of the serpent is ambiguous. It may be understood as you will be like God in all ways, and one of the consequences will be that you may recognize good and evil. It may also mean you will recognize good and evil like God and in so far be like God. Even a third sense may be found in the words: Good and evil are originally that which tastes good or bad (Deut. 1,39; Is. 7,15). According to popular belief, divine beings—elohim—enjoy supernatural food (Psalms 78,25). The serpent said, if you eat of this tree, you will certainly not die; on the contrary, you will have a wonderful experience. You have no idea what tastes good; this fruit is a divine delicacy. God knows this, but he does not want you to discover it. Your eyes will widen! The enjoyment of good food makes the eyes wide and bright (compare I Sam. 14,29).

Seduction needs to use a promise; the serpent must whet the woman's appetite. The mere prospect of intellectual enrichment would have left her unmoved.

> *⁶So when the woman saw that the tree was good for food, and that it was a dream to the eyes, and that the tree was desirable to look at, she took of its fruit and ate; and she also gave some to her husband who was with her, and he ate. ⁷Then the eyes of both were opened, and they knew that they were naked; and they sewed fig leaves together and made themselves aprons.*

It was not the first time that she had looked at the tree; but now it appears to her in a different light. As the awe of the prohibition is no longer so overwhelming, she does not gaze furtively at the tree, but openly and steadily. The order of words in Hebrew expresses how desire first sees the enticements; the object itself follows only then. She makes three observations. Obviously the tree is good to eat. Secondly it is a dream to the eyes; the Hebrew word means something that one wishes to see. He who has seen it once will always long for it. Someone who hears of it will wish: Oh that I could see it too! Yet these two qualities are also possessed by all other trees of the garden (2,9). This is one of the most subtle details; the prohibited fruit is after all no better than the permitted ones. As it is prohibited desire sees only its merits. Desire is all eyes and yet blind.

Therefore, the woman finds in it a third superiority; poor and self-deceiving, as it contains nothing new and only alters the expression: *desirable to look at.* Some translate "desired to make one wise", but this would be too weak for God-like knowledge (verse 5). However it may be explained, knowledge is the last object of the woman's desire.

The tree attracts her step by step like magic until she undertakes the fatal move with her hand, and then actions follow in quick succession; in half a verse everything is over. She creates an accomplice for herself. Later he casts the guilt back upon her.

Verse 7. This verse is full of bitter irony. These are the very words of the serpent. It had been right, but in a different sense. Consciousness of guilt causes a person to realize that he must hide something; he must hide himself, particularly from the eyes of him who gave the command. Thus in the presence of God not only men like Moses (Ex. 3,6) and Elijah (I Kings 19,13), but even the Seraphim (Is. 6,2) cover their faces. Before him even his servants and saints are not pure (Job 4,18 and 15,15). After their disobedience the first men became conscious that they must not appear naked before God, even that they must not appear at all before him. They try to cover themselves and to hide; they cover what according to later social convention must be covered. The connecting link between consciousness of guilt and consciousness of nakedness is the awe before the Holy. Fig leaves are the largest among leaves of Palestinian trees.

> ⁸And they heard the voice of the Lord God walking in the garden in the wind of the day, and the man and his wife tried to hide from the Lord God among the trees of the garden. ⁹But the Lord God called to the man, and said to him. "Where are you?" ¹⁰And he said, "I heard your voice in the garden, and I was afraid, because I am naked; and I hid myself."

The words *walking in the garden* do not refer to God , but to the voice (most Jewish commentators). *In the wind of the day.* The bad conscience is terrified even by rustling leaves and hears an accusation in the lightest gust of wind.

To hide from the Lord God is told in irony. Adam and Eve imagine themselves able to hide from the Lord God if they retreat into the garden.

Verse 9. This scene has been completely misunderstood as if God, lacking witnesses to the deed, wanted to elicit a confession or as if he asked for Adam's whereabouts due to lack of knowledge. When someone is called by a person from whom he wishes to hide, he does not reply: 'here I am.' Only children may play that way.

The Hebrew language uses a different word in inquiring for someone's location. The word used here mockingly and scornfully emphasizes the absence of a person from a place where he is expected or needed; compare Gen. 19,5 and many other passages. See also the frequent use of "Where is God"? Such questions serve as introduction for further speech (see Ex. 4,2).

Where are you? Are you whom I appointed as keeper of the garden not at your task? God can say this directly to Adam; he need not look for them nor find them. The omniscience and omnipresence of God are assumed. You are hidden; I saw it and knew it. God addresses only Adam because he had been commanded personally.

Verse 10. A rhetorical question may be answered by the other party as if it were real; perhaps he has or pretends no knowledge of what the questioner wants, or he wishes to gain a little time. If he hides himself because he is naked he would not have had to make an apron for himself. Was he not also naked when the commandment was given?

> ¹¹He said, "Who told you that you are naked? Have you eaten of the tree of which I commanded you not to eat?" ¹²The man said,

"The woman whom thou gavest to be with me, she gave me of the tree and I ate." [13]*Then the Lord God said to the woman, "What is this that you have done?" The woman said, "The serpent beguiled me, and I ate."*

God does not ask because he does not know, but that the evil-doer declare himself guilty. God calls it the tree of prohibition, not the tree of knowledge. The transgression brings the recognition of good and evil, and with it the fear of being seen by God, the moral and physical shame.

Verse 12. Obviously God knows everything. A denial is impossible. Adam tries to exonerate himself by blaming someone for whom he, as it were, had no responsibility; he represents the deed as having happened almost mechanically. Shortly before he had enthusiastically welcomed the woman as his long desired companion and as flesh of his flesh; now to the ingrate *she is the woman whom thou gavest to be with me.* It is almost God's own fault. *She gave me, and I ate.* He has really done hardly anything.

Verse 13. In Hebrew the woman's speech consists of only three words. Few words are spoken when no escape remains. *The serpent beguiled me* her talk has dissuaded me from fear of punishment (Spira).

Each party's share in the deed has been determined. It is unfortunate that the succeeding speeches of God have been regarded as pronouncement of sentences in analogy to human justice. No prohibition had been given to the serpent, so it could not be "punished"; the penalty for men was death as they had been advised in 2,17. How can new penalties be pronounced now? Aside from that no legal penalty begins: "Cursed be you. . . ."

Other evil consequences of an evil deed exist which automatically evolve from it, the consequences by which "it punishes itself", and the condemnation by one's own or other people's moral judgement; it brings regret, social banishment and contempt. These directly or indirectly are the "divine" punishments because God is both the creator of the laws of nature, the author of the bond between cause and effect, and the guardian of justice and morality. The following judgements must be understood in this sense.

Verses 2,16f were the example of a perfect law, a prohibition under threat of penalty. These divine speeches to the guilty are a supplement describing other consequences and adding a moral judgement. "The Law", as it is later understood by Tora and prophets, already confronts

the first man. Its most frequent form is found in Deuteronomy with its
curses at the side of judicial penalties. Here the great principle of
divine justice—retaliation—appears for the first time. Its linguistic
expression is the use of the same word for the deed and its consequences, measure for measure; as you have done so it shall be done to
you. Correspondence of the words expresses the anger of the legislator
who uses this method because nothing affects human feeling and
conscience more than this similarity. The penalty reveals itself as the
genuine and natural consequence of the deed through the use of the
same word, but the correspondence goes deeper. The penalty strikes
the evil-doer at his most vulnerable point and incontestably teaches
him the wickedness of his evil intent as well as his own impotence.
Here the important word is "eat"; you shall not eat—she gave me and I
ate—he beguiled me and I ate. It returns in the judgement.

> ¹⁴The Lord God said to the serpent. "Because you have done this,
> cursed are you among all cattle, and among all the beasts of the
> field; upon your belly you shall go, and dust you shall eat all the
> days of your life. ¹⁵I will put enmity between you and the woman,
> and between your seed and her seed; he shall bruise your head
> and you shall bruise his heel."

God begins with the serpent as the interrogation had led to it as
author of the deed. It is not asked, why have you done this? The animal
has no moral personality.

Old and new commentators understand these words to mean that the
serpent previously walked on legs. Yet if God would change the structure of one of his creatures he would be correcting himself. Today we
see the serpent crawling on its belly and it has always done so. The
meaning is rather that God's sentence cites the serpent's existing
nature: Crawl upon your belly and eat dust; that is your manner of life
and it will always be so; henceforth this will be interpreted as a curse. It
will be a reminder of your deed of dragging the first man down to you
into the dust. Because I call you cursed, everyone will look at you in
this way (Deut. 32,24 and Mic. 7,17). The motive for emphasizing this
aspect of the serpent—its poison is not mentioned—is the key word of
retaliation "eat". You beguiled the woman to eat of the fruit of the tree,
you whose nature it is to eat of the lowest and most despicable matter.

Among all cattle and among all the beasts of the field. The serpent
shall and will have a separate position among all the animals that share
the earth with man.

All the days of your life. As long as serpents are in existence. Redak: even in the Messianic time (Is. 65,25).

Verse 15. The mother plants the first antipathies into a child's soul; thus the enmity will be continued in the offspring. There will always be men and serpents. If the serpent is the inclination toward evil it would be even more certain that the struggle will never end and will have moral value. Man's body came from the dust, but he is also an "image of God". He shall always maintain opposition toward that which lives only in the dust and of the dust.

> ¹⁶To the woman he said. "I will greatly multiply your pain in childbearing; In pain you shall bring forth children, yet your desire shall be for your husband, and he shall rule over you."

This refers to all the troubles of womanhood, even before pregnancy. The woman cannot escape them according to her sexual organization and destiny. Woman feels "irresistibly" attracted to man; she must lean upon him as (4,7) a younger brother upon an older one. She knows, however, that by this she subordinates herself to him and must act according to his pleasure.

The general opinion is that all this is ordained as punishment for the woman. This interpretation is impossible for many reasons. The pronouncement does not refer to Eve's eating of the fruit. God himself had proclaimed as a blessing (1,28) that man shall be fruitful and multiply. The troubles of womanhood are inseparably connected with this.

God says this in parenthesis before turning from the serpent to Adam: concerning the woman; oh, if you had only known how much pain your first child will cause you! I need not punish you. Enough hardship is in store for you due to your constitution as woman. God speaks to her as every mother to her daughter. A punishment may perhaps be found in the fact that the woman is told so now.

I will greatly multiply is in the first person singular because it is God who created woman this way; it is he who causes the miracle of birth, who "opens the womb"; and sends the pain together with the blessing. The divine word refers to a permanent condition which cannot be imagined differently. It is an idle dream that woman, created to bear children, should have no discomfort, as vain as the dream of eternal youth or of a paradise; it would not agree with the realism and soberness of the Bible. A child, a new life, is the greatest blessing; it must be purchased through great pain.

It is a mistake to believe that the relation of woman to man is changed (from 2,20). Does the dominating position of man contradict her position as helper? Naturally the stronger, the protector, should be the leader. It is also never stated that man be master of the woman and that she must serve him. The whole idea must be discarded as if in Eve the entire female sex had been condemned to pain and humiliation forever. Nothing would have changed had she not eaten the fruit; even in the garden of Eden she would have given birth in pain and would have been subordinate to man. The loss caused by her transgression is described in that which follows.

> ¹⁷And to man he said, "Because you have listened to the voice of your wife, and have eaten of the tree of which I commanded you, 'you shall not eat of it', cursed is the ground because of you; in pain you shall eat of it all the days of your life; ¹⁸thorns and thistles it shall bring forth to you; and you shall eat the plants of the field. ¹⁹In the sweat of your face you shall eat bread till you return to the ground, for out of it you were taken; you are dust, and to dust you shall return."

This is finally a complete judicial decree. It refers to the express prohibition; it punishes through that which had been the cause of sin. The penalty is for Adam as an individual. The ground is cursed only for his lifetime. The first pious man born after Adam, Noah, redeems the ground from the curse (5,29). The idea that all mankind should suffer for ever for the deed of the one Adam has been introduced into the text from the outside.

The sin consisted in disobedience to God which was obedience to another voice: *you have listened to the voice of your wife.* Two voices spoke to man and he listened to the ungodly one. Only after the deed, when afraid of punishment, did he have an ear for the divine voice (verse 8). Nevertheless the other was the voice of the human being closest to him, of Eve. For this reason the seduction by the serpent takes its course through Eve. It would have offended the honor of God and been too shameful for man, had the serpent turned directly to Adam; it would have been necessary to state "you have listened to the voice of the serpent." Man to whom God has spoken so emphatically cannot sink that low, but the woman had heard of the prohibition only through the man.

In pain. The same word was used in verse 16; the back-breaking toil of man in the field is compared to the pain and labor of womanhood. *You shall eat of it* then you will taste the hard labor for bread. "You shall eat'', because you have eaten of the tree, used not less than five times as expression of retaliation.

Verse 18. *Thorns and thistles it shall bring forth to you.* Not as in paradise where I had beautiful fruit trees grow for you.

Verse 19. The train of thought is as follows: you will have trouble gaining food from the ground; you brought on it the curse of God so it will give fodder for animals grudgingly, thorns and thistles, for your effort. If you want bread, it will cost you much sweat because there is a great deal of labor from plowing to baking.

To dust you shall return it has been claimed that this sentence changes the former constitution of man and that death entered the world only through Adam's sin. The Bible very clearly indicates the opposite; the death of man is the consequence of his creation—everything returns to the place from which it has been taken; life is only a temporary separate existence of a piece of soil. The sinner and the innocent both die; the difference between them is only when and for what reason. This is certainly a somber view of man's destiny, but a necessary supplement to the happy view of chapter one. Life has the aspect of day and night; the Bible teaches the complete truth and can therefore not limit itself to the one or the other.

> ²⁰*Adam called his wife's name Eve, because she became the mother of all living.* ²¹*And the Lord God made for man and his wife skin garments., and clothed them.*

All living of course means only mankind. In Hebrew the word Eve can be derived from the word for living. The woman now gains a new importance for man; he recognizes in her the mother of the future generation through which he as mortal being will continue to live.

Verse 21. It seems strange that God makes garments for man. It is the only thing which he does not learn or invent by himself. God even clothes them in these garments. The verse rightly understood is the key to the whole story of paradise. Clothing is more than protection against cold or an ornament. Rank and dignity are marked by differences in clothing. The priests receive special garments "for glory and for beauty" (Ex. 28,2). Consequently the garments are a symbol of the dignity of man as man; nakedness is animal-like. Clothing is not a mere convention. It is a divine supplement to the creation, forced on man as little as the woman, but made necessary by his conduct.

Skin garments they cover the whole body and are directly upon his skin, as it were, a second skin.

God *clothed them*, performed their "investiture" as the first couple of future civilized mankind. This constitutes their higher dignity above the animal.

> [22]*Then the Lord God said, "Behold, Adam has become like one of us, knowing good and evil; and now lest he put forth his hand and take also of the tree of life, and eat, and live forever".* [23]*Therefore the Lord God sent him forth from the garden of Eden, to till the ground from which he was taken.* [24]*He drove out the man; and at the east of the garden of Eden he placed the cherubim, and a flaming sword which turned every way, to guard the way to the tree of life.*

In verses 17–19 it is already clear that man must leave paradise. Adam had been appointed as keeper of the garden of Eden and had proven a failure. He has eaten of the one tree which was prohibited to him; so the tree of life is also not safe from him.

Like one of us. The "us" must be understood as in 1,26; God speaks to those heavenly beings who surround him; such beings are mentioned in verse 24.

The tree of life Only now at the conclusion does this tree again appear. It makes the garden a paradise and motivates the expulsion of man. The tree is placed in paradise in order that man can never reach it. For a simple reason God did not forbid it previously. Only a person who knows that he must die and is afraid of death wishes to live forever. Man obtained this knowledge after he had eaten of the other tree. Threatening death for eating of the tree of life would have been absurd. It unambiguously states that eating of it would give life. Life means full life, in physical and mental health, a higher true existence (in many passages).

Possessing this fruit man would be protected against disease, old age, and death which is not the will of God. This is not the pagan envy of a deity which begrudges man the possession of immortality. The God of the Bible has created man and could have made this impossible for him by the manner of his creation. However the desire to live for ever and to live in a paradise should and could not be denied to him because this desire is included in being human.

Man imagines the achievement of immortality, in the analogy of the support of life, by eating a certain food; this leads to a tree with such fruit. The utopian wish for such a tree giving eternal life is smilingly answered by the divine wisdom: such a tree exists, but access to it is barred forever; for all practical purposes such a tree does not exist. Man shall not live forever. His mortality is not only a physical, but also a moral necessity. Death is the most effective threat against pride and sin. The tree of knowledge of good and evil demands as its necessary supplement a tree of life inaccessible to man.

Verse 23. Paradise was a test proving to man that he is not fit for it. The expulsion is neither a disgrace nor a punishment.

Verse 24. In all passages where they appear cherubim are close to the deity and its sanctuary which they carry and protect; compare with the cherubim of the tabernacle (Ex. 25,18ff etc.). The tree of life shall be inaccesible to man like God's dwelling place.

And a flaming sword which turned every way seems to be superfluous besides the cherubim. Grotius suggested that the cherubim were identical with the sword; instead of "and" he would translate "namely."

Concepts of an ideal condition of mankind in the beginning are spread throughout the world. Stories of various peoples have the idea in common that death and suffering did not originally exist, and afflicted mankind only later. Yet no story has been found which could be regarded as a source for the Bible. Some details may stem from outside of Israel and may be very old, as for example the cherubim. Certainly everywhere man dislikes hard labor and is afraid of death; he wishes that both did not exist. A paradise is wishful thinking placed into a beautiful age at the beginning.

The Biblical story opposes these dreams and is told with superior wisdom and an irony which is so subtle that even grown-up children do not yet understand it. They think that they are to be told a fairy tale; how happy man could have been without the sin of the first human couple. But no, the intention is entirely different. From the beginning man was created to toil for his bread, woman to bear children in pain, mankind to die. He is man and not God. His happiness consists in obedience to God's command. The desire for immortality on earth is arrogant and vain; man proved to himself that paradise is not for him. All phantasy is banished from the story, and in place of mythology we find religion, ethics, and psychology.

66287

FERNALD LIBRARY
COLBY WOMEN'S COLLEGE
NEW LONDON, N.H. 03257

Chapter 4

Cain And Abel. The Descendants Of Cain.

Now Adam had known his wife Eve, and she conceived and bore Cain, saying, "I have gotten a man with the help of the Lord."
²And again, she bore his brother Abel. Now Abel was a keeper of sheep, and Cain was a tiller of the ground.

Sexual union had probably taken place in Paradise and is not a consequence of the sin as man and woman had been created for it. It is also not thought of as substituting descendents for immortality which had been denied them.

I have gotten a man, produced a man; the Hebrew word is suggestive of the sound of the name Cain. The woman's exclamation uses the name "the Lord," which appears here for the first time without the additional "God". In 3,2 and 3 she and the serpent had suppressed the proper name of God. After the promise "you will have children" has been fulfilled she again acknowledges him in repentance and joy.

Verse 2. In Hebrew the name Abel means a puff of wind, frailty, or nothingness, this in view of his early death (Psalm 144,4). The two occupations of the sons are the most primary ones of mankind and supplement each other. Each of the sons assume a branch of their father's activities; the choice shows their character. Gentle Abel will be a shepherd; Cain disregards the fact that the ground is cursed (Rashi).

³In the course of time Cain brought to the Lord an offering of the fruit of the ground, ⁴and Abel made an offering too: of the firstlings of his flock and of their fat portions. And the Lord had regard for Abel and his offering, ⁵but for Cain and his offering he had no regard. So Cain was very angry, and his countenance fell.

Offerings are not instituted by God. Man toils, but then is surprised by the growth and blessing which he must ascribe to a higher power; he wants to express this feeling by an offering as sign of gratitude.

No reason for God's acceptance of Abel's offering and his disregard for that of Cain is mentioned. Perhaps an animal sacrifice is regarded as more meritorious than a vegetable offering as it testifies to a correct conception of the dignity of man; he shall stand in opposition to the animal in spite of the likeness between them. Nothing tells how the acceptance of the offering was recognized.

> *6The Lord said to Cain, "Why are you angry, and why has your countenance fallen? 7If you do well, will you not be accepted? And if you do not do well, sin is crouching at the door; his desire is for you, but you shall be his master.*

Verse 7. This is the most obscure verse in the entire book; a satisfactory explanation of the linguistic difficulties in the Hebrew text has not yet been found.

The second half of the verse is identical with 3,16. The relationship of older and younger brother is comparable to that of man and woman. The younger one has a desire to cling to the older; the older may guide him, make requests of him, and command him. The meaning seems to be: why do you angrily turn away? You could command him as your right; he would willingly obey you.

> *8Cain told it to Abel his brother. And when they were in the field. Cain rose up against his brother Abel, and killed him. 9Then the Lord said to Cain, "Where is Abel your brother?" He said, "I do not know; am I my brother's keeper?"*

Cain did not tell Abel God's entire speech, but that he had to obey him. *When they were in the field* following their occupations as usual.

Verse 9. Immediately after the deed God's voice is heard, see also 3,9. Cain replies: you ask as if I had to be his keeper. In Hebrew the word "I" emphatically used at the end of the sentence is the classical speech of egotism. It is a cunning protest against the inner voice which said: of course, you are your brother's keeper. The bad conscience would like to escape through a counter-question.

> *10And he said, "What have you done? The voice of your brother's blood is crying to me from the ground. 11And now you are cursed from the ground, which has opened its mouth to receive your brother's blood from your hand. 12When you till the ground, it shall no longer yield to you its strength; you shall be a vagrant and vagabond on the earth.*

God too answers with a question as 3,13. Do you believe that I need to ask at all? Another voice cries loudly to me—the blood of your brother.

Verse 11. This verse does not speak of a legal punishment for the murder, but of its moral consequence (see to 3,14). Retaliation is emphasized by the use of the word "ground". Cain had tilled the ground and had brought his offering from the ground; then he had let the ground drink his brother's blood.
Cursed from the ground, away from the ground.

Verse 12. Not as if the blood has poisoned the ground; it was well known that it had the opposite effect. The ground becomes less productive for Cain through his own bad conscience. As soon as he begins to work the ground, it seems to cry: murderer! Then his arms fall impotently. Language transposes psychological causes through metaphors into physical effects; compare Lev. 18,25 "the land vomits its inhabitants."
A vagrant and vagabond an alliterative pair of words in Hebrew; they express the necessity of roaming as a beggar.

> ¹³*Cain said to the Lord, "Is my guilt to great to be forgiven?*
> ¹⁴*Behold, thou hast driven me this day away from the ground;*
> *and from thy face I must hide; and if I am a vagrant and vagabond*
> *on the earth, it will come to pass that whoever finds me will kill*
> *me."*

This translation of verse 13 is preferrable to that of "my punishment is greater than I can bear"; because the latter would indicate no progress in thought and also be weak. The speech of Cain is again a question, but at the same time a confession and repentance.

Verse 14 Your words mean banishment above and below. God does not want the sinner as the sinner did not want God. When God hides his face from someone it indicates a withdrawal of protection and abandons him to the natural course of events. It is the same whether one says "God has hidden his face" or "The man must hide his face from God", if that were possible (Psalm 139,7). The roof protects only the person who places himself under it (Deut. 31,17). Cain deprived of God's protection becomes prey to the hostile forces of the world. He translates God's words into the language of desperation: *Whoever finds me will kill me.* His last word is the same as his deed.

> 15Then the Lord said to him, "Not so! If anyone kills Cain
> . . . Vengeance shall be taken sevenfold!" And the Lord set a
> sign for Cain, that not whoever came upon him would kill him.
> 16Then Cain went away from the presence of the Lord, and dwelt
> in the land of Nod, east of Eden.

As Cain repents he is paroled. The sentence cannot mean that six
more innocent people of the family of a slayer shall be killed. Such a
procedure for the sake of the murderer Cain would be revolting. *"Not
so! If anyone kills Cain . . .!* is an incomplete sentence containing a
threat (Rashi); compare II Sam.5,8.

Divine justice demands punishment for Cain by death; it is merely
postponed. *Vengeance shall be taken sevenfold* is an exaggerating
figure of speech.

God set a sign for Cain. The popular conception of a mark placed on
Cain's body to brand him as a murderer, must be abandoned. Should
such a mark protect him, how were he to prove that the sign be from
God if he were attacked? There are also linguistic reasons against this
interpretation. A "sign" indicates a foretold event (Ex. 3,12 and often).
God informs Cain that he will not be slain as he fears, but only after
seven—either generations or misfortunes.

Verse 16. In Hebrew the name Nod for the country sounds similar to
the word "vagabond" in verse 13. *East of Eden* constitutes a connection
with the story of paradise. This expulsion (verse 14) removes him still
further from Eden.

From Cain To Lamech

> 17Cain knew his wife, and she conceived and bore Enoch; and he
> built a city; and called the name of the city after the name of his
> son Enoch. 18To Enoch was born Irad; and Irad became the father
> of Mehujael, and Mehujael became the father of Methushael,
> and Methushael became the father of Lamech.

The question where Cain found a wife may find an answer in 5,1ff.
Adam had daughters; one of them became Cain's wife. If the unity of
mankind shall be expressed by descent from one couple, a marriage
between brother and sister in the second generation is unavoidable.
Enoch's name, "initiation," is appropriate for the first son of the first
begotten man. The city-building of Cain must refer to his condemnation. Although he must be a vagabond he wants to see his son settled.

Verse 18. Two of the names contain the word "el" God.

> ¹⁹*And Lamech took two wives for himself; the name of the one*
> *was Adah, and the name of the other was Zillah.* ²⁰*Adah bore*
> *Jabal; he was the father of those who dwell in tents and have*
> *cattle.* ²¹*His brother's name was Jubal; he was the father of all*
> *those who play the lyre and the pipe.* ²²*Zillah then bore*
> *Tubal-Cain; he was the forger of all instruments of bronze and*
> *iron. The sister of Tubal-Cain was Naamah.*

The Hebrew expression for "took wives for himself" is the same as in
6,2; thus it includes a disapproval of polygamy which Lamech
introduced.

Verse 20. The names of the three brothers are alliterative and also
sound somewhat like Abel in Hebrew.
Father of people of a certain occupation means the first in this
occupation.

> ²³*Lamech said to his wives:*
> *"Addah and Zillah, hear my voice;*
> *you wives of Lamech, hearken to what I say;*
> *I have slain a man for wounding me,*
> *a young man for striking me.*
> ²⁴*Because Cain is avenged sevenfold,*
> *and Lamech seventy-sevenfold."*

The connection to the preceeding is as obscure as is the meaning of
this song. There is general agreement about its antiquity; some scholars
regard it as the oldest piece of the Bible. It is the first example of
Hebrew poetry, so that Lamech might be called the inventor of poetry;
the intention may be to establish this.

> ²⁵*And Adam knew his wife again, and she bore a son and called*
> *his name Seth, for she said, "God has appointed for me another*
> *child instead of Abel, for Cain killed him.* ²⁶*To Seth also a son*
> *was born, and he called his name Enosh. At that time it was*
> *begun to call upon the name of the Lord.*

Seth—in Hebrew—is derived from the word "appointed". The mother cannot forget her murdered son or his killer for both had been her
children. She mentions all her sons in one sentence. The Hebrew name

Enosh is a synonym of Adam. The father and son of Seth have basically the same name "Man".

Verse 26 The last sentence has been explained as a statement on the history of religion. Yet "to call upon the name of the Lord" is to make an exclamation containing the name "Lord" (see my book Im Namen Gottes, page 27f.). This is a preliminary announcement of the exclamation of the second Lamech at the birth of his son Noah in 5,29 where the word "the Lord" reappears. Enosh is still alive at Noah's birth (5,29).

The name "the Lord" had been used no more after Cain. At Seth's birth the mother had only spoken of "God". By this remark the chapter closes with a word of hope; the name "the Lord" was not lost.

It was begun not that this happened for the first time since creation, but that a new epoch started the practice again! Just as Noah in 9,2 is not the first tiller of the soil, but the first since Adam and Cain.

The meaning of chapter 4 has often been discussed. It has been regarded as an attempt to describe the progress of civilization. This is incorrect as the Bible has exclusively religious and national interests. As a history of civilization, it would be rather poor, as it is limited to Cain and the sons of Lamech. The building of a city is a climax and would make a strange beginning.

The disobedience against God in the story of paradise is followed in the Bible by the story of a social crime, put into the most pointed form—murder among brothers. Cain is not a racial, but a moral type. Everything revolves around his deed; for its sake his genealogy is continued till Lamech and his song. The occupations of Lamech's sons must have some connection with it, even if we cannot yet find this connection. The story of paradise is deep, but clear. Chapter 4 is obscure and difficult. These figures may have had another significance in pre-Israelite folklore from which the Bible took them; it is the privilege of folkloristic research to discuss this meaning, but we are only concerned with the present text.

Chapter 5

Adam's Descendants

Ten generations from Adam through Seth to Noah follow and include Noah. In each case four facts are stated: 1) The length of the man's life before he begot the next one. 2) The length of his life afterwards begetting other sons and daughters. 3) The length of his life altogether. 4) His death. This presentation is completely uniform with a few exceptions. The nine generations from Shem, Noah's son, to Terach, Abraham's father, are a continuation (11,10–25), so that Abraham is the twentieth generation. The year of the great flood in this scheme is 1656. The idea that this number should constitute an era starting with Creation must be discarded. The Bible never uses such an era. An event is always dated in the years of a contemporary, so the flood started in the six hundredth year of Noah (7,6) etc.

The numbers are an artificial construction; this is incontestable regarding the two sets of 10 generations from Adam to Abraham. Thus it may be assumed that all such numbers are chosen for certain purposes. Adam shall obviously die within the first thousand years (year 930). Noah shall be the first man in the second millenium (born 1056) and shall die in the third millenium (year 2006). Real history is not so accommodating.

The phrase "he lived" followed by a number of years is important. Other Biblical passages show that the use of "he lived" before or after an event indicates this event as decisive in the life of a man and dividing it into two periods. The decisive event in these generations is always the begetting of the son who will continue the line. The meaning and purpose of their lives were fulfilled by that. Different expressions are chosen for Noah as the great event of his life was the flood (9,28).

The first generations shall live many years in order to fill the earth with sons and daughters, but they also fill it with violence and misdeeds.

There are ten generations in order to show God's patience (Aboth

V,2). He delays judgement as far as possible as later with Pharaoh by the use of ten plagues.

Chapter 5 represents the indispensable background for the great flood. Its monotony is impressive. The continuity must not be interrupted by a variety of events so as to create a conception of growth. Yet there is much material for thought. All generations except Noah see Adam die although he was created by God; so they too must expect death. They experience the removal of Enoch, an example of piety and an admonition to repentance. Methushelah begets a son late in life, yet sees him die while he himself dies only when the catastrophe is imminent (year 1656). One man is full of hope and pronounces a prophecy through the naming of his son. His prophecy is realized and God's world is saved by a pious man.

> ¹ his is the book of the descendants of Adam. When God created man, he made him in the likeness of God. ²Male and female he had created them, and he blessed them, and named them Man when they were created.

The Hebrew word "book" may also refer to a shorter document (Deut. 24,1). The sequence of generations through begetting begins. All later begotten men shall be images of God and so of the same kind as Adam. God's naming or changing a former name is always connected with the blessing of fertility and the promise of descendants (17,4 ff.). The name given by God appoints the person as an ancestor and assures that the family named after him will continue.

> ³When Adam had lived 130 years, he became the father of a son in his own likeness, after his image, and named him Seth. ⁴The days of Adam after he became the father of Seth were 800 years; and he had other sons and daughters. ⁵Thus all the days that Adam lived were 930 years; and he died.

Adam's being an image of God is transmitted to his son by begetting and thus it is assured that it will be true of all human generations because all human procreation is of the same kind.

Other sons and daughters are mentioned to explain 6,1.

> ⁶When Seth had lived 105 years, he became the father of Enosh. ⁷Seth lived after the birth of Enosh 807 years, and he had other sons and daughters. ⁸Thus all the days of Seth were 912 years; and he died.

⁹When Enosh had lived 90 years, he became the father of Kenan. ¹⁰Enosh lived after the birth of Kenan 815 years, and he had other sons and daughters. ¹¹Thus all the days of Enosh were 905 years; and he died.

¹²When Kenan had lived 70 years, he became the father of Mahalalel. ¹³Kenan lived after the birth of Mahalalel 840 years, and he had other sons and daughters. ¹⁴Thus all the days of Kenan were 910 years; and he died.

¹⁵When Mahalalel had lived 65 years, he became the father of Jered. ¹⁶Mahalalel lived after the birth of Jered 830 years; and he had other sons and daughter. ¹⁷Thus all the days of Jered were 895 years; and he died.

¹⁸When Jered had lived 162 years, he became the father of Enoch. ¹⁹Jered lived after the birth of Enoch 800 years; and he had other sons and daughters. ²⁰Thus all the days of Jered were 962 years; and he died.

²¹When Enoch had lived 65 years, he became the father of Methushelah. ²²Enoch walked with God after the birth of Methushelah 300 years; and he had other sons and daughters. ²³Thus all the days of Enoch were 365 years. ²⁴Enoch walked with God, and he was not, for God had taken him.

Verse 22. Enoch walked with God, the same expression for Noah in 6,9. It means moral conduct of life which finds favor in the eyes of God and has as consequence his intimate, protective friendship. Enoch is a forerunner of Noah. Noah's father Lamech expressed a Messianic hope by naming him Noah (see verse 29), as Jered had done by calling his son Enoch which in Hebrew means "beginning", "initiation". Through him the world should renew itself; it did so by his exemplary conduct.

Verse 24. Enoch walked with God until the end of his life which is told in unusual words; later the same expression is used for the end of the prophet Elijah (II Kings 2,3 ff.). His pious life is in contrast to the profane life of his contemporaries and thus implies an admonition for them. An early age already understood it this way (Sirach 44,16) and originated the concept that Enoch was removed beyond human ken into a higher world; there he was initiated into the mysteries of heaven in intimate contact with God and angels. He supposedly described his knowledge in books, which are the apocryphical writings, "the Book of Enoch" and others, ascribed to him. The Jewish Middle Ages are filled with fables about him, as are those of Islam in which he is called Idris.

On the other hand later Jewish tradition at times doubted his piety; it regarded him as a hypocrite who was taken away by an untimely death as punishment.

> 25When Methushelah had lived 187 years, he became the father of Lamech. 26Methushelah lived after the birth of Lamech 782 years; and he had other sons and daughters. 27Thus all the days of Methushelah were 969 years; and he died.
>
> 28When Lamech had lived 182 years, he became the father of a son, 29and called his name Noah, saying, "This one shall comfort us from our work and the toil of our hands out of the ground which the Lord has cursed." 30Lamech lived 595 years after the birth of Noah; and he had other sons and daughters. 31Thus all the days of Lamech were 777 years; and he died.

Methushelah reaches the highest age namely 969 years, so that he only dies in the year of the flood (1656).

Verse 29. What gives Lamech this hope? Noah is the first man born after the death of Adam and the ground was cursed only for Adam's lifetime. This Lamech is a counterpart to the Lamech in the lineage of Cain (4,23). The latter boasted of his sword; this one pronounces a prayer. The 777 years of this man may also allude to the seven and seventy-seven in the song of the earlier Lamech. The lineage of Cain begins with murder and ends in vengeance; although it contains the building of a city and inventions, it possesses no man of God. The genealogy of Seth seems without achievements for civilization, but it presents religious heroes like Enoch and Noah. The story begins with God and ends with "the Lord".

This one shall comfort us is not an etymology of the name "Noah", but is suggestive of it according to its Hebrew sound. Lamech's hope is fulfilled. Noah becomes a tiller of the soil and even plants the vine (9,20); when the ground produces this most noble fruit (Zech 8,12), it can no longer be cursed. Mourning ceases where wine is found.

> 32After Noah was 500 years old, Noah became the father of Shem, Ham, and Japheth.

Noah becomes a father only at the age of 500 years, so that his sons will not yet have children at the time of the flood.

There is a remarkable similarity, and in some cases even identity of names in the genealogies of Cain and Seth. Both contain Enoch and

Lamech; similar are Cain and Kenan, Irad and Jered, Mehujael and Mahalalel, Methushael and Methushelah. The ancient Babylonians, according to Berossus, told of ten kings ruling over Babylonia before the great flood; their combined rule in supposed to have lasted 432000 years. A certain similarity with names in the Babylonian report also exists.

The high ages reached by these generations are of course not historical. According to historical experience no man has reached an age of 200 years. Even a figure of 150 years cannot be verified; not to speak of 900 years and more. The human organism does not seem to permit an age of much over 100 years.

Antiquity did not object to these high figures, particularly as other nations used still higher ones. Compared with them the numbers in the Bible are moderate.

Chapter 6

The Depravity Of Mankind

When men began to multiply on the face of the ground, and
daughters were born to them, ²the divine ones saw the daughters
of men that they were strong; and they took to themselves women,
such of them as they pleased. ³Then the Lord said, "My spirit
shall never abide strongly in man, all the more since he is flesh,
but his days shall be a hundred and twenty years." ⁴The
Nephilim were on the earth in those days, and also afterwards
because the divine ones came in to the daughters of men, and
they bore children to them. These were the mighty men that were
of old, the men of renown.

An increase in population leads to an increase in sin.

Verse 2. The expression which we translate *the divine ones* in
Hebrew literally reads "the sons of God". Who are they? Some say they
were angels (already Philo, Josephus etc.). From this the idea of "fallen
angels" was derived. This interpretation is certainly wrong. The Bible
never thinks of angels as beings with sexual urges (see also Matthew
22,30); for the mind of Israel it is also inconceivable that angels would
rebel against God. Finally, if they are at fault, they should be punished
and not man. According to the whole context these "sons of God" must
be human beings. The flood shall punish the sins of man; therefore, his
depravity must be described. The "divine ones" were like God in their
own eyes, and yet of a very earthly humanity.

They took to themselves women such as they pleased, meaning
several, many. These sexual unions must have been of a nature which
could later be called "corrupt in God's sight"; "all flesh had corrupted
its way upon the earth" (6, 11f.). The Bible only generally hints at this
without glaring details.

The daughters of men *were strong,* not "fair" as often wrongly translated (see I Sam. 9,2). The word shall explain the resulting giants.

45

Verse 3. This verse is very difficult in language and meaning. In any case, the spirit of God and the flesh that is man are declared to be incompatible for any length of time. The spirit of God in the thinking of the Bible makes a man a prophet (Num. 24,2) or man of war and hero e.g. the "judges" (Judg. 3,10; 6,34; 11,29; 13,25); it is also the source of higher gifts in wisdom, art, and learning (Ex. 31,3; 35,31). Some persons among the first generations of mankind were intoxicated by their likeness to God and in a feeling of vigor generated and enhanced by the spirit of God, they fancied themselves to be "divine ones" and were regarded as such. Their conduct was that of "supermen" and began with the emancipation of the flesh. The daughters of men, of common men, became their prey. The expression "divine ones" may even be meant ironically (compare Psalm 82, 6f).

It seems that their long life is regarded as the cause of their sin; henceforth they shall grow no older than 120 years. This cannot be an age limit for all men as all succeeding generations live beyond this limit—not only from Noah to Terach (11,10–32), but also Abraham (175 years), Isaac (180 years), Jacob (147 years). These men receive divine revelations, but are not "sons of God". If the spirit of God is in a man, he dies before 120; Joseph (41,38) dies at the age of 110, and so Joshuah (Num. 27,18).

Moses is the first man after the flood to be called "a man of God", he indeed reaches an age of exactly 120 years (Deut. 31,2). Although his bodily vigor is undiminished (Deut. 34,7), he must die. Perhaps Elijah, another "man of God", is similarly 120 years old when he dies as only thus may he and his disciples know that his time has come (II Kings 2,3; 5).

Verse 4. The children of the "divine ones" and the daughters of the other men are nephilim, vigorous men of gigantic bodies and strength.

Men of renown like Nimrod (10,9) about whom popular tales were current. Nephilim are still mentioned at the time of Moses (Num. 13, 33); elsewhere they are called Refaim (Deut. 2,20) or Emim and Zamzumim. Og the king of Bashan, their last descendant, had "an iron bedstead, nine cubits long and four cubits wide," which was shown in Rabbah of the Ammonites (Deut. 3,11).

In those days may mean before the flood, and *afterwards* after the flood.

> ⁵*The Lord saw that the wickedness of man was great in the earth, and that every imagination of the thoughts of his heart was only evil all day long.* ⁶*And the Lord was sorry that he had made man*

on the earth, and it grieved him to his heart. ⁷So the Lord said, "I will blot out man whom I have created from the face of the ground, man and beast, and creeping things, and birds of the heavens, for I am sorry that I have made them." ⁸But Noah found favor in the eyes of the Lord.

The preceding verses reported the facts; now God's impression is given.

All day long Day as the time of activity is said in contrast to night. Only while asleep were they not wicked.

Verse 6. Pronouncements in Num. 23,19 and I Sam. 15,29 that God "is not a man who needs repent" do not contradict the much more frequent statements that God "repents" or "has repented" (I Sam. 15,11 in the same chapter! and often). The difference is not hard to discover. The first refers to the future, the latter refers to the past or the present. When prophets announce a decision of God for the future they say that God must be taken seriously; he is not like a man who says one thing today and the opposite to-morrow. The other passages teach that an imminent misfortune, although threatened by God, can be averted through prayer, repentence and good deeds. Similarly a man chosen by God may forfeit this by a change for evil. God's change reflects the altered actions of man (Jer. 18,7 ff.). It was the mistake of the prophet Jonah not to recognize this. No living religion of repentance and forgiveness is possible without such a conception of God. Yet the God of mercy is grieved that his creatures must perish.

To his heart. Differing from the heart of the wicked God's heart had plans for good and salvation. It was full of love; he mourns for his world. Not that God admits a mistake in creating man, but God's grief, anger, and sorrow are the counterpart to man's freedom even to do evil.

Verse 7. The animals shall be destroyed as they are created for the service of man; similarly the animals are saved with man (6,19.; Jon 4,11). The destruction is so radical, because the depravity of man and the grief of God are so great.

Verse 8. The only ray of hope promising a new future in this dark picture is Noah's favor in the eyes of God. The prophets never conclude without hope even following the most terrible threats. God's creation can never be so depraved that no slip remain for new growth (Is. 6,13).

Noah's Descendants

⁹*These are the descendants of Noah. Noah was a righteous man, blameless in his generations; Noah walked with God. ¹⁰And Noah became father of three sons: Shem, Ham, and Japheth. ¹¹Now the earth was corrupt in God's sight, and the earth was filled with violence. ¹²And God looked at the earth, and behold, it was corrupting itself, for all flesh had corrupted their way upon the earth.*

There are two elements in the flood; the destruction of all living and the rescue of Noah. Both must be motivated.

In his generations This expression will be explained in 9,28. The Midrash (Sanhedrin 108 a) debates whether this be absolute or relative praise; shall it mean even in this depraved generation! or in comparison with his evil contemporaries? Both opinions contain some truth. Noah is the only righteous man in his time, but he is not a pleader for sinners as Abraham, Moses, or Samuel.

Verse 9 states that God's favor in verse 8 was not without basis.

Verse 11. *In God's sight.* They did not believe God sees all and did not care for him or thought him indifferent to their ways.

Violence is tyrannical oppression of others and forceful seizure of their property; men took what they pleased, for example the wives of other men (verse 2). God reproaches them for social injustice only.

God's demands on man, as the prophet Micah expresses it are "to do justice, and to love kindness, and to walk in this way even outside the sight of man as God sees it"; this is how the famous passage in Mic. 6,8 should be understood and how mere morality becomes religion.

Verse 12. *All flesh* means all living beings, men and animals. It signifies the frailty common to both. The general depravity also consisted in abolishing the distinctions between animal and man; the ancient Jewish interpretation speaks of unnatural sexual vices. They had *corrupted their way*; everything contradicted its God given nature and had degenerated.

¹³*And God said to Noah, "The end of all flesh has been determined by me; for the earth is filled with violence through them; behold, I will destroy them, that is the earth. ¹⁴Make yourself an ark of gopher wood; make the ark tight, and cover it inside and outside with pitch. ¹⁵This is how you are to make it: the length of the ark 300 cubits, its breadth 50 cubits, and its height*

30 cubits. ¹⁶Make a roof for the ark, and finish it to one cubit from above, and set the door of the ark in its side; make it with lower, second, and third decks.

Here is the first usage of the term so important for later eschatology, *the end,* the great judgement (Dan. 8,17; Ezek. 7,2ff.; but already Amos 8,2). God says: I am not blind as the wicked believe; their measure is full; after ten generations my patience is at an end.

I will destroy them. The Hebrew uses the same word as in the description of man's corruption; it is another example of retaliation.

Verse 14. But Noah shall build himself an ark. The following is not a technically complete description. For that three verses would have been too brief.

Gopher wood is a kind of cedar. The ark is not a ship; it has neither a keel, nor a steering apparatus, neither mast nor sail. It shall be a house afloat which can protect its inhabitants during a flood and for this reason be made of wood.

Verse 14. *Make the ark tight* with papyrus fibres (Yahuda); this is the sense of the Hebrew, and not "make rooms" in it. Afterwards it is to be covered with pitch.

Verse 15. The size is unusually large, in accordance with the purpose.

Verse 16. *Roof* others translate the Hebrew word as window, an opening for light. This roof seems to extend down one cubit like a table cloth over a table's edge. See 8,13.

Now Noah shall learn the purpose of this structure.

¹⁷For behold, I will bring the flood of waters upon the earth, to destroy all flesh in which is the breath of life from under heaven; everything that is on the earth shall die. ¹⁸But I will confirm my covenant with you; and you shall come into the ark, you, your sons, your wife, and your sons' wives with you. ¹⁹And of every living thing of all flesh, you shall bring two of every sort into the ark, to keep them alive with you; they shall be male and female. ²⁰Of the birds according to their kinds, and of the cattle according to their kinds, of every creeping thing of the ground according to its kind, two of every sort will come in to you, to keep them alive. ²¹Also take with you every sort of food that is eaten, and store it up; and it shall serve as food for you and for them." ²²*Noah did this; he did all that God commanded him.*

The word translated by *flood* rather means "destruction" in Hebrew; it therefore need be explained by adding *of waters.* The Hebrew here uses a word for dying which indicates a slow death without the infliction of a wound, by loss of strength through lack of food. The first consequence of the inundation will be the loss of food supplies; men will be steadily weakened through hunger until they expire.

Verse 18. This verse does not refer to the covenant after the flood in chapter 9, but to the favor which Noah had found in the eyes of God (verse 8). That is already a covenant; God will now confirm it (see also to 9,9).

The others will only be saved "with Noah". The essence of the whole story is the preservation of the world for the sake of a pious man; all others live, so to speak in his shadow.

Verse 19. One couple of each species shall survive the flood and thus creation shall be preserved.

Verse 20. All of them will, guided by the instinct of self-preservation and attracted by Noah, enter the ark by themselves.

Verse 21. *For you* and your family *and for them* for the animals.

Verse 22. God had only "said" it (verse 13), but Noah takes it as a command; this is the exact opposite of the conduct of the serpent and Eve (3,3). The concluding sentence is therefore praise of Noah's obedience.

Chapter 7

Then the Lord said to Noah, "Go into the ark, you and all your household, for I have seen that you are righteous before me in this generation. ²Take for you seven pairs of all clean animals, the male and his mate; and a pair of the animals that are not clean, the male and his mate; ³and seven pairs of the birds of the air also, male and female, to keep their seed alive upon the face of all the earth. ⁴For yet seven days and I will send rain upon the earth forty days and forty nights; and every living thing that I have made I will blot out from the face of the ground." ⁵And Noah did all that the Lord had commanded him.

In 6,13 "God" spoke to Noah; here "the Lord" said; when man alone is addressed the name "the Lord" is used, but if animals are included as well (as in 6,20), the name "God". "The Lord" is the personal God; he speaks to man as a personality. The rest of creation merely possesses a general understanding of the divine ("God"); it is addressed through man whenever it is to receive a command. *Your household* has a moral connotation. The family of Noah is rescued with him for they have been educated by him and are not unworthy. God says: I have scrutinized all mankind and found nothing but wickedness; only you were righteous before my eyes which examine and judge everything. The wickedness of the evil and the virtue of the righteous appear before God simultaneously, one for extermination, the other for preservation.

This generation is said with angry disapproval.

Verses 2 and 3. These verses are not in conflict with 6,19-20; in the latter only two animals of each kind were taken, while here seven pairs of all clean animals. Chapter six speaks of the animals as creatures which should be preserved in their kinds through the flood. This chapter speaks of the animals which Noah shall take for himself (*for you*), for the sacrifices which he will offer after the flood (8,20) (Rashi and others). The reason for seven will be explained in 9,7; it will also be shown that as these seven pairs were sacrificed, an eighth pair was needed in the ark for preservation. Thus recognition is given Noah's piety as he will feel urged to bring a sacrifice; God permits this and even prepares for it. It would otherwise be impossible to sacrifice without entirely exterminating some species of animals. The expression *that are not clean* avoids the word "unclean", a Hebrew term specific for Israel's later religion and therefore not yet valid for Noah. The emphasis here is on the preservation of creation and in it nothing is "unclean" in itself.

Verse 3. The distinction between "clean" and "not clean" applies to the birds also as shown in 8,20. We will later find a representative of each in the raven and the dove.

To keep their seed alive as in 19,32.34 where a similar fear that the race might become extinct exists. They shall be kept alive for the sake of reproduction.

Verse 4. *Yet seven days* The end is near! But a last period of grace of one week (Rashi) as in Ex 7,25 is granted.

Every living thing The Hebrew drastically expresses this as everything that can stand upright.

The next paragraph seems to tell the same thing twice, once in verses 6–9 and then in verses 10–16. This fullness is a beautiful testimony to the thinking of the author and his concept of God. The pious man, the preservation of the creatures, and the merciful care for them are more important to him than the divine judgement; beginning with 6,13 he uses three times as many verses for a description of the ark and its inhabitants than for the flood.

Verses 7–9 report that all beings entered the ark. Yet when the last day has arrived and the catastrophe is about to start, God in his paternal mercy once more assures himself that all beings are really in the saving ark and none has been omitted. This is reported in verses 12–16.

> [6]Noah was six hundred years old; and the flood occured, water over the earth. [7]And Noah and his sons and his wife and the wives of his sons with him went into the ark, to escape the waters of the flood. [8]Of clean animals, and of animals that are not clean, and of birds, and of everything that creeps on the ground, [9]two and two, male and female, went to Noah, into the ark, as God had commanded Noah.

The flood occurs in Noah's six hundredth year, so all his ancestors, including the long-living Methushelah, had died and could not have been wicked.

Verse 7. The people enter the ark consciously; through God's revelation they know of the imminent flood, of its consequences and of the meaning of the ark. Only they enter *to escape the waters of the flood*. The animals are not aware of these facts and merely come to Noah, and then into the ark. Not that he had first entered the ark and expected them there; but before he entered they came to him. This expresses not merely that the animals seek companionship with man, but that it is this man Noah alone whom the whole animal kingdom, forgetting all enmities, obediently follows as their provider into the ark. It is a model for the general peace among all creatures in Messianic time. This is more than the peace in Adam's paradise. He who causes this miracle is a pious man who walked with God. And the animals even imitate the men who had gone before them and organize in couples as they had been created one for the other. Man is the model for the animal, rather than sinking to the animals' level (6,2). The scene of all animals, tame and wild, following Noah into the ark possesses much charm and simplicity which was well understood by many great painters.

> ¹⁰*And after the seven days the waters of the flood came upon the earth.* ¹¹*In the six hundredth year of Noah's life, in the second month, on the seventeenth day of the month, on that day all the fountains of the great deep burst forth, and the windows of the heavens were opened.* ¹²*And rain fell upon the earth forty days and forty nights.* ¹³*On the very same day Noah and Shem and Ham and Japheth, the sons of Noah, and Noah's wife and three wives of his sons with them had entered the ark,* ¹⁴*they and every beast according to its kind, and all the cattle according to their kinds, and every creeping thing that creeps on the earth according to its kind, and every bird according to its kind, every bird of every sort.* ¹⁵*They had come to Noah into the ark, two and two of all flesh in which there was the breath of life.* ¹⁶*And they that entered, male and female of all flesh, went in as God had commanded him, and the Lord locked behind him.*

Verse 11. In poetical and graphical language the waters are stored above the sky behind windows; when these are opened the waters fall (Is.24,18). This expresses powerfully the irruption of the flood as a gigantic catastrophe. The sparing use of such expressions heightens the effect. At the same time the *great* deep bursts forth; that is the answer to the *great* wickedness of man (6,5).

Verse 13. Noah and each of his sons have only one wife, compare Adam and Eve. The three families of nations, Japhethites, Hamites, and

Shemites, are each descended from one father and one mother. There are no descendants by second wives or maid-servants.

Verse 14. The birds as the freest and least tied to the ground enter last.

Verse 16. *The Lord locked behind him.* These words beautifully express the religious quintessence of the whole story. Everyone was in his place (verses 7–9), but at the last moment God wants certainty that no one is missing (verses 13–16). He is locking the door with his own hand. II Kings 4,21 is another example for locking from the outside. If someone who cannot protect himself must be left alone, he is temporarily locked in, so that he may be found unharmed upon return. In II Kings 4,21 a mother locks; here it is God. In a moment he will loosen the flood, but the waters will not be able to harm Noah and his family. God in effect seals the ark until he orders them to leave it. The elements will neither be able nor willing to break his seal. Noah's preservation achieved in a natural way by embarkation in an ark of wood shows the rationalism of our story; it is perhaps also a psychological necessity to conceive even miracles in a natural way.

> [17]*The flood was forty days upon the earth; and the waters increased, and bore up the ark, and it rose high above the earth.* [18]*The waters prevailed and increased greatly upon the earth; and the ark floated on the face of the waters.* [19]*And the waters prevailed so mightily upon the earth that all the high mountains under the whole heaven were covered;* [20]*the waters prevailed above the mountains, covering them fifteen cubits deep.* [21]*And all flesh perished that moved upon the earth, birds, cattle, beasts, all swarming creatures that swarm upon the earth, and every man;* [22]*everything on the dry land in whose nostrils was the breath of life died.* [23]*He blotted out every living thing that was upon the face of the ground, man and animals and creeping things and birds of the heavens; they were blotted out from the earth. Only Noah was left, and those that were with him in the ark.* [24]*And the waters were prevailing upon the earth a hundred and fifty days.*

Verse 18. The expression "prevailed" pictures the force of these floods. The story is a model of majestic simplicity (Dillmann). The verse emphasizes universality of the flood.

Verse 20. *Fifteen cubits;* four or five times as high as a man, so that everyone would drown.

Three different expressions indicate the death of all living creatures. The first signifies their pining away, the second that they have ceased to live, the third that they disappear from the earth.

Verse 22. *Everything on the dry land* excludes fish whose element is water.

Verse 23. This verse states that God's tragic resolution (6,7) has now been completely executed.

Verse 24. *Noah was left* an intentional and planned preservation; he is like the "remnant" of prophetical speech after catastrophe. Noah in the ark is a symbol of God's saving Providence and of comforting security (compare Psalm 46). The ark, as his house before the flood, was an island of virtue and fear of God in an ocean of wickedness and sin.

Verse 25. The waters rose no further after the forty days of rain; they remained at their height for 110 days; this totals 150 days. Was it not time to bring it to an end?

Chapter 8

*But God remembered Noah and all the beasts and all the cattle
that were with him in the ark. And God made a wind blow over
the earth, and the waters subsided;* ²*the fountains of the deep and
the windows of the heavens had closed, the rain from the heavens
was restrained,* ³*and the waters receded from the earth continual-
ly. At the end of a hundred and fifty days the waters had abated;*
⁴*and in the seventh month, on the seventeenth day of the month,
the ark came to rest upon the mountains of Ararat.* ⁵*And the
waters continued to abate until the tenth month; in the tenth
month, on the first day of the month, the tops of the mountains
were seen.*

The Hebrew does not say that God had forgotten Noah and merely
remembered him now; but, in spite of all this, God had not forgotten
Noah; after the predetermined time he brings a turn for the better. He
remembers the covenant 6,18 as Ex. 2,24 and often. In Jewish liturgy
God is praised as "He who remembers the covenant".

He *remembered Noah* for the promise had been made to him; the
family merely participates in his merit.

Verse 2. *had closed.* After forty days (7,12). God's wrath had come
over the earth; now his anger is calmed and he sends the healing wind.
The waters had risen for forty days; the descent is slower and more
gradual.

Verse 4. *The ark came to rest.* The Hebrew word for "came to rest"
sounds similar to the name "Noah."

Ararat is the name of a country (II Kings 19,37), Eastern Armenia.
Josephus (Antiquities I 3, 6) identifies the mountain as one which the
Armenians called Massis or preferably Ararat. It rises to a height of
16,000 feet near Erivan.

Verse 5. This verse represents the second stage in the descent of the waters. It reminds of 1,9 where the earth also became visible through the receding of the waters.

> [6]At the end of forty days Noah opened the window of the ark which he had made, [7]and released the raven; and it went to and fro until the waters were dried up from the earth. [8]Then he released a dove from him, to see if the waters had subsided from the face of the ground; [9]but the dove found no place to set her foot, and she returned to him to the ark, for waters were still on the face of the whole earth. So he put forth his hand and took her and brought her into the ark. [10]He waited another seven days, and again he released the dove out of the ark; [11]and the dove came back to him in the evening, and lo, in her mouth a freshly plucked olive leaf; so Noah knew that the waters had subsided from the earth.[12]Then he waited another seven days,and released the dove; and she did not return to him any more.

It is generally assumed that Noah sends forth the birds to discover whether the earth is dry so that he can disembark. Noah however will not disembark until told by God; Noah is not impatient. He waits no less than forty days before releasing the raven, then three times seven days with the dove; after the dove fails to return, he waits 56 days more until he disembarks. The raven is not sent out as a messenger who shall return with a report. No such purpose is mentioned regarding him in contrast to the dove (verse 8). The release of the raven occurs because the tops of the mountains have become visible. It is a first welcome to the earth which now emerges from the flood, a triumphal cry: land, land! The raven flying forth is a living banner which Noah hoists in celebration.

Verse 7. This verse describes the faithfulness of the raven as a living link between Noah and the earth which is slowly uncovered. The raven goes to and fro, as if to tell the one of the other until the earth is dry, and Noah disembarks. The dove is the more gracious bird, but the raven is more intelligent. The dove stays away as soon as she can set her foot on the ground. The Midrash thinks of the ravens of I Kings 17,4ff. The raven which returns so often and naturally receives food from Noah is the forefather of the ravens which God sends to bring bread and meat to the prophet Elijah at the brook Cherith in the time of famine. They repay to his descendant the support Noah gave their ancestor. The intelligent raven must have been regarded as a messenger and special favorite of God in Israel's folklore (see also Psalm 147,9 and Job 38,41). The two birds, dove and raven, are of the same size, but otherwise a contrasting pair beginning with their colors, black and white.

Verse 8. This verse explains the omission of the birds in verse 1. The animals which live on the ground cannot leave the ark until the earth is completely dry. Must the birds remain confined until then? Should they not be released as soon as the mountain peaks become visible? Like God who remembered man and animal, the pious Noah who "walks with God", remembers the birds and tries their release with one unclean and one clean bird. For "a righteous man has regard for the soul of his beast" (Prov. 12,10). The animals are grateful for the kindness and care.

The dove is released to see if the waters had subsided from the face of the ground. Noah, the man of the ground (9,20), looks forward to seeing the ground again. He wants to prepare himself for that festive moment. The first inquiry which is shy like the dove herself does not find a satisfactory answer. Therefore the dove must be sent again.

Verse 9. Helpfully and carefully Noah puts forth his hand to retrieve the dove as if regretting that he has troubled the little bird too soon.

Verse 11. The dove did not need to return, but does so out of gratitude in order to bring Noah the good tidings. *Evening* is the time when work ceases, trouble stops; man becomes pure again and hears the message of peace. *And lo* what a happy sight! The earth is green and reconsecrated, because oil is a sign of consecration.

Verse 12. The author lovingly uses as many verses for the episode of the birds as for the entire flood. The bird motif is older than the Bible, but is rather paltry in the Babylonian flood legend compared to this story. Although the dove has not returned Noah does nothing for the present, but lets a full month pass.

> [13]*In the six hundred and first year, in the first month, the first day of the month, the waters were dried from off the earth; and Noah removed the covering of the ark, and looked, and behold, the face of the ground was dry.* [14]*In the second month, on the twenty-seventh day of the month, the earth was dried out.*

In the first month, the first day of the month. Not only a new year for Noah begins, but it was New Year's Day for the whole world, the birthday of creation; on this very day the world rises again from the chaos of the flood. The removal of the ark's cover is Noah's New Year's celebration with which a renewed creation and a new life start. Now we may understand the arrangements in 6,16. The roof acted as a covering on top of the ark; Noah removes it, not because it hindered his view, but in honor of the day for which one removes the old garment as a woman removes the garment of her widowhood (38,14) or the garment of captivity (Deut. 21,13).

The last words of verse 13 picture the joy of the sight (1,30). Noah sees the grounds for which he had longed; see verse 8. This is God's New Year's present to him.

Verse 14. The Hebrew word for "dry" in this verse differs from that of verse 13; it means "so dry that it must rain again". It took 56 more days to reach this stage; this brings us to the second month which in Palestine is the month of rain. So as to end in the second month, the flood had to also begin in it. (7,11)

> ¹⁵Then God said to Noah, ¹⁶"Go forth from the ark, you and your wife, and your sons and your sons' wives with you. ¹⁷Bring forth with you every living thing that is with you of all flesh—birds and animals and every creeping thing that creeps on the earth—that they may move about on the earth, and be fruitful and multiply upon the earth." ¹⁸So Noah went forth, and his sons and his wife and his sons' wives with him. ¹⁹And every beast, every creeping thing, and every bird, everything that moves on the earth, went forth by families out of the ark.

Then God said not the "Lord" as in 7,1 because this speech concerns the animals as well as man; the personal name for God would not be fitting. The use of the different names for God is always intentional.

> ²⁰Then Noah built an altar to the Lord, and took of every clean cattle and of every clean bird, and offered burnt offerings on the altar. ²¹And the Lord smelled the pleasing odor and the Lord said to his heart. "I will never again curse the ground because of man, for the imagination of man's heart is evil from his youth; neither will I ever again destroy every living creature as I have done. ²²While the earth remains, seed time and harvest, cold and heat, summer and winter, day and night shall not cease."

Verse 21. This verse has been regarded as a crude ascription of human attributes to God. Yet smelling is no cruder than seeing or hearing.

A monologue of the Lord which gives us an insight into the depths of God's being follows. For the general meaning of this verse and Noah's sacrifice see 9,7. The Talmud regards the repeated "never again" as a formal oath (Is. 54,9). Indeed the later prophets will threaten all kinds of divine punishments, but never again a flood.

The flood does not change the course of nature. It is only a judgement for the living creatures, but for the earth it is a bath of purification which washes away its pollution and restores its purity (Num. 35,33 ff.). Therefore the waters even stood above the highest mountains for a long time (see also Ezek. 22,24).

Legends of a great flood, based on actual inundations, are found among many peoples. Most remarkable are the Indian, Greek, Babylonian and Sumerian legends. The Babylonian and Sumerian ones in their many versions show the most obvious parallels to the Biblical story. It is almost generally assumed that they are the source of it.

If this is true the Bible has made many changes. All polytheism has been eliminated. In the Babylonian legend the hero Ut-napishtim is saved for no apparent reason nor is a purpose for taking the animals into the ark given while the Bible speaks of preserving creation. The basic idea of the flood as a great judgement appears only as an afterthought in the Babylonian legend. Merely the general structure of the stories is the same. Almost all details differ.

The Babylonian story shows that such tales existed long before Israel among nations from whom Israel has borrowed other things as well. The Bible took the raw materials and thoroughly transformed them through its own characteristic spirit. The Babylonian story is mainly interested in epic narration. Deeper concepts have been relegated to the background or completely obliterated. The Bible clearly and decisively emphasizes religious ideas; it makes matter and form subservient to them. This proves the originality and energy of Israel's mind.

CHAPTER 9

The Covenant With Noah And His Sons

And God blessed Noah and his sons, and said to them, "Be fruitful and multiply, and fill the earth. ²The fear of you and the dread of you shall be upon every beast of the earth, and upon every bird of the heavens, upon every thing that creeps on the ground, and all the fish of the sea; into your hand they are delivered. ³Every moving thing that lives shall be food for you; as the green plants, I give you everything. ⁴Only you shall not eat flesh with its life, that is its blood. ⁵But for your blood, of every, life of you, I will surely require a reckoning; of every beast I will require it and of man; of every man's brother I will require the life of man. ⁶Whoever sheds the blood of man, by man shall his blood be shed; for God made man in his own image. ⁷And you be fruitful and multiply, bring forth abundantly on the earth and multiply in it."

It is the same blessing as given the first human couple (1,28) because a new beginning is made.

Verse 2. As man respectfully shies away from God, so the beasts will from man because he is an image of God (verse 6). His propagation, as desired by God, shall not be checked by the animals. The fullness of expression is to show that no being in any realm will be able to resist man (see Psalm 8). *Into your hands they are given* is the language of solemn investiture.

Verse 3. Although the animal is endowed with life it shall not be prohibited to man for food. Henceforth he may eat meat whereas so far he was dependent upon a vegetarian diet. A new relationship between man and animal is established and man's whole way of life is changed.

Verse 4. Life escapes from a body with the blood; therefore you may eat flesh, but not *flesh with its life, that is, its blood* (see after verse 7).

Verse 5 Man is compensated for refraining from animal blood by having the sanctity of his own blood guaranteed by God.

Of every life of you Everyone of you is a personality, and not like an animal just an example of a species.

I will surely require a reckoning of every man's brother regardless who has shed it, animal or man. A murderer and his victim are brothers. This looks back to Cain and Abel (compare Zech. 7,10).

Verse 6. This verse is a pointed statement of divine retaliation. The Hebrew words for blood and man have a similar sound. Punishment and deed shall completely correspond to each other.

Verse 7. You need not fear that beasts or murderers will kill you and go unpunished. This shall encourage you to multiply; you shall not decimate mankind by murder, but increase it by fertility (Midrash).

God's speech to Noah is related to God's monologue in 8,21-22; there, motivated by Noah's sacrifice (8,21), he had resolved not to let the regular order of the world cease, seed time and harvest, cold and heat, summer and winter, day and night. God had said this to his heart only, because the government of the world is his affair, but Noah's sacrifice also causes God to do something else, namely he permits man to eat meat. Man is informed of this by God for it concerns him. It is a covenant introduced by a blessing. The eating of animal meat is permissible as Noah had made an offering of them. The offering of animals is not derived from the human consumption of meat, but vice versa; due to man's offering of animals, he may be permitted to eat of them. Following Noah's sacrifice, God declares that he will give him the animals for food as a reward. This reflects the prophetic idea that God does not need the flesh of bulls (Psalm 50,13).

Noah brought his offering after the flood. Man had become too familiar with the animals contrary to his own better instincts (2,20). He had let himself be seduced by the serpent; finally in an accursed association "all flesh had corrupted their way." Now man and animal must be separated. It cannot be done more effectively than by giving animals to man for food like the plants of the field. The same Noah who had lived with the whole animal kingdom in the ark established by his offering the dignity of man in contrast to the animal. The permission to kill animals in order to eat their meat is also a bar against cannibalism. Only human life must be respected as holy. The Bible thus steers a middle path between cannibalism and Hinduism for which animal life is even more sacred than human life.

Noah is a pre-Israelite figure; one of those three famous men who can save sinners by their piety: Noah, Daniel, Job (Ezek. 14,14). The Hebrew Bible devotes a book to each of the other two; Noah is made part of the earliest history as the ancestor of a renewed mankind. Men, righteous before God, did not arise in Israel alone; they are descended from one perfectly righteous man from whom all nations are derived. Mankind shall find its higher moral unity not in Adam, the natural man, but in that pious father who by his offering brought about God's gracious resolution to preserve the world. Noah's offering is burnt completely on the altar; it is an expression of complete devotion to God and at the same time atonement and intercession for the other survivors. Job also brings such offerings (Job 1,5) as an atonement for possible sins of his children which they may have committed at their festivities, if only by thought. In the end Job's three friends must bring such offerings as atonement for their speeches (Job 42,8) and Job shall pray that they be accepted. The comparison with Job also shows the reason for "seven" sacrificial animals (7,2); regarding Job the number is motivated by his "seven" sons (Job 1,5). Noah too has seven members in his family, his wife, his three sons, and his sons' wives. At the beginning of a new period of mankind they shall stand atoned. The sacrifice of animals is regarded as a pre-Israelitic institution and Noah in the book of Genesis is a glorification of general human piety.

It is commonly conceded that the admonition against shedding the blood of man was appropriate for this moment. In the ark Noah and his family had been under the protection of God. Now they step out into the wide world. They are only one family which could easily be exterminated by wild beasts or by fratricide. The appropriateness of the other prohibition against eating blood is not so easily understood and has often been explained from primitive conceptions of life and soul or superstitions about blood as a "very special juice."

Notwithstanding all science it will always seem that the life of higher organisms escapes with their blood; therefore life and soul are said to be in the blood (Lev. 17,11). They are not identical with it, because the blood is matter, while life and soul are a force. Nevertheless in abbreviated language it may be said that life is blood (Lev. 17,14 and Deut. 12,23). The vigorous language of the people makes no subtle distinctions just as it calls bread (or even the millstone in Deut. 24,6) life. This is the psychological reason for which a murderer wants to see the blood flow to be satisfied, or even finds his highest triumph in drinking the blood of the enemy (Jer. 46,10). The thirst for human blood may find a substitute in the gushing blood of an animal. Eating blood may express a secret joy in killing and be an education for murder.

Thus the two prohibitions belong together. They are the most elementary demands of humanity in the literal sense of the word. They are pronounced when a human society is formed again. The permission to eat meat, but without its blood, and the prohibition against shedding human blood indicate the place of man within the world of the living, his relation to his fellow man and to the animal.

The atoning function of blood in the sacrificial cult is not a belief in a mystical-sacramental power inherent in it, but the permission to offer an animal as atonement to God in the place of man's forfeited life (Lev. 17,11). At the same time it is pedagogical wisdom to withdraw the blood from human consumption in this way. It is claimed for the altar, but not because the altar of God needs it. Deuteronomy again and again admonishes that the blood at slaughtering be poured out "like water" (Deut. 12,16 and often). This speaks cogently against the belief of any "holiness" inherent in it.

In summary: the reason for the prohibition of blood is of a moral character. The basic moral idea is very clear; mystical conceptions are consistently rejected. This is a rationalistic morality. The prohibition against consuming blood has decisively influenced the Jewish character. As it was carried to its logical conclusion in the Jewish method of slaughtering (shehita), it educated the Jew to keep away from brutality and savagery. The treatment of blood is one of the most glorious chapters in the Biblical and Jewish religion.

Noah laid the foundation to the prohibition against blood by his offering. For that reason he built an altar (8,20). If it were to be an offering according to Israelite principles, an altar would be necessary both for the burning of the offering, and for pouring out the blood.

Later Judaism regarded this passage as establishing fundamental ethics for every human being. It took the term "sons of Noah" as signifying mankind before Israel and outside of it; it found certain minimum demands of morality which every man must accept in this passage, the so-called "seven commandments given to Noah"; they are justice, the prohibitions of blasphemy, idolatry, murder, incest, robbery and consumption of the limb of a still living animal, and some similar actions. Even the early Church kept some of the horror of eating blood (Acts 15,29). All this is of course not really contained in the words of the Bible, but nevertheless in its true spirit.

The Promise Of The Covenant

God reassures Noah and his family by a declaration: Never again will there be a catastrophe that would destroy all flesh!

8Then God said to Noah and to his sons with him, 9"Behold, I establish my covenant with you and your descendants after you, 10and with every living creature that is with you, the birds, the cattle, and every animal of the earth with you, as many as came out of the ark, all living animals of the earth. 11I establish my covenant with you, that never again shall all flesh be cut off from the waters of the flood on, and never again shall there be a flood to destroy the earth."

God makes a covenant with the ancestor of a group only in so far as he is significant for the progress of religion: with Noah and his sons, with Abraham the ancestor of Israel (chapter 17), with Phinehas the priest (Num. 25,13, compare 18,19). They form the concentric spheres of mankind, Israel, priests. The reason in every case is religious and moral merit.

Verse 10. *And with every living creature* that has experienced the same catastrophe as you and shares the earth with man.

As many as came out of the ark. They had been preserved in the ark and shall be protected afterwards too.

Verse 11. God now informs man of his earlier decision (8,21f.) *From the waters of the flood on.* The waters of the flood are the great turning point in this history of the world. Two things are proclaimed: never again will there be a general catastrophe of any kind, and particularly never again a flood. This promise is called a covenant, meaning not a contract with mutual obligations, but only that God binds himself irrevocably.

12And God said, "This is the sign of the covenant which I make between me and you and every living creature that is with you, for all future generations: 13I have set my bow in the cloud, and it shall be a sign of the covenant between me and the earth. 14When I bring clouds over the earth and the bow is seen in the clouds, 15I will remember my covenant which is between me and you and every living creature of all flesh; and the waters shall never again become a flood to destroy all flesh. 16When the bow is in the cloud, I will look upon it and remember the everlasting covenant betweem between God and every living creature of all flesh that is upon the earth." 17God said to Noah, "This is the sign of the covenant which I have established between me and all flesh that is upon the earth."

Verse 17. God speaks again but to Noah alone; the covenant is ultimately made for this pious man.

Meaning of the Covenant and its sign The rainbow as a sign of the covenant has no parallels. Other signs are made by man, and remind him of a covenant with God as they are based on a commandment of his e.g. the circumcision or the sanctification of the Sabbath. A sign "to be seen" are the Ziziths, tassels on the garments which the Israelites should make and look upon in order to perform God's commandments and to become holy to him (Num. 15,37 ff.); similarly the phylacteries. The blood of the passover lamb in Egypt will be seen by God, but the Israelites shall put it on the doorposts. Man however does not make the rainbow nor shall he look upon it as reminder of an obligation.

The rainbow is exclusively a sign of God's love and faithfulness to his creation. As a reflection of the sun in the rainclouds it symbolizes mercy following judgement. Shining in its colors through clouds and tears of heaven it is a reflection of the divine which is ultimately love and mercy; it is the gracious glance appearing beneath somber brows. It signifies that the rain is over; the rain was a blessing. Established after the flood it teaches man the destructiveness of the powerful elements before showing him their benefit. The rainbow marks the completion of creation and its final seal, the last tender stroke of the brush.

This covenant reveals a great-hearted universalism. The world and mankind owe their preservation to a pre-Israelite hero and his virtue. It is a covenant with the entire living creation and has no prerequisites other than man's fulfilment of the most primitive demands of being human. Never again can all mankind become corrupt as it is descended from a Noah; scattered over the whole earth, it can no more band together for evil. All of this shows no trace of national particularism nor fervor for making religious converts.

Conclusion Of The Noah Story.

 [18]The sons of Noah who had gone forth from the ark were Shem, Ham, and Japheth. Ham was the father of Canaan. [19]These three were the sons of Noah; and from these the whole earth was peopled.

Verse 18. This will be followed by 1) an incident during which the three brothers act differently and which leads to a curse upon Canaan. 2) The list of all the nations scattered over the earth. These two verses prepare for both.

Verse 19. *Three sons of Noah.* A summation would not have been necessary as all three have been named. It shall rather emphasize that the whole world of nations is descended from only three men. Thus the blessing of verse 1 is fulfilled. The mention or omission of a number is intentional.

> ²⁰*Noah, the man of the soil, began to plant a vineyard;* ²¹*and he drank of the wine, and became drunk, and lay uncovered in his tent.* ²²*And Ham, the father of Canaan, saw the nakedness of his father, and told his two brothers outside.* ²³*Then Shem and Japheth took the garment, laid it upon both their shoulders, and walked backward and covered the nakedness of their father; their faces were turned away, and they did not see their father's nakedness.*

Noah is the man of the soil which was reborn after the flood. This is the fulfillment of 5,29 after the curse of 3,17.

Possession of a vineyard, enjoyment of its noble fruit, and rest in the peace of its shadow was a pleasure in the eyes of an Israelite and a Messianic wish (for instance I Kings 5,5;II Kings 18,31: Hos. 2,17). The vine is the sign of peace and prosperity (Zech. 8,12).

Verse 21. *Uncovered in his tent* is told as a mitigating circumstance. The inner warmth of the wine had caused him to throw off his garment. He celebrates the first vintage a little too freely.

Verse 22. Why did Ham enter while his brothers remained outside? Obviously he had first glanced into the tent from the outside and frivolously enjoyed his father's commencing drunkenness; he entered when the drunken man became unconscious, gloatingly ran out to let his brothers participate in the spectacle, insensitively assuming that they would enjoy this too. The effect is the opposite.

Verse 23. They took Noah's garment which Ham had carried out to confirm the story and had mockingly exhibited to them. Ham even completed the nakedness of his father. How surprised he must have been when the brothers took it so differently! They seize the garment from his hands, and cover their father again, acting with the greatest respect and caution.

²⁴*When Noah awoke from his wine and knew what his immature son had done to him,* ²⁵*he said,*
    "Cursed be Canaan; a slave of slaves shall he be to his brothers."
²⁶*He also said,*
    "Blessed be the Lord, the God of Shem;
    and let Canaan be their slave.
    ²⁷*God enlarge Japheth,*
    and let him dwell in the tents of Shem;
    and let Canaan be their slave."
²⁸*After the flood Noah lived three hundred and fifty years.* ²⁹*All the days of Noah were nine hundred and fifty years; and he died.*

Noah revives; the story expresses this nicely by letting his name disappear after he had planted wine and drunk of it; it reappears now after he has slept off his drunkenness. This was not the Noah we had known so far.

He *knew*, became aware of it. He vaguely remembers that Ham had been present when drunkenness began to overcome him. When he finds himself covered he understands everything. The different ways of his sons must have been known to him.

It has always seemed incomprehensible that Noah curses the seemingly completely innocent Canaan while it was Ham who had committed the deed. Another difficulty lies in the fact that otherwise the sons are always mentioned in the sequence Shem, Ham, and Japheth. If we assume this to be the order of their age can Ham be called here "his youngest son" as verse 24 is mostly translated?

It is twice stated: "Ham, that is the father of Canaan"; although as a genealogical statement it would be a superfluous addition to 10,6. However the explanation is that Ham acting thus showed himself as the true father of Canaan. The deed could be expected of the father of Canaan. Ham is not cursed so as to spare Ham's other sons. They shall not be included in the curse. It would be contrary to Israelite feeling for a father to curse his own son whatever he may have done, and even less for a deed against himself. Jacob does not curse Reuben for a similar deed.

In verse 24 we translate *what his immature son had done to him* (Rashi after Jer. 49,15). This remark does then not indicate a different order of age than the normal one: Shem, Ham, and Japheth.

Verse 25. *A slave of slaves.* He will be even a slave of their slaves, so the lowest slave (compare I Sam. 25,41).

Verse 26. As the curse is followed by a blessing, a new beginning is made. The Bible frequently congratulates and blesses someone by praising his God, the giver of all good (see 14,20; 24,27 and often). This fine expression assumes that the other person will ascribe his good fortune to his God and he is congratulated by entering into his sentiment. One rejoices with him in his own way. His conduct is ascribed to his God who can be congratulated on such a worshipper.

Verse 27. In Hebrew the word "enlarge" is a pun on the name Japheth. The wish is usually interpreted as may God give Japheth more living space, a doubtful translation of the Hebrew word. Clearly Japheth's religion ("God") is distinguished from that of Shem ("the Lord"). "God" is the more vague recognition of the divine. Japheth too possesses moral feeling, that is religion, as he has shown. May this finally lead him into the tents of Shem! This must not be understood as a Messianic hope that Japheth should convert to Shem's God and faith. He shall feel attracted to the tents of Shem, to his kind of family life (see Num. 24,5); this can be expected from him as he agrees with Shem on its first condition, respect for the father.

Verse 28. Noah is the only man who lived in two eras (11,10) and must be counted among two sets of fathers, one before and one after the flood. Thus both sets have 10 members: from Adam to Noah, from Noah to Terah.

The meaning of the story (Verses 18-29) The next chapter is a survey of the world of nations descended from the sons of Noah. In this world Israel felt itself in strongest moral contrast to Canaan, but attracted to the Japhethite nations. In order to explain these relationships the story reverts to the origins of mankind, where the trends were revealed. Canaan's sin is lack of shame, of sexual discipline which is regarded as frivolous. On the other hand the first commandment of Japhethite and Semitic morality is respect for the father. That is the theme of this story. The episode parallels the family life of the other legendary pious hero, Job. Job however does not participate in the drinking parties of his children, but later atones for blasphemous thoughts they may have had in their cups (Job 1,4f.). Here the father, Noah, becomes drunk. He does not cease to be a righteous man, yet he loses face. The Bible does not prohibit the drinking of wine, but describes its dangers.

The curse upon Canaan is very strong. When the Hebrew speaks of an attitude as deeply rooted and second nature it is said that this attitude existed from youth (8,21 and often) or even from the womb (Is. 48,8) and is inherited from the parents. The person is already the son of such people. This is used to strengthen praise as well as blame. A murderer is called "son of a murderer" (II Kings 6,32), a wise man "son of wise men" (Is. 19,11). Noah, in his curse, could of course not call Ham the son of a sinner; therefore he calls him, not less despicably, the father of Canaan. He curses him to be everyone's slave.

This curse is never later quoted as justification for hatred against Canaanites. It only serves to explain Canaan's character. Noah's pronouncement comes immediately upon having awakened from drunkenness, which does not make it exactly commendable.

On the other hand Shem is pictured as the link between Noah and Abraham keeping alive the faith in the "Lord". This is the most important idea of the story.

Blessing and curse by the father of all nations are as appropriate as those by Jacob and Moses at the end of their lives.

Chapter 10

The Descendants Of The Sons Of Noah.
These are the descendants of the sons of Noah, Shem, Ham and Japheth; sons were born to them after the flood.

It shall again be emphasized that every man is descended from a father and his three sons who alone have survived the flood. The chapter is divided into three parts corresponding to the three sons, but not in the usual order, Shem, Ham, and Japheth, but Japheth (verses 2–5), Ham (verses 6–20), Shem (verses 21–30); this corresponds to their distance from Israel and its interests. Japheth to whom Israel has no direct relations is most remote; then follows Ham with his sons Nimrod (Babel), Egypt and Canaan; then Shem down to Eber, the ancestor of the Ibrim to whom Israel itself belongs. The genealogy of Shem-Eber-Abraham may then follow in chapter 11. The order of the names is never that of birth; if someone named first is also the firstborn it must be expressly mentioned (verse 15). Each of the three groups is treated differently. The names of the sons are likewise used for the clans that called themselves after them. Even regional and political communities are briefly called after an ancestor who is the "father" of the region. Many of these names of peoples can no longer be identified.

²The sons of Japheth: Gomer and Magog and Madai and Javan and Tubal and Meshech, and Tiras. ³And the sons of Gomer: Ashkenaz and Riphath and Togarmah. ⁴And the sons of Javan: Elishah and Tarshish, Kittim and Dodanim. ⁵From these the coastland peoples spread in their lands, each with its own language, by their families, in their nations.

Gomer is now identified with the Gimirrai who appear in Assyrian texts and probably lived in Cappadocia. *Magog* (Ezek. 28,2; 39,6) are usually understood as the Scythians. *Madai* are certainly the Medes in Iran (II Kings 17,6). *Javan* are as undeniably the Greeks (Ionians), probably those of the Asia Minor coast and of Cyprus. *Tubal and*

71

Meshech are mentioned together in other passages also (often in Ezek. e.g. 27,13), probably living near the Black Sea. *Tiras* has been claimed for the Etruscans. *Ashkenaz* (Jer. 51,27), perhaps Phrygians or an Indo-German people; in late Hebrew it is the name for Germany. *Togarmah* seemed to have lived in Phrygia or Cappadocia (Ezek. 27,14.38,6); in late Hebrew it is the name for Turkey. *Elisha* (Ezek. 27,7) probably Alashia, mentioned in the El-Amarna letters and identical with Cyprus. *Tarshish* is frequently mentioned in the Bible and most likely Tartessus in South-Western Spain. Kittim, often mentioned, has been interpreted as Southern Italy. *Dodanim* should perhaps be read Rodanim from Rhodes, the Mediterranean island.

> *⁶And the sons of Ham: Cush, and Egypt, and Put, and Canaan. ⁷And the sons of Cush: Seba, and Havilah, and Sabtha, and Raamah, and Sabteca. And the sons of Raamah: Sheba and Dedan.*

Cush is without doubt Ethiopia. *Egypt* The Hebrew dual form of the name indicates the two parts into which the land was divided. *Put* Some scholars think of Punt as East Africa, others of Lybia. It is found many times in the Bible. *Canaan*, the name of the land which Israel later conquers. For the ancient Hebrew Canaan was a brother of Egypt. *Seba* (Psalm 72,10) perhaps on the Blue Nile. *Havilah* already used in 2,11, but not identified. *Sabtha* cannot be identified. *Raamah* (Ezek. 27,22) perhaps on the Arabian coast of the Persian gulf. *Sabteca* cannot be identified. *Sheba* often refers to a remote country from which caravans bring gold, precious stones and spices. The queen of Sheba, a contemporary of king Solomon, was famous. *Dedan* mentioned in other Bible passages, but not identified.

> *⁸Cush became the father of Nimrod; he began to be a mighty man on earth. ⁹He was a mighty hunter before the Lord; therefore it is said "Like Nimrod a mighty hunter before the Lord." ¹⁰The beginning of his kingdom was Babel, and Erech, and Accad, and Calneh, in the land of Shinar.*

Verse 9. Hunting was a favorite sport of the high and mighty in most ancient times; the Babylonian-Assyrian kings are frequently represented in this sport on their monuments. *Before the Lord* is a form of superlative: God who sees everything could not have found a mightier hunter (Ramban). Nimrod rose from hunter to king and ruler.

Verse 10 This verse is ironical. Babel is the city with the tower which was supposed to reach the heavens, but the people could not complete it as reported in the following chapter. *In the land of Shinar* confirms this as the same city (11,2), so there can be no mistake about an allusion to the following story. As that story is meant to ridicule the ambitions of man, the same is true of Nimrod; the height of his rule was a torso! It reflects on his "greatness" as a hunter as well.

> [11]*From that land Assyria went out and built Nineveh, and Reho-both-Ir, and Calah,* [12]*and Resen between Nineveh and Calah: that is the great city.*

Assyria, derived from Shem (verse 22), offers the first example of an exodus from Hamite bondage; the second are the Philistines (verse 14), and the third is Israel.

The four cities built by Assyria are obviously meant as a contrast to the four of Nimrod; Nineveh was truly *the great city* (Jon. 1,2, etc.). Some of the cities mentioned in these verses have been excavated. Representing Babel as the older city agrees with historical knowledge; it is also correct that Assyria freed itself from Babylonian rule only later; it finally conquered Babylon.

> [13]*And Egypt became the father of Ludim, and Anamim, and Lehabim, and Naphtuhim,* [14]*and Pathrusim, and Casluhim whence came the Philistines, and Caphtorim.*

Ludim, also in other Biblical passages, probably in lower Egypt. *Pathrusim* are the inhabitants of upper Egypt. The other peoples can hardly be identified with the exception of the *Philistines,* a nation often mentioned in the Bible, who gave their name to Palestine. *Caphtorim,* very likely Crete.

> [15]*And Canaan became the father of Sidon his first-born, and Heth, and the Jebusites, and the Amorites, and the Girgashites,* [17]*and the Hivites, and the Arkites, and the Sinites,* [18]*and the Arvadites, and the Zemarites, and the Hamathites. Afterwards the families of the Canaanites spread abroad.* [19]*And the territory of the Canaa-nites extended from Sidon, in the direction of Gerar, as far as Gaza, and in the direction of Sodom, and Gomorrah, and Admah, and Zeboim, as far as Lasha. These are the sons of Ham, by their families, by their languages, in their lands, and in their nations.*

Sidon was famous in antiquity as the capital of the Phoenicians. *Heth* probably the Hatti in Asia Minor whose culture is now well known through excavations. *Jebusites,* the inhabitants of Jerusalem (Judg. 19,10). *Amorites* in Canaan, but also east of the river Jordan. Only a few of the other peoples mentioned have been identified.

Verse 18. Because in the beginning all the Canaanites lived together, Sidon is mentioned as the first-born as the substitute of the father and leader of the brothers. From Sidon the Canaanites spread North and South. As Israel was the successor of Canaan the territory inhabited by both in succession is now described.

Verse 19. This verse defines "the land of Canaan" which Israel shall later conquer (Num. 34,2). Between the Mediterranean in the West and the Jordan in the East a boundary from North to South and in the South from East to West is needed.

> [21]*To Shem also, the ancestor of all the children of Eber, the elder brother of Japheth, children were born.* [22]*The sons of Shem: Elam, and Asshur, and Arpachshad, and Lud, and Aram.* [23]*And the sons of Aram: Uz, and Hul, and Gether, and Mash.* [24]*Arpachshad became the father of Shelah; and Shelah became the father of Eber.* [25]*To Eber were born two sons: the name of the one was Peleg, for in his days the earth was divided, and his brother's name was Joktan.* [26]*Joktan became the father of Almodad, and Sheleph, and Hazarmaveth, and Jerah,* [27]*and Hadoram, and Uzal, and Diklah,* [28]*and Obal, and Abimael, and Sheba,* [29]*and Ophir, and Havilah, and Jobab; all these were the sons of Joktan.* [30]*The territory in which they lived extended from Mesha in the direction of Sephar to the hill country of the East.* [31]*These are the sons of Shem, by their families, by their languages, in their lands, and in their nations.* [32]*These are the families of the sons of Noah, according to their descendants, in their nations: and from these the nations spread abroad on the earth after the flood.*

For the Book of Genesis Eber was the most important descendant of Shem. The faith in the Lord, the God of Shem (9,26) was preserved in his line; he is "the God of the Ibrim" of whom Moses speaks to Pharaoh (Ex. 3,18.5,3 etc.).

Verse 22. *Elam,* the land at the lower Tigris river and the North-East coast of the Persian Gulf with Susa as capital.

Asshur Assyria, the word at the same time designates the god, the country, and the capital city on the Tigris. It is the Asiatic power which destroyed Israel. *Aram* is Syria; the other names are hardly known or entirely unknown.

Verse 24. *Eber* has been identified by various scholars with the Habiri of the El-Amarna letters; the name has been explained as "the people from the other side" of the stream, either the Euphrates or better the Jordan.

Verse 25. *In his days* His name (Peleg-division) was acquired only later in his life.

Verses 26–29. In these verses most of the names are unknown. *Hazarmaveth* is Hadramaut in Southern Arabia. *Ophir* was known as the land of gold (I Kings 9,28 f.); its location has not been determined.

Verse 30. All these localities are unknown.

The Intention of the Chapter. God's original decision that man should fill the earth has been fulfilled. As different as mankind became in languages and countries it still is united by descent. All nations had their origins in family communities whose ancestors were the three sons of one man. Mankind is one just as there is only one earth, one heaven, and one creator. Such a conception in its universality, clarity, and decisiveness has not been achieved elsewhere. The cause for attribution to the individual ancestor can be neither race, nor language, nor the residence; for those differentiations came only later. Shem, Ham, and Japheth the ancestors were still sons of one house. The Bible derives all nations of the earth from them, but it does not intend to mention every nation. The sons of these three men are listed, but the genealogy is not always continued further. The total number is small in view of the numerous ones existing on the horizon of this author. Even the original inhabitants of Palestine who had disappeared before Moses like Rephaim, Emim, and others are missing; nor are all Canaanite tribes included. The ethnographic remarks shall serve a religious idea. They cannot be dated with certainty.

Jewish tradition often speaks of all nations in the world as "seventy nations". The song of Moses expressly states this as the opinion of the Bible (Deut. 32,8 f.). The number of the descendants of Jacob is seventy. The allusion in Deuteronomy to our chapter is shown by the terms used there, "separation", "distribution of the earth", and "boundaries of the peoples". Many attempts have been made to find the number seventy in our chapter. If all names are counted the result is 71; one must be eliminated. Perhaps it is Joktan who is completely absorbed in his sons: verse 29 *"all* these are the sons of Joktan." The others had more sons, even though they are not mentioned.

Chapter 11

Babel

> Now the whole world had one language and few words. ²And as
> men migrated to the East, they found a plain in the land of Shinar
> and settled there. ³And they said to one another, "Come, let us
> make bricks and burn them thoroughly." And they had brick for
> stone and bitumen for mortar.

One language and few words only a small vocabulary (Ehrlich). The
tone of irony which pervades the entire story is already sounded. The
language was unambiguous and the same for all; so it seemed easy for
them to unite also in will and action.

Verse 2. They migrated eastward as seen from Palestine. The plain is
between the Euphrates and the Tigris where Babylon was located.

Verse 3. Ancient writers testify that the surroundings of Babylon
were rich in asphalt. The simple and successful experiment came as a
happy surprise to man. It demanded only two operations and the result
was brilliant. The Hebrew expresses this by assonances which make
the words sound like a child's playsong; this cannot be imitated in
English. Bricks emancipated man from natural rock and the places
where it is found, one of the most consequential inventions ever made.

> ⁴Then they said, "Come, let us build ourselves a city, and a tower
> with its top in the heavens, and let us make a name for ourselves
> lest we be scattered abroad upon the face of the whole earth."
> ⁵And the Lord came down to see the city and the tower, which the
> sons of man had built. ⁶And the Lord said, "Behold, they are one
> people, and they have all one language; and this is only the
> beginning of what they will do; and nothing that they propose to
> do should now be impossible for them? ⁷Come, let us go down,
> and there confuse their language, that they may not understand
> one another's speech." ⁸So the Lord scattered them abroad from

there over the face of all the earth, and they had to leave off building the city. Therefore its name was called Babel, because there the Lord had confused the language of all the earth; and from there the Lord scattered them abroad over the face of all the earth.

They want to arouse the admiration of posterity by a tower rising to the skies. They did not want to climb into the heavens; this would have been senseless. The city shall keep them together; the tower is the impressive crowning of it.

Verse 5. *The Lord came down.* This is not the naive idea that God must go to the place in order to inform himself. He knows of the construction before descending, but a judgement demands a personal and formal investigation of the facts. The verse ironically implies that the tower supposed to reach the heavens is still far from there. Seen from above the gigantic structure is only a work of *the sons of man,* of these manikins.

Verse 6. The completion of the work shall be made impossible for them. Their present unity through a common language must be changed. God's course of action is clear.

Verse 7. God ironically imitates their "Come"; it is just as easy for him. He speaks to his heavenly court after having returned to heaven, as in 1,25 and 3,22 (Rashi). *Let us* is a humorous contrast to the constant "we" of the men (compare I Kings 22,20). The place which was intended to keep them together becomes the place of their complete dispersion.

Verse 8. Dispersion was the natural consequence of the confusion of languages.

Verse 9. The name Babylon really means "Gate of God". The meaning, which may have been known to the author, is here turned to a popular pun on the word twisting it into "Confusion" in order to discredit their undertaking.

Meaning of the Story. Few stories have been so completely misunderstood. Entitling it the story of "The Tower of Babel" was already erroneous.

If the tower had been the main concern, the conclusion would have read "they left off building the tower", but it is the city which is left unfinished and receives the nickname Babel. Some claimed that this is a story of an arrogant and conceited generation which like the Titans desired to storm the heavens and God feared that they might dislodge him. The confusion of languages and the dispersion of mankind would be a punishment for human presumption. The story is said to have originated from a mixture of amazement and horror produced in the Israelites, a tribe from the cultureless desert, when they saw the gigantic city of Babel and its enormous tower.

In reality the characteristic feature of that generation is anxiety and gregariousness. They do not want to penetrate the heavens, but to gather closely on earth for fear of becoming lost. Their dispersion is not a punishment destroying the original unity of mankind. The scattering of one nation is dispersal among others and means loss of its homeland, a misfortune and a punishment. The dispersion of mankind over the earth is an unavoidable consequence of their propagation and a fulfillment of the divine blessing: "be fruitful and multiply and fill the earth" (1,27;9,7). Otherwise there would be no need for the creation of so vast and wide an earth. The prophetic vision of the end of time never desires that all men live in one place and speak one language.

The construction of the gigantic city is an attempt, born of fear, to frustrate the divine plan. God's intention is achieved by thwarting this attempt. The defeat is brought about neither through external means as a collapse of their structure, nor by a prohibition, but in a most ingenious way, by the nature of man which evolves from the character of the undertaking. The attempt at artificial preservation of unity brings forth the variety of human minds leading to the diversity of languages. God, reason, and nature make the undertaking ridiculous.

The right mood is not anger or wrath as if it were moral depravity, but laughter; "he who sits in the heavens laughs" (Psalm 2,4).

The story condemns extreme centralization reaching its logical conclusion in a single world city with a skyscraper as its symbol; it would lead to gregariousness which feels safe only in crowding together and sees the ultimate goal in bringing all mankind under one tower. In brilliant irony following the pattern of retaliation the place of envisioned concentration becomes, even in its name, the point of dispersion. The gigantic city of Babylon and its temple towers high as the heavens made as little impression on the Bible as the pyramids, deemed unworthy of mention although much of the narrative is located in Egypt.

Numerous temple towers, called ziggurat, existed in Babylonia. Their ruins have been partly excavated.

Chapter 10 and 11 refer to each other frequently (see 10,19). The placement of chapter 10 before this one is a special refinement. The absurdity of the undertaking becomes obvious if we know the numerous nations into which mankind should grow.

The Descendants Of Shem.

The descendants of Adam to Noah (chapter 5) are now continued from Shem to Terah for nine generations. As Noah belongs to both lists (see 9,28f.) the number ten is again achieved. The ages at which the men of this list become fathers or die are lower than on the preceding list. One of the underlying ideas seems to be the presence of them all at the division of the earth under Peleg who is born 1758 and dies in 1997 (see 10,25).

> [10]These are the descendants of Shem. When Shem was a hundred years old, he became the father of Arpachshad in the second year after the flood; [11]and Shem lived after the birth of Arpachshad five hundred years, and had other sons and daughters. [12]Arpachshad had lived thirty-five years , and he became the father of Shelah; [13]and Arpachshad lived after the birth of Shelah four hundred and three years, and had other sons and daughters. [14]Shelah had lived thirty years, and he became the father of Eber; [15]and Shelah lived after the birth of Eber four hundred and three years, and had other sons and daughters. [16]When Eber had lived thirty-four years, he became the father of Peleg; [17]and Eber lived after the birth of Peleg four hundred and thirty years, and had other sons and daughters. [18]When Peleg had lived thirty years, he became the father of Reu; [19]and Peleg lived after the birth of Reu two hundred and nine years, and had other sons and daughters. [20]When Reu had lived thirty-two years, he became the father of Serug; [21]and Reu lived after the birth of Serug two hundred and seven years, and had other sons and daughters. [22]When Serug had lived thirty years, he became the father of Nahor; [23]And Serug lived after the birth of Nahor two hundred years, and had other sons and daughters. [24]When Nahor had lived twenty-nine years, he became the father of Terah; [25] and Nahor lived after the birth of Terah a hundred and nineteen years, and had other sons and daughters. [26]When Terah had lived seventy years, he became the father of Abram, Nahor, and Haran.

Verse 22 Nahor is also the name of a son of Terah (verse 26), that is of a grandfather and a grandson.

The Descendants Of Terah.

27Now these are the descendants of Terah. Terah was the father of Abram, Nahor, and Haran; and Haran was the father of Lot. 28Haran died before his father Terah in the land of his birth, in Ur of the Chaldaeans. 29And Abram and Nahor took wives; the name of Abram's wife was Sarai, and the name of Nahor's wife, Milcah, the daughter of Haran, the father of Milcah and Iscah. 30Now Sarai was barren; she had no child.

Verse 28 Haran dies before his father and so leaves to Terah the orphaned Lot who according to ancient family law became Terah's third son, so to say. For this reason the birth of Lot is reported here, and not after verse 30.

Ur of the Chaldaeans is the city of Ur on the lower Euphrates river. Excavations have shown high culture and art on this site as early as 4000 B.C.E. This ancient seat of culture as the home of Israel's ancestors is an attractive concept. Some scholars object to this identification and assign it to a place in North-Western Mesopotamia in the neighborhood of Haran (verse 31).

Verse 29. When Haran died and Terah took care of Lot, the brother Nahor took care of one of Haran's daughters by marrying her. Marrying the brother's daughter was always regarded as permissible and even meritorious. All this corresponded to ancient family law and was a necessary part of genealogies.

31Terah took Abram his son and Lot the son of Haran, his grandson, and Sarai his daughter-in-law, his son's Abram's wife, and they went forth together from Ur of the Chaldaeans to go into the land of Canaan; but when they came to Haran, they settled there. 32The days of Terah were two hundred and five years; and Terah died in Haran.

Nahor did not accompany them. The reason for Terah's departure from Ur is not mentioned. Perhaps it was the death of his son Haran or the barreness of Sarai or the place had become dangerous for Abraham's family according to 15,7. We are also not informed why wanting to go to Canaan they remained at Haran. Haran is the Carrhae of the later Greeks and Romans, an old city in Mesopotamia where Crassus and Caracalla lost battles and their lives.

Verse 32. Terah died long after Abraham's departure (12,4); he did not die in the land of his birth as his son Haran. In him the destiny of later Israel, his descendants, is reflected—migration, death, and burial in strange lands. His name has even been interpreted as "the migrant".

The Story Of The Fathers

Introduction

If the narrative of the patriarchs of the people of Israel is to be understood according to the original intent, it must be viewed with the eyes of a son of this people for whom it was first written. The following main ideas must be remembered while reading it.

The ancestral fathers are not the ultimate theme of the stories, but rather the God of the fathers; the God of Abraham who remained the God of Isaac and then became the God of Jacob. He proved himself to three successive generations; therefore their descendents possess the certainty of his unchanging faithfulness and love for all generations even in the most remote future.

How shall the people of Israel arrive at their claim of being sons of Israel with Canaan as their fatherland? Every Israelite is a member of a tribe; the ancestors of the twelve tribes were actually sons of Jacob who received the honorary name of Israel. Thus the people came into being. The country had been promised by the true and only God, creator of heaven and earth, to their first ancestor as to a faithful and worthy servant. A covenant was made with him to this effect. The promise was repeated to his son and his son's son as a triple assurance never to be broken. God fulfilled the promise when the descendants had grown to a people matured by experience and equipped with laws.

The story of the patriarchs presents a religious and moral interpretation of the national interests of this people. It shall create faith, humility, gratitude, and obedience toward the Lord of the universe, the God of the Fathers.

The promise is given the fathers ten times while in actual view of the land; they already dwelled in it. The conception of a Promised Land is of extraordinary importance. It should prohibit any imperialistic wish for expansion; for God had promised this land only. Later kings thus undertook conquests as their private enterprise which found no echo in the consciousness of the people.

Israel's history begins with a promise. This shall determine its whole character, just as the Lord God is called "he who will come." Faith must be proven by unshakable confidence. The story of the fathers is an education in patience. Every great thing is realized slowly and in the face of obstacles. Abraham reaches a hundred years before the birth of the son without whom the promise would have been pointless. Isaac is married twenty years before the birth of Jacob. Jacob must labor for two seven year periods before the birth of Joseph, the son of his beloved Rachel. Furthermore the sons are endangered before the father can be certain of their future. Isaac is to be sacrificed; Jacob is forced to flee and upon his return must be in doubt over the fate of his family; Joseph is long believed lost. The life of each patriarch consists of a chain of delays, trials, and afflictions.

In spite of this Abraham, Isaac, and Jacob do not doubt their destiny or the divine promises. Thus they become the fathers of Israel, not only through procreation, but through faith. God chose Israel as his people for the sake of the fathers; he loved them and elected them, because they elected and loved him and lived for the future.

No other people possesses an epic like that of Israel's patriarchs which reflects an unlimited devotion to nation and people. They and most particularly Abraham, believed in the people and its future, although this man was separated from its realization by centuries. Even with the last of them the promised people were only a small group. If Israel is to understand the meaning of its existence, it must be told of its fathers. In Hebrew the word 'father' is by coincidence the first word in the dictionary.

A family story confronts us; the choice of wives and the birth of sons is therefore of greatest importance. Three elements fill the soul of the Israelite—his God, his people, and his country. The fathers to whom God had promised the land represent in themselves the promise of the people. The ultimate subject of the tales is God. This is clearly indicated and constitutes the uniqueness of the story. The God who is eternal and One makes of history a meaningful plan extending through generations. He is the supernatural and holy God; this guards against all nationalism. National interests shall not be taken as the measure of all things; deification and worship of one's own nation with all its human weaknessses and errors is prevented.

Some have doubted that the patriarchs were historical. It is not our task to examine this question. The conditions reported however agree surprisingly well with the cultural conditions of the ancient Near East as discovered by archaeology. The patriarchs could indeed have lived in this period.

Chapter 12

The Entrance Into Canaan

Now the Lord said unto Abram, "Go from your country and your kindred and your father's house to the land that I will show you. ²And I will make of you a great nation, and I will bless you, and make your name great, and be a blessing. ³I will bless those who bless you, and him who curses you, I will curse; and by you all the families of the earth will bless themselves."

Abraham shall not remain in Haran. Whatever had been Terah's intentions in moving to Haran, it had not been a divine command that had driven him on. He, therefore, did not continue to Canaan (11,31) but halted halfway. God not only accepts man's plans if they are reasonable, but also brings them to completion by making them an impulse in a soul which is receptive to his call. At first Canaan had been a mere human goal. Now through God's call to Abraham it is made a part of a magnificent divine plan and becomes the Promised Land. The Lord was not an unknown God to Abraham, but a heritage from former generations.

The divine call to Abraham means: cut all your ties and go without looking back. It is the call to God's chosen to go his way. *From your country*—he must give up all economic, social, political, and emotional ties. *From your kindred*—from the circle of related people. From your *father's house*—leaving father and mother signifies breaking the strongest bond of natural belonging. It is a great paradox that the history of a people which finds its strength in the family and in loyalty to the past must begin through a break with tradition and ancestors, for God calls.

To the land which I will show you—The meaning is not which I will not yet announce by name, so that Abraham must depart without knowledge of his destination. It rather means 'I shall inform you about it by showing it to you. When you arrive, I shall say to you—see this land, enjoy its sight in the thought that I shall give it to you' (see verse 7 and 13,14ff.).

Verse 2 A land requires a people. *A great nation* indicates one both numerous and great in inner values (see Deut. 4,6). This is an amazing promise to a man who is already advanced in years and whose wife (11,30) has been barren.

I shall bless you—first of all I shall provide for wordly wealth and children. Abraham was indeed wealthy (12,16) and his wealth is ascribed to God (24,1). However he had possessed wealth before departing from his home (verse 5) and the possibilities of further enrichment were outweighed by all which had to be abandoned. His earthly fortune was also never of such magnitude that "all the families of the earth" could have regarded it as the ideal for their aspirations. He is respected, but his position in the world is rather modest. He is an immigrant, a foreigner without land who must express his gratitude for a burial place. He experiences painful trials and losses. The simple happiness of a son is only given at an advanced age and almost again taken from him. The blessing must, for all these reasons, refer to a later time, long after his life, to the special destiny of the people who shall grow from him. In response to his faith in the future, Abraham is identified with the future people.

I will make your name great is also an extraordinary promise. Otherwise only God is 'great' obliging everyone to recognize his majesty. This also alludes to the story of the tower of Babel (11,4); not a tower shall bring a "name" to a people, but an Abraham (Procksch).

Be a blessing is the strongest promise; it is almost a command by God to history, in the manner of his words during creation. Abraham's glory shall not depend upon the judgement of men who may be misled by appearances. It shall possess fullest reality, you shall be the cause and measure of all blessing.

Verse 3. To bless a great man means to recognize him admiringly as blessed by God. One sees in him an example which shall be imitated; in other words one blesses oneself. He who blesses Abraham will see his wish fulfilled by God. In contrast a person who curses Abraham, the man blessed by God, is an enemy of God and will come to know through his own experiences the true source of blessing and curse.

And by you all the families of the earth shall bless themselves or "be blessed". Both translations are possible. The first would mean that all people will say among themselves of Abraham, would that our people be blessed like him. The second would mean: all peoples will be blessed through you as a consequence of their relation to you, even if they do not recognize the true relationship of cause and effect. This blessing is repeated when Abraham shows himself as an example of moral and religious greatness (18,18 and 22,18). It is confirmed for the two other patriarchs of the future people, Isaac in 26,4 and Jacob in 28,14. These five passages belong together like the promises of land and nation.

The speech of God abounds in blessing. The word 'bless' occurs five times as the word 'light' occurs five times in the story of the creation. A second world is called into being through Abraham, a world of blessing for man by man. It is an expression of a great-hearted religious universalism, not surpassed by any of the prophets. It is stated at the beginning of Israel's history.

> ⁴*So Abram went, as the Lord had told him; and Lot went with him. Abram was seventy-five years old when he departed from Haran. ⁵And Abram took Sarai his wife, and Lot his brother's son, and all their possessions which they had gathered, and the persons that they had gotten in Haran; and they set forth to go to the land of Canaan, and they came to the land of Canaan. ⁶Abram passed through the land to the place of Shechem, to the oak of the oracle. At that time the Canaanites were in the land! ⁷Then the Lord appeared to Abram and said: "To your descendants will I give this land." So he built there an altar to the Lord, who had appeared to him. ⁸Thence he removed to the mountain on the east of Bethel, and pitched his tent, with Bethel on the west, and Ai on the east; and there he built an altar to the Lord and called on the name of the Lord. ⁹And Abram journeyed on, still going toward the Negeb.*

Now Lot has his great hour. He follows no divine call; nor must he leave a father. The motive of Abraham is love of God; that of Lot is loyalty toward a close relative (Compare Ruth and Naomi). As Abraham was an old man this action of faith is all the greater.

Verse 5. They take all their possessions which shows that the departure is final. *The persons that they had gotten in Haran* is best explained by referring to the people who had joined them out of personal affection and conviction. Abraham and Sarah had gained hearts and souls for themselves and for their cause; the proselyte is as old as Judaism. The Midrash states, "he who teaches a man, in a way creates him."

Schechem is in the middle of Canaan (see Josh. 20,7) and was probably a religious and political center since most ancient times. Its distinctive mark was an *oak of the oracle* (35,4 and Judg. 9,37). The tree was most likely regarded as seat of divine life which explains the severity of Biblical law against worship of or under trees.

At that time the Canaanites were in the land does not indicate that they were no longer in the land when the Book of Genesis was written; then it would be a superfluous remark as the whole story of the fathers presupposes that the land was occupied by the Canaanites after whom it was named. As in a similar sentence in II Sam. 23,14 ff. our attention shall be drawn to the paradoxical situation. Abraham builds an altar and has a divine revelation in the very center of the country in the midst of pagan religious life, with Canaanites surrounding him.

Verse 7. Here, at the place of Canaanite worship, Abraham gains the certainty that this must become the land of the true God and that he is selected to be the ancestor of the chosen people. After he has left his old home, he immediately receives a new one from God. The altar is Abraham's response to the divine revelation and a protest against Canaanite worship. In a manner he hoists the flag of his God over the land of Canaan. All three patriarchs erect such altars.

Verse 8. Abraham marks the land as the future dwelling place of his descendants by also pitching his tent. Here he builds a second altar; the human residence and the place of the divine belong together. Thus he *calls on the name of the Lord* means he gave thanks. Abraham sets an example for the future people of Israel. Upon its arrival in the Promised Land, it shall build an altar (Deut. 27,2) and Joshuah does so (8,30).

Verse 9. The Negeb is the dry land of southern Canaan. Abraham passes through the entire Promised Land unto its end.

The Journey To Egypt

[10]*Now there was a famine in the land. So Abram went down to Egypt to sojourn there, for the famine was severe in the land.* [11]*When he was on the verge of entering Egypt, he said to Sarai, his wife: "I know that you are a woman beautiful to behold;* [12]*and when the Egyptians see you, they will say: "This is his wife"; then they will kill me, but they will let you live.* [13]*Say you are my sister, that it may go well with me because of you, and that my soul may be revived on your account."*

Each of the patriarchs experiences a famine in Canaan. Egypt, fertile by the Nile river and the granary of the ancient world, then attracted the neighboring Semitic tribes.

Verse 12. The Egyptians will do this according to their manner and habit. The most certain way of seizing a married woman was to remove her husband; compare the story of David and Uriah in II Sam. 11.

Verse 13. Henceforth he will not live with her as husband and wife; a brotherly relationship shall take the place of a matrimonial one. The bride is called sister (Song. 4,9 etc.) when love which restrains itself is to be expressed. Then Abraham does not think of the later 'gifts' of Pharaoh. The soul revives when anxiety is removed. Abraham does not feel happy about the matter. The request itself is expressed in a reluctant manner, true to life, concisely, in four words; all the more numerous are the words of the surrounding framework.

> *14When Abram entered Egypt the Egyptians saw that the woman was very beautiful. 15And when the princes of Pharaoh saw her, they praised her to Pharaoh. And the woman was taken into Pharaoh's court. 16And for her sake he dealt well with Abram; and he got sheep, oxen, he-asses, manservants, maidservants, mules, and camels.*

Verse 15. The courtiers of Pharaoh say of her among themselves that this would be a woman for his majesty. *The woman was taken into Pharaoh's court.* It must be understood that everything was done in a pleasing and courteous form as suitable to a royal court. The husband neither caused the matter nor could he hinder it.

Verse 16. The language of this verse is intentionally ambiguous. Pharaoh did not 'buy' his wife from Abraham. Such bluntness is not the manner of a royal court. Nevertheless, Abraham owes all his wealth to consideration for Sarah; at a hint from above the man is favored in his legitimate occupation as cattle-breeder; perhaps grazing lands were given him through contracts, so that he finally had rich herds. The productive animals to which the servants and maids belong are mentioned first, then the animals used for transportation. These are not direct gifts of Pharaoh; gold and silver which could certainly have been expected are missing.

> *17But the Lord afflicted Pharoh and his court with great afflictions, because of Sarai, Abram's wife. 18So Pharaoh called Abram and said, "What is this you have done to me? Why did you not tell me that she is your wife? 19Why did you say 'She is my sister', so that I took her for my wife? Now then, here is your wife, take her and*

go." *²⁰And Pharaoh gave men orders concerning him: and they accompanied him on the way with his wife and all that he had.*

Pharaoh's courtiers are to suffer with him as they participated in the intrigue. God intervenes to save the wife of his chosen friend, the mother of Israel, from disgrace and to protect the legitimate marriage.

Verse 18. Pharaoh's words are not a harsh rebuke and an expulsion from the country. He would not openly admit his weakness. It is a dismissal with hidden irony. He saves face unto the last and the couple is led from the land with an honor guard.

The Meaning and Purpose of the Story. This story has aroused much indignation and is said to show low moral standards. Even the Jewish commentator Ramban said, "Our father Abraham committed a great sin in exposing his wife to moral danger out of fear that he would be killed. He should have trusted in God." Abraham has been defended by claiming that he did not exactly lie, or that a white lie in danger of death is permissible. The incorruptible truthfulness of the Bible is to be praised because it does not pass in silence over the mistakes of one of its heroes.

We shall discuss Abraham's ambiguous action in connection with chapter 20. Here we may inquire whether Abraham seems to care less for Sarah's womanly honor if he calls her his sister. How ancient Israel thought in this regards is shown in Chapter 34.

The story shows that Israel's women can be certain that God will protect them in the greatest danger and is strong enough even against Pharaoh. He needs no help in this from human ambiguities or white lies.

God sends a famine soon after Abraham has become acquainted with Canaan so that the patriarch be a sojourner in Egypt and experience God as his protector in a foreign land against its mighty ruler. He shall also learn that Canaan is not a paradise; the land is never praised to the patriarchs for its advantages. Yet he returns to it after the famine has passed. He shall specifically return from Egypt as an example for his descendants. This Pharaoh subdued by afflictions is a forerunner of the Pharaoh of Moses.

Chapter 13

Separation From Lot and Renewed Promise Of The Land.
So Abram went up from Egypt, he and his wife, and all that he
had, and Lot with him into the Negeb. ²And Abram was very
weighty in cattle, in silver, and in gold. ³And he journeyed on
from the Negeb as far as Bethel, to the place where his tent had
been in the beginning, between Bethel and Ai, ⁴to the place where
he had made an altar at the first; and there Abram called on the
name of the Lord. ⁵And Lot, who went with Abram, also had
flocks and herds and tents, ⁶so that the land could not bear both of
them dwelling together; for their possessions were so great that
they could not dwell together, ⁷and there was strife between the
herdsmen of Abram's cattle and the herdsmen of Lot's cattle. At
that time the Canaanites and the Perizzites dwelt in the land.

Verse 2. *Weighty in cattle, silver, and gold* Abraham's journeys were
bothersome due to his many possessions; but he was also a man of
consequence. The Hebrew word combines both meanings as the
English weighty. Abraham departs from Egypt like later the people of
Israel (Ex.12,36).

Verse 4. The return of Abraham to Bethel is a home-coming; *called
on the name of the Lord* is a prayer of thanksgiving.

Verse 5. *Who went with Abram* Lot had not yet left Abraham and this
brought him wealth also (see 12,16).

Verse 6. It is usually claimed that the land did not provide enough
space, fodder, and water for the two families with their big herds;
consequently there was strife between the herdsmen over grazing
rights and wells. Yet it is hard to believe that the land could not
accomodate two more families. Land here as often means its inhabitants; the people could not "bear" them because they had become too
rich. Abraham and Lot could also not dwell together; strife existed

between their herdsmen; finally Canaanites and Perizzites were present. The importance of each point becomes clear from Abraham's speech.

> *8Then Abram said to Lot, "Let there be no strife between me and you, between my herdsmen and your herdsmen; for we are kinsmen. 9Is not the whole land before you? Separate yourself from me. If you take the left hand, then I will go to the right; or if you take the right hand, then I will go to the left." 10And Lot lifted up his eyes and saw that the Jordan valley was well watered everywhere like the garden of the Lord, like the land of Egypt, in the direction of Zoar; this was before the Lord destroyed Sodom and Gomorrah. 11So Lot chose for himself all the Jordan valley; and Lot journeyed east; thus they separated from each other. 12Abram dwelt in the land of Canaan, while Lot dwelt among the cities of the valley and moved his tent as far as Sodom. 13 Now the men of Sodom were wicked, great sinners against the Lord.*

Abraham suggests that both leave the place. The real reason for this was not the strife of the herdsmen, but the envy and fear of the natives for whom they had become too rich. Similarly the Philistines later say to Isaac, "Go away from us; for you are much too strong for us." (26,12 ff.) They might have born Abraham alone, so he could have said to Lot, "You see that we are too many; you must look for another place." Abraham's generosity makes Lot's cause his own. Lot cannot remain, so he will not stay either; they might have moved away without separation, but there is also strife between their herdsmen. "It is good and pleasant when brothers dwell together" (Psalm 133,1), but only without strife.

Verse 9. As the strife might repeat itself elsewhere Abraham suggests separation.

The real motive of Abraham is the presence of the Canaanites and Perizzites (see 34,30). Abraham does not want to live among people to whom he or his relatives are unacceptable. He does not wish mere tolerance. He abandons the place of the tent and the altar although he had journeyed through half the country for their sake. Abraham's conduct shows not only peacefulness and forbearance, but also pride, delicacy, and unselfishness.

Verse 10. *Before the Lord destroyed Sodom and Gomorrah.* If Lot is enchanted with the flourishing scenery, the reader needs an explanation for the contrast to the present condition. No one has seen the proverbial paradise, but Egypt is well known. Both comparisons may be understood as exclamations of Lot. They teach the Israelite reader that once Canaan too had a paradise-like region which needed no rain (Deut. 11,10 ff.); its fate is a warning (Deut.29,23). It extended to Zoar, the south-east end of the present Dead Sea.

Verse 12. In 19,1 Lot dwells only at the gates of Sodom (Chiskuni).

Verse 13. Lot had examined the land, but not the inhabitants as he should have done (Bechor Shor). Ezek. 16,49 tells more of Sodom, "this was the guilt of your sister Sodom. . . .pride, surfeit of food, and prosperous ease, but she did not aid the poor and needy. They were haughty and did abominable things. . . .".Other prophets also speak of Sodom and Gomorrah as well-known places of evil. The Sodomites were like Noah and Nimrod proverbial figures of ancient legend.

> ¹⁴The Lord said to Abram, after Lot had separated from him, "Lift up your eyes, and look from the place where you are, northward and southward and eastward and westward; ¹⁵for all the land which you see I will give to you and to your descendants for ever. ¹⁶I will make your descendants as the dust of the earth; can one count the dust of the earth? So your descendants also cannot be counted. ¹⁷Arise, walk through the length and the breadth of the land for I will give it to you." ¹⁸So Abram moved his tent and came and dwelt by the oaks of Mamre, which are at Hebron; and there he built an altar to the Lord.

All divine revelations to Abraham take place after a separation, a renunciation, or a sacrifice and serve as consolation and reward.

Verse 15. *For ever.* Lot lives for the moment, Abraham for eternity.

Verse 17. Unlike Moses who must be content with a distant view Abraham shall feel the land under his feet, symbolically taking possession of it.

Verse 18. Mamre like Shechem is the name of a person (14,13;24) and of a place (23,19;35,27). The place derives its name from the person. It is identified with Hebron where the patriarch's permanent home and later grave will be. Hebron is in a fertile valley south of Jerusalem and still exists as a city.

Chapter 14

The Expedition For The Liberation Of Lot

It happened in the days of Amraphel king of Shinar, Arioch king of Eliasar, Chedorlaomer king of Elam, and Tidal king of Goiim; ²they made war with Bera king of Sodom, Birsha king of Gomorrah, Shinab king of Admah, Shemeber king of Zeboim, and the king of Bela (that is, Zoar). ³All these were neighbors in the Valley of Siddim (that is, the Salt Sea). ⁴Twelve years they had served Chedorlaomer, but in the thirteenth year they rebelled.

Amraphel may be identical with Hammurabi the great ruler of Babylon in the 18th century B.C.E. Arioch is perhaps king Eri-aku of the Babylonian city Larsa (Ellasar). Chedorlaomer is a true Elamite name according to archaeology. Tidal may be the name of a Hittite king.

Verse 2. These four great kings of the east did not come to war against five little kinglets in a corner of Canaan. According to verses 5-7 they came to conquer the Rephaim, Zuzim, Emim, Horites, Amalekites, and Amorites; these nations occupied the whole region east, south, and southwest of Canaan. Only after these nations had been subdued, did the kinglets of the five cities at the southern end of the Dead Sea meet the victors to fight in the Valley of Siddim.

The names *Bera* and *Birsha* kings of Sodom and Gomorrah seem to be derived from the words for evil and wickedness in Hebrew.

Verse 3. The *Salt Sea* or later Dead Sea is the end of the geological rift through which the River Jordan flows. Its surface is 1275 feet below the level of the Mediterranean. It is called Salt Sea because of its high mineral content.

⁵In the fourteenth year Chedorlaomer and the kings who were with him came and subdued the Rephaim in Ashteroth-karnaim, the Zuzim in Ham, the Emim in Shave-kiriathaim, and the Horites in their Mount Seir as far as El-paran on the border of the

wilderness; ⁷then they turned back and came to En-mishpat (that is, Kadesh), and subdued all the country of the Amalekites, and also the Amorites who dwelt in Hazazon-tamar.

Ched-or-laomer is designated as the leader; the other kings only accompany him. The *Rephaim* are often mentioned in the Bible as a people of giants. Except for the Zuzim, the other nations and the localities are also often mentioned.

⁸Then the king of Sodom, the king of Gomorrah, the king of Admah, the king of Zeboim, and the king of Bela (that is, Zoar) went out and joined battle with them in the Valley of Siddim, ⁹with Chedorlaomer king of Elam, Tidal king of Goiim, Amraphel king of Shinar, and Arioch king of Ellasar, four kings against five. ¹⁰Now the Valley of Siddim was full of asphalt pits; and as the kings of Sodom and Gomorrah fled, they fell into them, and the rest fled to the mountain. ¹¹So they took all the goods of Sodom and Gomorrah, and all their provisions, and went their way; ¹²they also took Lot, the son of Abram's brother, who dwelt in Sodom, and his goods, and departed.

The Bible ridicules these little potentates; their enterprise is megalomania. They too are "kings" even favored by the odds of five against four. The proud military expedition comes to a quick and sorry end.

Verse 10. It is not necessary to report their defeat; after having set themselves in martial array they flee immediately. Two kings fall into asphalt pits, probably handicapped in their flight by wide royal garments. They are stuck in the gluey mess and climb out to stand there dirty and dripping. This is robust humour as in Ex. 9,11. The other kings run to the mountains and forsake their comrades.

Verse 11. Some people of the enemy army do this, (see verse 15).

¹³Then one who had escaped came and told Abram the Hebrew, who was living by the oaks of Mamre the Amorite, brother of Eshcol and Aner; these were allies of Abram. ¹⁴When Abram heard that his kinsman had been taken captive, he led forth his trained men, born in his house, three hundred and eighteen of them, and went in pursuit as far as Dan. ¹⁵And he divided his forces against them by night, he and his servants, and routed them and pursued them to Hobah, north of Damascus. ¹⁶Then he

brought back all the goods, and also his kinsman Lot he brought
back with his goods, and the women and the people.

Verse 13. *The Hebrew* thus the refugee refers to him.

Verse 14. Abraham feels challenged as one of his kinsman is in
captivity, he must free him. As ancestor of Israel he sets the first
example for liberation and redemption of captives, later regarded as
one of the most sacred obligations. The situation demands extraordinary action, so Abraham appears as a changed man. He who had
previously avoided all strife draws the sword and sets out in pursuit.
     Dan is probably the city of that name on the north-eastern border of
Canaan.

Verse 15. *Against them,* just as "they took" and "they went" in
verses 11 and 12; who is meant? It is usually assumed that they were
the four kings of the East. But they should have been mentioned
expressly as verse 10 deals with something else. The taking of goods
and even provisions also seems odd and petty. All objections disappear
and the whole chapter becomes understandable if "they" are unknown
persons, the camp followers and marauders of the big army. They loot
and flee and are pursued by Abraham unto Dan, and later Hobah. We
have not to be informed of the return route of the great eastern kings'
army.

> [17]*The king of Sodom went out to meet him after his return from*
> *"the defeat of Chedorlaomer and the kings who were with him"*
> *at the Valley of Shaveh (that is, the King's Valley).* [18]*And*
> *Melchizedek king of Salem brought out bread and wine; he was*
> *priest of God Most High.* [19]*And he blessed him and said,*
>   *"Blessed be Abram by God Most High,*
>   *owner of heaven and earth;*
>   [20]*and blessed be God Most High,*
>   *who has delivered your enemies into your hand!"*
> *And Abram gave him a tenth of everything.*

Verse 17. This verse seems to refute our interpretation of verse 15.
Does it not claim that Abraham and his 318 men defeated Ched-or-
laomer and all the kings with him. This is the extravagant language the
folks at home use to greet the returning warriors. On such occasions the
greatest exaggerations are everywhere permissible. Compare I Sam.
18,7: "Saul has slain his thousands and David his ten thousands"; so
many Philistines probably did not even exist. The king of Sodom who

has in the meantime recovered from his asphalt bath is the official
orator. His speech is as boastful as his behaviour in verse 8.

Verse 18. Salem is very likely an old name for Jerusalem (see Psalm
76,3); used here, as the word meaning peace fits into the setting. An
honored guest is welcomed through the symbolic ceremony of bringing
forth wine and bread over which a priest pronounces blessings.
Melchizedek's conception of God is universalistic; his "God Most
High" is the Lord of heaven and earth, yet not their creator as in chapter
1, merely their owner.

Abraham gives him a tithe. It looks as if Melchizedek of whom
nothing had been said previously appeared only for the sake of the
tithe. Abraham understands at once. Thus Melchizedek is the first
person in whom 12,3 becomes fulfilled.

Melchizedek lived in Israel's memory as an ideal priest (Psalm
110,4); in Christianity (Hebrews 7,1ff.) he became a prototype of the
Messiah.

> ²¹*And the king of Sodom said to Abram, "Give me the persons,
> but take the goods for yourself." ²²But Abram said to the king of
> Sodom. "I have sworn to the Lord God Most High, owner of
> heaven and earth, ²³that I would not take a thread or sandal-
> thong or anything that is yours, lest you should say, 'I have made
> Abram rich.' ²⁴Save only that which the young men have eaten,
> and the share of the men who went with me; let Aner, Eshcol, and
> Mamre take their share."*

The incident just described had been observed with uncomfortable
feelings by the king of Sodom. The sly priest with his unctious
blessing, a way of seeking bakshish, had gotten the better of him. The
tithe was given at his expense as it was his property which Abraham
had retrieved. It seemed that Abraham had thus indicated his right of
possession and wanted to keep the rest. The king tries to save at least
the most valuable part for himself. He is generously willing to leave the
goods to Abraham. The brief and sullen speech, not sweetened by
polite phrases, seems to say that these pious gestures are mutual aid at
his expense. Unfortunately he can do nothing else about it.

Verse 22. Abraham not only declines the offer, thus rejecting the
implied suspicion, but does so through a solemn oath. The words of the
oath at the same time turn to Mechizedek and acknowledge that both of
them stand on the same religious ground; nevertheless Abraham
emphazises his particular creed. He repeats "owner of heaven and

earth" and accepts "God Most High", but refers these general names to the Lord, his God. The relationship of Abraham and Melchizedek is similar to that of Moses and Jethro (Ex. 18).

A thread or a sandal-thong are minimal and stand for "nothing". Abraham wants to owe nothing to a Sodomite. None of the goods of the evil city shall remain in his hands.

Verse 23. This verse intimates that Abraham as the victor could have disposed of everything. He had rightfully given a tithe to the priest; the king of Sodom really had no claims to anything and had on his part been enriched by Abraham.

The Meaning Of The Chapter. This chapter has been the subject of many controversies. Most of the arguments against its credibility and historicity result from wrong interpretation. The expedition of four mighty kings against the tiny territory of five kinglets as well as their supposed defeat by Abraham's 318 men would indeed be impossible. Yet an expedition of rulers of Mesopotamia to the west agrees with their generally known policy of expansion. Abraham does not miraculously defeat them, but recovers spoil from marauders. Only the king of Sodom celebrates this as a "victory over Chedorlaomer and the kings with him". This chapter, whether historical or not, is in every respect sensible and true to life.

The chapter characterizes Abraham as a man who has liberated his brother's son, not as a military hero. He is a man who by virtue of his conduct and faith stands among his contemporaries as a priestly and royal personality.

Lot thought that he had chosen best by living near Sodom; he had left his father's brother in the belief that he would not need him again. Now he is carried off as captive, and no one but Abraham appears as his redeemer. Abraham had avoided envy and strife over property, yet he draws his sword for the unfortunate. Lot suffered by going to Sodom, but Abraham was blessed by going to Hebron. He found allies there, Aner, Eshcol, and Mamre who loyally stand by him in an emergency.

Arrogant and pretentious, Sodom receives a lesson; it is chastised by four great powers. Insult is added to injury by the incident of the asphalt pits. The climax is the reply of Abraham to the king of Sodom.

The little war ends in blessing and peace. Abraham is revealed as a magnanimous man, acting vigorously and wisely on earth, and yet a man oriented toward heaven. A king of the Philistines justifiably aspires to his friendship (21, 22 ff.), and the inhabitants of Hebron will call him a prince of God (23,6).

Chapter 15

The Covenant With Abraham.

After these things the word of the Lord came to Abram in a vision, "Fear not, Abram, I am your shield; your reward shall be very great." ²But Abram said, "O Lord God, what wilt thou give me, for I continue childless, and the steward of my house is Eliezer of Damascus?" ³And Abram said, "Behold, thou hast given me no offspring; and the man born in my house will be my heir." ⁴And behold, the word of the Lord came to him, "This man shall not be your heir; but one who comes forth from you shall be your heir." ⁵And he brought him outside and said, "Look toward heaven and number the stars—if you are able to number them." Then he said to him, "So shall your descendants be." ⁶And he believed the Lord, and he reckoned it to him as righteousness.

The first verse expressly indicates that the chapter is a vision. As it might frighten Abraham, God begins, *Fear not!*

Verse 2. *What wilt thou give me?* is not the blunt question, what will I get? Abraham has a petition, but his humility and respect hinders him from direct and bold expression. He clothes it in words of doubt, resignation, and even rejection. I need no thing as I have no children and at present am well cared for by my steward. *Eliezer* "God helps", perhaps the servant had received this name from Abraham. In later Israel it became very popular.

Verse 3. As Abraham receives no answer and may think that he has not spoken clearly, he pauses and begins again. He wants a son, but dares not to pronounce the word son and only approaches it by circumlocutions. Abraham does not doubt God's promises of descendants. Yet will he live to transmit his heritage to them? He says, I already see, as it were, Eliezer as my heir!

Verse 4. Abraham has hardly finished when God interrupts him by 'no, no, that will not happen' (Ramban).

Verse 5. As often in prophetic visions an idea is illustrated through action (compare Jer. 25,17). The image of the countless stars of heaven here appears for the first time. As heaven and earth belong together this image supplements that of the dust of the earth (13,16). It is more brilliant and lively, therefore more impressive and permanent. Looking up to the heavens and stars means looking up to God who resides above them.

Verse 6. Abraham is definitely re-assured by God's answer to his timid protest. He trusts God who replies, 'I shall remember this.' The verse has no relation to the dogma of "justification by faith." (Romans 4)

Righteousness is a claim to recognition and reward, earned by his conduct (Deut. 9,4; Psalm 106,31). God leaves neither good will nor thought unrewarded.

> 7*And he said to him, "I am the Lord who brought you from Ur of the Chaldaeans to give you this land to inherit it."* 8*But he said, "O Lord God, how am I to know that I shall inherit it?"* 9*He said to him, "Bring me a thirdborn heifer, a thirdborn she-goat, a third-born ram, a turtledove, and a young pigeon."* 10*And he brought him all these, cut them in two, and laid each half over against the other; but he did not cut the birds in two.* 11*And when birds of prey came down upon the carcasses, Abram drove them away.*

Verses 1-6 dealt with the descendants; the land is inseparable from them. This sentence spoken by God will often be quoted later. Beginning with the Exodus the incessantly repeated fundamental fact of Israel's history is that "It was I, the Lord, who brought you from Egypt." The "I" states his power based in his personality; and so the final goal is guaranteed by this "I am the Lord." The use of a similar sentence here marks the Exodus statement as mere repetition and Abraham's exodus as model for that from Egypt. Ur of the Chaldaeans was for Abraham what Egypt is for Israel. Certain dangers must have existed for Abraham in Ur. Thus God speaks to the man who trusts him; even before announcing the troubled times in Egypt (verse 13), God offers comfort and hope.

Verse 8. This parallels verse 2. Following verse 6 these words cannot express doubt or lack of confidence. After the promise of descendants has been illuminated by the image of the sky covered with stars, Abraham asks that the second promise about the land also be made impressive. The spoken word supplemented by a visible image will be better remembered.

Verse 9. This is no sacrifice as nothing is burned; there is no altar, nor is blood poured out.

Thirdborn animals were regarded as particularly strong and fat (Bechor Shor).

Verse 10. Cut in two they are *laid each half over agains the other.* They have only been separated to be joined again. This too is only a vision. Such brothersome actions on the part of Abraham are unnecessary; the request to imagine them is sufficient.

Verses 7 ff. are a continuation of the dialogue between God and Abraham; the subjects are not even mentioned again, (compare Jer 25,15;17).

> *¹²As the sun was going down, a deep sleep fell upon Abram; and lo, a dread and great darkness fell upon him. ¹³Then he said to Abram, "You shall know that your descendants will be sojourners in a land that is not theirs, and will be slaves there, and they will oppress them, for four hundred years; ¹⁴but I will bring judgement on the nation which they serve, and afterwards they shall come out with great possessions. ¹⁵As for yourself, you shall go to your fathers in peace; you shall be buried in a good old age. ¹⁶And they shall come back here in the fourth generation; for the iniquity of the Amorites is not yet complete."*

The sun had not set, so the darkness falling upon Abraham was not the natural one of night. It is a deep sleep filled with anxiety in which Abraham receives the revelation (compare Job 4,12-16).

Verse 13. When I promised that your descendants would inherit the land I must add that for a long time they will remain sojourners like you. The *land that is not theirs* is not only Egypt; four hundred years are too much for the Egyptian bondage. According to the numbers in the Bible Israel's stay in Egypt could not have lasted more than about 215 years, as Moses, who leads the exodus, was the grandson of Kohath, who had gone there with his grandfather Jacob. The four hundred years here may indicate the point at which reckoned from this moment their sojourn will be at an end, (Ibn Ezrah).

Verse 14. *The nation which they serve* are the Egyptians.

Verse 15. The divine speech concludes with comforting and almost poetical words. The word peace appears appropriately for the first time in the Bible, when it speaks of the first patriarch returning to his fathers. He will be the unrivalled model for *a good old age.*

Verse 16. The fourth generation are the Amorites (Ramban). God permits three generations to continue in sin; then they have proved incorrigible, and the cup overflows (Ex. 20,5).

> *17When the sun had gone down and it was dark, behold a smoking fire pot and a flaming torch passed between these pieces. 18On that day the Lord made a covenant with Abram, saying, "To your descendants I give this land, from the river of Egypt to the great river, the river Euphrates, 19The Kenites, the Kenizzites, the Kadmonites, 20the Hittites, the Perizzites, the Rephaim, 21the Amorites, the Canaanites, the Girgashites, and the Jebusites.*

Verse 17. The fiery spectacle is best presented in complete night.

Verse 18. The epochal event is the covenant; God bestows the land on Abraham's descendants. He will never revoke this promise. A covenant is not a contract with mutual obligations as such are not mentioned on the part of Abraham.

The borders of the Promised Land are described. The river of Egypt may refer to the Nile or the Wadi El Arish, an oasis fortified by ancient Egypt. This extended territory has never been reached by Israel, except perhaps under King Solomon (I Kings 5,4).

It was a theoretical claim.

Verses 19-21. Ten nations; the number is a poetical exaggeration about the land as the stars of heaven are about the number of his descendants. The first three nations and the Rephaim are mentioned only here.

The Meaning of The Chapter. This chapter contains only visions and speeches. Abraham becomes a confidant of God who lets him know his hidden decrees. "The word of the Lord came to him" is a technical term of prophecy. Descendants and land are promised. Abraham can easily imagine the fulfillment of the promise of descendants. As soon as he has a son, the natural progression from one generation to the next will continue, and a great people will finally exist. Abraham requests no sign for this, God gives him one as gracious encouragement. Yet how

shall Abraham imagine his descendants possessing the land in which
he is only a sojourner? God's answer initiates Abraham into the principles of divine decrees; in a few words it presents a complete philosophy of history.

The descendants will grow into a people outside of Canaan; there
they will be enslaved and oppressed so as to prevent their absorption
and permanent settlement in that land. Later they will return to Canaan
as a nation and will seize the land. This will not be a deprivation of
legitimate owners, as the former inhabitants will have lost their claims
through their sins. God is long-suffering and allows time to repent to
the former owners of the land. Will Israel have to suffer those years
underservedly and really bear the sins of the Canaanites? That is divine
justice and wisdom. No one may be given someone else's property, but
property is not inalienable. God allows a people to keep a land or takes
it from them according to moral principles. Further "no nation is born
in a day". The suffering of the future heirs is the price of their freedom.
God will also judge the oppressor although he was his tool; for he acted
for his own interests and overstepped all bounds. Thus the Lord,
creator of heaven and earth and judge of the universe, allots everyone
his due. The later prophets teach this as well (e.g. Amos 9,7ff; Is 10,5ff
ff; Jer. 27,4 ff.).

The divine plans are communicated to Abraham in a mysterious way
to make him conscious of their importance (Job 4,12ff.) Abraham is not
to bring a sacrifice, but to perform a symbolic act as in Jer. 34,17ff. The
animals, with the exception of the birds, are cut in two and laid out so
that something can pass between them. The fiery apparition passing
through means that the living God passes through the times of oppression and unites those who are separated. The halves of the animals
belong together. It is a symbol of establishing a covenant, as in Jer. 34.
The Hebrew speaks of "cutting" a covenant. The birds, however, are
not cut in two. A bird is a symbol of freedom (see 8,7 ff; Lev. 14,7).
Therefore the undivided birds symbolize the generation of liberation
from Egyptian bondage, the fourth generation. The three other animals
must represent the three generations of oppression, expressed by their
being cut to pieces. The bird of prey descending upon the carcasses
(verse 11) is the oppressor who would devour the people. The memory
of Abraham and of the promise given to him does not allow this to
happen.

Day and night play a part in the vision; the sun in particular is
mentioned. Both phases of its setting are indicated, the beginning
when the sun slowly sinks below the horizon (verse 12), and the end
when the sun has disappeared (verse 17). This must be understood in

the spirit of Is. 60,19. When the sun sinks for the descendants of Abraham, or has completely disappeared, "the Lord will be your everlasting light . . . your sun shall never go down . . . and your days of mourning shall be ended."

Chapter 16

The Birth Of Ishmael. Hagar's Flight.

Now Sarai, Abram's wife, bore him no children. She had an Egyptian maid whose name was Hagar; ²and Sarai said to Abram, "Behold now, the Lord has prevented me from bearing children, go in to my maid; it may be that I shall obtain children by her." And Abram harkened to the voice of Sarai. ³So, after Abram had dwelt ten years in the land of Canaan, Sarai, Abram's wife, took Hagar the Egyptian, her maid, and gave her to Abram, her husband, as a wife.

After God's promise Abraham can expect a son; but the fulfillment is delayed in so far as it is not Sarah *Abraham's wife* who becomes the mother. Sarah probably brought this maid from her home at her marriage (compare 29,24.29).

Verse 2. Isaac and all descendants are due to God's special providence, as the mother was first barren. God's blessing does not consist in the suspension of a natural law, but in letting it take its course after it had been suspended. The removal of the obstacle is recognized as God's work. Sarah, who naturally knew of God's promise, was convinced that Abraham would have a son, though perhaps God did not want her to be the mother. She suggests a way to a kind of indirect motherhood and Abraham agrees.

Verse 3. As this is a legal action the persons and their relationships to each other are exactly defined. Sarah as wife must not only give permission, but formally presents her maid to her husband, that is without renouncing her own rights as wife. In this way, Hagar became a wife of Abraham and any son born by her his legitimate son. Sarah acts not for her own sake, but out of love for Abraham; she tactfully hides this under her own desire for a child. Showing similar affection, Abraham had not taken this way out for his own sake. Otherwise he should have made the suggestion himself. All this is based on family law as it existed during the period of Abraham. The Code of Hammurabi deals with such situations in several paragraphs.

After Abram had dwelt ten years in the land of Canaan Both Abraham and Sarah had expected children only in Canaan, but now ten years had already passed. In later Jewish law a man could divorce his wife if childless after ten years.

> ⁴*And he went in to Hagar, and she conceived; and when she saw that she had conceived, she looked with contempt on her mistress.* ⁵*And Sarai said to Abram, "May the wrong done to me be on you! I gave my maid to your embrace, and when she saw that she had conceived, she looked on me with contempt. May the Lord judge between me and you!"* ⁶*But Abram said to Sarai, "Behold, your maid is in your power; do to her as you please."* *Then Sarai dealt harshly with her, and she fled from her.*

Verse 4. Hagar refused or neglected to give her mistress due respect, as she well knew that her legal status would change with the birth of a child. According to the popular notion, barrenness is a disgrace for a woman (19,31; 30,1.23), so Sarah could be treated contemptuously.

Verse 5. The slave maid probably felt encouraged by her intimacy with Abraham, as Sarah appeals to the omniscient judge. She has brought this sacrifice; but isn't the girl still her maid?

Verse 6. Abraham leaves it to Sarah to act as judge; Sarah makes her aware that she is still a slave. An ill-treated slave naturally flees.

> ⁷*The angel of the Lord found her by a spring of water in the wilderness, the spring on the way to Shur.* ⁸*And he said, "Hagar, maid of Sarai, where have you come from and where are you going?" She said, "I am fleeing from my mistress Sarai."* ⁹*The angel of the Lord said to her, "Return to your mistress and submit to her."* ¹⁰*The angel of the Lord also said to her, "I will so greatly multiply your descendants that they cannot be numbered for multitude."* ¹¹*And the angel of the Lord said to her, "Behold you are with child, and shall bear a son; you shall call his name Ishmael; because the Lord has heard your affliction.* ¹²*He shall be a wild ass of a man, his hand against every man and every man's hand against him; and he shall dwell in front of all his kinsmen."*

An angel appears for the first time. The Hebrew word means messenger; God has many different kinds of messengers.

Hagar shall bear Abraham a son in his house; he shall also be circumcised. Hagar must not flee before this occurs, so God's messenger calls her back.

Verse 8. The questions of the angel are a way to start a conversation (see 3,9) and also reproach her "are you not the maid of Sarah who should be at home with her mistress?"

Verse 11. A promise or a threat is made credible by describing its results beforehand. So in the case of the prophesied birth of a child its name is already given (17,19).

God has heard your affliction. Your submission is not asked because God approves of your oppression; but it is necessary for his plans.

Verse 12. Your son will be an image of unrestricted freedom. The wild ass is a beautiful shy animal, but vigorous and unmanageable so the son will fight everyone. *In front of all his kinsmen.* Ishmael's territory will be a barrier against Egypt (see 25,18).

> *13So she called the name of the Lord who spoke to her, "Thou art a God of seeing"; for she said, "Have I not seen here after him who sees me?" 14Therefore the well was called Beer-lahairoi; it lies between Kadesh and Bered. 15And Hagar bore Abram a son; and Abram called the name of his son, whom Hagar bore, Ishmael. 16Abram was eighty-six years old when Hagar bore Ishmael to Abram.*

It must be true as she has even seen him in contrast to "God has heard your affliction" (verse 11). The next sentence is very difficult, but it is certain that the word "to see" is used in different meanings: I was permitted to look after him, who saw me and my misery, who befriended me.

Verse 15. Abraham gives the boy the name of verse 11. Hagar must have informed him of these events.

The episode is a necessary part of Abraham's story and follows almost logically. Abraham shall have a son and heir; his birth by Sarah shall be delayed so as to be more appreciated. This is achieved by Abraham begetting a son, but from a maid, Hagar. When Hagar becomes pregnant, jealousy is a natural consequence; she flees as any ill-treated slav'e, but she must return so that her son may be born in Abraham's house. This is brought about by a divine messenger. The well gives greater reality to the apparition by localizing it.

Chapter 17

The Covenant Of Circumcision.
    *When Abram was ninety-nine years old the Lord appeared to
    Abram and said to him, "I am God Almighty, walk before me, and
    be whole. ²And I will make my covenant between me and you,
    and will multiply you exceedingly." ³Then Abram fell on his face;
    and God spoke with him saying, "Behold my covenant is with
    you, and you shall be father of a multitude of nations. ⁵No longer
    shall your name be called Abram, but your name shall be
    Abraham; for I have made you the father of a multitude of
    nations. ⁶I will make you exceedingly fruitful; and I will make
    nations of you, and kings shall come forth from you. ⁷And I will
    establish my covenant between me and you and your descend-
    ants after you throughout their generations for an everlasting
    covenant, to be God to you and to your descendants after you.
    ⁸And I will give to you and to your descendants after you, the
    land of your sojournings, all the land of Canaan, for an everlast-
    ing possession; and I will be their God."*

    God's revelation is dated in the ninety-ninth year of Abraham one
year preceding the birth of Isaac. The last arrangements must be made
before Sarah conceives. They shall renew their matrimonial union; the
true son will not only have Abraham as father, but also Sarah as
mother.
    God here first uses of himself a name which is generally translated as
the Almighty; its linguistic derivation and original meaning have not
yet been satisfactorily explained.
    Walk before me, and be whole parallels the call of 12,2. If you want to
become whole which is my request from you, you must walk before me;
you must place yourself under my exclusive supervision, guidance,
and protection. The image is taken from the shepherd who walks
behind his herd directing it by his calls (48,15), or from the father
under whose eyes the child walks. It is more than the walking "with"
God of Enoch and Noah who were practically lead by the hand.

When questions arise you shall take directions only from God and be devoted to him without reservation. This word does not refer to moral conduct, for that would be too insignificant in this situation and is self-understood. The high demand corresponds to God's, "Be you mine, and I will be yours."

Verse 2. *My covenant* the special covenant which I have readied for my chosen one (as Num. 25,12). It is a gift of divine grace and parallels the gift of the land.

Verse 3. This is Abraham's answer to God's call. Words would be too feeble. In 12,4 he goes without words, here he prostrates himself. Falling on one's face before God shows both awe before his majestic manifestation which blinds like the sun and also humility and gratitude (see I Kings 18,7 and I Sam. 25,23 for falling down before a human being).

This covenant shall enhance that of Noah which merely dealt with the survival of mankind, but it is also a harbinger of the covenant with Israel at Mount Sinai which will designate this people as priests of mankind, close to God. God is meaningful for man only as God of a covenant, as a power with which he can have a personal relationship; he must be the same God as the Creator and Master of the universe.

Verse 4. *The father of a multitude of nations* is usually explained as referring to the nations aside from Israel which are derived from Abraham, the descendants of Ishmael, Keturah (25,1), and Esau. However, the number of these nations is small; furthermore the Hebrew words do not express the promise of descendants. The reference is not to physical fatherhood, but figuratively Abraham shall become the spiritual father of converts from a multitude of nations. They will confess the God of Abraham, and thus become the equals of Abraham's "seed". He will be the father of all the faithful.

In order to express this idea a new name is formed for him. Abram meant "high father"; Abraham seems to be an augmented form of the word, "higher father". Emphasis is achieved by lengthening the word; the old name disappears and is never again used.

God makes a twofold covenant with Abraham, with him personally, and with his descendants; one covenant refers to all mankind, the other to this single people. The two cannot be separated as Israel is to become the priest of mankind. The universal and the national idea stand side by side as at the covenant on Mount Sinai (Ex. 19,5f.).

Verse 6. *Kings shall come forth from you.* The Bible sees kingship as the climax of national development. This is not the opinion of Samuel in I Sam. 8.

Verse 7. *Your descendants after you.* You shall never lack descendants who will continue the covenant.

> ⁹*And God said to Abraham, "As for you, you shall keep my covenant, you and your descendants after you throughout their generations.* ¹⁰*This is my covenant, which you shall keep, between me and you and your descendants after you: Every male among you shall be circumcised.* ¹¹*You shall be circumcised in the flesh of your foreskins, and it shall be a sign of the covenant between me and you.* ¹²*He that is eight days old among you shall be circumcised; every male throughout your generations, whether born in your house, or bought with your money from any foreigner who is not of your offspring,* ¹³*both he that is born in your house and he that is bought with your money, shall be circumcised. So shall my covenant be in your flesh an everlasting covenant.* ¹⁴*Any uncircumcised male who is not circumcised in the flesh of his foreskin shall be cut off from his people; he has broken my covenant."*

Verse 9. God will fulfill his part of the covenant. Abraham must contribute something according to his abilities; namely the circumcision. The covenant is always called God's covenant; man is not a partner whose obligation is really an equivalent return. Yet, to God's offer 'You shall be mine', he shall answer 'I will be yours.' Circumcision shall be a covenant of God with Abraham and with all succeeding generations; he enters into it before the son and heir is born. The circumcision elevates him to hereditary nobility; it will have greater meaning for him and his descendants if he is already God's nobleman upon begetting a son.

Verse 11. *You shall be circumcised in the flesh of your foreskins* This mark cannot be laid aside or effaced.

Verse 12. The eight days are only applicable to later generations.

Verse 14. A male who was uncircumcised and has wilfully remained so will be punished by being "cut off" from his people. The expression is taken from the felling of a tree (Deut. 19,5) and refers to the strokes of

fate which will fell him unless turned aside by God. This is an ingenious idea in the true prophetic spirit; such blows strike every man, but
for the Israelite they are raised to a matter of conscience. If he has
broken God's covenant, he shall regard them as a punishment, which
had been foretold to him. It is therefore a very general threat of divine
judgement which may occur in many different ways.

> ¹⁵And God said to Abraham, "As for Sarai your wife, you shall
> not call her name Sarai, but Sarah shall be her name. ¹⁶I will bless
> her; moreover, I will give you a son by her. I will bless her and she
> shall be a mother of nations; kings of peoples shall come from
> her." ¹⁷Then Abraham fell on his face, and laughed, and said to
> himself, "Shall a child be born to a man who is hundred years
> old? Shall Sarah who is ninety years old bear a child?" ¹⁸And
> Abraham said to God, "Oh that Ishmael might live in thy sight!"
> ¹⁹God said, "No, but Sarah your wife shall bear you a son, and
> you shall call his name Isaac. I will establish my covenant with
> him as an everlasting covenant for his descendants after him.
> ²⁰As for Ishmael, I have heard you; behold, I will bless him and
> make him fruitful and multiply him exceedingly; he shall be the
> father of twelve princes, and I will make him a great nation. ²¹But
> I will establish my covenant with Isaac, whom Sarah shall bear to
> you at this season next year."

Verse 15. Sarah in Hebrew means "princess".

Verse 16. Her first blessing will be a son following barrenness, the
other further descendants from this son. God pronounces the word son
before Abraham for the first time. The suspense which had dominated
the entire life of the patriarch is now released.

Verse 17. This disclosure is as overwhelming as that of verses 1–3;
Abraham again falls on his face in humility and gratitude.
Laughed is jubilant.
Abraham's questions do not imply doubt and still less that this
cannot happen. Abraham, who had abandoned all for such a promise,
cannot possibly now question the power of Almighty God and
disbelieve his promise. Furthermore he has had a son at the age of
eighty-five. Sarah had not mentioned advanced age as an obstacle 16,2;
her words rather indicate the opposite: if God were willing she might
give birth. Great happiness is often hidden behind exclamations of
doubt, even if the good fortune had been strongly desired or indeed

secretly expected. Should that be true? Is it possible? Can it really happen to me? I cannot believe it! This restrains his happy excitement and protects him from an abundance of emotion which might later embarass him even if he need not fear disappointment or envy.

Furthermore, God only speaks to a soul which is receptive, gives prohibitions merely to him who is willing, makes promises only to a believer. Their objections are not a denial of his power, but are based upon a feeling of their own inadequacy, upon the resistance of the world, upon the analogy of other experiences. They want to be reassured. They do not doubt, but would like to know how it will happen.

Verse 18. Abraham had said all this to himself as such a speech would be improper before God. He expresses his feelings differently before him; he would be happy if the son whom he has would stay alive. This is not meant seriously but is only a way of declaring the gift as too great without declining it.

Verse 19. God repeats the promise and gives it greater certainty by already informing him that the son shall be called Isaac—laughter, rejoicing. This is a brilliant refinement of divine gaiety. God too "laughs", is happy, with the father. Not only will he be a son of Sarah, but he shall take your place concerning the covenant. I will speak of him as I speak of you.

Verse 20. *I have heard you* alludes to the name of Ishmael, "God hears" (16,11). A great abundance of blessing is showered on Ishmael; the climax is that his sons will already be princes.

Verse 21. The essence and value of the divine covenant could not be expressed more clearly. All worldly greatness will be the portion of the son of Hagar (verse 20), of the children of this world. Yet, it is only a temporal grant when compared with the eternal future which will be the portion of the chosen son; all princely crowns cannot outweigh the divine crown. Ishmael's descendants will reach their climax in the next generation (25,12 ff.), whereas the people of the promise will grow slowly.

²²*When he had finished talking with him, God went up from Abraham.* ²³*Then Abraham took Ishmael his son and all those born in his house or bought with his money, every male among the men of Abraham's house, and he circumcised the flesh of their*

foreskins that very day, as God had said to him. 24Abraham was ninety-nine years old when he was circumcised in the flesh of his foreskin. 25And Ishmael his son was thirteen years old when he was circumcised in the flesh of his foreskin. 26That very day Abraham and his son Ishmael were circumcised; 27and all the men of his house, those born in the house and those bought with money from a foreigner, were circumcised with him.

Abraham immediately obeys the commandment. This is so important in both his life and that of his son, Ishmael, that their ages are given.

The Meaning Of Circumcision.

Circumcision is found among many other peoples; it has existed from antiquity until today in different parts of the world.

Its meaning in our chapter is simple and clear. It is a sign of the covenant between God and Abraham and his descendants. The covenant shall be marked on their bodies and thereby be permanent. Circumcision signifies God's possession of Abraham and his people. Like a seal, it is impressed upon every boy soon after his birth at his genitals, the organ of reproduction of the generations. Due to its nature it can neither be removed nor denied. The Israelite cannot be withdrawn from belonging to God.

Here the circumcision seems related to the change of Abram's name to Abraham. The new name is a kind of second birth; it establishes a filial relationship to God which every man who takes Abraham, the believer, as his father can join. The new creation, expressed for Abraham by a change of name, is repeated in every generation by circumcision.

The performance of circumcision indicates willingness to enter into the covenant with God and to preserve it. It is a symbol of obedience; therefore, remaining uncircumcised becomes an image for hardness of heart (Deut. 10,6 and often) in Biblical language. Likewise "stiffnecked-ness" refuses to listen to a call and is therefore an image of obstinacy. Circumcision is submission of inborn nature to a divine call. Descent by birth means much, but not all. The admonition of the prophets (already Deut. 10,16; 30,5 f.) to circumcise the heart was naturally not meant as an abrogation of the circumcision of the body.

Circumcision shall apply to all male members of the household (verse 12), even to the unfree men born in the house or bought. The reason is that they are born in *your* house and bought with *your* money. The reception into the house is raised into a higher sphere through circumcision.

Thus foreign stock also becomes a servant of God and the servant of the house its child; this shall insure humane treatment. The servant, even if not of "the seed of Abraham", becomes a member of the family and the nation. For this reason the word slave is intentionally avoided in this chapter.

Circumcision shall be performed on the eighth day after birth because the child is regarded part of its mother during the first week (Ex. 22,29f; Lev. 22,27).

Circumcision is a national and religious symbol and remains such beyond the people that are descended from Abraham by birth. Every stranger who submits to it receives Abraham as his father and becomes an Israelite.

Any explanation by sanitary considerations is to be rejected as not Biblical. It is also of no importance whether Israel appropriated circumcision from other people, perhaps from the Egyptians. It has a distinct character in Israel which can have been borrowed as little as Israel's God and the specific relationship to Him.

Chapter 18

The Angels Visit With Abraham

And the Lord appeared to him by the oaks of Mamre, as he sat at the door of his tent in the heat of the day. ²He lifted up his eyes and looked, and behold, three men stood in front of him. When he saw them, he ran from the tent door to meet them, and bowed himself to the earth, ³and said, "My Lord, if I have found favor in your sight, do not pass by your servant. ⁴Let a little water be brought, and wash your feet, and rest yourselves under the tree, ⁵while I fetch a morsel of bread, that you may refresh yourselves, and after that you may pass on - since you have come to your servant." So they said, "Do as you have said."

By the covenant of circumcision Abraham had entered into closest relationship with God; he had become his servant and confidant. The reward for his zeal and for the performance of the circumcision is a new revelation; it follows immediately, so that it can be said; the Lord appeared *to him* and not "to Abraham". God appears to him through three men; the closer a person's relationship to God, the more human is the form of God's manifestation. To a man remote from God, revelations are more impersonal. These men are messengers of God; in their human way they wash their feet and eat. Yet, as we shall see, Abraham immediately knows with whom he must deal. We may even assume that the first verse indicates Abraham had been informed of God's decision (verses 17–20) and therefore expected messengers of God, dispatched for Sodom and Gomorrah.

Verse 2. *He ran from the tent door to meet them.* To meet an honored guest one hurries a shorter or longer distance according to his rank, similarly one escorts him when he departs (verse 16). Abraham knows the nature of his guests and his deep bow before God's messengers corresponds to falling on his face before God (17,3;17).

Verse 3. He addresses them *My Lord.* Abraham never calls himself the servant of a human being or addresses a man as his master, neither

116

the Hittites (chapter 23), nor Abimelech (chapters 20.21). How then could he have done so with complete strangers had he not known who they were? He asks them not to pass by him; he knows that they are only passing and their destination. This delightful scene is usually assumed to illustrate Abraham's generous hospitality. However, Abraham does not live in a region where travellers are so rare; he cannot possibly have received every passer-by in this exuberant manner. Yet, he recognizes the messengers of God and does not want them to go without having brought forth his petition. His invitation shall make verses 23ff possible and prepare for it.

Verse 4. They must show patience; it will not be long. The wanderer who walks in sandals must first be given water to wash his feet (19,2 and often). *Rest yourselves under the tree* avoids asking them to enter into the tent. For this reason the meeting takes place in the heat of the day. Abraham makes them understand that he knows the urgency of their assignment and he will not detain them long. Bread restores the tired wanderer more quickly than anything else as Plutarch also states. Abraham speaks only of bread, unassumingly. The Talmud draws the lesson: a pious man promises little and gives much; a wicked man does the opposite. Their courteous answer consists in asking that he do no more than he had said.

> 6And Abraham hastened into the tent to Sarah, and said, "Make haste: three measures of fine meal groats, kneed it and make cakes." 7And Abraham ran to the herd, and took a calf, tender and good, and gave it to the servant and hastened to have it prepared. 8Then he took curds, and milk, and the calf which he had prepared, and set it before them: and he stood by them under the tree while they ate.

Sarah shall have a share in entertaining the distinguished guests. This also prepares for verse 9.

Verse 7. Bread is baked in the tent and therefore the business of the wife and her maids. The meat is provided by the man who disposes of the herd. *Hastened* used three times indicates that great men need not wait.

Verse 8. Respectfully, Abraham himself sets the meal before his guests. He stands ready to wait on them further.

> [9]They said to him, "Where is Sarah your wife?" And he said, "She is in the tent." [10]He said, "I will come back to you next year, and Sarah, your wife, shall have a son." And Sarah heard it at the tent door behind him. [11]Now Abraham and Sarah were old, advanced in age; it had ceased to be with Sarah after the manner of women. [12]So Sarah laughed to herself, saying, "After I have grown withered, shall I have pleasure, and my husband is old?"

Not that they miss Sarah or asked for her well-being, but the question is a way of beginning a conversation.

Verse 10. This verse presents a lively, personal manner of speaking. *I will come back* anyone who comes to you next year, and in my case it would be a return, will see a son from Sarah.

Verse 11. *Advanced in age*, in those years during which nothing further may be expected of life. With a child life would really only begin. Even if the years of both were no obstacle, Sarah's condition contradicted such a hope.

Verse 12. *Sarah laughed to herself* refers to 17,17. *Saying*, refers to the succeeding half doubting, half questioning exclamation: Should that be possible? This was expressed by laughter not by actual words.

> [13]The Lord said to Abraham, "Why did Sarah laugh, and say, 'Shall I indeed bear a child, now that I am old?' [14]Is anything too hard for the Lord? At the appointed time I will return to you next year, and Sarah shall have a son." [15]But Sarah denied, saying, "I did not laugh," for she was full of awe. He said, "No, but you did laugh." [16]Then the man got up from there and looked toward Sodom; and Abraham went with them to set them on their way.

Sarah's laughter is interpreted by the guest as the laughter of an older woman. It is to be understood that when told she will have a child she questions, Shall I yet bear a child? At my age? The guests have heard Sarah laughing, not speaking.

Verse 15. Sarah denies her laughter not because of her fear of punishment, but out of respect. It shows good breeding to feel shamed when reprehended by a distinguished man, and to say "I did not do it." It is actually not a concealment, but a confession that she had done wrong (Isaac Arama). She would have preferred not to have laughed. Abraham says nothing which is understandable in the light of the preceding chapter 17. For him the prophecy is not new while Sarah only now receives the good tidings; she shall be on the same level as Abraham, as previously when her name too was changed.

Her reaction corresponds to that of Abraham. She too "laughs", but is horrified in feminine modesty to discover that her laughter has been heard; therefore she does not want to admit it. The man of God disputes her denial not as a reprimand which would have been rather petty, but he regards her laughter as important for it shall justify the name Isaac—laughter. Through this announcement the men have not only delivered their message to Sarah, but have made a generous return for the hospitality they received and can depart.

Verse 16. Abraham escorts them on their way in the same manner as he had gone to meet them (verse 2); this also affords him an opportunity to speak his mind regarding their destination.

> *[17]The Lord had said, "Shall I hide from Abraham what I am about to do? [18]Seeing that Abraham shall become a great and mighty nation, and all the nations of the earth shall bless themselves by him. [19]Because I have chosen him, that he may charge his children and his household after him to keep the way of the Lord by doing righteousness and justice; so that the Lord may bring to Abraham what he has promised him."*

If all this were a deliberation by God on the way to Sodom, it should somehow be disclosed to Abraham. This is not done and yet in verse 24 he shows himself well informed. Verses 17–21 are therefore a decision reached in heaven before the beginning of the story and only reported now. Such a deliberation in heaven precedes every divine judgement; see the great flood in 6,5–7 or the confusion of languages in 11,6f. The divine revelation of verse 1 must have referred to it, but the reader was left to take its contents from the following section and from verses 17–21, namely the disclosure that God had resolved on judgement over Sodom and Gomorrah.

This cannot have come as a surprise to Abraham. The evil of these cities was constantly before his eyes; he realized that they were ready for destruction. When the three men appear, he immediately knows who they are and acts accordingly. He is happy that they pass his house; this would not have been necessary for their mission. He realizes it to be a hint of his share in the matter which shall consist of intercession in the last moment. Therefore he stops the wanderers; the meal is served only so that he may escort them afterwards. It shows great art of narration to mention the divine decision at his moment when the important conversation is about to begin and the wonderful, still thriving region lies before the eye, but every further step brings catastrophe nearer.

Abraham by his circumcision had become worthy of deeper initiation into God's decrees. "Surely the Lord God does nothing, without revealing his secret to his servants and prophets" (Amos 3,7). Amos did not discover this truth, but found it in existence; otherwise his own appearance could not be understood. Abraham is the first confidant and prophet of God, though not in the sense of warning his people of a divine judgement as his people do not yet exist. Out of him shall grow a people which through its tradition and education will render God-sent prophets and warners possible. They appear when the ground has been prepared by the moral idea of justice and righteousness in imitation of the way of God, the all-just judge of the world. Israel becomes great by producing the prophets, a blessing for all peoples of the earth. The purpose for which Abraham had been called will be fulfilled.

> 20Then the Lord said, "The outcry against Sodom and Gomorrah, how great it is! and their sin how very grave! 21I will go down to see whether they have worked destruction according to the outcry which has come to me; and if not I shall consider."

Verse 21. *I will go down to see* God is thoroughly informed, but it is the conscientious manner of a judge to establish the facts in person (Rashi). As the Bible assumes that the cry of the oppressed reaches heaven and is heard by God, so he must also be able to see from there.

They have worked destruction for themselves. These two verses are by no means a definite and unalterable death decree. The sentence is held in abeyance, written but not yet signed. This is the true meaning of the whole chapter. God wants intercession and Abraham shall be its mouthpiece. Man shall be the voice of humanity in God's council and court. God will not only listen, but even provoke him to speak. His voice is after all another voice of God himself. (Compare God and Moses in Ex. 32,10).

> 22So the men turned from there, and went toward Sodom; but Abraham still stood before the Lord.

From there the way branched off to Sodom; two of the men went on, while the third remained with Abraham. Now, when alone with

Abraham, he is called the Lord. It is not as if he were God in person walking on earth in a body, but because he may speak for God with authority. Abraham still wants to say something; this agrees with God's intention who expectantly turns to him.

> ²³Then Abraham drew near, and said, "Will you indeed destroy the righteous with the wicked? ²⁴Suppose there are fifty righteous within the city; will you then destroy and not spare the place for the fifty righteous who are in it? ²⁵Far be it from you to do such a thing, to slay the righteous with the wicked, so that the righteous fare as the wicked! Far be that from you! Shall not the judge of all the earth do right?" ²⁶And the Lord said, "If I find at Sodom fifty righteous in the city, I will spare the whole place for their sake."

Abraham drew near—he dared it. The motive and purpose of the visit of the three men with Abraham is revealed. For the first time man not only answers in a discussion with God, but begins the discussion; God designed this. Abraham shall have a voice in God's court. For this reason God had appeared to him in the shape of men who visit with him, eat at his table, and converse with him in the greatest affability; even some teasing of Sarah is added. All this shall give Abraham courage so he may dare speak to God as man speaks to his fellow.

Abraham's speeches are humble questions as if he wanted to be respectfully certain of the standards for the sentence. He acts like a guest admitted to the heavenly court, always conscious of the immeasurable distance between the Lord of the universe and himself, a worm on the ground. He must overcome his own resistance for every new question. He begins no less than six times, cautiously feeling for the next rung. If he should be refused, he does not want to expose himself to it too early, but he also stops at the right moment.

Abraham expresses two ideas: 1) the righteous, whom he believes to exist among every people, must not be destroyed with the wicked. This is strongly rejected as incompatible with the righteousness of the judge of the universe. It is self-evident that no righteous man will be destroyed. 2) The existence of a number of righteous should be reason for mercy. This mercy is not sought, as often assumed, for the wicked; it is incorrect to speak of Abraham's intercession for the sinners. Justice demands punishment of the guilty as much as acquittal of the innocent. The righteous of a community by their virtue protect and save the community as such, the place which would otherwise perish from the face of the earth. Abraham does not speak of sparing the sinners, but always of sparing the city. The question revolves around the number of righteous a community must contain in order to be spared.

Abraham begins with fifty. This might find its explanation according to Amos 5,3. There we see that a larger city is supposed to furnish 1000 armed men, a smaller city 100; fifty would be half of that. Abraham's question is: what if righteous and unrighteous counterbalance each other?

Abraham's first speech is most detailed and clever; it begins with the generally accepted thought that as it is the duty of a human judge to acquit the righteous, how much more is it to be expected of God (20,4)? Is he not the judge of all the earth? This seems to agree with God's own thought. Did he not choose Abraham to charge his children to do righteousness and justice (verse 19)? Nevertheless God does not take up this idea in the following. He is in no need of Abraham's appeal to his righteousness; his seeming failure to have heard it is a subtle reprimand for Abraham.

Verse 25. *Far be that from you.* Then man would draw the conclusion that is is senseless to strive for righteousness (Mal. 3,14).

> ²⁷And Abraham answered and said, "Behold, I have taken upon *myself to speak to the Lord. I who am but dust and ashes.* ²⁸Suppose five of the fifty righteous are lacking? Will you destroy the *whole city for the lack of five?" And he said, "I will not destroy it* if I find forty-five there." ²⁹Again he spoke to him and said, *"Suppose forty are found there." He answered, "For the sake of* forty I will not do it." ³⁰He said, "Oh let not the Lord be angry, and I will speak. Suppose thirty are found there." He answered, "I will not do it, if I find thirty there." ³¹He said, "Behold, I have taken upon myself to speak to the Lord. Suppose twenty are found there." He answered, "For the sake of twenty I will not destroy it." ³²He said, "Oh·let not the Lord be angry, and I will speak again only this once. Suppose ten are found there." He said, "For the sake of ten I will not destroy it."

Abraham tries five times and God always answers briefly and graciously: Even then . . . .

Verse 27. *I who am but dust and ashes.* This is an expression of deepest humility. Dust is the lowest form of matter upon which everyone steps, and ashes are the last worthless remnant of it.

Verse 28. Timidly Abraham subtracts only five, but does not speak of the resulting forty-five, he merely mentions the lacking five. Can it fail for five? Later he gathers enough courage to reduce the figure by tens. Monotony is artfully avoided through a few variations.

Abraham's "haggling" is deeply moving as its intention is to save places of civilization as long as they can still be supported by righteous men; as magnificent is the unshakable patience of divine grace. Abraham halts at ten; ten may be regarded as the smallest number still capable of organization, of influencing a greater number or of representing the whole if necessary.

[33]*And the Lord went his way when he had finished speaking to Abraham; and Abraham returned to his place.*

The conversation had produced complete agreement, and they separate in inner harmony.

Chapter 19

The Destruction Of Sodom And Gomorrah.

The two angels came to Sodom in the evening; and Lot was sitting in the gate of Sodom. When Lot saw them, he rose to meet them and bowed himself with his face to the earth, ²and said, "Behold, there are my lords; turn aside, I pray you, to your servant's house, and spend the night, and wash your feet; then you may rise up early and go on your way." They said, "No, we will spend the night in the town square." ³But he urged them strongly; so they turned aside to him and entered his house; and he made them a meal, and baked unleavened bread, and they ate.

The two angels arrive in the evening to make the following incident possible. Lot is sitting in the gate and cannot miss the strangers.

Verse 2. Lot resides in a house, not in a tent like Abraham. In spite of Chapter 14 he has really settled down in Sodom and has even given his daughters to Sodomites in marriage. Yet, in the eyes of the natives he remains the foreigner without full citizenship (verse 9).

Verse 3. A first refusal is often not taken seriously (33,10). Unleavened bread is prepared quickly.

⁴But before they lay down, the men of the city, the men of Sodom, both young and old, all the people from every corner, surrounded the house; ⁵and they called to Lot, "Where are the men who came to you tonight? Bring them out to us, that we may know them." Lot went out of the door to the men, shut the door after him, ⁷and said, "I beg you, my brothers, do not act wickedly. ⁸Behold, I have two daughters who have not known man; let me bring them out to you, and do to them as you please; only do nothing to these men, for they have come under the shelter of my roof."

Unnatural sexual desire is awakened; it is regarded as typical of Canaan (Lev. 18,24 ff); young and old men of the city, even from the remotest quarters, pour out like dogs and shout their vice in public. Is. 3,9 shows that this vice of Sodom had become proverbial; they were "men of Sodom".

Verse 6. Lot shows courage by going out to meet the excited crowd and even shutting the door behind him. He protects his guests with his own body; he tries to dissuade the people.

Lot's offer cannot be taken seriously. With the unnatural bent of the Sodomites he knows that they would not accept. He wants to stress that under no circumstances will he deliver the men. This is emphasized by mentioning the highest price. The later action of his daughters toward him appears like retaliation.

Under the shelter of my roof. The roof protects a guest and refugee like a sanctuary.

> *9But they said, "Stand back!" and they said, "This fellow came to sojourn, and he would play the judge! Now we will deal worse with you than with them." Then they pressed hard against the man Lot and drew near to break the door. 10But the men put forth their hands and brought Lot into the house to them and shut the door. 11And they struck with blindness the men who were at the door of the house, both small and great, so that they wore themselves out groping for the door.*

A foreigner who should be happy to be tolerated will usurp the highest native office .

Verse 11. The Hebrew term indicates a delusion in seeing rather than actual blindness (compare II Kings 6,18).

> *12Then the men said to Lot, "Have you any one else here? Sons-in-law, sons, daughters, or any one you have in the city, bring them out of the place; 13for we are about to destroy this place, because the outcry against its people has become great before the Lord, and the Lord has sent us to destroy it." 14Lot went out and said to his sons-in-law who had married his daughters, "Up, get you out of this place; for the Lord is about to destroy the city." But he seemed to his sons-in-law to be jesting.*

The above incident has made the wickedness of the Sodomites so apparent that God's judgement seems justified before the world and its execution cannot be further delayed.

Verse 13. This verse takes us into the heavenly court where offended morality has cried out against Sodom and Gomorrah. The angels are messengers of the heavenly court for the execution of a catastrophe.

Verse 14. *Sons-in-law who had married his daughters.* Others translate "who were to marry his daughters." But the next verse seems to distinguish the two daughters who are still at home from those who were already married. Their husbands, born Sodomites with typical self-assurance, do not believe in a catastrophe and perish in it.

> ¹⁵*Morning dawned and the angels urged Lot, saying, "Arise, take your wife and your two daughters who are here, lest you be consumed for the guilt of the city."* ¹⁶*As he lingered, the men seized him and his wife and his two daughters by the hand, the Lord being merciful to him, and they brought him forth and set him outside the city.* ¹⁷*And when they had brought them forth to the outside, he said, "Flee for your life; do not look back or stop anywhere in the valley; flee to the hills, lest you be consumed."*

Verse 16. Lot shows lack of resolution and his inability to abandon everything. He, in contrast to Abraham, is pictured as a man who likes to live well (13,10ff.), is soft, vaccilating, and timid (Procksch). Wife and daughters are saved with him just as it had been with Noah's wife, sons and their wives.

Verse 17. Be satisfied to save your life; don't bother about your property (Rashi). *Do not look back* from anxiety for your sons-in-law in the city; looking back also means delaying (Rashbam)

> ¹⁸*Then Lot said to them, "Oh no, my lords;* ¹⁹*behold, your servant has found favor in your sight, and you have shown me great kindness in saving my life; but I cannot flee to the hills, lest the worst hit me, and I die.* ²⁰*Behold, yonder city is near enough to flee to, and it is a little one. I would prefer to flee there—is it not a little one?—and my life will be saved."* ²¹*He said to him, "Behold I grant you this favor also, that I will not overthrow the city of which you have spoken.* ²²*Make haste, flee there; for I can do nothing till you arrive there." Therefore the name of the city is called Zoar.*

Verse 19. Lot introduces his petition by gratefully acknowledging all that they have already done for him which practically obliges them to grant this request. Lot, exhausted by anxiety and the hurried flight, is out of breath and afraid that if he climb a hill, he will suffer a stroke. We may imagine Lot as a rather portly gentleman. In spite of all its horror the narrative is not without a shade of irony. He pants and cannot go further; the farthest is that little city. It is near and small, its sinfulness cannot be great (Rashi). It is a matter of life and death, but in reality even now he can hardly depart from the lovely valley.

Verse 21. The petition is granted. The angel can do so, as he has been assigned to destroy Sodom with its surroundings, but also to save Lot.

Verse 22. Zoar means small.

> ²³The sun had risen over the earth when Lot came to Zoar. ²⁴Then the Lord rained on Sodom and Gomorrah brimstone and fire from the Lord out of heaven; ²⁵and he overthrew those cities, and all the valley; and all the inhabitants of the cities, and what grew on the ground. ²⁶But Lot's wife behind him looked back, and she became a pillar of salt.

As Lot is safe the work of destruction may begin.

Verse 24. *Brimstone* is sulphur; the fire ignites the sulphur. The cities return to primeval chaos in which nothing grew on earth and no man cultivated the soil.

Verse 26. Her motive in turning around and the method of her becoming a pillar of salt are not mentioned. The legend probably originated with a pillar of salt existing in the region.

> ²⁷And Abraham went early in the morning to the place where he had stood before the Lord; ²⁸and he looked down toward Sodom and Gomorrah, and toward all the land of the valley, and beheld, and lo, the smoke of the land went up like the smoke of a furnace.

We must not forget that Abraham, not Lot, is the main person in the story. Chapter 18 had left the fate of the cities in suspense. Abraham had gone home in deep anxiety, knowing that the matter would be decided during the night. Therefore he rises early, and with sorrow and terror views the catastrophe.

Abraham is the only witness of the disaster; later generations will learn of it through him (18,17f). To that end none of the refugees had

been allowed to look back; Lot's wife who had nevertheless done so,
had become a pillar of salt.

> ²⁹So it was that, when God destroyed the cities of the valley, God
> remembered Abraham, and sent Lot out of the midst of the over-
> throw, when he overthrew the cities in which Lot had dwelt. ³⁰Lot
> went up out of Zoar, and dwelt in the hills with his two daughters,
> for he was afraid to dwell in Zoar; so he dwelt in a cave with his
> two daughters.

Abraham had tactfully not petitioned for the life of his brother's son
in chapter 18, because he had interceded for the sake of a principle.
God, however, had also seen this advocate of survival as a man, an
individual with human and family ties; so he had allowed his nephew,
Lot, to be led from the scene of destruction. The motive for saving Lot is
his relationship to Abraham. He was not without merit as he had once
accompanied him into strange lands.

Verse 30. Lot will soon be mentioned no more, therefore we must
still be told about his descendants (after 11,27 as in 22,20 ff. for Nahor
and Betuel). Only then will the line of descendants of Terach be
complete.

> ³¹And the first-born said to the younger, "Our father is old, and
> there is not a man on earth to come in to us after the manner of all
> the earth. ³²Come, let us make our father drink wine, and we will
> lie with him, that we may bring offspring into the world through
> our father." ³³So they made their father drink wine that night; and
> the first-born went and lay with her father; he did not know when
> she lay down or when she arose. ³⁴And the next day, the firstborn
> said to the younger, "Behold, I lay last night with my father; let us
> make him drink wine tonight also; then you go in and lie with
> him, that we may bring offspring into the world through our
> father." ³⁵So they made their father drink wine that night also;
> and the younger arose, and lay with him; and he did not know
> when she lay down and when she arose. ³⁶Thus both the daugh-
> ters of Lot were with child by their father. ³⁷The first-born bore a
> son, and called his name Moab; he is the father of the Moabites to
> this day. ³⁸The younger also bore a son and called his name
> Ben-ammi; he is the father of the Ammonites to this day.

The conduct of Lot's daughters has been severely critized as motivated by hostility against the nations of Moab and Ammon. It is claimed that this story of their origin by incest was invented to insult them.

The action of the daughters in the opinion of the Bible is to their credit. They do not act to satisfy sexual lust, but to fulfill their destiny as women and to preserve the family. All their scruples disappear as they must reach the highest goal of womanhood. They sacrifice themselves for it and their action testifies to magnificent heroism. The original Hebrew more clearly expresses their struggle to overcome a deep-seated physical reluctance. *There is not a man on earth.* Their father seems to be the only survivor and uncertain of his consent they use cunning to achieve their goal just as Tamar in regard to her father-in-law, Judah (chapter 38).

Lot, in contrast to his daughters, plays a rather sorry part. He loves his cups upon which his daughters rely. Should one ask the source of wine in the cave, it may be assumed that Lot, in spite of all the excitement, had not forgotten to bring some.

Verse 33. This also ridicules Lot; he noticed nothing whereas Noah in awakening at least realized what had happened to him (9,24). The two stories are related and each follows a catastrophe.

Verse 34. The younger seems to be more timid and needs to be urged again.

The Meaning and Character of Chapter 19

This narration definitely shows legendary touches. It is the only chapter in the book of Genesis in which miracles occur; the transformation of Lot's wife into a pillar of salt, and perhaps the blinding of the Sodomites, must be called miraculous. There is also the fiery rain of sulphur destroying the region, and finally the story of Lot's daughters. The story, although occuring in the utmost South of Palestine, has the character of Northern Palestine which was fonder of miracles. The legendary features are, however, organically connected with the whole trend of the story. Abraham by circumcision had become the confidant of God; thus he received a voice in the divine council before the execution of judgement. God's message to him takes the most intimate and personal form. The judgement concerns cities in the neighborhood of Abraham and of the land promised to his descendants; as a warning the ruins may always remain before their eyes. Here had dwelt Lot who had been saved for the sake of Abraham—proof of the patriarch's worth in God's eyes.

Now Lot may disappear from the narration as it had been his part in the story to afford an opportunity for showing Abraham's consequence in God's eyes. Abraham's national importance lies in being the physical ancestor of the people of Israel, his religious importance in following God's call, his universal moral importance in showing his attitude to the world around him to which his brother's son, Lot, is the connecting link. Chapter 13 shows Abraham as a man of peace, chapter 14 as a selfless helper, and finally chapters 18 and 19 as representative of humanity in God's court, an educator toward virtue and righteousness which are "the ways of God." God's choice of him as a source of blessing for all the world may only be fully understood through this last element.

Chapter 20

Abraham And Sarah With Abimelech.

From there Abraham journeyed to the territory of the Negeb; and
dwelt between Kadesh and Shur; and he sojourned in Gerar. ²And
Abraham said of Sarah his wife, "She is my sister." And Abimelech king of Gerar sent and took Sarah. ³But God came to Abimelech in a dream by night and said to him, "Behold, you are a dead
man, because of the woman you have taken; for she is a man's
wife." ⁴Now Abimelech had not approached her; so he said,
"Lord, will you slay innocent people? ⁵Did he not himself say to
me 'She is my sister'? And she herself said, 'He is my brother.' In
the integrity of my heart and the innocence of my hands I have
done this." ⁶Then God said to him in the dream, "Yes, I know that
you have done this in the integrity of your heart, and it was I who
kept you from sinning against me; therefore I did not let you touch
her. ⁷Now then restore the man's wife; for he is a prophet, and he
will pray for you, and you shall live. But if you do not restore her,
know that you shall surely die, you, and all that are yours."

Abraham leaves Hebron, the location of the story since 13,18. The
Midrash thinks because he disliked the region after the destruction of
Sodom and Gomorrah; it was now so depopulated that he could no
longer show hospitality. The real reason is that Isaac may be born in the
land of the Philistines to fulfill 15,13 ff.

He *sojourned in Gerar* in Hebrew has the connotation of staying
somewhere as a stranger.

Verse 2. The Egyptian adventure (12,10 ff.) repeats itself, and is here
assumed as known.

Verse 3. *God came to Abimelech.* He receives a warning from beyond
in a dream which impresses him so strongly that he cannot disregard it.
You are a dead man Your life is a in danger, namely if you keep the
woman.

131

Verse 4. *Will you slay innocent people* The king identifies himself
with his people who would have to suffer with him (see also verse 9).
The thought reminds of 18,23ff. The deity is a righteous judge, also in
Abimelech's opinion.

Verse 5. *In the integrity of my heart* unsuspectingly; although a
heathen, he assumes God judges according to the intention.

Verse 6. God knows this and need not be told; he had kept him from
the sin of adultery.

Verse 7. Restore the woman; this is necessary so the husband may
intervene with me to forgive you. He will do so successfully because he
is a prophet. If he prays for you, you will live. Nothing can give greater
satisfaction to the insulted party than to be asked to pray for the
offender. It will be the strongest proof for God that the insulted man is
reconciled; then God can no longer be angry either. Abraham is called a
prophet in consequence of chapter 18. A prophet is not so much a man
who speaks to God as a man whom God answers (Ex. 19,19).

> *8Abimelech rose early in the morning, and called all his servants,
> and told them all these things; and the men were very much
> afraid. 9Then Abimelech called Abraham, and said to him,
> "What have you done to us? And how have I sinned against you,
> that you have brought on me and my kingdom a great sin? You
> have done to me things that ought not to be done." 10And Abime-
> lech said, to Abraham, "What were you thinking of, that you did
> this thing?"*

The servants are as God-fearing as the king.

Verse 10. The questions in verse 9 are only rhetorical reproaches that
do not require an answer. As Abimelech wants the reason for
Abraham's inexplicable conduct, he begins again with a real question
(verse 10): What profit or what consequences did you expect?

> *11Abraham said, "Because I thought, There is no fear of God at all
> in this place, and they will kill me because of my wife. 12Besides
> she is indeed my sister, the daughter of my father, but not the
> daughter of my mother; and she became my wife. 13And when
> God caused me to wander from my father's house, I said to her,*

> *'This is the kindness you must do me: at every place to which we come, say of me, 'He is my brother.' "*

Abraham has two answers. The first shamefacedly confesses that he has sinned by an unfounded suspicion. Abimelech and his servants have proven that there is true fear of God in this place.

Verse 12. According to II Sam. 13,13 such a marriage with a half-sister might have been permissible in ancient times although in contradiction to the laws Lev. 18,9 11; 20,17; Deut. 27,22.

Verse 13. Abraham's words are adapted to heathen conceptions. It shall sound as if God's call had brought him into an embarassing situation forcing him to leave his secure home and to wander in strange, dangerous lands.

> *¹⁴Then Abimelech took sheep and oxen, and male and female slaves, and gave them to Abraham, and restored Sarah his wife to him. ¹⁵And Abimelech said, "Behold, my land is before you; dwell where it pleases you." ¹⁶To Sarah he said, "Behold, I have given your brother a thousand pieces of silver; it is your vindication in the eyes of all who are with you; and before every one you are righted." ¹⁷Then Abraham prayed to God; and God healed Abimelech, and also healed his wife and female slaves so that they bore children. ¹⁸For the Lord had closed all the wombs of the house of Abimelech because of Sarah, Abraham's wife.*

Verse 16. Abimelech explains to Sarah that the gifts to Abraham shall vindicate her; people shall not think meanly of her, as he had to restore her with large presents (Rashi). Abimelech's invitation to dwell in the land is an offer of friendship to Abraham.

Verse 18. We now hear what had happened to Abimelech and his wives; they had become sterile.

The Meaning Of The Story.

This story is apparently a repetition of the occurrence in Egypt related in 12,10ff. The intention of the Bible is to demonstrate the different reactions of Pharaoh and Abimelech in the same situation. Pharaoh releases Sarah because the Lord had visited him and his house with great plagues. No deity warns him or speaks to him. He speaks for himself alone and not for his country. He has given preferment to

Abraham in advance and offers neither apology nor satisfaction. Abraham gives him no answer at all and must finally leave the land with Sarah.

The Pharaoh of Abraham is a forerunner of the Pharaoh of Moses. He does not know of God, fear of God, or sin. No deity appears to him because a Pharaoh regards himself as god. Only plagues will be effective with him; it is sufficient to report these and their success.

Abimelech is different; he does not wish to commit a sin. He wants to keep his heart and hands clean. He can be warned by the deity and his servants show the same religious attitude. He not only corrects his mistake, but beyond this gives Abraham compensation. Abimelech who abhors sin and fears God may reproach Abraham, who in turn must justify himself. Abraham has sinned by using a lie, perhaps a white lie, or by expressing himself ambiguously. He deserves blame, but only by a person qualified to reproach him, therefore he is once more brought into the same situation and this second time he will have no excuse. In Egypt he might have claimed lack of fear of God; a Pharaoh was not fit to pronounce moral reproaches and his servants had only appeared when his sexual appetite needed pandering. In the other country fear of God exists; the servants support their king in it; Abimelech by his reply shows his receptivity for a word of God and a sensitive conscience, and finally acts corespondingly. Abraham must confess that he wrongly suspected the land with its people and gives Abimelech highest satisfaction by intervening as a prophet on his behalf.

Sarah is not hurt in either case; thus the Bible demonstrates again that God does not need the cunning or the lies of humans by which they seek to come to his aid.

The story is a credit to the Philistine king in contrast to the Egyptian. Abraham too is not left in shame. It is the refinement and tenderness of God's wisdom that although Abraham is the guilty sinner he shall pray for Abimelech. Abraham will have to speak to God, just as Abimelech, "Lord wilt thou slay innocent people?" He will then have to continue, 'Did I not tell him that she is my sister, and she that I am her brother?' In other words Abraham's intercession must first implore pardon for himself. A prayer for someone else must begin with a confession of ones own unworthiness (see 18,27). Abraham might have been able to justify himself before Abimelech as people do in order to save face, but with God this will not prevail. This expresses the Bible's real opinion of Abraham's conduct and is his punishment. Abraham's closeness to God is stressed by this demand for his intercession. He is a prophet and mediator as in the preceding story.

As all the women in Abimelech's house can now give birth, the story of the following chapter is prepared. God can certainly not refuse Abraham what he had given others through Abraham's intervention and could Abraham show himself more worthy of a son than by asking the same for others?

Chapter 21

The Birth Of Isaac. The Dismissal Of Hagar And Ishmael. The Covenant With Abimelech.

The Lord remembered Sarah as he had said, and the Lord did to Sarah as he had spoken. ²And Sarah conceived and bore Abraham a son in his old age at the time of which God had spoken to him. ³Abraham called the name of his son who was born to him, whom Sarah bore him, Isaac. ⁴And Abraham circumcised his son Isaac, when he was eight days old, as God had commanded him. ⁵Abraham was a hundred years old when his son Isaac was born to him. ⁶And Sarah said, "God has made laughter for me; every one who hears it, will laugh with me." ⁷And she said, "Who has said to Abraham that Sarah would suckle children? Yes, I have born him a son in his old age.

At last the often promised event occurs; it had been long and eagerly expected and upon it the whole future depended; an heir is born to the first ancestor of the people. In Hebrew the diction approaches poetical rythm. The phrase "The Lord remembered" is later the cue for Israel's redemption from Egypt (50,24 f.; Ex. 4,31). The appearance of the first heir at the beginning of Israel's history is like the appearance of the redeemer in Egypt. The Lord God of Israel is the faithful God; he keeps his word and being all-powerful can fulfill it.

Verse 2. *A son in his old age.* The birth of Isaac which makes the later nation possible is even more appreciated, as it is late and an unexpected gift of God.

Verse 3 and 4. Every detail is carefully noted.

Verse 5. The remarkable and impressive age of exactly one hundred years stresses the late arrival of the first heir.

Verse 6. Both parents are happy, but to the father fall the duties connected with the joyous event, the prosaic side of life; while the mother who moreover is resting reflects on the poetical aspect of the moment. These two verses are her song of joy. Verse 7 refers to her laughter in 18,12ff. Now she may openly show her happiness; she will find her joy reflected in everyone's face; not as some translate "they laugh about me."

Verse 7. The answer to this question of Sarah is no one but God (Rashi). The verse praises God without mentioning his name.

> *8And the child grew and was weaned; and Abraham made a great feast on the day that Isaac was weaned. 9But Sarah saw the son of Hagar the Egyptian, whom she had borne to Abraham, have his play. 10So she said to Abraham, "Cast out this slave woman with her son; for the son of this slave woman shall not be heir with my son Isaac." 11And the thing was very displeasing to Abraham on account of his son. 12But God said to Abraham, "Be not displeased because of the lad and because of your slave woman; whatever Sarah says to you, do as she tells you, for through Isaac shall your descendants be named. 13And I will make a nation of the son of the slave woman also, because he is your offspring." 14So Abraham rose early in the morning, and took bread and a skin of water, and gave it to Hagar, putting it on her shoulder, along with the child, and dismissed her. And she departed and wandered in the wilderness of Beer-sheba.*

The weaning of children was delayed many years; in the modern Near East it is sometimes done only after four years. Abraham made this an occasion for a "great feast" as great people (verse 22) were invited as guests.

Verse 9. *Have his play.* It is usually assumed that he made sport of Isaac. In the context it means that he boasted of his earlier birth. He followed the example of his mother in this (16,4). A direct allusion to verse 6 must be assumed; he laughed at Sarah and her joyful "laughter"; therefore her indignation.

Verse 10. Sarah does not mention Ishmael by name, but speaks contemptuously of "the son of this slave woman". She emphasizes this, assiduously mentioning Isaac by name. Sarah demands that Abraham expel the slave woman and her son. She herself could no longer dispose of her as Hagar had given Abraham a son. She does not want Ishmael and Isaac to share Abraham's heritage, his possessions. This is not greed or avarice, but the conviction that Ishmael may lay claim to leadership of the tribe and to God's promises (15,4), particularly to Canaan, the Promised Land. Permitting this, Sarah would deny her call to be the ancestress of the people. There is no other way left but to cast out both son and mother.

Verse 11. The suggestion of throwing out his own flesh and blood is repugnant to Abraham's instincts of fatherly love and grieves him.

Verse 12. God comforts him. More than one sentiment depressed Abraham; his son was a little boy who needed care and should not be separated from the mother. Even if only a slave woman, she was nevertheless his concubine, and would now lose her master and protector. The Bible has Abraham express only the motive that is decisive for him, while God indicates the other considerations. Sarah is right in so far as the succession shall rest on Isaac.

Verse 13. The boy whom Sarah had contemptuously called "the son of the slave woman" shall not lack a future. As he too is Abraham's physical descendant, he shall not be denied the greatness connected with this and grow into a nation.

Verse 14. The apparently circumstantial report of Abraham's actions illustrates his merciful care. Abraham gave Hagar bread and water, probably instructing her to use them sparingly; then he arranges them carefully on her shoulder so that her hands are free. Finally he places her child into her hands. *He dismissed her* is milder than Sarah's "Cast her out."

> [15]When the water in the skin was gone, she put the child under one of the bushes. [16]Then she went and sat down over against him a good way off, about the distance of a bowshot; for she said, "Let me not look upon the death of the child." And as she sat over against him, she lifted up her voice and wept.

She ran out of the water as she lost her way. She still carefully places the child in the shade under bushes. Although she says that the child will die and that she does not want to see it die, she sits within sight waiting for help. This is the moving lack of logic of a mother's heart; she sits far enough away to be able to let her tears run freely.

17But God heard the voice of the lad; and an angel of God called to Hagar from heaven and said to her, "What troubles you, Hagar? Fear not; for God has heard the voice of the lad where he is. 18Arise, lift up the lad, and hold him fast with your hand; for I will make him a great nation." 19Then God opened her eyes, and she saw a well of water; and she went and filled the skin with water, and gave the lad a drink. 20And God was with the lad, and he grew up; he lived in the wilderness, and became an expert with the bow. 21He lived in the wilderness of Paran, and his mother took a wife for him from the land of Egypt.

God's pity is even greater than a mother's love (Is 49,15) and he is strong enough to help. Even if she did not want to hear the lad cry, God has heard him. *Where he is* he is not forsaken or lost, although you have forsaken him. Should something great become of the boy his mother must lift up the child and guide his steps with a firm hand.

Verse 19. After her desperate mood has been allayed by this announcement of a magnificent future, the present emergency is redressed; comfort becomes help. No miracle takes place as the well is not created just now; Hagar had merely not seen it in her desperation. God's encouragement opens her eyes.

This incident of Ishmael's childhood is told in such detail that it may become a life-long comfort to him. He will remain in the desert and will often thirst, but God who saved him once will not let him perish.

Verse 21. The wilderness of Paran is near Egypt whence his mother, in place of the father, gets him a wife. Hagar had been an Egyptian herself. She acts in contrast to Abraham (24,3) and consciously separates herself from his house. Neither mother nor son understood or were fit for its destiny.

22At that time Abimelech and Phicol, the commander of his army, said to Abraham, "God is with you in all that you do; 23now therefore swear to me here by God that you will not lie to me or to my offspring or to my posterity, but as I have dealt loyally with you, you will deal with me and with the land where you have sojourned." 24And Abraham said, "I will swear." 25But Abraham complained to Abimelech about a well of water which Abimelech's servants had seized. 26Abimelech said, "I do not know who has done this thing; you did not tell me, and I have not heard of it until today."

At that time returns us to an earlier event, the feast at the weaning of Isaac (verse 8), to which the great men of the country had been invited. Abimelech and his military aid Phicol say, *God is with you* as a form of congratulation for Abraham on his home life that is so grandly presented to them. What good fortune to have a son at the age of hundred! He continues, half seriously, half jokingly, 'Old friend, you have lied to me when you said that Sarah is your sister; you must not do so again. You must swear to me here on the spot.' The emphatic, but half humorous wording almost makes it a reproach and covers his desire to keep Abraham's friendship. One must be on good terms with such a favorite of the gods. As I have shown loyalty to you, you must be loyal to me and my country. You were a stranger and I, on my part, have shown you the kindness due to a stranger. In summary—the whole speech of Abimelech might be called a toast at the festival table, friendly, but full of pointed remarks.

Verse 24. Abraham's reply is short, as if to say, alright; but first he still has to make a complaint.

Verse 25. Both men speak plainly, Abimelech of lying, Abraham of stealing. This was done by Abimelech's servants, but he, as master, is responsible.

Verse 26. The thrust had gone home. Embarassed Abimelech stammers some insufficient excuses.

> [27]Abraham took sheep and oxen and gave them to Abimelech, and the two made a covenant. [28]Abraham set seven ewe lambs apart. [29]And Abimelech said to Abraham, "What is the meaning of these seven ewe lambs which you have set apart?" [30]He said, "These seven ewe lambs you will take from my hand, that it be a witness for me that I dug this well." [31]Therefore that place was called Beer-Sheba; because there both of them swore on oath. [32]So they made a covenant at Beer-sheba. Then Abimelech and Phicol, the commander of his army, rose up and returned to the land of the Philistines. [33]Abraham planted a tamarisk tree in Beer-sheba, and called there on the name of the Lord as the Everlasting God. [34]And Abraham sojourned many days in the land of the Philistines.

In their friendly exchange Abraham had indicated to Abimelech that the kindness shown him in the land of the Philistines had not been quite perfect; furthermore he had demonstrated to him who had accused him of lying how easily a person can be entangled in a lie. Finally, he has him swear, without being aware of it, that he will desist from future expropriation. Abraham does not bluntly demand an oath; he delicately brings it about. He gives Abimelech a leave-taking present, reciprocating that of 20,14: he presents sheep and cattle, but neither man-servants nor maid-servants, for the patriarch does not make a gift of people. Thus they have made a covenant after the feast and exchange of gifts, and promised friendship to each other.

Verse 28. Abraham uses this gift to make Abimelech's confession as unforgettable as if he had sworn an oath. Namely Abraham retains seven ewe lambs.

Verse 29. Abimelech is astonished and asks for its meaning.

Verse 30. Abraham explains it as a "witness". As Abimelech raises no objection the number seven makes this an oath (compare 31,51 ff.), because in Hebrew "to swear" literally means to state something seven times. This was regarded as the strongest form of affirmation.

Verse 31. *Beer-sheba* "well of seven" or "well of the oath." The place is the southern extremity of Palestine (from Dan to Beer-sheba).

Verse 33. The tree shall be a permanent memorial of the event; therefore Abraham here calls on God as the Everlasting. The wood of a tamarisk tree is very durable; as an evergreen it symbolizes God's eternity. (Delitzsch).

Verse 34. This is stated now, although it must have happened following 20,15 in acceptance of Abimelech's offer. It shall explain verse 23: you have sojourned in my country. Verses 22 ff. take place in Beer-sheba where Abraham now remains (22,19).

The chapter is a prelude to the next. It shows Abraham at the height of good fortune and prestige. The coming events will therefore be still more painful to him.

Chapter 22

The Binding Of Isaac For Sacrifice.
> *After these things God tested Abraham, and said to him, "Abraham!" And he said, "Here am I!" ²He said, "Take your son, your only son, whom you love, Isaac, and go to the land of Moriah, and bring him there for a burnt offering upon one of the mountains of which I shall tell you."*

After these things always indicates a surprising turn of events. After Isaac has finally been born the story might continue smoothly, but everything once more becomes uncertain. *God tested Abraham.* The reader shall know from the outset, what Abraham does not know: that the stupendous demand made of him shall be only a test. God's trials make apparent the mettle of a man, how far his obedience to God will go (Ex. 16,4; Deut. 8,2). The intention is not an actual sacrifice, but to show Abraham's reaction. This reminds us of the book of Job. It is the same problem; is there an unconditional devotion to God which could sacrifice everything and survive the hardest test? The test in that book is undertaken by one of God's subordinates, Satan, here, as the Hebrew remains ambiguous, by God himself or also merely by an angel. The similarity to the story of Job can already be found in chapter 21. In both a description of domestic happiness and of high prestige serves as foil for the impending trials. In each case a family feast has preceded immediately. The heir has been born to Abraham; he has concluded an alliance with the king of the country; he has planted a tree as a symbol of permanence; then he must learn that in matters of this world no permanence exists.

The conversation with God occurs at night (verse 3). When a person of higher rank calls by name and the person of lower rank answers "Here am I", it indicates that the lower one expects a command and declares himself willing to obey even though its contents are yet unknown to him. There are many Biblical examples for such a call of God, of a father, or of a king. However, to be called by name is also a sign of familiarity, love, and distinction (Ex 31,2;Is 40,26 and often).

God knows his own and "Here am I" is the most adequate answer a man can give him.

Verse 2. The demand now follows, but only hestitatingly, slowly becoming clearer and more exacting until it finally culminates in the name—Isaac. For this name contains all of Abraham's felicity (Midrash; Rashi).

Your only son The ascending line of demands reminds of 12,1; the reference to that passage becomes incontestable by the use of the same Hebrew word for go. This Hebrew phrase is rare, and in fact is only used in these two passages. It is Abraham's destiny to depart from that which has become dear to his heart, these two are the most bitter separations, there from his parents, his past, here from his whole future, his son.

Bring him there for a burnt offering. Abraham must assume that he shall bring Isaac as a burnt offering, but the decisive word "to me" which in Hebrew would be indispensable is missing. Abraham may understand the unusual expression as veiled language designed to spare his feelings.

> *3So Abraham rose early in the morning, saddled his ass, and took two of his young men with him, and his son Isaac; and he cut the wood for the burnt offering, and arose, and went to the place of which God had told him. 4On the third day Abraham lifted up his eyes and saw the place afar off. 5Then Abraham said to his young men. "Stay here with the ass; I and the lad will go yonder and worship and come again to you."*

Abraham rose early. God's will shall not be delayed. Abraham, who is a great lord, cuts the wood himself, showing eagerness to obey God's command; no stranger's hand shall participate in this noble deed. The preparations are described in detail, because Abraham could not and would not discuss the matter with anyone and had to keep it all to himself. The easiest way to pass such difficult hours is to keep oneself busy. These exertions of Abraham are more moving than any analysis of his feelings would have been.

Verse 4. Three days are often the period for the preparation of important events. Abraham shall also be given time so that God may see whether he remains firm in his resolution; his deed must not be a rash action. Earlier the place had been called "one of the mountains". Abraham now views it differently, for him it is *the* place. As soon as he sees it, he makes his arrangements.

Verse 5. Feeling that he will receive a great revelation, one way or the other, he wants to be alone with his sacrifice and with God as Moses on Mount Sinai (Ex. 19,12 f.). *Yonder* is spoken with a gesture which leaves the destination undefined *We will worship* By the preparations the servants saw that it would be more. *And we will again come to you* Indeed Abraham speaks the truth even if unintentionally.

> ⁶*And Abraham took the wood of the burnt offering, and laid it on Isaac his son, and he took in his hand the fire and the knife. So they went both of them together.* ⁷*And Isaac said to his father Abraham, "My father!" And he said, "Here am I, my son," He said, "Behold, the fire and the wood; but where is the lamb for a burnt offering?" Abraham said, "God will provide himself the lamb for a burnt offering, my son," So they went both of them together.*

Isaac carries the wood for the sacrifice like a man sentenced to be crucified carries his own cross (Breshith Rabba).

A prize question for all the great poets of world literature would be the topic of Abraham and Isaac's conversation as they walked to the place where the father should sacrifice his son. Here is the absolute and final solution. We find the full artlessness of a child who is neither dull nor precocious; Isaac asks a question which is almost inevitable in view of the situation, and the reply expresses submission to God. Artistically this dialogue achieves a further delay leaving the reader in suspense. It is also admirable how this precise moment has been chosen to let the son speak, so that he is no longer only a silent object. This removes the burden of emotion from the end of the story where a less skilful narrator would have placed it. The father's answer seems evasive, yet very nearly leads to the solution, only to break off and leave both of them again to their thoughts. An atmosphere of anxiety lies over the scene.

Verse 7. Isaac begins timidly as if he had struggled with himself, whether to speak without being asked. Abraham's "Here am I, my son" expresses many things—an apparent surprise, a resignation gained long ago, and a kind condescension to the child. He had been ready for this difficult moment and had already prepared the answer. The question is that of a child who sees something curious and asks the father who is supposed to know everything; yet it is a question which breaks Abraham's heart.

Verse 8. Abraham's reply seems clear and can satisfy a child who just wants any answer, however it contains many meanings. It may express no more than, Do not worry; there will be a sacrifice. It may mean that this is an offering of a special kind; God has reserved the choice for himself; I myself do not yet know; therefore I did not bring a lamb. It may even by a wish and a prayer: May God provide the lamb!

This dialogue is the only one between Abraham and Isaac reported in their whole story. It begins "my father" and ends "my son". The information given consists in the single sentence "God will provide"; that is the end of all wisdom. They had stopped for this conversation as if the child has wanted to say: Wait! We have forgotten something; it seems that we will have to turn back. Now he is satisfied; both are again "together" and continue on their way. A deep silence returns until they have arrived; there will be no more words, only action.

9When they came to the place of which God had told him, Abraham built an altar there, and laid the wood in order, and bound Isaac his son, and laid him on the altar, upon the wood. 10Then Abraham put forth his hand, and took the knife to slay his son.

Every detail is methodically reported as in verse 3. We shall see that Abraham acts as God had commanded him. His labor takes hours and as no voice from heaven is heard, Abraham can no longer doubt that his son Isaac shall be the sacrificial lamb. He binds him. Judaism calls this greatest deed of faith of its first ancestor by the word Akedah, the "binding". This action which deeply touches the father's heart is for God sufficient sacrifice; he values the intention as the deed.

Verse 10. A single phrase characterizes Abraham's superhuman intention and expresses the deep emotion of the narrator, of the reader, and of the father; earlier it had always been Isaac his son (verses 3;6;9); here it is only *his son*. A father shall slay his son! Nothing could be more horrifying to an Israelite. Such a deed was a terrible consequence of paganism (Deut. 12,31ff). Every word breathes terror: knife—slay—son. Abraham was resolved to perform the extreme deed and was already in the midst of its execution; any doubt of his sincerity is removed. The son who lets himself be bound, put on the altar, and waits for the deadly blow is as great as the father. We humans have not been the only ones to follow this scene anxiously; a heavenly audience has seen it from above, with tension, and sympathy. It was "A spectacle worthy of God, namely a man bravely facing his misfortune" (Seneca).

> [11]*The angel of the Lord called to him from heaven, and said,*
> *"Abraham, Abraham!" And he said, "Here am I".* [12]*He said, "Do*
> *not lay your hand on the lad or do anything to him; for now I*
> *know that you fear God, seeing you have not withheld your son,*
> *your only son, from me."*

Abraham's name is called twice in anxiety as it might be too late.
Abraham, receptive to any divine call, again answers with "Here am I."
The trial shall not go further.

Verse 12. *Now I know.* I have always known, or now it has been
demonstrated. Rashi explains it as: now I have an answer for those who
wonder why I love you. Now *they* see that you fear God in the fullest
sense of the word.

You have not withheld your son . . . you have brought him and
were willing to sacrifice him; by this you have indeed given him up
completely. God wanted only proof of your obedience to his voice, not
the blood of the lad.

Abraham's religion is manly and heroic, but does not disown natural
human feelings. Abraham loved God so much that he gave up his own
son so that all his followers may know the highest good, but also realize
that love of God must never lead to sacrifice of human beings.

> [13]*And Abraham lifted up his eyes and looked, and behold, behind*
> *him was a ram, caught in a thicket by his horns; and Abraham*
> *went and took the ram and offered it up as a burnt offering instead*
> *of his son.* [14]*So Abraham called the name of that place The Lord*
> *will see; whereas it is said this day "On the mount of the Lord it*
> *will be seen."*

The altar shall not have been built in vain; the demand for a sacrifice
in verse 2 shall not go completely unheeded either. An animal is
offered in place of the son; every sacrifice is a substitute for a man.

Verse 14. *The Lord will see.* He is the omniscient, guiding, saving
Providence. *Whereas it is said this day.* A later time has coined a
phrase alluding to Abraham's experience, but varying his words.

On the mount of the Lord it will be seen. There everything is
revealed. "God sees" is the essence of religion, creating fear of him and
confidence in him. To see God is the deepest longing of a soul that is
kindred to God. Abraham's story teaches that God is to be experienced

in sacrifice, with a certainty which grows as the sacrifice becomes greater. Moriah is a summit of religious experience. *It* will be seen; the subject is intentionally not mentioned. Everything stands revealed there; both the character of the man who goes there as well as the essence of the divine.

> ¹⁵*And the angel of the Lord called to Abraham a second time from heaven,* ¹⁶*and said, "By myself I have sworn, says the Lord, because you have done this, and have not withheld your son, your only son,* ¹⁷*I will indeed bless you, and I will multiply your descendants as the stars of heaven and as the sand which is on the seashore. And your descendants shall possess the gate of their enemies,* ¹⁸*and by your descendants shall all the nations of the earth bless themselves, because you have obeyed my voice." So Abraham returned to his young men, and they arose and went together to Beer-sheba; and Abraham dwelt at Beer-sheba.*

Verse 16. God takes an oath, the only formal one in the story of the patriarchs; it is referred to later in numerous passages. The oath summarizes all former promises in the most emphatic form. Heaven and earth are used to describe the innumerable hosts of the people, the "ten thousand thousands of Israel" of Num. 10,36; they will irresistibly defeat their enemies.

Verse 18. Triumph over the enemy shall not be the last word. It shall rather be the promise of 12,2: a blessing for all the nations of the earth. Beer-sheba was the birthplace of Isaac who been restored to his father.

> ²⁰*Now after these things it was told Abraham, "Behold, Milcah also has borne children to your brother Nahor:* ²¹*Uz the first-born, Buz his brother, Kemuel the father of Aram.* ²²*Chesed, Hazo, Phildash, Jidlaph, and Bethuel.* ²³*Bethuel became the father of Rebekah. These eight Milcah bore to Nahor, Abraham's brother.* ²⁴*Moreover, his concubine, whose name was Reumah, bore Tebah, Gaham, Tahash, and Ma'achah".*

The paragraph begins with the same phrase as verse 1 in order to create a contrast. Not only had Isaac remained alive, but we shall already learn the name of his future wife. Eight sons of Milcah plus four sons of the concubine make twelve, the same number as used with Ishmael (25,16) and later with Jacob. Reumah's position is parallel to that of Hagar. The ratio of two to one in the number of children of the main wife to those of the concubine is similar to the ratio of the children of the wives and concubines of Jacob (chapters 29.30). Only Rebekah is important as she is the daughter of the son of Abraham's brother.

Chapter 23

The Buying Of A Family Tomb.

Sarah lived a hundred and twenty-seven years; these were the years of the life of Sarah. ²And Sarah died at Kiriath-arba (that is, Hebron) in the land of Canaan; and Abraham went in to mourn for Sarah and to weep for her. ³And Abraham rose up from before his dead, and said to the Hittites, ⁴"I am a stranger and a sojourner with you; give me property with you for a burying place, that I may bury my dead out of my sight." ⁵The Hittites answered Abraham, speaking to him, ⁶"Hear us, my lord; you are a prince of God in our midst. Bury your dead in the choicest of our sepulchres; none of us will withhold from you his sepulchre that you could not bury your dead."

Sarah shall die before Rebekah succeeds her; for this reason her age is stated; this is otherwise never done for a woman. Isaac, who was born when his mother was ninety years old, marries at the age of forty (25,20).

Verse 2. At the end of the preceding chapter Abraham dwelt in Beer-sheba (22,19). The family must since have returned to Hebron, their former place of residence; later Abraham dies there. The name Kiriath-arba is derived from a man by the name of Arba who was the greatest among the Anakim (Josh. 14,15). Another explanation is "city of the four" (men) (35,27). *In the land of Canaan* in added in contrast to 21,34; it shall state that the mother of the nation died and was buried in the Promised Land. *To mourn* refers to the mournful lamentations for which professional mourning women were hired in later times (Jer. 9,16; compare II Chron 35,25). Abraham holds obsequies in honor of his wife; following them he must bury her.

Verse 3. *Abraham rose up* because mourners sat on the ground upon which the body had been laid. Hittites appear regularly among the inhabitants of Canaan.

The following negotiation has been misunderstood. Abraham is full of dignity and refinement without submissiveness. The Hittites address him as my lord in every speech, but he never reciprocrates or calls himself their servant. Abraham knows his station and that it is below his dignity to put on an air of obsequiousness.

Verse 4. *I am a stranger and sojourner among you.* This shall immediately state his true relationship to those whom he is addressing. It is upright and astute thus to pronounce that which they anyhow think in their hearts without saying it. The words express his legal position in relation to the Hittite population and the authorities of Hebron. He had no seat in their councils and no property rights, a privilege of natives. Ownership of land is a higher status than mere residency as it ties a man to a place. A dead body needs this because it can no longer move; therefore Abraham asks for property as a burial place. He cannot leave his dead wife above ground. He desires the field of Ephron, but cleverly first turns to the community to obtain general approval which may also have been legally necessary. Land might pass into the hands of strangers only with the consent of the community.

Give me. Terms like buying and selling do not appear in the chapter; gentlemen do not transact business, but make each other "presents", although they carefully watch that the counter-present at least has the same value.

Verse 6. The Hittites cannot deny that according to the letter of the law he is a stranger among them and stands beneath them, the natives. They, however, say that another order of rank exists and in this you are a prince of God. This phrase never occurs again; it was either coined by them or applied to Abraham only at this moment. It honors them as well as him. They comprehend that they have before them an extraordinary man, belonging to a world in which he is not only a citizen, but a prince; it is an honor for them to have him in their midst. His strangeness, separating him from them even in the grave, generates not antipathy, but respect. Thus the common people recognize a great personality which they cannot fully comprehend, but nevertheless on the whole value quite correctly. They see the man serve a God who is strange to them and so they bow before a dignity which has not been bestowed by man.

How generous is their statement "in our midst" against his "with you," for us you are no outsider; you are different, but for that very reason you shall completely belong to us. It is especially tender to tell him so while he mourns. Abraham receives this title of honor from "pagans". With similar nobility of feeling they offer to accept his wife among them after death as they accept him while alive.

> *7Abraham rose and bowed to the Hittites, the people of the land. 8And he said to them, "If you are willing that I should bury my dead out of my sight, hear me and entreat for me Ephron the son of Zohar, 9that he may give me the cave of Machpelah, which he owns; it is at the end of his field. For the full price let him give it to me in your midst as a possession for a burying place."*

Abraham bows in gratitude for the offer. *The people of the land* seems to be a term and official title for the state or city assembly as it was in later times (Salzberger).

Verse 8. Abraham treats their offer as not meant seriously, but anyhow they are willing to help him in his pious purpose and do not refuse him a grave in their territory.

Verse 9. As the lot is at the end of his field it will be easier for Ephron to part with it. He can hardly refuse after what has been said. It also flatters him to have Abraham ask the assembly in his presence to entreat him. *He may give me* shall not be misunderstood, so Abraham immediately interprets it by *for the full price,* to be paid in good money without discount. They perhaps intentionally did not hear that he wants a permanent possession which is legally incontestable. It is a refinement that now he uses their phrase "in your midst"; this way I shall remain with your for ever.

> *10Now Ephron was sitting among the Hittites; and Ephron the Hittite answered Abraham in the hearing of the Hittites, of all who went in at the gate of his city, 11"No, my lord, hear me; I give you the field, and I give you the cave that is in it; in the presence of the sons of my people I give it to you; bury your dead." 12Then Abraham bowed down before the people of the land, 13And he spoke to Ephron in the hearing of the people of the land, "But if you will, hear me: I will give the price of the field; accept it from me, that I may bury my dead there."*

Ephron, thus indirectly addressed, does not wait for the intervention of the assembly. Not wanting to be surpassed in generosity, he says: it is given to you (three times "given"); all Hittites shall be witnesses. He does not, like Abraham, say the cave at the end of the field, but no, the field and the cave.

Verse 13. *A gift. I cannot accept that.* Ephron shall favor him and accept payment. *That I may bury my dead there.* Agreement as to its use is as important as the sale itself. The decisive moment, tensely watched by the audience, has come in this duel of compliments. What price will Ephron ask? How will he express himself? How will Abraham react?

> [14]*Ephron answered Abraham, saying to him,* [15]*"My lord, listen to me; a piece of land, worth four hundred shekels of silver, what is that between you and me? Bury your dead."* [16]*Abraham agreed with Ephron; and Abraham weighed out for Ephron the silver which he had named in the hearing of the Hittites, four hundred shekels of silver, according to the weights current among the merchants.*

Verse 15. Ephron equals the situation. He does not crudely state its price, but treats money as a trifling matter in an offhand manner. According to other prices mentioned in the Bible (e.g. Lev. 27,16) a price of four hundred shekels for a useless field is exorbitant, and Ephron may have named it with palpitation.

Verse 16. Abraham agrees without wincing; he pays him the amount demanded before witnesses and in current coin, on the spot. One may imagine Ephron greedily watching whether Abraham weighs it out correctly.

> [17]*So the field of Ephron in Machpelah, which was to the east of Mamre, the field with the cave which was in it and all the trees which were in the field, throughout its whole area, was made over* [18]*to Abraham as a possession in the presence of the Hittites, before all who went in at the gate of the city.* [19]*After this, Abraham buried Sarah his wife in the cave of the field of Machpelah east of Mamre (that is, Hebron) in the land of Canaan.* [20]*The field and the cave that is in it were made over to Abraham as a possession for a burying place by the Hittites.*

The lot is described in legal terminology. The witnesses are also mentioned. Everything is oral; no document is drawn. This cave is supposed to be located beneath the Ibrahim mosque above the city of Hebron. Strangers are admitted only to the entrance of the courtyard, but the shrines of the patriarchs in recesses of the wall are known to be empty.

The Intention Of The Chapter.

It has been claimed that the buying of a family tomb shall constitute the legal basis for Israel's right to dwell in the land. Yet possession of a small lot gives no right to the whole. The Israelites never use this argument upon entering the land.

The motive is first of all simply the one given by Abraham. He wants a burial place for Sarah. The purchase is made in her honor and is testimony of his love beyond death. Therefore it deserved a separate chapter like the marriage of the son. (chapter 24)

This tomb shall also serve other purposes; Abraham, his son and grandson with their wives will be buried in it, and thus the cave of Machpelah becomes a resting place of the patriarchs and their wives. It will like a magnet attract the generations who live abroad in Egypt and will unite the descendants when they later live in the land. Canaan becomes the land of the fathers for Israel through the tomb of the fathers, "land where my fathers died."

The purchase does not create a legal title in the eyes of the world, but it binds the heart.

Ephron's offer to give the lot to Abraham as a present was naturally to be taken with as little seriousness as the invitation of the Hittites to bury Sarah with them. Abraham would have lost their respect by accepting it like a beggar. Such generous offers are only made to a man who will surely not avail himself of them. The price is expressly stated as in 33,19 for the burial place of Joseph (see 48,22), and in II Sam 24,24 for the threshing-floor of Arauna, the site of the Temple. As David says, one must not make an offering of something received as a gift; a tomb is as sacred as the altar. It must be legitimate property, purchased at ones own expense.

Abraham, however, wants to express something additional by this formal purchase. According to God's grant the whole land of Canaan belongs to Abraham, but only in his own belief. By paying for a lot he respects the present legal condition and expresses his own legal correctness. This is the attitude of all three patriarchs, "because the guilt of the Amorite is not yet full."

Chapter 24

The Wooing Of Rebekah.

Now Abraham was old, well advanced in years; and the Lord had blessed Abraham in all things. ²And Abraham said to his servant, the oldest of his house, who had charge of all that he had, "Put your hand under my thigh, ³and I will make you swear by the Lord, the God of heaven and the God of earth, that you will not take a wife for my son from the daughters of the Canaanites, among whom I dwell, ⁴but will go to my country and to my kindred, and take a wife for my son Isaac."

At Abraham's age his concern about a wife for Isaac seemed justified. As God had blessed him in all things, everyone would have liked to be related to him by marriage; his agent will be able to bear himself accordingly.

Verse 2. *The oldest of his house.* The first in rank shall substitute for his master; his name is intentionally not mentioned as his person shall be completely absorbed in his task. He is Abraham's servant and wants to be nothing else (verse 34). This longest chapter in Genesis is a fitting monument for the faithful and intelligent servant.

Put your hand under my thigh. Jewish commentators (ibn Ezrah and others) see in this gesture a symbol of homage.

Verse 3. If Abraham has his servant swear by the Lord, he must have been a believer (see 12,5).

Verse 4. The patriarchs as well as the Mosaic Law abhor marriages with Canaanites; this is due neither to concern over racial purity, nor differences in religion, as the relatives of Abraham also worship foreign gods (Josh. 24,2; compare Gen. 31,30), but to immoral practices resulting from them (Deut. 12,31).

Abraham has the servant solemnly swear because he will more easily obtain a hearing if he can refer to an oath; the relatives will not wish him to break it.

> [5]The servant said to him, "Perhaps the woman may not be willing to follow me to this land; must I then take your son back to the land from which you came?" [6]Abraham said to him, "See to it that you do not take my son back there. [7]The Lord, the God of heaven, who took me from my father's house and from the land of my birth and who spoke to me and swore to me, 'To your descendants I will give this land', he will send his angel before you, and you shall take a wife for my son from there. [8]But if the woman is not willing to follow you, then you will be free from this oath of mine; only you must not take my son back there." [9]So the servant put his hand under the thigh of Abraham his master, and swore to him concerning this matter.

Verse 7. God cannot be inconsistent; it would endanger and falsify his whole plan for our future. *The God of heaven* who rules above the earth, and can guide his own everywhere, even abroad, so that they reach their goal by a happy combination of circumstances. This God has many times shown Abraham that he has plans for him.

Verse 8. *You will be free of this oath of mine* not to take a Canaanite woman, but Abraham is certain this will not be necessary. The foresight and conscientiousness of the servant are shown by considering all possible alternatives in advance.

Verse 9. These were naturally not the only words exchanged between them. Abraham must have told the servant of the granddaughter of his brother, asked him to woo her, to inquire of her character; he also must have given him additional instructions as to his conduct.

> [10]Then the servant took ten camels of his master's camels and departed, taking all kinds of choice things from his master; and he arose, and went to Mesopotamia, to the city of Nahor. [11]And he made the camels kneel down outside the city by the well of water at the time of evening, the time when women go out to draw water.

The camels with the necessary attendants are a considerable caravan; the servant shall act as agent of a rich and important man. The *choice things* are to serve as gifts which he may later distribute (verses 22;53).

¹²*And he said, "O Lord, God of my master Abraham, grant me success today, I pray thee, and show steadfast love to my master Abraham. ¹³Behold, I am standing by the spring of water, and the daughters of the men of the city are coming out to draw water. ¹⁴Let the maiden to whom I shall say, 'Pray, let down your jar that I may drink' and who shall say, 'Drink, and I will water your camels also'—let her be the one whom thou hast appointed for thy servant Isaac. By this I shall know that thou has shown steadfast love to my master."*

The servant prays to the God of his master for a favor for his master.

Verse 14. The sign which the servant asks and the following scene have not been completely understood in their wisdom and refinement. Why shall the solution depend upon a sign and why does he not immediately approach the family? The reason is the same as for the oath in verse 4. He wants to present his later request as God's will which they cannot refuse. The clever servant is worthy of his master. No task requires more delicacy and greater diplomacy than that of a matchmaker. Even a disguised refusal would be an insult. This way he may be certain of acceptance. Not that the servant will be satisfied with any girl; he wants Rebekah; it is she whom he will test. No other girl from Nahor's town would have suited Abraham, even if she had passed the test.

Furthermore if the question would have merely been giving a drink to a poor, thirsty traveller, no girl could have refused. Yet Abraham's first servant is not a poor wretch; he appears as master of a large caravan and as he is at a public well, he might expect the reply, "Please, help yourself!" Besides he had been at the well a good while. Parallels from the Talmud which has preserved many fragments of ancient life will explain this scene. There we find that respect is shown by younger persons to their elders through willingness to serve and courteously assist; the simplest service consists in offering a drink of water. The request of Abraham's servant is therefore a test of Rebekah's training in respect for old age.

This alone would not have been an adequate test. The girl shall even seek further opportunity for assistance. If she offers to water the camels without being asked then she is appointed by God for Isaac; she is well bred, charitable, circumspect, and has a heart even for animals. The servant not only fulfills his master's orders, but goes further. Abraham desired this marriage; if he only knew whether it also has the blessing of heaven as marriages are made in heaven. He wants to learn whether God shows *steadfast love to his master.*

> ¹⁵Before he had done speaking, behold, Rebekah, who was born to Bethuel, the son of Milcah, the wife of Nahor, Abraham's brother, came out with her water jar upon her shoulder. ¹⁶The maiden was very fair to look upon, a virgin, whom no man had known. She went down to the spring, and filled her jar, and came up. ¹⁷Then the servant ran to meet her and said, "Pray give me a little water to sip from your jar." ¹⁸She said, "Drink, my lord"; and she quickly let down her jar upon her hand and gave him a drink. ¹⁹When she had finished giving him a drink, she said, "I will draw for your camels also, until they have done drinking." ²⁰So she quickly emptied her jar into the trough and ran again to the well to draw and she drew for all his camels.

At this moment Rebekah appears. A picture of the lovely maiden is drawn before our admiring eyes in a few short lines.

Verse 17. The servant runs to meet her, courteous on his part, in order to save her steps with the filled jar. He politely asks only for a sip of water.

Verse 18. She addresses him as lord. The servant may recognize her good training in proper respect by both her words and deeds. As she thus honors the old servant, she will certainly respect the master of the house and her husband. She will make a good daughter-in-law as well as a good wife.

Verse 19. She waits until he has finished drinking, as it is not fitting to talk while another eats or drinks. She draws water for his ten camels as he had wished, no small labor with the drinking capacity of a camel; she acts quickly and eagerly.

> ²¹The man gazed at her in silence to learn whether the Lord had prospered his journey or not. ²²When the camels had done drinking, the man took a gold ring weighing a half shekel, and two bracelets for her arms weighing ten gold shekels, ²³and said, "Tell me whose daughter you are. Is there room in your father's house for us to lodge in?" ²⁴She said to him, "I am the daughter of Bethuel the son of Milcah, whom she bore to Nahor." ²⁵She added, "We have both straw and provender enough, and room to lodge in."

In silence Neither by gesture, nor by word had he encouraged her to do more.

Verse 22. A ring designed to fasten the two parts of a veil on the bridge of the nose. The servant does not yet give her this jewelry, but holds it in his hand while he inquires, "To whom am I giving this?" This is the generous gift of a noble lord who splendidly repays the most trifling favor.

Verse 24. It might seem odd that she calls herself *the daughter of Bethuel the son of Milcah whom she bore to Nahor* instead of giving her parents' name. According to 11,29 her father came from a marriage, famous in the region, between uncle and orphaned niece by which Nahor had fulfilled a pious duty toward his deceased brother Haran. This had become a byname for Bethuel. Unwittingly she characterizes herself as an equal of Isaac.

> ²⁶*The man bowed his head and worshipped the Lord,* ²⁷*and he said, "Blessed be the Lord, the God of my master Abraham, who has not forsaken his steadfast love and his faithfulness to my master. As for me, the Lord has led me in the way to the house of my master's kinsmen."* ²⁸*Then the maiden ran and told her mother's household about these things.* ²⁹*Rebekah had a brother whose name was Laban; and Laban ran out to the man, to the spring.* ³⁰*When he saw the ring and the bracelets on his sister's arms, and when he heard the words of Rebekah his sister, "Thus the man spoke to me", he went to the man; and, behold, he was standing by the camels at the spring,* ³¹*He said, "Come in, O blessed of the Lord; why do you stand outside? For I have prepared the house and a place for the camels."*

It is indeed good fortune to be guided straight to the house of Abraham's kinsfolk! This is God's work who protects his master.

Verse 28. *Her mother's household.* She must first tell the incident to her mother (Rashi), or better in order to show the beautiful jewelry to her mother. (Ramban)

Verses 29–31. These verses are full of humor. Laban is in a great hurry. These were the thoughts which went through his mind while he ran. If only the man has not yet left, but there he stands by the camels at the spring. So generous a man must be blessed by the Lord.

> ³²*So the man came into the house; and he ungirded the camels, and they gave straw and provender for the camels, and water to*

wash his feet and the feet of the men who were with him. ³³The food was set before him to eat; but he said, "I will not eat until I have told my errand." He said, "Speak on."

It is also humor that "the man" does not make himself known to Laban who is so talkative in his eagerness, but follows him silently.

Verse 33. The conscientious servant will not eat before he has discussed his errand. The following narrative (verses 34–48) repeats verses 12–27. Everything depends upon the impression which the incident will make upon the family; for they have to decide. The reader shares the servant's tension after having lived through the incident with him.

³⁴So he said, "I am Abraham's servant. ³⁵The Lord has greatly blessed my master, and he has become great; he has given him flocks and herds, silver and gold, manservants and maidservants, camels and asses. ³⁶And Sarah my master's wife bore a son to my master when she was old; and to him he has given all he has. ³⁷My master made me swear, saying, 'You shall not take a wife for my son from the daughters of the Canaanites in whose land I dwell; ³⁸but you shall go to my father's house and to my kindred and take a wife for my son.' ³⁹I said to my master, 'Perhaps the woman will not follow me.' ⁴⁰But he said to me: 'The Lord before whom I have walked, will send his angel with you and prosper your way; and you shall take a wife for my son from my kindred and from my father's house; ⁴¹then you will be free from my oath, when you come to my kindred; and if they will not give her to you, you will be free from my oath.'

Verse 34. Previously verse 2 had described the position of trust enjoyed by him, but here he modestly only mentions that he is a servant. On the other hand he is more eloquent in describing the greatness of his master. All his wealth will be inherited by his son, who still lacks a wife.

Verse 37. The matter is very serious for Abraham; so he had me swear an oath. This must be very flattering for them.

Verse 39. Cleverly everything in verse 5 ff. which might endanger his mission is omitted; he completely passes over the possibility of Isaac's return to Haran; the hearers might become suspicious or feel their country slighted.

Verse 41. You have done your duty if you go to my family and are not to be blamed if you are unsuccessful.

> ⁴²"I came today to the spring, and said, 'O Lord, the God of my master Abraham, if now you will prosper the way which I go, ⁴³behold, I am standing by the spring of water; let the young woman who comes out to draw water, to whom I shall say, 'Pray give me a little water from your jar to drink,' ⁴⁴and who will say to me, 'Drink, and I will draw for your camels also,' let her be the woman whom the Lord has appointed for my master's son.' ⁴⁵Before I had done speaking in my heart, behold, Rebekah came out with her water jar on her shoulder; and she went down to the spring and drew. I said her, 'Pray let me drink.' ⁴⁶She quickly let down her jar from her shoulder and said, 'Drink, and I will give your camels drink also.' So I drank, and she gave the camels drink also. ⁴⁷Then I asked her and said, 'Whose daughter are you?' She said, 'the daughter of Bethuel, Nahor's son, whom Milcah bore to him.' So I put the ring to her nose and the bracelets on her arms. ⁴⁸Then I bowed my head and worshipped the Lord and blessed the Lord, the God of my master Abraham, who had led me by the right way to take the daughter of my master's kinsmen for his son. ⁴⁹Now then, if you will deal loyally and truly with my master, tell me; and if not, tell me; that I may turn to the right hand or to the left."

Verse 48. The servant effectively concludes his report; he almost puts the answer as God-willed into the mouth of the parents.

Verse 49. They cannot permit him to leave in search of a wife elsewhere. It would be rebellion against God.

> ⁵⁰Then Laban and Bethuel answered and said, "The thing comes from the Lord; we cannot speak to you bad or good. ⁵¹Behold, Rebekah is before you, take her and go, and let her be the wife of your master's son, as the Lord has spoken." ⁵²When Abraham's servant heard their words, he bowed himself to the earth before the Lord. ⁵³And the servant brought forth jewelry of silver and of gold, and raiment, and gave them to Rebekah; he also gave to her brother and to her mother costly delicacies.

Laban is mentioned first. In this house the efficient Laban is master (verse 31). The father Bethuel could of course not be passed by as his approval is indispensable. The old man must only nod his head and perhaps sign the papers. After this strenuous activity he retires, leaving the rest to the son and the womenfolk; so he is mentioned no more.

God has spoken! expresses the main idea of the whole story. To produce their acknowledgement of this, the servant had not only reported the incident, but even provoked it. He expected to come to people with whom he would have gained his point, as soon as he could persuade them that God had spoken and decided; they cannot possibly obstruct a marriage apparently made in heaven. Abraham's confidence had been justified; in master and servant piety and cleverness worked harmoniously together.

Verse 52. The pious servant first thanks God; his previous talk of God had not been pretense. Only now is he again called Abraham's servant; his gratitude also came from the soul of his master.

Verse 53. He unpacks presents for Rebekah, for the brother and the mother. These are voluntary gifts, not legal payment as has been claimed; they were the spontaneous expression of happiness about the successful match. They are intended to create an atmosphere of joy, cordiality and familiarity. Rebekah's gifts are presented in the name of the bridegroom. All this is timeless, universal, human custom.

> *54And he and the men who were with him ate and drank, and they spent the night there. When they arose in the morning, he said, "Send me back to my master." 55Her brother and her mother said, "Let the maiden remain with us a while, a year or ten months; after that she may go." 56But he said to them, "Do not delay me, since the Lord has prospered my way; let me go that I may go to my master." 57They said, "We will call the maiden and ask her." 58And they called Rebekah and said to her, "Will you go with this man?" She said, "I will go."*

Finally the servant accepts food, drink, and hospitality for himself and his men, so that he may depart the next morning as his work is finished.

Verse 55. Her brother and mother do not want to part from Rebekah so suddenly. This explains the presents to them. They have a different relationship to her than the father; he is rather glad to see her taken off his hands; but she was a helper for the mother, and the brother feels himself to be her protector. The presents shall comfort them and bring about willingness. They are still uncertain whether to let her go with this stranger immediately.

Verse 56. As the servant wants to bring her with him, he would have to wait such a long time; the conscientious man will not do so; a faithful messenger reports accomplishments without delay.

Verse 57. Rebekah when asked, simply replies yes. The worthy old man had gained her confidence; it might as well be done quickly. This too is a fine feature of her character. They ask her in his presence so that he will not believe her influenced by them (Redak).

> *59So they sent away Rebekah, their sister, and her nurse, and Abraham's servant and his men. 60And they blessed Rebekah, and said to her, "Our sister, be the mother of thousands of ten thousands; and may your descendants possess the gate of those who hate them." 61Then Rebekah and her maiden arose, and rode upon the camels and followed the man; thus the servant took Rebekah, and went his way.*

Leave must be taken. Rebekah also had other maidservants with her (see verse 61); but only the nurse, as a person of confidence and in view of 35,8 is mentioned.

Verse 60. Rebekah shall become the ancestress of a great people. As the second part of the verse is almost a literal repetition of 22,17 the servant must have told of the promise and Isaac's divine calling. It is the ultimate destiny of Isaac's family. Their wish asks that it may come about through her (Rashi).

> *62Now Isaac had come from the well Lehai-roi and was dwelling in the land of the Negeb. 63And Isaac went out for a walk in the fields in the evening, and he lifted up his eyes and looked and behold, there were camels coming. 64Rebekah lifted up her eyes, and when she saw Isaac, she bent to the side from the camel, 65and said to the servant, "Who is the man yonder, walking in the field to meet us?" The servant said, "It is my master." She took her veil and covered herself.*

Before the servant returns to Abraham, Isaac and Rebekah meet on the way; this forms a counterpart to the meeting at the well. In 25,11 Isaac dwells at this well, Lehai-roi.

Verse 63. It seems to have been Isaac's habit to walk shortly before sunset; he was a friend of nature (27,27).

Verse 64. *She bent to the side from the camel* in order not to be seen (Onkelos), similar to the following veiling.

Verse 65. Her first glance had told her that this man is to be respected. Only now she inquires who he is. Then she covers herself, aware that he is her bridegroom; this is an oriental custom, a trace of which still survives in the Jewish custom of "veiling" before the wedding. It shows her modesty.

> ⁶⁶*And the servant told Isaac all the things that he had done.* ⁶⁷*Then Isaac brought her into the tent of Sarah his mother, and took Rebekah, and she became his wife, and he loved her. So Isaac was comforted after his mother's death.*

Another motive for the marriage was the death of a deeply mourned mother which had orphaned the son. Rebekah shall replace her, as she was close to her by descent and similar in character.

The sequence in verse 67 shows a sense of reality; he took Rebekah as his wife, he loved her. In modern fiction it would be reversed.

The charming and artful narrative shall be a counterpart to chapter 23, funeral and wedding. The word God is not even mentioned there, but is here the decisive element. God's action is however brought about by man. God is the interpretation and recognition of events as a higher destiny. Both chapters reflect the same spirit. They picture family life free of sentimentality, full of dignity and charm, and show the deeper sympathies of the Bible. The story of God's friend, Abraham, could not have been concluded more beautifully. It is fit that he appear no more, not even to receive the report of the servant or to bless his son or grandson. His final order given in loving concern for the son, and appealing to God is his testament and the last word which we hear from his mouth.

Chapter 25

The Other Descendants Of Abraham.
Abraham took another wife, whose name was Keturah. ²She bore him Zimran, Jokshan, Medan, Midian, Ishbak, and Shuah. ³Jokshan was the father of Sheba and Dedan. The sons of Dedan were Ashurin, Letushim, and Le-ummim. ⁴The sons of Midian were Ephah, Epher, Hanoch, Abida, and Eldaah. All these were the children of Keturah. ⁵Abraham gave all he had to Isaac. ⁶But to the sons of the concubines which Abraham had, Abraham gave gifts, and while he was still living he sent them away from his son Isaac, eastward to the east country.

It has always appeared surprising and unbelievable that Abraham marries again after Sarah's death and has half a dozen sons, although forty years earlier he regarded himself as too old for children (17,17). However, the Hebrew phrase at the beginning of this verse does not imply that he married again after the death of his first wife, but on the contrary that she was still alive. Chronologically the passage lies before chapter 23 or chapter 17 or perhaps even before chapter 14. In view of the barrenness of Sarah, it would be unlikely for Abraham to have had no children from concubines as this was not objectionable. Abraham must have been regarded as the ancestor of numerous non-Israelite clans. The design of the author prohibited an earlier report, therefore it has been mentioned at the end.

Verses 2–4. Most of these names are otherwise unknown with the exception of Midian.

Verse 6. The children of concubines were not entitled to inheritance, but Abraham gives them presents. He sends them off, so that they may not be in the way of the real heir.

⁷These are the days of the years of Abraham's life which he lived, a hundred and seventy-five years. ⁸Abraham passed away and died in a good old age, an old man and full of years, and was gathered to his people. ⁹Isaac and Ishmael his sons buried him in the cave of Machpelah, in the field of Ephron, the son of Zohar the Hittite, before Mamre, ¹⁰the field which Abraham purchased from the Hittites. There Abraham was buried and Sarah his wife. ¹²After the death of Abraham God blessed Isaac his son. And Isaac lived at the well Lahai-roi.

Verse 8. Abraham *passed away* gently, without disease or pain, from natural infirmity. *In a good old age* which was not marred by misfortune and sorrow according to the promise in 15,15. *Full of years* a longer life would not have offered him more. *He was gathered to his people* is not identical with dying or being buried, as both are additionally mentioned here and many other times. It can only refer to a reunion of the soul, of the transfigured personality, with the souls of the ancestors; like them he belongs to the dead and is counted with them.

Verse 9. Isaac and Ishmael the two real sons meet again at the grave.

¹²And these are the descendants of Ishmael, Abraham's son, whom Hagar the Egyptian, Sarah's maid, bore to Abraham. ¹³These are the names of the sons of Ishmael, named according to their descendancy: Nebaioth, the first-born of Ishmael; and Kedar, Adbeel, Mibsam, ¹⁴Mishma, Dumah, Massa, ¹⁵Hadad, Tema, Jetur, Naphish, and Kedmah. ¹⁶These are the sons of Ishmael, and these are their names, by their villages and by their encampments, twelve princes according to their tribes. ¹⁷These are the years of the life of Ishmael, a hundred and thirty-seven years; he passed away and died, and was gathered to his people. ¹⁸They dwelt from Havilah to Shur, which is opposite Egypt in the direction of Asshur; he was lying before all his people.

Ishmael had to be characterized as son of Abraham, so to show the fulfillment of the promise of 17,20, and as son of Hagar so not to be reckoned as real heir. He was not equal to Isaac, because his mother was an Egyptian and a maid of Sarah.

Verse 13. The formula "these are the names" occurs only with the legitimate descendants of Abraham. In Israel names were important for the distribution of the land. Each Israelite had to indicate the genealogical descent from which he derived his claim to land. If this phrase is also used of the descendants of Ishmael and Esau, it shows that they too had a claim to the land promised to Abraham. They are also his offspring (21,13). Therefore the territories of the Ishmaelites and Edomites, in a wider sense, belong to the land of Canaan, particularly to the south and southwest. They are the outposts of the Semites in the direction of Egypt which corresponds to their descent from Abraham and an Egyptian mother.

Verse 16. This verse stresses that the promise of "twelve princes from Ishmael" (17,20) was fulfilled. They dwelt in stationary encampments and never achieved urban settlement.

Verse 18. Here Asshur cannot mean Assyria. It must have been the name of an Egyptian frontier town.

Ishmael's privilege, derived from being Abraham's son, was spent by fathering twelve distinguished sons; it comes to an end in the next generation. No nation, land, or empire of Ishmael has ever existed. They were the true Bedouins, but conscious of a common descent.

Isaac And His Sons

Abraham only had one son who was the true heir. Isaac has two sons of equal birth, twins from his only wife. Their rivalry develops into a varied story, rich in ideas; finally Jacob emerges as the only worthy son. Isaac's story might be called the father's blessing. He receives it and transmits it. He is blessed for the sake of Abraham; God rewards his servant in the faithful son. He is the blessed of the Lord (26,29), and as a blessed man he blesses his own sons. Nowhere else is the word blessing found so often.

This results in a minor role for the second patriarch when compared with the first and the third. He is neither an independent and clear cut personality, nor does he have varied and original experiences like them. The Bible does not offer exhaustive biographies of the patriarchs, but demonstrates the share of each in the greater design. Abraham and Jacob are the cornerstones, while Isaac links one to the other. His life runs smoothly and does not break with the past. He is born in Canaan, dies there, and need not emigrate like the other two. His name was not changed either.

> [19]These are the descendants of Isaac, Abraham's son: Abraham fathered Isaac, [20]and Isaac was forty years old when he took to wife Rebekah, the daughter of Bethuel the Aramaean of Padan-Aram, the sister of Laban the Aramaean.

Verse 20. The round numbers connected with Isaac are remarkable. He marries at 40, has a son with 60, dies at 180.

> ²¹And Isaac prayed to the Lord for his wife, because she was barren; and the Lord granted his prayer, and Rebekah his wife conceived. ²²The children struggled together within her; and she said, "If it is thus, for what am I yet?" So she went to inquire of the Lord. ²³And the Lord said to her,
> "Two nations are in your womb, and two peoples, born of you, shall be divided;
> The one shall be stronger than the other, the elder shall serve the younger."

And Isaac prayed. The Hebrew word indicates urgent prayer (Rashi).

Verse 22. She feels herself pregnant with twins and sees her destiny as mother of one heir of the promises endangered. She questions: What purpose has life then? She wants advice from God whether the prospective dilemna can be solved.

Verse 23. The answer is a rhythmical sentence, foretelling a struggle between the peoples of Edom and Israel. Even now the children are called the elder and the younger, due to the slight difference in the time of their birth. The prophecy refers to the peoples, not to Esau and Jacob. They never served one another; only the parents interpreted it this way.

> ²⁴When her days to be delivered were fulfilled, behold there were twins in her womb. ²⁵The first came forth red, all his body like a hairy mantle; so they called his name Esau. ²⁶Afterwards his brother came forth, and his hand had taken hold of Esau's heel; so his name was called Jacob. Isaac was sixty years old when she bore them.

Verse 25. *He came forth red.* Plainly an allusion to the red pottage in verse 30. The Hebrew word for red is also a pun on Esau's other name "Edom"; it reminds of the Hebrew for blood and of Esau's savageness. The statement that his body was *like a hairy mantle* plays on his third name Seir, his being a hunter and woodsman. He receives the name Esau which has no apparent meaning.

Verse 26. An accident is given as reason for Jacob's name. It shall be understood as "He takes by the heel". This unmistakably hints at the

ʄuture character of the new-born; Jacob who contests the precedence of
his brother even tries to hold him back at birth (Hos. 12,4). The incident
itself is physically impossible.

> ²⁷When the boys grew up Esau was a skilful hunter, a man of the
> field, while Jacob was a quiet man, dwelling in tents. ²⁸Isaac loved
> Esau, because he ate of his game; but Rebekah loved Jacob.

A man of the field roving about like the animals of the field which he
chased. But Jacob was a quiet man which indicates the opposite, a
peaceful, harmless, gentle man with a simple, well regulated way of
life.

Dwelling in tents. He was a shepherd (Rashbam; see 4,20). The two
brothers go different ways like Isaac and Ishmael, and even Cain and
Abel.

Verse 28. This verse prepares us for chapter 27. Isaac liked the taste
of game.

> ²⁹Once when Jacob was boiling pottage, Esau came in from the
> field, and he was famished. ³⁰And Esau said to Jacob, "Let me
> gulp some of that red pottage, for I am famished!" Therefore his
> name was called Edom. ³¹Jacob said, "First sell me your birth-
> right." ³²Esau said, "I am going to die; of what use is a birthright
> to me?" ³³Jacob said, "Swear to me first." So he swore to him, and
> sold his birthright to Jacob. ³⁴Then Jacob gave Esau bread and
> pottage of lentils, and he ate and drank, and rose and went his
> way. Thus Esau despised his birthright.

The episode shows the character of the brothers by an example and
also explains the name Edom (the red one). It continues the story of
their birth in a renewed attempt of Jacob to be regarded as the firstborn.

Verse 30. Let me gulp. The Hebrew expression is taken from the
feeding of animals and characterizes the uncontrolled gluttony as well
as the vulgar language of Esau. Edom is the usual name for the nation
derived from Esau. This interpretation shall express ridicule and repul-
sion for the hated neighbor; he loves red and that is blood.

Verse 32. I am going to die. In my dangerous occupation I constantly
risk death so that I may even die before our father (ibn Ezra).

Verse 33. Jacob demands a formal oath because the birthright is not something concrete (Seforno), or in case Esau should repent after having eaten (Redak).

Verse 34. *He ate and drank, and rose and went.* This depicts the rude fellow and his pretense not to care for the birthright. *Esau despised his birthright* is the final judgement of the Bible (Rashi). The attitude of Esau to his privilege explains and excuses the preference of the mother for Jacob.

Chapter 26

Isaac The Blessed Son

Now there was a famine in the land, beside the former famine that was in the days of Abraham. And Isaac went to Gerar, to Abimelech king of the Philistines. ²And the Lord appeared to him, and said, "Do not go down to Egypt; dwell in the land where I shall tell you. ³Sojourn in this land, and I will be with you and will bless you; for to you and your descendants I will give all these lands, and I will fulfill the oath which I swore to Abraham your father. ⁴I will multiply your descendants as the stars of heaven and will give to your descendants all these lands; and by your descendants all the nations of the earth shall bless themselves: ⁵because Abraham obeyed my voice and kept my charge, my commandments, my statutes, and my instructions."

The first verse establishes an inner relationship between the two famines. As calamities they were alike, but this time things will go differently. We are immediately prepared for the similarity, but also the differences in the experiences of Abraham and Isaac. Isaac goes to Abimelech, the king of the Philistines. This may be the Abimelech of Abraham's time or all the kings of the Philistines might have had the same name.

Verse 2. The first divine revelation to Isaac at the beginning of his career is parallel to that of Abraham (12,1f), but Abraham shall depart; Isaac shall stay.

Verse 3. *I will be with you* is said by God to a person setting out on a journey; he shall know that God will accompany and protect him, even if the journey be difficult and dangerous. It therefore prepares for Isaac's adventures in the land of the Philistines. Isaac shall be aided as the son of Abraham to whom God had given his promises.

Verse 4. The entire promise to Abraham is repeated to Isaac and later to Jacob, so it may afterwards be said that God has sworn thus to all three fathers (for instance 50,24).

Verse 5. The renewal of the promises is not automatic; it is a reward for Abraham's obedience, particularly for the sacrifice of chapter 22, from which the first half of this sentence is literally taken (22,18). The different expressions indicate that Abraham had conducted his life according to specific instructions from God as they had been given to him or as he might have surmised them. The various terms are similar to those of the later law. The abundance stresses that Abraham's conduct pleased God in every way; the promise of blessings for the son appears fully justified.

> *6So Isaac dwelt in Gerar. 7When the men of the place asked him about his wife, he said, "She is my sister"; for he feared to say, "My wife", thinking, "lest the men of the place should kill me for the sake of Rebekah"; because she was fair to look upon. 8When he had been there for a long time, Abimelech king of the Philistines looked out of a window and saw Isaac fondling Rebekah his wife. 9So Abimelech called Isaac and said, "Behold, she is your wife; how then would you say "She is my sister?" Isaac said to him, "Because I thought 'lest I die because of her.'" 10Abimelech said, "What is this you have done to us? One of the people might easily have lain with your wife and you would have brought guilt upon us." 11So Abimelech warned all the people saying, "Whoever touches this man or his wife shall be put to death."*

Isaac follows the divine admonition to remain in Canaan.

Verse 8. The real relationship remained hidden for a long time until Abimelech accidentally discovered it. The couple might have believed itself safe by that time.

Verse 10. *You would have brought guilt upon us.* Responsibility and punishment fall upon the entire people as in 20,9. Therefore the succeeding warning by the king.

> *12And Isaac sowed in the land and reaped in the same year a hundred-fold. The Lord blessed him, 13and the man became rich, and gained more and more until he became very wealthy. 14He*

*had possession of flocks and herds and a great household so that
the Philistines envied him.* *¹⁵Now the Philistines had stopped and
filled with earth all the wells which his father's servants had dug
in the days of Abraham his father.* *¹⁶And Abimelech said to Isaac,
"Go away from us; for you are much mightier than we."*

God fulfilled the second promise: I shall bless you.

Verse 14. Gold and silver are not mentioned, only wealth growing
from the soil despite the famine. They envy him as the brothers envy
Joseph.

Verse 15. The Philistines attempt to make his stay there impossible.
Here we learn that Abraham's servants had dug wells. The modern
Arabs filled the wells on the pilgrimage road unless they received the
required toll (Knobel). *And filled with earth all the wells* assiduously;
their rude vandalism was foolish. God's blessing could not be stopped.

*¹⁷So Isaac departed from there, and encamped in the valley of
Gerar and dwelt there.* *¹⁸And Isaac had dug again the wells of
water which had been dug in the days of his father Abraham; for
the Philistines had stopped them after the death of Abraham; and
he gave them the names which his father had given them.* *¹⁹But
when Isaac's servants dug in the valley and found there a well of
living water,* *²⁰the herdsmen of Gerar quarreled with Isaac's
herdsmen, saying, "The water is ours."* *So he called the name of
the well Esek (contention), because they contended with him.*
*²¹Then they dug another well, and they quarreled over that also;
so he called its name Sitna (enmity).* *²²And he moved from there
and dug another well, and over that they did not quarrel; so he
called its name Rehoboth (room), saying, "For now the Lord has
made room for us, and we shall be fruitful in the land."* *²³From
there he went up to Beer-sheba.*

Verse 18. These are the wells mentioned in verse 15 (Rashi). Verse 18
does not immediately follow verse 15 because before telling of the
digging of new wells it shall be mentioned that Isaac tried to restore
those of his father and re-established his memory by giving them the
old names. The request of Abimelech as well as Isaac's departure must
have occurred only afterwards.

Verse 19. The first time, not as in verses 21.22 "they dug a well", but *they dug in the valley and found a well* which had been there earlier (Redak); this makes it possible for the herdsmen of Gerar to claim it.

Verse 22. They do not quarrel over the third well because he had gone out of their way.

Verse 23. Isaac returns to Canaan and the place of his birth. His migrations come to an end.

> ²⁴*And the Lord appeared to him the same night and said, "I am the God of Abraham your father; fear not, for I am with you and will bless you and multiply your descendants for my servant Abraham's sake."* ²⁵*So he built an altar there and called upon the name of the Lord, and pitched his tent there. And there Isaac's servants dug for a well.*

After the famine and the experience of enmity Isaac has a reassuring revelation of the Lord in the night following his arrival. Isaac's migrations are introduced (verse 2) and concluded by a divine blessing.

Verse 25. First he builds an altar, and only then his tent.

> ²⁶*Now Abimelech had come to him from Gerar with Ahuzzath his adviser and Phicol the commander of his army.* ²⁷*Isaac said to them, "Why have you come to me, seeing that you hate me and have sent me away from you?"* ²⁸*They said, "We have plainly seen that the Lord is with you; so we say, let there be an oath between you and us, and let us make a covenant with you,* ²⁹*that you will do us no harm, just as we have not touched you and have done to you nothing but good and have sent you away in peace. You are now the blessed of the Lord."*

Verse 27. As Isaac is in his own territory he may speak more frankly and reproach them. You come seeking my friendship, although you sent me away in an unfriendly manner.

Verse 28. A question requires an answer, an accusation a defense. The reply of Abimelech must contain an apology and an explanation for their former behaviour. *We have plainly seen* all the time; we were not blind to your success as you perhaps think. It would be useless to deny it. They intentionally speak of *the Lord* as they want to emphasize the special favor of his God. Their speech is not quite clear which reflects their halting embarassment. After this confused speech, their confession sounds all the happier: you are indeed a man blessed by the Lord.

> ³⁰So he made them a feast, and they ate and drank. ³¹In the morning they rose early and took oath with one another; and Isaac set them on their way, and they departed from him in peace. ³²That same day Isaac's servants had come and told him about the well which they had dug, and said to him, "We have found water." ³³He called it Shibah therefore the name of the city is Beer-sheba to this day.

As a wise and peace loving man Isaac acquiesces in the situation and invites them for a meal of reconciliation.

Verse 33. This is the well of verse 25. The good news were a satisfaction for Isaac while the guests were present; they are witnesses and have not protested. For this reason the result of the digging had not been mentioned in verse 25.

> ³⁴When Esau was forty years old, he took to wife Judith the daughter of Be-eri the Hittite, and Basemath the daughter of Eli the Hittite; ³⁵and they made life bitter for Isaac and Rebekah.

If Esau married (like his father in 25,20) at the age of forty, Isaac was now 100 years old. This prepares for 27,1.

Verse 35. This verse obviously prepares for 27,46 ff.

The Meaning Of The Chapter.

This chapter describes the whole life of Isaac as son of Abraham. Everything which follows in chapters 27-36 is not his story, but that of his sons Jacob and Esau. After he had blessed them, Isaac disappears completely except for the report of his death (35,28f.). On the one side he is the father of his sons, on the other side the son of his father.

Abraham had not blessed his son as Isaac and Jacob will. A man like Abraham need not bless by words; his life is a blessing for those who observe it. This was also the meaning of 12,2 "Be a blessing"; therefore in 25,11 "After the death of Abraham God blessed Isaac," which is a counterpart to 24, 67, "Isaac was comforted after his mother's death". Comfort for the death of a mother can be found only in the love of a wife, another female being; but the father's death puts the son into his place. Chapter 26 is the detailed execution of the preliminary statement in 25,11. Isaac acquires his blessings for the merits of his father.

An emergency is created so that God may reveal himself to Isaac and promise him aid. A famine offers the proper occasion; it forces the departure which necessitates divine protection. Isaac shall not go to Egypt like his father, but remain in the land of the Philistines as Abimelech has shown that he will respect and honor the son of Abraham. A Pharaoh would not have fitted this purpose (12,15 ff.); God promises to be with him, and to bless him.

These are the two sides of God's guardianship as in the priestly blessing (Num. 6,24)—"The Lord bless you and keep you". Abimelech fully justifies the confidence placed in him. Things need not proceed as far as in chapter 20; he gives the strictest public warning not to molest the man and his wife, showing the same fear of God which animated him in chapter 20. Thus all three episodes are needed in the story of Abraham-Isaac; each refers to the preceeding one.

Now blessings in form of wealth are reported in verses 12-22. Some readers will be surprised to find Isaac sowing and harvesting, while we know the patriarchs so far only as herdsmen. Yet this would not preclude tilling of the soil; it is also clearly limited to this land and this year. There is no mention of the purchase of land.

The Philistines would have done well to hold on to a man who obviously brought blessing to their land. Instead they envy him, the inevitable consequence of success.

The other aspect of divine care is Isaac's success with his wells. Bread and water are in Biblical thinking the blessing of God, for instance Ex. 23,25. Isaac's father had dwelt and acquired wealth in foreign countries in time of famine. He also dug wells there, and so had not only labored for himself, but also for the land of his residence. He had been able to take his herds, his gold and silver with him, but the wells he had to abandon. They give water to the inhabitants long after he has gone. The envious Philistines had stopped the wells; although in their blind hate they harmed themselves. They found courage for their vandalism only after Abraham's death, for he was too great for them while alive; Abimelech had even asked him to stay in the land. Now they desired to extinguish his name; as it was connected with the wells they believed to achieve this goal by destroying them. A name could be most certain of perpetuation if its bearer had provided a well or spring. This patriotic service, this glory of Abraham the stranger, makes the true Philistines as restless as his wealth. Isaac's first concern is restoring the memory of his father. Had Isaac been a less noble character, *he* would have destroyed the wells before his departure or would have rejoiced in seeing them stopped as a punishment for the ungrateful people. Only afterwards does he dig his own wells. He *found there a well of living water* is a unique expression (verse 19). It is a contrast to the former water which has been restored after Abraham's death and also indicates that respect and preservation of the father's work will see a living success in his own work. The Philistines force him to depart, stop the wells of his father, and contest two of his own. They let him work, see him succeed, and then claim the results.

Only at the third time do they desist. Does Abimelech's request for Isaac's departure not contradict the praise given him above? Abimelech had to consider public opinion which had become excited over the wealth and influence of the stranger. The king tries to act as loyally as possible. He does not exactly banish Isaac but only says, "Go away from us", from Gerar; nor does Isaac for the time being leave the land of the Philistines. God was always with him, so there occurs a second divine revelation at the conclusion of this blessed career.

Now Isaac, as Abraham (21,22 ff.), receives a visit by Abimelech and his great men; but Abraham had invited Abimelech and had been the one to remind him of earlier injury. Here the situation is reversed, and therefore the visit is to Abimelech's credit. He is ashamed of the Philistines and wishes to reconcile Isaac. Perhaps he brings a third person as a representative of the population. They have recognized that Isaac, blessed by God, could not be harmed. The saying of Prov. 16,7 finds fulfillment in Isaac: "When a man's ways please the Lord, he makes even his enemies to be at peace with him." The reconciliation should not be ascribed merely to Isaac's love for peace. He possesses this virtue, although mostly from the necessity of withdrawing before powerful odds. Yet he does not reject the hand which offers peace, offered only as God's blessing has so visibly been showered upon him. All conflicts in the story of the patriarchs end in harmony and reconciliation. Regarding Abraham this is true of his conflicts with Pharaoh, Lot and Abimelech; regarding Isaac of his conflict with Abimelech; regarding Jacob of his conflicts with Laban and Esau; regarding Joseph of his conflicts with the brothers.

The renewal of the place name Beer-sheba fits well here. Isaac gives the name permanence *to this day* (verse 33). His loyalty as a son equals the devotion by which the father had made the son the aim of his life.

This chapter has special significance as Isaac is the first son since God made a covenant with Abraham, and exemplifies two fundamental conceptions of Israel and its religion; "the God of the father" and "the merit of the father."

Divine guidance and blessing in this story are in harmony with rational and psychological causation. No miracles occur; but it is miraculous that fruit comes out of seed, and that water springs from the solid soil, although it happens each day; but human toil also contribute. Isaac owes his success, aside from the blessing and the example of the father, to his piety and enduring industry. He is not faultless. He too speaks a lie, a complete one, not a half truth as Abraham. The Bible need not emphasize this especially after its severe treatment of Abraham. The report itself implies the blame.

Chapter 27

Isaac, The Blessed Son, Blesses His Sons (27-28,9)

When Isaac was old and his eyes were dim so that he could not see, he called Esau his older son, and said to him, "My son"; and he answered, "Here I am." ²He said, "Behold, I am old; I do not know the day of my death. ³Now then, take your weapons, your quiver and your bow, and go out to the field, and hunt game for me, ⁴and prepare for me savory food, such as I love, and bring it to me that I may eat; that I may bless you before I die."

When Isaac was old and his eyes were dim is deliberately mentioned at the outset to explain his inability to recognize Jacob, as well as his feeling of imminent death.

Verse 2. I want to do something before my death; it requires preparation on your part.

Verse 3. Every word sounds the call for gay hunting, Esau's favorite occupation.

Verse 4. Pronouncing a blessing requires high spirits as body and soul are so closely connected; this is promoted by a feeling of physical comfort created by the pleasant stimuli of food, drink, and smell. Their effect is greater if they come from the person to be blessed and produce a bias in his favor. Isaac wanted to give Esau an opportunity to do him a service, and thus to be prejudiced on his behalf (Seforno).

⁵Now Rebekah had listened when Isaac spoke to his son Esau. So when Esau went to the field to hunt for game and to bring it, Rebekah said to her son Jacob, "I heard your father speak to your brother Esau, ⁷'Bring me game, and prepare for me savory food, that I may eat it, and bless you before the Lord before I die.' ⁸Now therefore, my son, obey my word as I command you. ⁹Go to the flock, and fetch me two good kids, that I may prepare from them savory food for your father, such as he loves; ¹⁰*and you shall bring it to your father to eat, so that he may bless you before he dies."*

Rebekah waits until Esau has gone. She has good reasons to desire the father's blessing for Jacob; the younger one deserves it for his character and conduct. Esau is unworthy as he had made himself unfit as heir of the divine promise by his marriages; she also mistakes the prophecy of 25,23 as referring to the brothers themselves. Consequently, she believes it permissible to promote the divine plans even against her husband who in his weakness favors Esau. Jacob is *her son.*

Verse 7. Only Rebekah says: *before the Lord* which betrays her thoughts. The last blessing of a father must have the approval of God.

Verse 8. *As I command you.* This shall silence any resistance of Jacob.

Verse 9. *Two good kids* to select the most suitable pieces. She also thinks of the hairy skin.

¹¹*But Jacob said to Rebekah his mother, "Behold, my brother Esau is a hairy man, and I am a smooth man.* ¹²*Perhaps my father will feel me, and I shall seem to be mocking him, and bring a curse upon myself, and not a blessing,"* ¹³*His mother said to him, "Upon me be your curse, my son; only obey my word, and go, fetch them to me."* ¹⁴*So he went and took them and brought them to his mother; and his mother prepared savory food, such as his father loved:* ¹⁵*Then Rebekah took the best garments of Esau her older son, which were with her in the house, and put them on Jacob her younger son:* ¹⁶*and the skins of the kids she put upon his hands and upon the smooth part of his neck;* ¹⁷*and she gave the savory food and the bread which she had prepared, into the hand of her son Jacob.*

She has given a command, and as son he must obey his mother; but has she considered the following difficulty?

Verse 12. He may accidentally feel me when I present the food to him.

Verse 13. A curse would be only a wish, which a third person might ward off by a declaration of willingness to accept it as the guilty party.

If the effectiveness of blessing and curse depends upon consciousness of merit, Rebekah testifies against her own endeavor.

Verse 14. The Hebrew text is very terse; it was difficult enough for Jacob, but his mother wants it, and it is she who prepares the meal.

Verse 15. She interchanges her two sons by putting the garment of the older on the younger. According to verse 27 the garments had a good odor; they were probably stored with scented herbs or even perfumed, as in Talmudic times. For the blind man touch and smell take the place of sight. Rebekah thought of the one, Jacob of the other.

Verse 16. Rebekah covers Jacob's hands as Isaac will take something from them, and his neck because he will embrace him.

Verse 17. Bread belongs to meat; later (verse 25) wine is also added. The actions of the mother are described in detail; she is busy and anxious for success, in contrast to Jacob's passivity. She even puts everything into his hand.

> ¹⁸So he went in to his father, and said, "My father"; and he said, "Here I am; who are you, my son?" ¹⁹Jacob said to his father, "I, Esau, your first-born. I have done as you told me; now sit up and eat of my game, that you may bless me." ²⁰But Isaac said to his son, "How is it that you have found it so quickly, my son?" He answered, "Because the Lord your God granted me success."

Cautiously and uncertainly Jacob announces himself by only one word—my father. Should the father recognize his voice he can still withdraw (Luzzato). As Isaac hears himself addressed—my father, he believes it to be Esau; but wonders at his early return.

Verse 19. Jacob gathers courage and speaks the fatal lie which will cost him twenty years of his life.

Verse 20. As Jacob speaks of game Isaac asks how he was able to find it so rapidly. The deception might have failed at this point, but Rebekah and Jacob had prepared an answer as the question could be foreseen. *The Lord your God* shows obsequiousness, respect, courtesy, or flattery. He does not say "I", but "you" had good luck.

> ²¹Then Isaac said to Jacob, "Come near, that I may feel you, my son, to know whether you are really my son Esau or not." ²²So

Jacob went near to Isaac his father, who felt him and said, "The voice is Jacob's voice, but the hands are the hands of Esau." ²³*And he did not recognize him because his hands were hairy like his brother Esau's hands; so he blessed him.*

Isaac is reassured about the hurried return as the stated reason is credible; but he has become suspicious of the identity of the person standing before him for another reason.

Verse 22. The Bible intentionally calls the false Esau by his true name Jacob. However, the matter was decided for Isaac because he had made the question dependent upon feeling him. When he says: *the voice is Jacob's voice* he thinks of the words he had heard, and finds this surprising, but not decisive. He relies more on touch, particularly regarding Esau, who has a mark on his body. Jewish interpreters (Rashi and others) think that the Hebrew word does not refer to the voice which might possibly have been similar in both or could be imitated by Jacob, but the manner of speech and the language, "The Lord your God"—please, "sit up", did not sound like Esau, but like Jacob.

Verse 23. Recognition is usually by sight; but for Isaac touch must take its place. The verse emphasizes its inadequacy; we shall pity the blind man. *He blessed him* is not yet the real blessing, but the Hebrew word means also to welcome, to recommend, to thank, namely for having done as he had asked and in such a surprisingly short time.

²⁴*He said, "Are you really my son Esau?" He answered, "I am."* ²⁵*Then he said, "Bring it to me, that I may eat from my son's game and bless you." So he brought it to him, and he ate; and he brought him wine, and he drank.* ²⁶*Then his father Isaac said to him, "Come near and kiss me, my son."* ²⁷*So he came near and he kissed him; and he smelled the smell of his garments, and blessed him, and said, "See the smell of my son is as the smell of a field which the Lord has blessed!*

Verse 24. This is more a statement than a question and no confirmation is needed beyond a simple yes.

Verse 25. Then everything is alright and I may begin. *My son's game* is said tenderly.

Verse 26. Isaac kisses his son before blessing him as Jacob later his grandchildren (48,10).

Verse 27. Isaac is affected by the smell of the garments. Isaac is happy about the smell of the fields as he was a man of the fields, as friend of nature (24,63). Esau was to bring him some of this smell by the game. It is true to life that in breathing the precious smell, the expression of his delight changes imperceptibly into the blessing itself:

> ²⁸*May God give you of the dew of heaven,*
> *and of the fatness of the earth,*
> *and plenty of grain and wine.*
> ²⁹*Let peoples serve you,*
> *and nations bow down to you.*
> *Be lord over your brothers,*
> *and may your mother's sons bow down to you.*
> *Cursed be every one who curses you,*
> *and blessed be every one who blesses you."*

He wishes him a paradise which does not need rain and is drenched by the dew of heaven.

Verse 29. The second part of the blessing means dominion. This blessing is of a political nature and has no bearing on Jacob as an individual. It may allude to the subjection of Edom by David (II Sam. 8,14).

> ³⁰*As soon as Isaac had finished blessing Jacob, when Jacob had long ago gone out from the presence of Isaac his father, Esau his brother came in from his hunting. He also prepared savory food, and brought it to his father. And he said to his father, "Let my father arise and eat of his son's game, that you may bless me."* ³²*His father Isaac said to him, "Who are you?" He said, "I am your son, your first-born, Esau."* ³²*Then Isaac trembled violently, and said, "Who was it then that hunted game and brought it to me, and I ate it all before you came, and I have blessed him?—yes, and he shall be blessed."*

Jacob had not just left, so that he was nearly caught as is usually explained. Esau does not enter immediately after him, but only returns from hunting; it still took considerable time until he could bring the prepared meal to his father. Jacob was far away (verse 42), so that they did not meet each other. For this reason Esau has no idea that Jacob had preceded him.

Verse 32. Isaac does not ask: who are you, my son? For now he thinks it must be a stranger who speaks, even if he addresses him: my father.

Verse 33. The last words show that Isaac has now recognized who had been there previously. Retracting the blessing would imply cursing of Jacob and the father cannot bring himself to that. He sees a divine decree in his mistake and resigns himself to it. It makes him tremble to think that he had felt no inner inhibition in giving the blessing. Only the mother can have contrived this; thus she has gotten her way (Rashbam).

> *34When Esau heard the words of his father, he cried out with an exceedingly great and bitter cry, and said to his father, "Bless me, even me also, my father!" 35But he said, "Your brother came with guile, and he has taken away your blessing." 36He said, "Is he not rightly named Jacob? For he has supplanted me these two times. He took away my birthright; and behold, now he has taken away my blessing." Then he said, "Have you not reserved a blessing for me?"*

Esau speaks four times; he by all means wants a blessing too. He fights desperately against the entanglement which he has brought upon himself by despising the birthright.

Verse 35. Isaac is the first to mention the brother. Now it is clear that it was not only Jacob's voice. I cannot conceal from you that it was not a stranger, but your brother. Esau's indignation can break forth without having to guess.

Verse 36. The question already contains the answer. His name expresses his guile. The Hebrew is not only a pun on the name Jacob, but also on the two words blessing and birthright which contain in Hebrew the same letters, only in different sequence. This is the grim wit of anger and indignation, but also an acceptance of these events. *Have you not reserved a blessing for me?* He would like to help the father, perhaps a loophole can be found.

> *37Isaac answered Esau, "Behold I have made him your lord, and all his brothers I have given him for servants, and with grain and wine I have sustained him. What then can I do for you, my son?" 38Esau said to his father, "Have you but one blessing, my father? Bless me, even me also, O my father." And Esau lifted up his voice and wept.*

Isaac has (in verse 29) formulated the relationship of the two in such a way that no quibbling is possible; he had additionally bestowed grain and wine upon him.

Verse 38. The question is justified as Jacob later has a blessing for each one of his twelve sons.

> ³⁹*Then Isaac his father answered him,*
>
> *"Behold, of the fatness of the earth shall your dwelling be,*
> *and of the dew of heaven on high.*
> ⁴⁰*By your sword you shall live,*
> *and you shall serve your brother;*
> *but when you break loose*
> *you shall break his yoke from your neck."*

Some interpreters rather translate: "away from the fatness of the earth shall your dwelling be etc.," but this would be a curse, and not a blessing and would mock Esau's expectations. Nor is there a land which is "away from the dew of heaven." Isaac wants to say that the first part of Jacob's blessing can also be pronounced for him. Indeed modern travellers describe some part of Edom as very fertile.

Verse 40. You will live trusting your sword and inseparable from it, but you will not be free. Then comes the bitter core of the matter which Esau cannot be spared: you must serve your brother; yet this is immediately mitigated by a hope that he may throw off this yoke. This will happen *when you break loose*; it seems to say the same as *you shall break his yoke.* Jewish interpreters have thought that it will depend upon Jacob's conduct and that the words shall be translated: if you have justified complaints of too great severity.

> ⁴¹*Now Esau hated Jacob because of the blessing with which his father had blessed him, and Esau said to himself, "The days of mourning for my father are approaching; then I will kill my brother Jacob." ⁴²But the words of Esau, her older son, were told to Rebekah; so she sent and called Jacob, her younger son, and said to him, "Behold, your brother Esau comforts himself by planning to kill you. ⁴³Now, therefore, my son, obey my voice; arise, flee to Laban my brother in Haran. ⁴⁴And stay with him a while, until your brother's fury turns away; ⁴⁵until your brother's anger turns away, and he forgets what you have done to him; then I will send,*

*and fetch you from there. Why should I be bereft of you both in
one day?"*

I will kill my brother Jacob a cruel phrase not mitigated by the
sentiment of the preceding clause.

Verse 43. People flee abroad before a threat of death as Moses, David,
and Jeroboam.

Verse 44. *A while* This means a few days; she says this to comfort
him on the separation which will be hard.
It cannot be meant seriously as the anger of Esau will not vanish so
quickly. Nevertheless, Rebekah knows him sufficiently well to say that
his anger will eventually disappear.

Verse 45. I would be bereft of you both in one day, as Esau would
have to flee if he killed his brother or become a victim of vendetta. Her
words skillfully appeal to Jacob's love for his mother, but show that she
also cares for Esau.

> [46]*Then Rebekah said to Isaac, "I am weary of my life because of
> the Hittite women. If Jacob marries one of the Hittite women such
> as these, one of the women of the land, what good will my life be
> to me?"*

Rebekah's words are to be understood as the beginning of a longer
speech the contents of which can be taken from the following. She
suggests an emigration to Haran without revealing the true cause to
Isaac. Nevertheless this also is sincerely meant, therefore the notice in
26,34. Rebekah appeals to Isaac's reverence for his father and his
intentions (24,3). By her words *of the women of the land* she suggests a
solution.

Chapter 28

Then Isaac called Jacob and blessed him, and charged him, "You shall not marry one of the Canaanite women. ²Arise, go to Paddan-Aram to the house of Bethuel, your mother's father; and take as wife from there one of the daughters of Laban your mother's brother. ³God Almighty bless you and make you fruitful and multiply you, that you may become a company of peoples. ⁴May he give the blessing of Abraham to you and to your descendants with you, that you take possession of the land of your sojournings which God gave to Abraham!" ⁵Thus Isaac sent Jacob away; and he went to Paddan-Aram to Laban, the son of Bethuel the Aramaean, the brother of Rebekah, Jacob's and Esau's mother.

Isaac acts like his own father.

Verse 3. He charges Jacob to marry; it necessarily follows that he wishes him numerous descendants.

Verse 4. *The blessing of Abraham* as contrast to his own blessing. Esau had renounced his claim to the "blessing of Abraham" by marrying Canaanite women. Esau knows that this land is destined to become the abode of a people which is not interbred with Canaanites and shall establish a specific way of life, but he does not feel himself fit for that. Isaac, by expecting Jacob not to marry a Canaanite woman, shows that he probably always regarded him as the chosen one. The last word that we hear from him is the name of his father, Abraham, similarly his first word had been (22,7) my father. The father was the standard and the content of his entire life.

Verse 5. *Jacob's and Esau's mother* implies blame for Esau; he too could have married someone from there (Ramban).

⁶Now Esau saw that Isaac had blessed Jacob and sent him away to Paddan-Aram to take a wife from there, and that as he blessed him he charged him, "You shall not marry one of the Canaanite women," ⁷and that Jacob had obeyed his father and his mother and gone to Paddan-Aram. ⁸So when Esau saw that the Canaanite women did not please Isaac his father, ⁹Esau went to Ishmael and took to wife, besides the wives he had, Mahalath the daughter of Ishmael Abraham's son, the sister of Nebaioth.

The lengthy sentence corresponds to the tortuous considerations of Esau.

Verse 7. Jacob's obedience is emphasized in contrast to Esau.

Verse 8. Now Esau must acknowledge that his father was serious in disapproving of his marriages (26,35); he tries, as the good son, at least of his father, to efface the bad impression.

Verse 9. Jacob marries a daughter of the mother's brother, thus Esau goes and marries a daughter of the father's brother, to please the father (Verse 8), and to spite the mother. But he did not consider that Ishmael's mother as well as the wife (21,21) had been Egyptian women, and that Egypt and Canaan were brothers. For this reason his wife is also called *the sister of Nebaioth;* she is from the same Egyptian mother as this first-born son. Esau had first married Canaanite women, daughters of the country; only now he goes some distance, but not too far, only to Ishmael! Even that needs long and twisted deliberation. How insignificant when compared to the distant Paddan-Aram of Jacob which for this reason is mentioned four times.

The Meaning Of The Paternal Blessing.

Issac blesses twice, in chapter 27 Jacob as well as Esau, in 28, 1–4 only Jacob. The two blessings are entirely different. Chapter 27 is marked by constant repetition not only of the names Isaac, Rebekah, Esau, Jacob, but also of the terms of relationship, father, mother, son, brother. A different tendency is indicated and confirmed by the unlike contents of the blessings. The one intended for Esau, but mistakenly pronounced over Jacob, and the one belatedly pronounced over Esau speak of two matters: wealth of the soil and dominion over the other. However the final blessing of Jacob deals with neither the one nor the other, but contains the following elements—divine blessing, fertility and growth into a great nation, and possession of the land of Canaan by the descendants. Not a word of this occurred in chapter 27.

The divine blessing for Abraham as it is expressly called is repeated here. Isaac himself had received this blessing from God (26,3 ff; 24), and now gives it as a wish to Jacob. It is the blessing of the ancestor of the chosen people, and Jacob is destined to be the third patriarch. As Isaac never speaks of it to Esau, either the alleged or the real one, it can never have been his intention to transmit this privilege to the older son even it he had the power to do so. It can also not have been Rebekah's intention to deprive Esau of this blessing. Not the birthright, but only fitness and merit could have been decisive for this choice. Should one of several brothers be chosen, the scrutiny might start with the older one as in the case of David. Under equal conditions Esau would have received preference, but he had shown no capacity, inclination, or understanding for it. The patriarchs must not become related by marriage to the people of the land which their descendants shall possess. They shall remain separate and free as Israel shall be built on different conceptions of family and morality; and in addition they shall receive the land of Canaan as a possession bestowed upon them by God through their fathers, not through Canaanite mothers. Thus only Jacob could receive the "blessing of Abraham".

The bargaining about the birthright is no more than a symptom of the different minds of the brothers which becomes apparent in their childish games. The fact that Esau was the first-born could not be undone by anyone; therefore he continues to be called the first-born later (Bechor). The birthright (bechoro) is however different. It may also indicate first place in descent, but furthermore refers to certain privileges and material advantages. These can by taken from the firstborn and transferred to another person (see I Chron. 5,1). Only the "birthright" can have been involved in the bargain between Jacob and Esau. It could be transferred, it could also be abandoned. It became valid after the father's death whose position the first-born received. When Jacob says to Esau "Sell me your birthright", he means after the father's death I shall be regarded as the first in inheritance. He may further claim to be in command of the house. Esau answers "I shall anyhow not survive our father; of what use is the birthright to me?"

In summary, chapter 27 had dealt merely with the relationship of the two brothers to each other, a matter inside the family and the different attitude of the parents to it; therefore the constant repetition of father, mother, son, brother. Isaac had no reason to deprive Esau of this precedence as he did not love Jacob more than his brother, unlike Jacob's own later preferences for Joseph (37,3); nor is Jacob the son of a favorite wife (Deut. 21,16).

Isaac need not stress the disposition of the paternal inheritance; it naturally belongs to the first-born, so the privilege of dominion is more strongly emphasized. Rebekah thinks differently guided by the divine oracle "the elder shall serve the younger," and the inclination of her heart. She justifiably loves Jacob. She could not bear to see her innocent, peaceful son serve his savage and rude brother. As the latter has flung away the spiritual precedence, he shall not have secular precedence either. As the blessing of the father before his death would come to this, she substitutes Jacob through trickery. The trick succeeds, and Isaac cannot revoke the blessing.

Yet all human stratagems are vain. Jacob does not profit by having bought the birthright. He has merely incurred the deadly hatred of his brother, so he, son and heir of a wealthy father, must flee from the parental home and native land. He is forced to do twenty years' service abroad for a begrudging relative who cheats him.

He must earn everything by his own hard toil. Upon his return he must tremble for his life, and humble himself deeply before his more powerful brother. Rebekah had deceived herself by relying on the divine oracle; it referred not to persons, but to the later peoples. A human blessing is only an empty wish if God does not confirm it. Isaac's fault was that he wanted to bless Esau secretly without the presence of the brother and the mother, so Rebekah might say: "do you want to conceal this from us? Then I shall see to it that you will bless Jacob without noticing it." The high value which all parties set on the father's blessing is the only commendable part in this tragedy.

Jacob is the third patriarch and can be the last because in his twelve sons "the house of Israel" becomes established. With Abraham and Isaac the future of the people had always hinged on one son. The following story must answer two questions: How did Jacob get twelve sons, and how did he obtain the name Israel by which the people and its tribes are called!

Jacob's Emigration 28,10–22

> [10]Jacob left Beer-sheba, and went toward Haran. [11]And he came to a certain place, and stayed there that night, because the sun had set. Taking of the stones of the place, he put them at his head and lay down in that place to sleep.

Beer-sheba was the residence of the father (26,23) and Haran is located in Paddan-aram.

Verse 11. This verse seems to say that he places stones by his head, perhaps as protection against wild animals.

12And he dreamed that there was a ladder set up on the earth, and the top of it reached to heaven; and behold, the angels of God were ascending and descending on it! 13And behold, the Lord stood above it and said, "I am the Lord, the God of Abraham your father and the God of Isaac; the land on which you lie I will give to you and to your descendants; 14and your descendants shall be like the dust of the earth , and you shall spread abroad to the west and to the east and to the north and to the south; and by you and your descendants shall all the families of the earth bless themselves. 15Behold, I am with you and will keep you wherever you go, and will bring you back to this land; for I will not leave you until I have done that of which I have spoken to you." 16Then Jacob awoke from his sleep and said, "Surely the Lord is in this place, and I did not know it." 17And he was afraid, and said, "How awesome is this place! This is none other than a house of God, and this is the gate of heaven."

Jacob is about to exchange his native land for a foreign country. He shall be told that God will protect him there too, and that he will be accompanied by angels. The ascending angels are those of the native land, the descending ones those of the foreign country. They change at the border as every land due to its different conditions of life and dangers needs other angels (Midrash, Rashi). The image expresses the same idea as the following speech of God. It is created by the Bible only for this moment in sympathy for Jacob who is abandoned and afraid.

Verse 13. The fugitive wories whether he will ever see this land again. Not only that, but it will belong to you and your descendants! Be not mislead by now sleeping on its ground like a homeless beggar and as you think for the last time. This should on the contrary be a symbol of permanent possession for you, as I will keep my promises.

Verse 14. Jacob is not only a fugitive, but also without family; therefore the second theme of all promises is an abundance of descendants.

Verse 15. turns from the distant future to Jacob's present situation, promising him protection for his person. In this dream the departing blessing of the father (verses 1 ff.) is repeated and confirmed.

Verse 16 the exclamation shows that Jacob had thought disparagingly of the place; he apologizes; *I did not know.*

Verse 17 Jacob's words show the deep impression he had received by the vision; they breathe the same divine majesty and tenderness. *Gate of heaven* is as unique as the image of the ladder.

> *¹⁸So Jacob rose early in the morning and he took the stone which he had put at his head and set it up for a pillar and poured oil on top of it. ¹⁹He called the name of the place Bethel; but the name was Luz at first.*

The erection of stones as monuments at the scene of important events is a custom frequently mentioned in the Bible. They were viewed with respectful awe called forth by reminiscence. It is a general human feeling, ancient as well as modern. The Talmud prescribes special benedictions upon seeing places where Israel experienced a miracle.

Here the act introduces the following vow (see 31,13). In Bethel Jacob takes leave of his home land. Should he return to this place, his prayer will have been heard, so he marks the spot. The stone shall remind him of his vow. Jacob had treated it slightingly, not knowing of the presence of God. Awakening he is frightened and anoints the stone to atone for it. He now recognizes the place as holy, wishes to treat it correspondingly, and gives it a suitable name: Bethel, "house of God". He will later (35,14) erect another monument in the same place concluding the fulfilment of his vow. In Babylonian-Assyrian documents we also find the pouring of oil on a stone as dedication.

The city is in the neighborhood, but Jacob had slept in the open. In later times we find a recognized sanctuary at Bethel (Judg. 20,18; 26ff); its founding is here ascribed to the vow of the third patriarch.

> *²⁰Then Jacob made a vow, saying, "If God will be with me, and will keep me in this way that I go, and will give me bread to eat and clothing to wear, ²¹so that I come again to my father's house in peace, then the Lord shall be my God, ²²and the stone which I have set up for a pillar, shall be God's house; and of all that you give me I will give the tenth to you."*

This vow, the first in the Bible, has been misunderstood as if Jacob set a number of conditions before deciding to acknowledge the Lord as his God. Yet all he wishes is to be protected on the way, abroad, and to survive. The "conditions" only mean, if I stay alive. This does not imply that he would otherwise not be willing, but rather not be capable of doing it. Jacob's words are a model vow; they imply the confession that the fulfillment depends upon God alone. He wishes to stay alive to be able to serve God. It is not an offer of an exchange of inferior goods, but the self-dedication of the whole man, if God will grant it to him.

Jacob had been deeply affected by the divine promises. The vision occurred not only for the glorification of this place, Bethel, but of the entire land. Jacob now realizes that he will be able to belong to God only in this land promised to the fathers and now to him, not abroad. This place is the center of the land. Jacob's wishes are no more than the divine promise translated into a prayer beginning with "if". Bread and clothing are the indispensable necessities of life, and Jacob will rest satisfied with them. *The the Lord shall be my God.* I will speak of him as my God, so that the God of Abraham and Isaac will also have become the God of Jacob, as far as it is a matter of human effort. These words express the whole inner development which Jacob shall undergo.

Verse 22. The new inner relationship to God shall also be expressed concretely: 1) by a lasting memorial, the stone. Jacob's words in verse 17 were not only an empty exclamation. 2) by the tithe which shall mark all which will become his as an undeserved gift of God.

This story shows no trace of the desecration of Bethel by Jeroboam who established the worship of golden calves there (I Kings 12,29), nor of the vehement attacks of the prophets against this (e.g. Amos 5,5; Hos. 4,15).

Chapter 29

Jacob With Laban

Then Jacob went on his journey, and came to the land of the people of the east. ²As he looked, he saw a well in the field, and lo, three flocks of sheep lying beside it; for out of that well, the flocks were watered. The stone on the well's mouth was large, ³and when all the flocks were gathered there, the shepherds would roll the stone from the mouth of the well, and water the sheep, and put the stone back in its place upon the mouth of the well.

The first Hebrew words of verse 1 reflect the high spirits which mark Jacob's departure after his comforting experience. As God promised to be with him everywhere, Jacob, the settled "dweller of tents" (25, 27), joyfully goes into the wide world which is Paddan-aram for him.

Verse 2. Quarrels easily arose when the flocks were watered (Ex. 2, 16 ff.); to preserve peace, the well was closed by a stone which was removed when everyone was present. This also protected it from use by wild animals. The stone must be large, so as not to be arbitrarily removed by an individual.

⁴Jacob said to them, "My brothers, where do you come from?" They said, "We are from Haran." ⁵He said to them, "Do you know Laban the son of Nahor?" They said, "We do." ⁶He said to them, "Is it well with him?" They said, "It is well; and see, Rachel his daughter is coming with the sheep!" ⁷He said, "Behold, it is s.'ll high day; it is not time for the animals to be gathered together, water the sheep, and go, pasture them." ⁸But they said, "We cannot, until all the flocks are gathered together and the stone is rolled from the mouth of the well; then we water the sheep."

Jacob addresses the shepherds affably as "my brothers"; but these dull people, stupid like their sheep, answer every question lazily with

193

only a word or two as if each word were a dollar. As Jacob hears them mention Haran he asks for Laban, obviously assuming that the first immigrant and founder of the family must be well known.

Verse 6. If you want to talk here comes someone.

Verse 7. Jacob's heart beats quicker; he would prefer no witnesses at the meeting and therefore would like them to move on; he cleverly knows how to accomplish this. His speech is impatient and peremptory; you are bad shepherds!

Verse 8. They acknowledge the superiority of this domineering stranger and condescend to explain.

> *9While he was still speaking with them, Rachel came with her father's sheep; for she kept them. 10Now when Jacob saw Rachel the daughter of Laban his mother's brother, and the sheep of Laban his mother's brother, Jacob went up and rolled the stone from the well's mouth, and watered the flock of Laban his mother's brother. 11Then Jacob kissed Rachel, and wept aloud. 12And Jacob told Rachel that he was her father's kinsman, and that he was Rebekah's son; and she ran and told her father.*

Rachel is coming from the pasture.

Verse 10. The feeling of kinship, the memory of his native country, and of his mother at home rises in Jacob; this is the daughter of the brother of his mother! The sheep belong to the brother of his mother. This must be the girl intended for him (28,2); she looks pretty, but the author saves this for verse 17. Chilvalry and love multiply Jacob's strength; although three shepherds could not accomplish it, he rolls the large stone from the mouth of the well, disregarding local custom. Then he waters the sheep of Laban his mother's brother. Love breaks all rules. By this action Jacob shows himself as son of his mother who once had given water to the stranger and his camels. Surely she had told her son of it. Heaving and casting of a heavy stone is the simplest proof of bodily strength, as often in Homer.

Verse 11. Naturally Jacob told Rachel who he was before or during the work. Verse 12a occurs before verse 11 or 10. But the present order of the verses expresses the vividness of the impulse more strongly. He weeps for joy (Biur), because he has reached his goal (Skinner), or

because of the contrast between his home and his present situation. As
he came empty-handed (Rashi), he thought how once the servant of his
grandfather came with jewels and presents, while he possesses
nothing. 'The son of Rebekah is here' is big, impressive news! They had
undoubtedly often spoken of her wooing and departure from her
parents' home.

> *13When Laban heard the tidings of Jacob his sister's son, he ran to
> meet him, and embraced him and kissed him, and brought him to
> his house. Jacob told Laban all these things, 14and Laban said to
> him, "Well, you are my bone and my flesh!" And he stayed with
> him a full month.*

Overflowing cordiality is suspicious with a man like Laban. He
thought that the servant of the house had once come with ten loaded
camels, how much more would the son of the house bring! (Rashi)

When *Jacob told Laban all these things*, the domestic events which
had brought him here, Laban's amiability disappears completely.

Verse 14. Laban, masterfully characterized, is from beginning to end
a selfish, greedy, exploiting, distrustful peasant who nevertheless
maintains appearances, a type which may have been familiar to the
author. Economical, cautious in his words and a sly fox he always
leaves room for a different interpretation. His first words are half sweet,
half sour. They may mean: You are most welcome; or that it may be true
that you are my sister's son; as you were sent by her you may stay for a
visit. Actually he does not even say so much. Jacob stays a full month.

> *15Then Laban said to Jacob, "Because you are my kinsman,
> should you therefore serve me for nothing? Tell me what shall
> your wages be?" 16Now Laban had two daughters; the name of the
> older was Leah, and the name of the younger was Rachel. 17Leah's
> eyes were gentle, and Rachel was beautiful and lovely. 18Jacob
> loved Rachel and he said, "I will serve you seven years for your
> younger daughter Rachel." 19Laban said, "It is better that I should
> give her to you than to any other man; stay with me." 20So Jacob
> served seven years for Rachel, and they seemed to him but a few
> days because of the love he had for her.*

Jacob cannot have failed to make himself useful. He himself was a
shepherd and in his love for Rachel (Ramban) he wanted to help her
and be close to her. Laban recognized in him a good worker and liked

to keep him. Equivocal as the word brother is, he might perhaps have liked to hear the answer, "Certainly, I am your kinsman and will always be glad to serve you for nothing." The possibility that Jacob as a volunteer might leave any time may also not have suited him.

Verse 16. The name Leah has been interpreted as either cow or lady; Rachel means an ewe. We already know of Rachel, but did not yet know that she is the younger one which is indispensable for the following narrative.

Verse 17. The opening words are usually translated as Leah's eyes were weak or dim, without brilliance. However an ancestress of Israel would not be described as ugly; Leah later shows herself no less high-spirited than Rachel. The Bible wants to mention something exquisite of them both. *Beautiful* the Hebrew word refers to the figure, the proportions of the limbs. *Lovely* refers to the subjective impression of the person looking at her.

Verse 18. Jacob loves Rachel and will serve seven years for her. This is not meant as a price paid for the bride as such a custom never existed in Israel. It would also be rash of Jacob to make the highest offer immediately instead of waiting to hear Laban's demands and then try to lower the price.

This is rather an example of a motive which is a favorite one in the poetry, legend, and fairy tales of all peoples and ages—the testing of the suitor, the bride as a reward for a deed of valor or hard work as price for the bride. Other examples in the Bible are Josh. 15,16 (Caleb's daughter) and I Sam. 17,25 (Saul's daughter). Jacob, in the youthful fire of his love, offers to do the utmost in his power, to serve for seven long years.

The words *For your younger daughter Rachel* show the passion of the suitor for the object of his love, for her and for no one else. The scene at the well had been a prelude, but there the motive had only been a feeling of kinship, and the deed had been an isolated act of valor. This labor inspired by love is more sober, but also infinitely harder. Jacob personifies the heroism of prosaic labor; its loyalty and perseverance come from the quiet glow of steady devotion to an ideal. Deep feeling and suppressed poetry come to light in these words.

Verse 19. This is a masterfully ambiguous answer, seemingly full of honesty and well acted composure. Laban has expected this proposal for a long time and has prepared his reply. It is in fact the rule in the region that cousins marry each other. As natural as Laban's answer sounds, does he really promise him Rachel or does he directly tie Jacob's stay to it? Almost condescendingly he says, "stay."

Verse 20. The years pass quickly for Jacob because he does his work happily. Later (31,38 ff.) we shall hear how much toil and perseverance the service meant for him.

> *21Then Jacob said to Laban, "Give me my wife that I may go in to her, for my time is completed." 22So Laban gathered together all the men of the place and made a feast. 23But in the evening he took his daughter Leah and brought her to Jacob; and he went in to her. 24Laban gave his maid Zilpah to his daughter Leah to be her maid.*

My wife she had become his by Laban's promise as Jacob had understood it.

Verse 22. On such an occasion one cannot be closefisted; everyone in town is invited, yet Laban schemes.

Verse 23. As the bride is veiled he succeeds in substituting Leah in the evening, and Jacob, completely unsuspecting, drunk of love and blind from love, allows himself to be deceived.

Verse 24. A maid is part of the dowry; she therefore remains inseparable from the wife.

> *25And in the morning, behold, it was Leah; and Jacob said to Laban. "What is this you have done to me? Did I not serve with you for Rachel? Why then have you deceived me?" 26Laban said, "It is not so done in our place, to give the younger before the first-born. 27Complete the week of this one and we will give you the other also in return for serving me another seven years." 28Jacob did so and completed her week; then Laban gave him his daughter Rachel to wife. 29Laban gave his maid Bilhah to his daughter Rachel to be her maid. 30So Jacob went in to Rachel also, and he loved Rachel more than Leah, and served him for another seven years.*

As chapter 27 is known to the reader he will think of retribution. Jacob had disguised himself to deceive his father: now he is deceived by the veil and takes the older daughter instead of the younger. Jacob is indignant; this is fraud.

Verse 26. Laban does not apologize, but claims to have acted correctly. Besides he does not want to refuse him Rachel.

Verse 27. Wait the week of the wedding, then you shall get the other too, but it has also been understood to mean the seven years of service. The wedding might have taken place sometime before the completion of the seven years. Laban remits nothing of his claim. His only concession is that Jacob shall get Rachel at once, but in return for seven more years of service. Jacob is married to two sisters at the same time, contrary to later law (Lev. 18,18). Laban has deceived not only Jacob, but also Rachel.

> *31When the Lord saw that Leah was unloved, he opened her womb; but Rachel was barren. 32And Leah conceived and bore a son, and she called his name Reuben (See, a son); for she said, "Because the Lord has seen my affliction; surely now my husband will love me." 33She conceived again and bore a a son, and said, "Because the Lord has heard that I am unloved, he has given me this son also"; and she called his name Simeon (Hearing). 34Again she conceived and bore a son, and said, "Now this time my husband will be devoted to me, because I have born him three sons"; therefore his name was called Levi (Devotion). 35And she conceived again and bore a son, and said, "This time I will praise the Lord"; therefore she called his name Judah (Praise); then she ceased bearing.*

The wife unloved due to no fault of her own is compensated by the just God and preferred by him, so that the husband must love her as the mother of his children (compare I Sam. 1).

The names of the sons are pairs of corresponding ideas: Seeing —Hearing, Devotion—Praise. The original meaning of the names cannot be recognized.

Chapter 30

When Rachel saw that she bore Jacob no children, Rachel envied
her sister; and she said to Jacob, "Give me children, or I shall
die." ²Jacob's anger was kindled against Rachel, and he said,
"Am I in the place of God, who has withheld from you the fruit of
the womb?" ³Then she said, "Here is my maid Bilhah; go in to
her, that she may bear upon my knees, and even I may have
children through her." ⁴So she gave him her maid Bilhah as a
wife; and Jacob went in to her. ⁵And Bilhah conceived and bore
Jacob a son. ⁶Then Rachel said, "God has judged me, and has also
heard my voice and given me a son"; therefore she called his
name Dan (He judged). ⁷Rachel's maid Bilhah conceived again
and bore Jacob a second son. ⁸Then Rachel said, "With divine
wrestlings I have wrestled with my sister, and have prevailed"; so
she called his name Naphtali (Wrestling).

Rachel is unhappy about her barrenness and envies her sister which
is human and most natural. A childless wife has failed; everything else
which the world may offer her is only a substitute. Rachel not only cries
for a child, but for a son whom she would like to bear for "Jacob." It is a
matter of honor for her to become likewise the mother of tribal chiefs in
Israel (See 25,22) The love of her husband is not enough.

Verse 2. Jacob understands her complaint as if she regarded him at
fault or believed him weary of her. He replies indignantly which must
have been very depressing for her, "It is God who denies you
children!" Rachel had only wanted to prepare for a different step (verse
3).

Verse 3. She makes the suggestion once proposed by Sarah (16,2).
This is also a way of becoming a mother.

Verse 5. She always mentions God in the names which she gives to
the sons as a reply to Jacob's words in verse 2.

Verse 6. *God heard my voice.* She had cried to him too.

Verse 8. *Divine wrestlings* a wrestling for God; see our later discussion. The two names again form a pair, Judgement and Strife.

> ⁹*When Leah saw that she had ceased bearing children, she took her maid Zilpah and gave her to Jacob as a wife.* ¹⁰*Then Leah's maid Zilpah bore Jacob a son.* ¹¹*And Leah said, "Good Fortune!" so she called his name Gad (Fortune).* ¹²*Leah's maid Zilpah bore Jacob a second son.* ¹³*And Leah said, "Happy am I! For the women will call me happy"; so she called his name Asher (Happy).*

Rachel complains that she can bear no children, Leah that she can bear no more.

Verse 11. In Is. 65,11 Gad is a deity whose worship is frequently attested in Phoenicia, Syria, and Arabia.

Verse 13. The two names are again a pair of related ideas; Good Fortune and Happiness.

> ¹⁴*In the days of wheat harvest Reuben went and found mandrakes in the field and brought them to his mother Leah. Then Rachel said to Leah, "Give me, I pray, some of your son's mandrakes."* ¹⁵*But she said to her, "Is it a small matter that you have taken away my husband? Would you take away my son's mandrakes also?" Rachel said, "Then he may lie tonight with you for your son's mandrakes".* ¹⁶*When Jacob came from the field in the evening, Leah went out to meet him, and said, "You must come in to me; for I have hired you with my son's mandrakes." So he lay with her that night.*

The mandrakes which Reuben finds in the days of the wheat harvest, May or June, occur also in Song.7,14. They frequently grow in Israel and neighboring countries; their fruits are like smooth little apples of a dirty yellow color and the size of a musk nut. They are regarded as a pain-relieving narcotic and as an aphrodisiac. This however does not justify the claim that Rachel asks for them to become fertile. She says nothing of that nature, nor are the following births, of Leah or Rachel, ascribed to this effect. The births are rather attributed to God who is made the subject of the events with even greater emphasis than previously.

The opposite occurs as Leah bears children for giving the mandrakes away, while Rachel does not become fertile for a long time. Besides Jacob, this vigorous young man who afterwards hires himself out again for many more years of hard service, was neither weak nor senile.

Verse 15. *You have taken away my husband.* As Rachel married Jacob who was already Leah's husband. She, not Rachel, always speaks of him as "my husband" (29,32 and 34;30,15,18,20). She regards it her destiny to bear the children who will be the tribal ancestors of Israel according to the divine promise which cannot have remained unknown to her. After four sons her fertility stops; she worries, but provides for further births by giving her maid to Jacob. This means a greater sacrifice of pride for her than for Rachel who saw no other possibility of getting children. With four sons she had already regarded Jacob as completely her own. Yet she is willing to share him with her maid. She had prayed to God to be rewarded for this; God who heard Rachel (verse 6), also hears her (verse 17). She finds her reward not in the births of her maid, but in Issachar (Reward) to whom she herself ʒives birth.

One might even question whether the old identification of the flowers with mandrakes as an aphrodisiac is necessary. The situation is no more erotic than flowers generally are. Little Reuben, as small children do, brings some flowers of the field to his mother while Rachel is present. Each woman immediately thinks how nice it would be to offer them to the husband. When Rachel expresses this wish Leah replies, "Have you not his love already?" Nevertheless she does not refuse her, Give him flowers, if he only remains my husband. Rachel reciprocates through a greater sacrifice. She will be content to present only a sign of love to her husband.

Verse 16. *I have hired you* said in preparation for the name Issachar.

> [17]And God harkened to Leah, and she conceived and bore Jacob a fifth son. [18]Leah said, "God has given me my hire because I gave my maid to my husband"; so she called his name Issachar (Hire). [19]And Leah conceived again, and she bore Jacob a sixth son. [20]Then Leah said, "God has endowed me with a good dowry; this time my husband will appreciate me because I have born him six sons"; so she called his name Zebulun (Dowry). [21]Afterwards she bore a daughter and called her name Dinah. [22]Then God remembered Rachel, and God harkened to her and opened her womb. [23]She conceived and bore a son, and said, "God has taken away

my reproach"; ²⁴and she called his name Joseph (Addition), saying, "May the Lord add to me another son!"

Verse 20. The Hebrew name Zebulun is a double play on words; on
dowry, and on a word which probably means appreciation. God is the
subject as with Issachar and "my husband" also occurs in the explanation. The two names, Issachar and Zebulun express the idea of hire and
gift.

Verse 21. With all her children Leah reaches the significant number
of seven.

Verse 23. This name is in Hebrew again a play on two words, "to take
away", and "to add". Fourteen years after Jacob and Rachel met she
bears her first son. She has waited as long as he served for her; both are
models of perseverance.
Of Jacob's twelve sons (35,22) Leah bore six, Rachel two, Zilpah,
Leah's maid two, Bilhah, Rachel's maid two. The wives together eight,
which is twice as many as the maids; Leah with her maid eight which is
twice as many as Rachel with her maid. In the case of Issachar and
Zebulun Leah had hired the husband and stands in the place of Rachel;
so each one really has four. That may be the intention of the episode of
the mandrakes. The sacrifice of the wives in letting their maids take
their places are the "divine wrestlings" (verse 8), a wrestling for the
divine blessing of children.
The marriages of Jacob form a counterpart to chapter 27. There two
brothers fight for the father's blessing, here two wives for the
possession and love of the husband. In both cases the formal right is on
the side of the older, of Esau as the first-born, of Leah as the legitimate
first wife. Each time the younger one has a better moral claim, Jacob as
the heir of the divine promises, Rachel as the beloved wife. In each
story occur substitution and deception. The one fraud is punished by
the other, as indicated by the use of the same Hebrew word in 27,35 and
29,25. Jacob, formerly the guilty party, is now the victim. The girls are
innocent. Thus Leah is not repudiated and is first remembered by God;
Rachel also does not remain forsaken. Her long wait is a punishment
and a test for Jacob.
The story must know of the prohibition against marrying two sisters
simultaneously, but God educates men through their trespasses and
sufferings; and the letter of the law is not the last word. Thus Rachel
finally triumphs. The underlying emotions are only intimated in the
story; namely the persevering loyalty of the patriarch whom even mean

fraud cannot divert from his purpose; the wives' jealous longing to become the mother of his children; their wrestlings for God; their triumphant happiness; the tender play with love flowers; and above all God's justice and loving care.

The Labor Contract verses 25–42

²⁵When Rachel had born Joseph, Jacob said to Laban, "Send me away, that I may go to my own home and country. ²⁶Give me my wives and my children for whom I have served you, and let me go: for you know the service which I have given you." ²⁷But Laban said to him, "If you will allow me to say so, I have learned by divination that the Lord has blessed me because of you." ²⁸Then he said, "Name your wages from me; I will give." ²⁹Jacob said to him, "You yourself know how I have served you, and how your cattled fared with me. ³⁰For you had little before I came, and it has increased abundantly; and the Lord has blessed you since I came. But now when shall I provide for my own household also?"

If Jacob quickly accepts the offer to continue serving Laban for wages and has a proposition ready, it proves that his talk of leaving was only an introduction to negotiations. He takes the birth of the first child by his favorite wife as occasion; he now has a family and longs (28,21) for his home remembering his youth in familiar surroundings. Joseph shall grow up there too.

Verse 26. It must have been controversial whether Jacob could take his wives and children with him after the completion of his period of service. Otherwise Jacob's secret flight and Laban's claim in 31,43 could not be understood. Jacob obliges Laban by requesting formal permission, but also makes his own point of view perfectly clear; it is his good right because of his services. His thrice repeated "service" indicates that he will now deal with their relationship realistically without the fancy notions of a lover.

Verse 27. Laban does not hear well, when he dislikes something. He never repeats the words of the other party so not to let himself be bound by them. He only speaks in half-finished sentences which do not concede anything and permit him to withdraw. His answer here is extremely tricky. He speaks to Jacob as to a superior. Laban needs Jacob, however his politeness contains a hidden irony; in contrast to Jacob's constant mention of his "services", he assures him that he feels as his servant; yet, he continues piously raising his eyes to heaven, "the blessing came from above". He speaks of the Lord to please Jacob, but his own religious ambiguity expresses itself in his pagan talk of divination. He wants Jacob to stay, but does not frankly say so and let the other side gain the upper hand.

Verse 28. Jacob does not want to accept such vague advances. Laban finally brings himself to a positive offer, but as briefly as possible; each word, particularly the last "give", without an object, comes from the bleeding heart of a miser.

Verse 29. Before Jacob consents he must still correct Laban's speech, no blurring of the facts! It was my toil as you well know. He becomes very plain-spoken and openly contrasts the former and the present wealth of Laban.

Verse 30. What did you have when I arrived and what do you have now? Do not forget this, even if *the Lord has blessed you*, a fact which a man like Jacob naturally does not deny. He does not, like Laban, say the Lord has blessed you because of me, but only: *since I came.*

> *[31]He said, "What shall I give you?" Jacob said, "You shall not give me anything; if you will do this for me, I will again feed your flock and keep it: [32]let me pass through all your flock today, removing from it every speckled and spotted sheep, and every reddish lamb, and the speckled and the spotted among the goats; and such shall be my wages. [33]So my righteousness will answer for me later, when it comes to my wages with you. Every one that is not speckled and spotted among the goats and reddish among the lambs if found with me, shall be counted stolen."*

To this fervent speech Laban, not wanting to dwell on the past, replies with a heavy heart in only three words with the repeated question, "What shall I give you?" Then Jacob suggests that he "give" nothing; nothing shall pass from the hand of the one to the hand of the other.

Verse 32. They shall start from the present status. After Jacob's explicit declaration of verse 31, this verse does not mean that the eliminated animals shall be his share, but those born in the future with these colors.

Verse 33. If all of these are eliminated, I will start with nothing. If you ask from where shall such animals come in the future, let that be my worry. I will trust in my righteousness.

God has blessed me for your benefit so far and will do the same for my benefit. This righteousness will testify for me at the time of payment. No non-colored animal will remain in my possession; otherwise you may count it as stolen; this word will be the basis for Laban's later accusation against Jacob.

³⁴Laban said. "Well, may it be as you have said." ³⁵And that day he removed the he-goats that were speckled and spotted, and all the she-goats that were speckled and spotted, every one that had white on it, and every lamb that was reddish, and put them in charge of his sons; ³⁶and he set a distance of three days' journey between himself and Jacob; and Jacob fed the rest of Laban's flock.

The answer of the cautious Laban is again as brief as possible and intentionally unclear as in 29,19. His deceitful words mean, it would indeed be nice if you have good luck with future births.

Verse 35. Laban removes the animals, closely watching their sex of which Jacob had not spoken, to prevent the future birth of colored animals. He gives the eliminated animals to his sons.

Verse 36. He takes another precaution by setting a distance of three days between the herds.

³⁷And Jacob took fresh rods of poplar and almond and plane, and peeled white streaks in them, exposing the white of the rods. ³⁸He set the rods which he had peeled in front of the flocks in the runnels, that is, the watering troughs where the flocks came to drink. And since they bred when they came to drink, ³⁹the flocks bred in front of the rods and so the flocks brought forth striped, speckled, and spotted. ⁴⁰And Jacob separated the lambs, and set the faces of the flocks toward the striped and all the reddish in the flock of Laban; and he put his own droves apart, and did not put them with Laban's flock. ⁴¹Whenever the stronger of the flock were breeding Jacob laid the rods in the runnels before the eyes of the flock, that they might breed among the rods, ⁴²but for the feeble of the flock he did not lay them there; so the feeble were Laban's and the stronger Jacob's. ⁴³Thus the man grew exceeding-

ly rich, and had large flocks, maidservants, menservants, and camels and asses.

It has been claimed that Jacob used a trick which might be called a fraud in order to influence the births in his favor. Indeed the belief in such practices has always been widely spread. If these things occasionally happen, they are too rare to be used as a successful principle of breeding and have never been applied as such. Shepherds, peasants, businessmen may be superstitious—according to the principle "If it does not help it will not hurt". They may surround their activities with pious, mystical, or irrational accessories, but among every people and in all ages they are practical, realistic men who rely only on certainties.

In 31,10ff. Jacob himself gives a different explanation; the deity is supposed to have caused this play of color to have shown it to him. Here is no contradiction between profane and religious explanation; two different aspects of the same events are reported in separate parts of the narration. Thus Jacob after the dream, which the Bible for good reasons reports only later, sets these rods into the watering troughs as a gesture which shall not bring forth the miracle, but only accentuate it. Similarly Moses and Aaron stretch out their staff or their hand for the plagues in Egypt. Nothing is more exclusively in God's power than life, breeding, and giving birth. Only he can cause spotted cattle to be born. People, seeing Jacob's action and taking it for the cause, might have believed that the rods brought about the abnormal births. Even the old cattlebreeder, Laban, never thinks of blaming Jacob for this. The story is an example of Jacob's trust in the promised divine aid and transforms a folkloristic superstition through higher religion.

Verse 40. This verse is very difficult. How could there still be striped and reddish animals in Laban's herd as they had been eliminated (verse 35) and graze three days' distance away? I know no satisfactory explanation.

Verse 42. This action of Jacob is a concession to Laban, so that he may at least get some animals.

Chapter 31

Jacob's Flight.

Now Jacob heard that the sons of Laban were saying, "Jacob has taken all that was our father's; and from what was our father's he has gained all this wealth." ²And Jacob saw by Laban's face that he did not regard him with favor as he did before. ³Thus the Lord said to Jacob, "Return to the land of your fathers and to your kindred, and I will be with you."

Now master of maidservants and manservants Jacob has become a big lord. His wealth will diminish the inheritance of the sons.

Verse 2. Jacob hears the loud talk of the young folks. The cautious old man is quiet, but cannot hide his dark looks at the daily losses.

Verse 3. Jacob might not have been concerned about the young folks, but the face of the old man is a graver matter; it is time to make an end. A divine revelation comes to Jacob at just the proper moment, according to 28,15.

The land of your fathers only said of Jacob. It is his fatherland as he is the first whose father and grandfather have resided in the same land. Jacob feels loyalty to it; abroad he longs for it and would prefer never to leave it 37,1;46,3. Two motives for returning combine, a practical consideration and a religious impulse as frequently. His flight from home had been determined by several causes.

⁴So Jacob sent and called Rachel and Leah into the field where his flock was, ⁵and said to them, "I see by the face of your father that he does not regard me with favor as he did before. But the God of my father has been with me. ⁶You know that I have served your father with all my strength; ⁷yet your father has made sport of me and changed my wages ten times, but God did not permit him to harm me. ⁸If he said, 'The spotted shall be your wages', then all the flock bore spotted; and if he said, 'The striped shall be your wages', then all the flock bore striped. ⁹Thus God has taken away the cattle of your father and given them to me. ¹⁰In the mating season of the flock I lifted up my eyes, and saw in a dream that the he-goats which leaped upon the flock were striped, spotted, and mottled. ¹¹Then the angel of the Lord said to me in the dream, 'Jacob', and I said 'Here I am!' ¹²And he said, 'Lift up your eyes and see, all the goats that leap upon the flock are striped, spotted, and mottled; for I have seen all that Laban is doing to you. ¹³I am the God of Bethel, where you annointed a pillar and made a vow to me. Now arise, go forth from this land, and return to the land of your birth.' "

Rachel is mentioned first; as she is the main wife (46,19); Jacob had remained so long for her sake. *Into the field* where no one can listen. *Where his flock was,* the object of the conflict, but *his* flock as he will explain. Jacob must persuade his wives as he cannot force them to emigrate to a foreign country; it brought them into inner conflict.

Verse 5. He does not refer to the evil talk of the sons, as only the father is decisive; he interprets his unfriendly face accordingly. Jacob knows that his success angers him, but that is God's doing.

Verse 6 He purposely always says "Your father".

Verse 7. After these generalities he explains the source of the colored animals. Jacob wants to speak of two things; Laban's constant changes of terms, and the reason why this did not help him. Only two of the 'ten' changes are mentioned; the big number is an emphatical exaggeration. Laban could find occasion for changes after every birth as Jacob had innocently set no time limit to the conditions or to the length of his service. Only here when Jacob wants to complain to his wives are the changes reported. They had not profited Laban as God did not allow this to happen.

Verse 8. Laban's conditions are described with dramatic vividness. The colors of the animals changed in my favor, regardless of his stipulations.

Verse 10. Jacob explains this, and makes it impressive through speaking in a particularly circumstantial and solemn way.

Verse 11. An angel of God expressly calls his attention to it, so that he may not think the dream meaningless, but as an intentional arrangement.

Verse 12. Jacob does not speak of the rods of which his wives surely knew; it again proves that the rods were not the cause in his eyes.

Verse 13. The stone which you marked for your return awaits you; "I am waiting for you there." *From this land* where they treat you so badly into the land which is your home. The long skillfully composed speech terminates with an unspoken question which puts a decision before the women.

> *14Then Rachel and Leah answered him, "Is there any portion or inheritance left to us in our father's house? 15Are we not regarded by him as foreigners? For he has sold us, and has been using up the money given for us. 16All the property which God has taken away from our father belongs to us and our children; now then, whatever God has said to you, do."*

Jacob's speech has stirred them, and the divine call effects the women as a command. With passionate, indignant words they side with their husband; Rachel leads.

Verse 15. Is this the action of a father? He sold us as if we were slaves, for the price of the services of our husband.

Verse 16. This verse is certainly an exaggeration caused by their excitement.

> *17So Jacob arose, and set his sons and his wives on camels; 18and he drove away all his cattle, all his livestock which he had gained. the cattle in his possession which he had acquired in Paddan-Aram, to go to the land of Canaan to his father Isaac. 19Laban had gone to shear his sheep, and Rachel stole her father's Terafim. 20And Jacob stole the heart of Laban the Aramaean, in that he did not tell him that he intended to flee. 21He fled with all that he had: he arose and crossed the River, and set his face to the hill country of Gilead.*

Verse 18. Jacob only took his rightfully acquired property.

Verse 19. Shearing the sheep was a gay occasion with guests; it was the shepherd's harvest festival. The celebration occurs at a distance from the residence and is a well suited motive for absence.

The word "to steal" is the important word of the succeeding narration, particularly in the dispute between Jacob and Laban. A servant who leaves secretly is always suspected of having taken something unlawfully; the master immediately investigates whether anything is missing. Thus Laban's pursuit is motivated in a human way. *Terafim* are according to parallel passages religious objects, often used for oracles. They seem to have had the shape of a human figure, but must have been small enough for Rachel to hide them under her seat. Whatever else has been said about the word is only guesswork.

This report shall throw light on Laban's religion. Rachel's motive was either to take revenge on her father or (Rashbam) to prevent his inquiry from the Terafim about their flight. He hears of it anyhow as the large caravan could not go unnoticed. Perhaps she wanted to have religious objects of her home with her in a strange country as in the times of the kings women married into Israel imported the religious cults of their own lands.

The Bible calls Rachel's action "stealing" without circumlocution and thus stigmatizes it.

Verse 20. The secret departure of Jacob is also called "stealing"; namely of Laban's heart. The phrase is used in II Sam. 15,6 for Absalom's deceptive activities through which he tried to win the people to his cause. In later Hebrew it became an established term for creating a false assumption in someone. The following words shall characterize the reproach of Laban in verses 26 f. as unjustified and unreasonable. Jacob had no choice but to flee and therefore must dissemble.

Verse 21. *The River* can only be the Euphrates.

> ²²When it was told Laban on the third day that Jacob had fled, ²³he took his kinsmen with him and pursued him for seven days and followed close after him into the hill country of Gilead. But God came to Laban the Aramaean in a dream by night, and said to him, "Take heed that you say not a word to Jacob, either good or bad." ²⁵And Laban overtook Jacob. Now Jacob had pitched his tent in the hill country, and Laban with his kinsmen encamped in the hill country of Gilead.

Verse 24. *Take heed that you say not a word to Jacob* cannot mean *not speak to him at all,* but as we will see in verse 29, he shall not harm him, not take anything from him, nor try to force his return. It is not correct that Laban shall abstain from judgement concerning Jacob's flight, because he does not do so although he repeats the divine speech literally (verse 29), nor does he acquiesce in Jacob's flight; on the contrary he expresses his opinion profusely. The deity intervenes on behalf of Jacob at two decisive moments—when in danger of not getting any profit, and now again as he stands to lose everything; God had promised to be with him until he has safely returned home.

26And Laban said to Jacob, "What have you done, that you have stolen my heart, and carried away my daughters like captives of the sword? 27Why did you flee secretly, and cheat me, and did not tell me, so that I might have sent you away with mirth and songs, with tambourine and lyre? 28And why did you not permit me to kiss my sons and daughters farewell? Now you have done foolishly. 29It is in my power to do you harm; but the God of your father spoke to me last night, saying, 'Take heed that you speak to Jacob neither good nor bad!' 30And now you have gone away because you longed greatly for your father's house, but why did you steal my gods?" 31Jacob answered Laban. "Because I was afraid, for I thought that you would take your daughters from me by force. 32Any one with whom you find your gods shall not live. In the presence of our kinsmen point out what I have that is yours, and take it." Now Jacob did not know that Rachel had stolen them.

Laconic Laban becomes eloquent at the end. The divine warning makes him powerless, so he first puts on an air of sweetness which hardly conceals his anger. Amiable regrets are in the end followed by his trump card which he had readied from the beginning. He starts with the mildest reproach and closes with the crudest—theft. What have you done, and what have you lost by your folly!

Verse 27. You have cheated me, deprived me, not yourself, of a nice leave-taking party which I would have arranged if you had told me. He could not even kiss his sons, his grandchildren goodbye! Here he shows sincere sentiment as proven by putting his grandchildren first.

Verse 29. A higher power forbids his taking revenge. Laban calls it the *God of your father,* meaning Abraham.

Verse 30. The anger of Laban is discharged in mocking words which in Hebrew are long and drawn out. This mother's pet wants to go home! Now without transition, his final triumph. He does not speak of Terafim, but says "my gods", in order to enhance Jacob's supposed misdeed.

Verse 31. Jacob is indignant and repays him in the same coin. In his tenderness for his daughters, Laban might have gone so far as to keep them back and thus to crown his former fraud. Similarly exaggerating Jacob calls this "to take them from me by force." I, a thief? No, you are a robber; at least you would be capable of that.

Any one with whom you find your gods shall not live. According to widely spread conceptions of the time and its common law, the theft of sacred objects was punishable by death as we find in Hittite laws. Jacob's indignation was sincere, not pretended as that of Laban—had he only known the truth! We anxiously follow Laban's search.

> *33So Laban went into Jacob's tent, and into Leah's tent, and into the tent of the two maidservants, but he did not find them. And he went out of Leah's tent and entered Rachel's. 34Now Rachel had taken the Terafim and put them in the camel's saddle, and sat upon them: Laban felt all about the tent, but did not find them. 35And she said to her father, "Let not my lord be angry that I cannot rise before you, for the way of women is upon me." So he searched, but did not find the Terafim.*

It seems as if Rachel was first passed; in fact Laban went into Jacob's tent, then into Leah's, and from there, as is expressly stated, into Rachel's, finally into that of the two maidservants. The reader whose heart beats anxiously in Rachel's tent has the satisfaction of following Laban into the last tents. Each woman had her own tent, so that the husband could be alone with her (Ramban).

Verse 34. In verse 30 the Bible clearly mocks: a god who can be stolen! Now one who can be sat upon! Even worse a woman is supposed to have been seated upon him when "the way of women" was upon her!

Verse 35. Respectfully she calls her father "my lord". The failure of the search is once more stressed at the end. After her theft, Rachel must tell a lie. Laban is cheated by the very daughter whom he made the object of a fraud. The Midrash, demanding a punishment for every sin says (Bereshith Rabba): for this behavior Rachel died soon afterwards. Perhaps this is really the intention of the Bible.

> ³⁶Then Jacob became angry, and upbraided Laban; Jacob said to Laban, "What is my offense? What is my sin, that you have hotly pursued me? ³⁷Although you have felt through all my goods, what have you found of all your household goods? Set it here before my kinsmen and your kinsmen, that they may decide between us two. ³⁸These twenty years I have been with you; your ewes and your she-goats have not miscarried, and I have not eaten the rams of your flocks. ³⁹That which was torn by wild beasts I did not bring to you; I bore the loss of it myself; of my hand you required it, whether stolen by day, or stolen by night. ⁴⁰Thus I was; by day the heat consumed me, and the cold by night, and my sleep fled from my eyes. ⁴¹These twenty years I have been in your house; I served you fourteen years for your two daughters, and six years for your flock, and you have changed my wages ten times. ⁴²If the God of my father, the God of Abraham and the Fear of Isaac, had not been on my side, surely now you would have sent me away empty-handed. God saw my affliction and the labor of my hands, and rebuked you last night."

Now Jacob's blood is boiling. He had suffered the search and contained himself during it. As soon as his innocence has been revealed, he pours out his indignation at the offensive suspicion, and adds all the anger suppressed over these long years. He speaks as man to man, therefore expressly the names. Am I a criminal or villain that you went after me in hot pursuit?

Verse 37. Did you find anything by the insulting search of my belongings?

Verse 38. I a thief? After being the most conscientious servant for twenty years. There would have been plenty of opportunity to harm you. On the contrary I have kept your property from damage and loss, more than my duty. I nursed the ewes and she-goats when they were breeding, so that they did not miscarry; or—as miscarriages cannot have been lacking in all those years (Abrabanel)—you never heard of them. I did not eat the fat rams. This must not be taken literally, as if this was the good right of a shepherd, but is meant as a challenge: are they not there; have they perhaps disappeared into my stomach?

Verse 39. When an animal was lost or torn by a wild beast, I did not regard myself free from responsibility according to law, or was allowed to free myself from it by bringing evidence that it was torn (Ex 22,12); *I bore the loss of it myself* because you did not recognize an "act of God" (Seforno). Growing emphatic Jacob uses ancient poetical language in Hebrew.

Verse 40. He explains in rhythmic sentences, outdoing Laban's words in verse 27, what all this meant to him. One must remember the extraordinary differences in temperature between day and night in the Near East (compare Jer. 36,30).

Verse 41. The twenty years need elaboration, because Jacob wants to speak of his flock for which the first fourteen years need not be considered.

Verse 42. The *Fear of Isaac* refers to Isaac's experience when he was bound to be sacrificed in chapter 22 (ibn Ezra). The trip to Mount Moriah and the terrible hour when Isaac had lain bound on the altar, apparently demanded by God as a sacrifice, must have been decisive for his whole life and thought.

You would have sent me away empty-handed not like a faithful servant Deut. 15,13) who brought you so much profit.

> [43]Then Laban answered and said to Jacob, "The daughters are my daughters, the children are my children, the flocks are my flocks, and all that you see is mine. But what can I do this day to these my daughters, or to their children whom they have born? [44]Come now, let us make a covenant you and I; and let it be a witness between you and me."

Laban has no defense. He can only cover his retreat with a general empty claim which he does not substantiate and pretends not to press. How could I intend to do evil to your wives (Rashi); they are my daughters and the children are born by them (Bechor Shor). *Today* as circumstances have developed.

Verse 44. Keep what you have and we will part in peace. As it was not yet certain, it is intentionally not said what the witness shall be.

The Concluding Of An Alliance verses 45–54

[45]So Jacob took a stone and set it up as a pillar. [46]And Jacob said

to his kinsmen, "Gather stones," and they took stones and made a
heap: and they ate there by the heap. ⁴⁷Laban called it Jagar-
sahadutha but Jacob called it Galed. ⁴⁸Laban said, "This heap is a
witness between you and me today." (Therefore they named it
Galed, ⁴⁹and Mizpah, for they say "The Lord watch between you
and me, when we are absent one from the other.") ⁵⁰"If you
ill-treat my daughters, or if you take wives besides my daughters,
although no man is with us, remember, God is witness between
you and me." ⁵¹Then Laban said to Jacob, "See this heap and the
pillar, which I have set between you and me. ⁵²This heap is a
witness, and the pillar is a witness, that I will not pass over this
heap to you, and you will not pass over this heap and this pillar
to me, for harm. ⁵³The God of Abraham and the God of Nahor, the
Gods of their father, judge between us." So Jacob swore by the
Fear of his father Isaac, ⁵⁴and Jacob slaughtered on the mountain
and called his kinsmen to eat bread; and they ate bread and
tarried all night on the mountain.

The passage contains some annotations which interrupt the
speeches. Antiquity did not possess graphic aids like marginal notes
and parentheses. Such remarks introduced by "therefore. . . . " are
very frequent. Verse 47 contains the only Aramaic word in the five
books of Moses: Jagar-sahadutha. This as well as the remark "the Gods
of their father" finds its explanation in the different religious attitude of
Jacob and Laban. The latter is a polytheist who knows and recognizes
the Lord (24,50;30,27) but differentiates in him the God of Abraham
who had followed this God's call (12,1), and the God of his own
grandfather Nahor who had remained in Haran, (see Josh. 24,2). He also
calls Terafim his gods and practices divination. The expression "the
Gods of our father" was therefore necessary because naming two Gods
is unusual and requires explanation.

It is a covenant between two religiously different parties. In such a
case it was the general practice in antiquity to call on the deities of both
parties to guard the treaty. We find this in a state treaty between Ramses
II of Egypt and the king of Heta, also in the state treaties discovered in
Bogazköy and in the El-Amarna letters. Laban expresses himself in this
way and calls upon each God of the the ancestors of both parties. Jacob
swears only by the God of his father Isaac, in whom the faith of
Abraham had been continued.

Verse 45. Jacob, accepting Laban's suggestion, erects a stone as a
pillar, as "the witness." Laban had suggested both witness and a

covenant. To the latter belongs a meal and for this Jacob has a heap of stones gathered as a table.

Verse 46. Now when friendship prevails, Jacob calls Laban and the relatives with him his kinsmen.

Verse 47. Each one names the heap in his own language, Laban in Aramaic. The Bible characterizes Laban as a foreigner, different from Jacob in language and faith.

Verse 48. Laban by the Aramaic name concurs in Jacob's interpretaion of the Hebrew Galed. Both mean heap of witness.

Verse 49. This calls forth an interpretation of Mizpa as "watchpost". The whole verse and already the end of verse 48 is in parenthesis as shown by the use of the term "the Lord", otherwise avoided in the entire story, particularly in the mouth of Laban, even in verses 50 and 53. It is a popular Israelitic saying, "May the Lord watch between you and me". Mizpa, a hill looking far into the land, shall remind of God in heaven from whom one cannot hide.

Verse 50. Only here begin the words of Laban for which the heap of stones shall be the witness. Two miseries can come over a wife in the house of her husband, ill-treatment or demotion from the position as the main wife. For this reason Laban had given maidservants to his daughters who might serve as concubines. He could be sure of them as they had grown up with their mistresses and were obedient. Such stipulations have also been found in texts from Bogazköy.

Verse 51. Laban recognizes the heap as well as the pillar.

Verse 52. This verse may be understood, contrary to the usual interpretation, as an obligation of Jacob and Laban to pass this border in order to aid each other in an emergency (Hiskuni). That would be a real alliance.

Verse 54. This verse does not speak of a sacrifice, but of fraternization after peace-making; a common meal unites the two parties. The most essential part of any meal was bread. It takes place on the mountain where Jacob had pitched his tent (verse 25) and he was the host. Laban stays over night as guest and departs only the following morning.

Chapter 32

*Early in the morning Laban arose, and kissed his grandchildren
and his daughters and blessed them; then Laban departed and
returned home. ²Jacob went on his way and angels of the Lord met
him; ³and when Jacob saw them, he said, "This is God's camp!"
So he called the name of that place Mahanaim (Two Camps).*

Laban kisses his grandchildren, as he had said in 31,28, a pleasant
trait, making him similar to Jacob (48,8 ff.); it is hard for him to part
from the grandchildren who are even mentioned before his daughters.
He blesses them; inspite of all he wishes them the best.

Verse 2. This verse reminds us of 28,11 ff.; again angels descend,
while the angels who had protected him abroad ascend. Thus God has
really brought him back, and as those angels had protected him against
Laban, these will protect him against Esau.

Verse 3. *Jacob saw them* but the vision is not elaborated as the dream
in 28,11 ff. He calls the place "Two Camps" after the twofold appearance of angels.

The Meaning Of The Story.

Laban the Aramaean and Jacob, the father of the future Israel, part
from each other in peace after an argument and conclude an alliance.
Laban charges Jacob always to keep his daughers in due state, as they
now go abroad; he takes the heap of stones as a witness for this and
calls upon the omniscient God as guardian. The covenant consists in
the obligation either to come to each other's aid beyond this border in
case of an emergency or to respect this border. The God of each party is
called as judge regarding this obligation. Nothing is written, but pillars
of stone become documents; they are erected at the place of the covenant and their names are a play on the names of the localities of the
covenant namely: Gilead—Galed; Mizpah—Mazevah (pillar). The story
is written in honor of the ancestral mothers of Israel and their children.

If Laban and Jacob are not sovereigns they are nevertheless the fathers and grandfathers of the ancestors of kings.

Jacob's Meeting With Esau

4Jacob sent messengers before him to Esau his brother in the land of Seir, the country of Edom, 5instructing them, "Thus you shall say to my lord Esau: 'Thus says your servant Jacob. I have sojourned with Laban and stayed until now; 6and I have gotten ox and ass, flocks, manservant and maidservant; and I have sent to tell my lord, in order that I may find favor in your sight.'"

Jacob sends messengers to express his submissiveness. Although Esau resides in another country, Jacob reports to him as he enters the homeland.

Verse 5. The messengers shall use the exact words of Jacob; above all they shall repeat that he calls Esau his lord and himself his servant. Hereby Jacob surrenders the claim derived from the father's blessing and revokes that fraud. He tries to represent himself, his experiences, and his condition as insignificant.

I have sojourned with Laban may sound as if it had been a brief visit which had been extended a little longer; or he may want to gloss over his former flight and give a different interpretation to his service with Laban. He merely calls him Laban, speaking of him cooly as if of a stranger. *I stayed until now* it had not been his intention to flee from Esau permanently.

Verse 6. Jacob wants to speak of his large possessions as modestly as possible, therefore the singular forms of ox, ass, etc. His precious camels (verse 16) are not mentioned at all. Yet these words open the attractive prospect of presents for Esau; first Jacob wants to discover where he stands. He hopes that Esau will graciously take note. He is careful with his expressions in order not to go too far.

7The messengers returned to Jacob, saying, "We came to your brother Esau, and he is coming to meet you, and four hundred men with him." 8Then Jacob was greatly afraid and distressed; and he divided the people that were with him, and the flocks and herds and camels, into two camps. 9thinking, "If Esau comes to the one camp and destroys it, then the camp which is left will escape."

Whereas he had not spoken of Esau as his brother before the messengers, they unaffectedly do so. The Midrash interprets it as: we came to your brother, but what a brother, Esau! The report of the messengers does not indicate whether they spoke to him in person, or his answer to their words, or any suspicions they may have of his intentions. The narration is brief and indefinite so as not to weaken the following story.

Verse 8. Jacob fears the worst in spite of the promise of divine protection. It is the physical fear which comes naturally over even the bravest man who may be confident of success (Abrabanel)

Verse 9. The word "camp" has here not completely lost its military meaning. Even if Jacob throws himself, his wives and children on the mercy of his ferocious brother, his stalwart men will not let themselves be killed without resistance. As the Midrash expresses it, Jacob prepares to meet Esau in three ways, by battle, by presents, and by prayer. The second camp may be able to excape while Esau is occupied with the first, or perhaps his rage will be satiated by one camp. Jacob, his wives, and children do not belong to the camps; they will meet Esau regardless of the outcome. Jacob tries to achieve the rescue of at least a part of the people and cattle; not everything must fall to Esau, a feature true to life. Jacob is afraid, but no coward; he is prudent and circumspect inspite of his worries. Finally he puts his trust in God to whom he now turns in prayer.

> ¹¹And Jacob said, "O God of my father Abraham and God of my father Isaac, O Lord who did say to me, 'Return to your country and to your kindred, and I will do you good', ¹¹I am not worthy of the least of all the steadfast love and all the faithfulness which you have shown to they servant for with only my staff I crossed this Jordan: and now I have become two camps. ¹²Deliver me, I pray you, from the hand of my brother, from the hand of Esau, for I fear him, lest he come and slay us all, the mothers with the children. ¹³But you did say, 'I will do you good, and make your descendants as the sand of the sea, which cannot be numbered for multitude.'"

This model prayer begins with an appeal to God, but can only plead God's relationship to him, not his own merit. God has been the God of Abraham and Isaac, of Jacob's grandfather and father. Jacob is a link in a natural chain, a grandson; his prayer appeals to historical precedent ; God must remain true to himself. God had also requested Jacob's return and promised his protection.

Verse 11. Should this appeal sound presumptuous Jacob corrects himself immediately. God owes him nothing, but has indeed done more than enough. Jacob has been able to return, and in what grand state! No one could set out poorer than he, with only a staff in his hand. Now he has such abundance that he had been able to divide it into two camps. This shows an overflowing measure of God's true, unmerited, and disinterested love towards me, your servant; for I am and want to be "your" servant. This alludes to his constant use of the words master and servant in regard to Esau. All this is more than God had promised and Jacob could expect; it is out of proportion to his importance and merit. The words are a classical expression of humility before God. Worry over his great possessions, half of which he expects to lose does not stifle Jacob's gratitude for God's rich gifts. He tried to belittle his possessions only before Esau.

Verse 12. His life is endangered, so after this introductory statement, Jacob offers his petition, the cry of his bitter need. Fear of the ferocious brother puts strong words into Jacob's mouth, which perhaps are a popular phrase for complete, merciless destruction; he will slay us all, the mothers with the children.

Verse 13. After your promises that is impossible! Jacob's prayer has been criticised for not conceding the wrong he has done; it does not show the humility of a repentant sinner facing the holy God. However a man cannot be expected to confess his sins in his cry for help; it would even be suspect were he to do so. It means more that Jacob reckons only with God's mercy and faithfulness; praying at this time is characteristic of him. He takes appropriate precautions, considers every possibility, and omits nothing which might win Esau, but anyone who merely observes him in his dealings with Esau and the world and does not see him standing before God, would know him imperfectly.

> *14So he lodged there that night, and took from what he had gotten a present for his brother Esau. 15two hundred she-goats and twenty he-goats, two hundred ewes and twenty rams. 16thirty milch camels with their colts, forty cows and ten bulls, twenty she-asses and ten he-asses. 17These he delivered into the hands of his servants, every drove by itself, and said to his servants. "Pass on before me, and put a space between drove and drove." 18He*

instructed the foremost, "When Esau my brother meets you, and
asks you, 'To whom do you belong? Where are you going? And
whose are these before you?' ¹⁹Then you shall say, 'They belong
to your servant Jacob; they are a present sent to my lord Esau; and
moreover he is behind us.'" ²⁰He likewise instructed the second
and the third and all who followed the droves, "You shall say the
same thing to Esau when you meet him. ²¹and you shall say,
'Moreover your servant Jacob is behind us.'" For he thought, "I
may appease him with the present that goes before me, and
afterwards I shall see his face; perhaps he will accept me." ²²So
the present passed on before him; and he himself lodged that
night in the camp.

As yet Jacob receives no answer to his prayer. He anyhow prepares to
win Esau by sending him a rich present and ransom. By a concrete act,
he designates himself as Esau's vassal (II Kings 17,3). He sends five
kinds of animals, male and female in the proper proportions, not only
for consumption, but to present Esau with the most complete breeding
stock. He conveys a part of his whole property to him. Together these
are 550 animals, a princely "present".

Verse 17. The manner of presentation is important for its full effect.
Each drove is a sufficient present in itself. Each time Esau shall think
that this is all; when another drove appears he shall be overwhelmed
and exclaim with wide eyes, "Still more?"

Verse 18. The instructions of Jacob to the servants are clever. They
shall act (Abrabanel) as if they do not know Esau who will meet them
and ask them questions, but their answers shall, seemingly without
intention, express all the respect of Jacob for his brother; each time they
shall say that he himself follows them. His mood will continue to
improve with each drove until Jacob finally appears.

Verse 21. None of them must fail to say, "From your servant for his
lord!" Esau's countenance can mean life or death (Prov. 16,14 ff.) for
Jacob. He approaches him like a superior being; it is already a favor to
be allowed into his presence "to see his face".

Verse 22. Jacob spends this night in the camp in order to make
arrangements for his family.

²³The same night he arose and took his two wives, his two maids,
and his eleven children, and crossed the ford of the Jabbok. ²⁴He

*took them and set them across the stream, and everything that he
had he let go ahead.*

Eleven children sons, not counting Dinah. The Jabbok is an eastern
tributary of the Jordan. Jacob crosses the ford alone to see (Ramban)
whether it is passable. Afterwards he lets all he has precede him in
preparation for verse 25.

> *25Jacob remained alone; and a man wrestled with him until the
> breaking of the day. 26When he saw that he did not prevail against
> him, he touched the hollow of his thigh; and Jacob's thigh was put
> out of joint as he wrestled with him. 27Then he said, "Let me go,
> for the day is breaking." But Jacob said, "I will not let you go,
> unless you bless me." 28He said to him, "What is your name?"
> And he said, "Jacob." 29Then he said, "Not Jacob—it will once be
> said—shall be your name, but Israel (He Strives With God), for
> you have striven with God and with men, and have prevailed."
> 30Then Jacob asked him, "Tell me, I pray, your name." But he
> said, "Why is it that you ask my name?" And there he blessed
> him.*

The Hebrew word for wrestling through its sound reminds of the
name of the river, Jabbok, perhaps even of Jacob's name. The sudden
appearance and attack by "the man" is to enhance the impression of the
mysterious nightly incident. "The man" is (verses 29.30) undoubtedly
an angel.

Verse 26. *When he saw that he did not prevail* against Jacob. He
intended to prevail, but found Jacob so strong that he recognized it as
God's will that he should fail.

Verse 27. *Let me go;* it is time that we cease (Rashbam). Jacob
answers, *"I will not let you go unless you bless me."* A wonderful
phrase; the victor is not satisfied before the defeated has blessed him,
provided we can speak of a victor and a defeated at all. This request for
a blessing is different from the one before the father.

Verse 28. *"What is your name?"* not that the angel does not know it,
but he wants the known fact confirmed by the other party before
commenting on it (compare Ex. 3,13;4,2; Gen. 3,9).

Verse 29. This verse does not duplicate 35,10 but prepares for that
passage.

It will once be said. "The man" speaks like a prophet, as he himself is not authorized to give the new name. The blessing by the angel consists in the promise of a blessing by a higher one (like Num. 6,22f).

Verse 30. Jacob wants to know whom he shall thank and honor by a gift when the promise comes about similar to Manoah in Judg. 13,17; the answer must be understood as declining an intended honor (compare 33,15).

> ³¹*Jacob called the name of the place Peniel (Face of God), saying, "For I have seen God face to face, and yet my life is preserved." ³²And the sun rose upon him as he passed Penuel, limping because of his thigh. ³³Therefore to this day the Israelites do not eat the sinew of the hip which is upon the hollow of the thigh, because he touched the hollow of Jacob's thigh on the sinew of the hip.*

Jacob names the place. *My life is preserved* not only refers to the divine apparition which might have been deadly, but to the promise; he must remain alive to see it fulfilled, as Manoah's wife reasonably argues in Judg. 13,23.

Verse 33. This is the ischiadic nerve.

The Meaning Of The Story.

Jacob's struggle by night has found varied interpretations. The context, however, is decisive, and the end clearly indicates the purpose of the story. Jacob implored God to save him from Esau. Such a prayer expects a response, 'I will come, I am here.' Where is the answer? The struggle shall give it.

Although the omnipotent God has many ways of helping Jacob, he carefully chooses the one which is most appropriate to the situation, and of the greatest educational value for the persons concerned. Therefore he does not perform a miracle, perhaps carry Jacob off in a cloud, suddenly equip him with gigantic strength, deprive Esau of his strength, or place an obstacle in Esau's way. Divine wisdom knows a manner of salvation which surprises but is at the same time psychologically true.

When Esau later sees Jacob he runs to meet him, embraces him, and both weep. How astounding! What brought the sudden change in this man, thirsting for revenge with his four hundred warriors?

Following his vow to slay Jacob he should have rejoiced to see him finally in his hands; Jacob had trembled in anticipation of this hour since his messengers had returned. The presents could mean little to Esau who could soon take all which Jacob possessed. Esau becomes disarmed when he finally sees Jacob, dragging himself forward, bowing down to the ground seven times, behind him a crowd of women and children. This limping, defeated man, hobbling forward with difficulty is hardly the same Jacob who had once been so agile, against whom he had trained his warriors. God saved Jacob by making him weaker and thus defeats Esau's purpose. He feels himself vanquished by seeing a vanquished man before him. Jacob is defeated at his thigh, lamed in the very foot in which the root of all their enmity had lain (25,26). This is not "Jacob who takes by the heel".

The salvation of Jacob is his lameness. As he cannot yet recognize this, his confidence is restored by the promise of a new name. No man thus designated for greatness can perish. This name contains a vocation and a future for him and for all his descendants. The Bible intends the name Israel to mean: fighter with God and God's fight. First of all it applies to Jacob who has fought with something superhuman, until the break of the day without being defeated. He who persists in fighting through the night deserves such a name. It was also a fight of God. God, the divine in Jacob, had fought and won. Jacob had gained strength and perseverance from his awareness of something divine in him which must not and could not be defeated. He felt a divine vocation to become the third ancestor of a people of God who shall conduct "the wars of God". He fights for God, with God's help. The new name removes the evil interpretation of the name Jacob in 27,36, and in addition is the triumph of spirit over nature and innate character.

Jacob has understood this. *The sun rose upon him* means a new day, a new life dawns on him after the night of struggle; Penuel is the scene of a psychological regeneration, inspite of the lameness in his thigh. Now he is prepared to meet Esau; as he has seen God face to face, he will be able to look into the face of his brother. Weakened in body he has become psychologically invincible. The man of God effects both, a wondrous dubbing of a knight.

Jacob's opponent was sent by God as shown by verse 29 (35,10). The wrestling with Jacob is willed or permitted by God. "The man" is of the same type as the angel who strikes Job, stands in the way of Balaam, and tests Abraham; he too is a "Satan". The Midrash says (Bereshith Rabba) that it was Esau's angel. This, of all interpretations, is truest to the meaning of Scripture. "Satan" is also a divine fighter; always representing a cause which is relatively valid. Esau's cause was relatively just; he had good reason for anger against the brother who had cheated him. When anxious Jacob prays: "save me from my brother", a voice in the heavenly council, where no one is unrepresented, must have asked "Does Jacob deserve to be heard, is this not his due?" God must have answered the accuser as in the book of Job: "You advocate of Esau, see whether you can prevail over Jacob, whether he will surrender, and destroy my plan to make him Israel. If he prevails, then touch him on his thigh so that this may become his salvation from Esau." God's messenger is the spirit, and cause of Esau, the shadow which had pursued Jacob twenty years, and now looms large as a giant. Finally in prevailing, he becomes Israel. Awareness of an eternal destiny and a resolution to live for it carry the day. His former deed against Esau is neither justified, nor atoned by this and only Esau can forgive it. Making peace with God's representative is a prelude to reconciliation with the brother.

God answers a man if he prays by searching himself, becoming his own opponent; this self searching must be relentless, even if it lessens some of the buoyancy of his native, earthly being. The more joyfully will the soul breathe the light of a new life. The struggle is set in the night of need and in solitude. The remark about the sinew in verse 33 stands in a most appropriate place and shall perpetuate the spirit of the story. The slaughtering for each meal shall recall to the people, who call themselves Israel, the hour when this name was first pronounced and the struggle of their ancestor. The sinew, which is thrown away, symbolizes a reprehensible ambition cast off; it may mean that Israel will loose the race after the good things of this world. It is a sign and symbol similar to the unleavened bread which reminds of the suffering in Egypt. The story is a counterpart to the binding of Isaac, Peniel to Moriah where God sees and is seen. Abraham is an almost superhuman hero of religion; while Jacob is humanly closer to us.

Chapter 33

*Jacob lifted up his eyes and looked, and behold Esau was coming,
and four hundred men with him. So he divided the children
among Leah and Rachel and the two maids. ²And he put the
maids with their children in front, then Leah with her children,
and Rachel and Joseph last of all. ³He himself went on before
them, bowing himself to the ground seven times, until he came
near to his brother. ⁴But Esau ran to meet him, and fell on his
neck, and kissed him, and they wept.*

Esau is not appeased by the presents as he brings four hundred men
with him (Seforno).

Verse 2. He places those dearest to him at the end, not that they may
be struck last, but so that they may be presented last, in verse 6; the
others shall appear like forerunners.

Verse 3. This is the climax of self-abasement. The spectator must
follow this scene with the greatest tension and anxiety. It is the first
meeting of the two hostile brothers, one of whom had sworn to kill the
other! The moment is decisive for Jacob's fate which now depends on a
glance of Esau. Should he yet be full of old hatred and nod to his men,
all will be lost.

Verse 4. The miracle happens; Esau acts like a changed man. The
Midrash questions Esau's kisses. Kisses or bites? This biting skepticism
is to be understood by interpreting the brothers as their respective
nations, and from Israel's experiences with Edom. Jacob also weeps; he
is saved. The change in Esau's mood can only be explained through the
sight of his lamed brother; the savage is sentimental, as quick to anger
as in overflowing compassion and tenderness; one reconciles us to the
other. Mutual courtesies follow.

*⁵And when Esau raised his eyes and saw the women and the
children, he said, "Who are these with you?" Jacob said, "The*

children whom God has graciously given your servant." Then the maids drew near, they and their children, and bowed down: ⁷Leah likewise and her children drew near and bowed down, and last Joseph and Rachel drew near, and they bowed down. ⁸Esau said, "What do you mean by all this company which I met?" Jacob answered, "To find favor in the sight of my lord." ⁹But Esau said, "I already have much, my brother; keep what you have for yourself." ¹⁰Jacob said, "No, I pray you, if I have found favor in your sight, then accept my present from my hand; for truly to see your face is like seeing the face of God, with such favor have you received me. ¹¹Accept, I pray you, my gift that is brought to you, because God has dealt graciously with me, and because I have enough." Thus he urged him, and he took it.

The first courtesy is Esau's question about the women and children which Jacob answers with thanks to God because "children are a gift of God".

Verse 6. So far they stood back and now draw near after this introduction at a gesture of Jacob; they bow respectfully to the mighty brother-in-law and uncle.

Verse 7. The Midrash nicely remarks that little Joseph placed himself bravely before his beautiful mother in case the savage man should cast his eyes upon her.

Verse 8. The inquiring about the family was only an introduction to the more important one about the presents.

Verse 9. Courtesy demands that Esau first decline. The deep impression the rich present had made on him is betrayed by his addressing Jacob as his brother at last.

Verse 10. Jacob must pretend to take this seriously. Therefore he urges him with many words: 'you do me a favor by accepting this gift of homage.' It is the dutiful expression of gratitude for having been permitted to appear before him and for having been taken back into his grace. Nevertheless, Jacob is cautious in expression; he does not call Esau a god, but only compares his appearance before him with the appearance before a god. The brother's face as he had last seen it had haunted him as a terrifying memory. (32,21).

Verse 11. This present means no loss for him as God has given him so much; he would still be well provided. Esau says: 'I have much, (and can therefore use more).' Jacob; 'I have everything which I need, and can therefore give without worry.'

And he took it the brevity of this is characteristic of Esau. Seforno contrasts it to II Kings 5,16.

> ¹²Then he said, "Let us journey on our way, and I will go at your side." ¹³But he said to him, "My lord knows that the children are frail, and that the flocks and herds giving suck are a care to me; and if they are overdriven one day, all the flocks will die. ¹⁴Let my lord pass on before his servant, and I will lead on slowly, according to the pace of the cattle which are before me and according to the pace of the children, until I come to my lord in Seir." ¹⁵So Esau said, "Let me leave with you some of the men who are with me." But he said, "What need is there? Let me find favor in the sight of my lord."

Esau gives no counter present, but in order to do something, offers to accompany Jacob with all his men, which costs nothing.

Verse 13. Jacob feels uneasy about this offer and declines it, addressing him again as "my lord", and giving reasons which Esau cannot very well contest.

Verse 14. Esau shall go; Jacob will follow him to Seir; but he sets no time limit for this.

Verse 15. Esau must out of courtesy make his offer a second time. He will at least give Jacob an escort of part of his people, but Jacob declines with thanks.

> ¹⁶So Esau returned that day on his way to Seir. ¹⁷But Jacob journeyed to Sukkoth, and built himself a house, and made booths for his cattle. Therefore he called the name of the place Sukkoth (Booths). ¹⁸And Jacob came peacefully to the city of Shechem, which is in the land of Canaan, when he came from Padan-aram; and he camped before the city. ¹⁹And from the sons of Hamor, Shechem's father, he bought for a hundred pieces of money the piece of land on which he had pitched his tent. ²⁰There he erected an altar and called it El-Elohe-Israel (God is the God of Israel).

Verse 17. The report that Jacob builds a house is meant as a reproach. Like Lot in Sodom he prepares himself for permanent residence while Abraham and Isaac had felt themselves strangers in the land and dwelt in tents.

Verse 18. *Peacefully* expresses Jacob's intentions towards the country and the people which is later acknowledged by Shechem's father (34,21). He returns as a changed man into the land of Canaan which he had left after a fraud. He does not intend to join the city people and encamps before the city.

Verse 19. This verse presents proof of Jacob's peaceful and honest conduct towards his neighbors.

Verse 20. In dedicating the altar, Jacob pronounces this sentence: 'God is the God of Israel', thus professing the God who had appeared to him, and his own name Israel.

Chapter 34

Dinah

Now Dinah the daughter of Leah, whom she had borne to Jacob, went out to visit the women of the land; ²and when Shechem, the son of Hamor the Hivite, the prince of the land, saw her, he seized her and lay with her and raped her. ³And his soul was drawn to Dinah the daughter of Jacob; he loved the maiden and spoke tenderly to her. ⁴So Shechem spoke to his father Hamor, saying, "Get me this maiden for my wife." ⁵Now Jacob had heard that he had defiled his daughter Dinah; but his sons were with his cattle in the field, so Jacob held his peace until they came.

Dinah is called daughter of Leah, so that Simeon and Levi, her revengers, were full brothers (Ramban). Debouching a virgin of a noble family is an insult. The choice of words in the Hebrew text shows (compare 27,46) disapproval of her visit with the women of the land.

Verse 2. The result is that Shechem *seized her* unlawfully. It was a case of rape. The beauty of the girl had captivated him, but afterwards he recognizes the harm he has done and with whom he is dealing.

Verse 3. His soul cannot free itself from Dinah the daughter of Jacob, a girl of equal birth, but of a family with different notions. He knows that he must propose to her father (Ex. 22,15f). *He spoke tenderly to her*, promises to marry her.

Verse 5. Before the two parties meet, we see how the other side viewed the affair. The affect on Jacob, the father, is shown by the crass expression *he had defiled her*, which pictures his indignation. He might have felt impelled to act immediately, yet she is not only his daughter, but also the sister of his adult sons; they have a voice in the matter. Jacob waits for them which prevents his taking the first step, a dangerous move for a stranger.

6And Hamor the father of Shechem went out to Jacob to speak with him. 7The sons of Jacob came in from the field. When they heard of it the men were indignant and very angry, because one had wrought a shameful deed in Israel by lying with Jacob's daughter, for such a thing ought not to be done.

Fortunately Jacob was relieved from action by Hamor's visit which gave a different aspect to the matter. Proposing was the task of the father although, as shown by verse 11, Shechem had accompanied him. Father and son have discussed the matter at home. They will declare Shechem's intention to marry her and will accept any conditions; therefore he must be present.

Verse 7. *The men;* this word is used because they had been touched in their honor. The act is a crime against Israel, against the sanctity which is the honor of our people, against the chastity of our women! Their exclamation is the judgement of Scripture, explaining that the brothers were right in being deeply concerned about the incident. The fathers had not wanted to marry Canaanite women, now shall the only daughter be good enough for a Hivite.

8But Hamor spoke with them, saying, "The soul of my son Shechem longs for your daughter; I pray you, give her to him in marriage. 9Make marriages with us; give your daughters to us, and take our daughters for yourselves. 10You shall dwell with us; and the land shall be open to you; dwell and trade in it, and get property in it."

Hamor discovers a situation different than expected. He only wanted to speak with Jacob, but finds himself facing the whole family. He must arrange his speech correspondingly, namely sue for Dinah on behalf of his son, which he does briefly, and propose a general interchange between the tribes by marriage and commerce. His many words concentrate on making this sound attractive and profitable for the house of Jacob. Courteously, he makes his Hivites the object; the Israelites may choose their daughters.

11Shechem also said to her father and to her brothers, "Let me find favor in your eyes, and whatever you say to me I will give. 12Ask of me ever so much as marriage present and gift, and I will give according as you say to me; only give me the maiden to be my wife."

Young Shechem whose happiness is at stake cannot remain silent. Hamor had addressed the sons; he expressly turns to "her" father and brothers. His offer is purely personal as he can make no proposition for the whole tribe.

Verse 12. The marriage present is a gift to the father for the virgin, but not a price paid to him. The other gifts are the customary presents for the bride as well as the other members of the family (24,53).

> [13]The sons of Jacob answered Shechem and his father Hamor deceitfully. Thus they spoke because he had defiled their sister Dinah. [14]They said to them, "We cannot do this thing, to give our sister to one who is uncircumcised, for that would be a disgrace for us. [15]Only on this condition will we consent to you: that you will become as we are and every male of you be circumcised. [16]Then we will give our daughters to you, and we will take your daughters to ourselves, and we will dwell with you and become one people. [17]But if you will not listen to us and be circumcised, then we will take our daughter, and we will be gone."

On the other side the sons reply, and take the delicate matter from the father's shoulders. Jacob remains silent till the end in verse 30. *Deceitfully* is the same Hebrew word which was used of Jacob in 27,35 and of Laban in 29,25. All these passages refer to each other. Jacob had deceived his father; for that he had been deceived by Laban. He shall still have occasion to experience deceit in his children and condemn it. This will be the complete repudiation of his lying.

Verse 14. They deem it below their dignity to reply to Shechem's additional offer; first a question of principle must be solved. Their concern is of a higher nature than money.

An uncircumcised husband for their sister would be a disgrace for them; it would elicit disgraceful comments. As only one family of Jacob existed, circumcision must have been regarded even by strangers as an honor and a duty of this family which they are expected to maintain.

Verse 16. According to the manner of negotiations, the men repeat Hamor's offer, but enlarge on it with deceitful cordiality; *we will become one people.* They disdain to speak of trading (verse 10). They do not merely concern themselves with the question of Shechem and Dinah. Nor have they demanded his circumcision, but only expressed themselves negatively in verse 14. That is the deceit in their speech; for

their deed comes later. Shechem, an uncircumcised man, has dishonored their sister, which is irreparable.

> *18Their words pleased Hamor and Hamor's son Shechem. 19And
> the young man did not delay to do the thing, because he had
> delight in Jacob's daughter. Now he was the most honored of all
> his family.*

Their reasons convince both Hamor and Shechem. Obviously the
refusal is not social arrogance of the family, but results from higher
necessity. The disgrace would also be attached to the son-in-law. Had
they not been so particular with her husband, he could not have been of
much consequence. They must be glad that the obstacle is not
insurmountable as differences of "race" or alien "blood" would have
been. Indeed, differences of race have never been an obstacle to joining
Israel which did not know the concept of purity of blood. The prohibition against marrying Canaanites has a religious foundation. (Ex. 34,12
ff; Deut. 7,3) while that against marrying Ammonites and Mohabites
has (Deut. 23,4 ff.) moral reasons. Circumcision turned a man of foreign
origin into an Israelite (Ex. 12,48).

Verse 19. Shechem wanted immediate action, a resolution by the
people. The present ruler, the most honored of his subjects, and future
ruler agree in the matter; the latter even urges it. This already prepares
for the consent of the people of Shechem.
He may even have assured Jacob and his sons that his own example
would be effective.

> *20So Hamor and his son Shechem came to the gate of their city
> and spoke to the men of their city, saying, 21"These men are
> friendly with us; let them dwell in the land and trade in it, for
> behold, the land is large enough for them; let us take their daugh-
> ters in marriage, and let us give them our daughters. 22Only on
> this condition will the men agree to dwell with us, to become one
> people: that every male among us be circumcised as they are
> circumcised. 23Will not their cattle, their property and all their
> beasts be ours? Only let us agree with them, and they will dwell
> with us." 24And all that went out of the gate of his city hearkened
> to Hamor and his son Shechem; and every male was circumcised,
> all that went out of the gate of his city.*

They present the matter faithfully, but try to win their fellow-nation-
als by the clever manner of their report. These people are friendly and

sincere. There is enough room for them. They first propose trade and only then marriage which requires something on their part. Everything is presented as if the initiative were on their side. They do not speak of the case of Shechem and Dinah at all. Finally, once more they emphasize the great material advantages of such a union, exaggerating as if they would get all the property of these people in this way. The words reveal the true thinking of these Canaanites. It is good business and therefore worth some religious concession. The whole speech is craftily arranged.

Verse 24. The assembly agrees and the circumcision is executed, so the request cannot have appeared to them as odd or too hard. Circumcision was a custom like any other one for them.

> ²⁵*On the third day, when they were sore, two of the sons of Jacob, Simeon and Levi, Dinah's brothers, took their swords and came upon the city unawares, and killed all the males.* ²⁶*They slew Hamor and his son Shechem with the sword, and took Dinah out of Shechem's house, and went away.* ²⁷*And the sons of Jacob came upon the slain, and plundered the city, where their sister had been defiled;* ²⁸*they took their flocks and their herds, their asses, and whatever was in the city and in the field;* ²⁹*all their wealth, all their little ones and their wives, all that was in the houses, they captured and made their prey.*

Verse 25. *Dinah's brothers;* they wanted to revenge their sister's honor. They are the brothers closest after Reuben in whom initiative and energy seem to have been lacking (compare Judg. 5,15 f.). Taking their swords expresses resolution in the face of all scruples. *Unawares* implies a judgement. They fall on the defenseless people without risk to themselves.

Verse 27. The other sons of Jacob complete the action as it was done against a hostile city; the justification was that here their sister had been dishonored.

> ³⁰*Then Jacob said to Simeon and Levi, "You have brought trouble on me by making me odious to the inhabitants of the land, the Canaanites and the Perizzites; my numbers are few, and if they gather themselves against me and attack me, I shall be destroyed, both I and my household."* ³¹*But they said, "Should he treat our sister as a harlot?"*

Jacob is indignant over Simeon and Levi and describes the possible consequences to them. All his words are pathetic and drastic.

Verse 31. The sons answer in the same vein. Jacob has no reply to their question; there was no way out of the dilemna.

The Intention Of The Story

After Jacob's troubles with Laban and Esau are over, sorrowful trials in his own house and through his own children begin: through his sons—Reuben, Simeon, Levi, Joseph, Benjamin—and his daughter. The sorrow which she brings, lies in the nature of her sex. The persons are described true to life—the passionate and easy-going young nobleman, the farsighted practical father, the irreconcilable brothers for whom the family honor defiled in their sister can be cleansed only by the blood of a whole guilty city. Their guile was derived from their somber resolution. Pretending religious scruples they trap the unsuspecting opponent whom they could not have otherwise overcome. Jacob is in a dilemma; he cannot disapprove of his sons defense of their honor. Purity of the family must be the foremost consideration for him too, as his clan had been chosen for this. Yet his house must live in peace with the heathen neighbors. Violence and bloodthirst must be hateful to him, even if he now suppresses his feelings and withholds his curse over the evildoers until his deathbed (49,5 ff.). Dinah plays a passive role. We hear nothing of her further fate.

Chapter 35

Jacob's Journey To Bethel And Hebron

God said to Jacob, "Arise, go up to Bethel, and dwell there; and make there an altar to the God who appeared to you when you fled from your brother Esau." ²So Jacob said to his household and to all who were with him, "Put away the foreign idols that are among you, and purify yourselves, and change your garments; ³then let us arise and go up to Bethel, that I make there an altar to the God who answered me in the day of my distress and has been with me wherever I have gone." ⁴So they gave to Jacob all the foreign idols that they had, and the rings that were in their ears; and Jacob hid them under the oak which was near Shechem.

Jacob's vow (28,20ff.) requires fulfillment after his happy return home. He now performs a pilgrimage, the model for all later pilgrimages. This is the key to all which follows. Experiences like those of chapter 34 may be conclusive to the fulfillment of a duty which had been undertaken toward God. Jacob might ascribe some of the guilt in the defilement of Dinah to himself. He should have watched his daughter more closely. He had too trustfully settled near Shechem. His deliverance consists in a renewal of his attachement to God which occurs in the pilgrimage. The contents characterize the call as coming from God. A summons to a pilgrimage is always a divine voice. This is a personification like the fatherland, the country, the home "call".

Go up to Bethel. Sacred spots are located on high places, so that going to them may lead upward.

And dwell there, waiting for the revelation of verse 9 which will repeat the former one. Remember your former danger and deliverance.

Verse 2. Appearing before God, the pure and holy one, requires purification, (see e.g. Ex. 19,10). Jacob extends the divine call, which apparently had been addressed to him alone, to all who belong to his house.

The people of his household shall first remove the idols of other countries which are in their midst. This includes (verse 4) ornaments in the form of heathen idols derived through trade with foreign nations. In daily life they might be overlooked or could perhaps not be avoided. Yet if one is to appear before the God of Israel, he must recognize them as symbol and cause of pagan "impurity" which is to be removed. Nothing like that shall be found in Israel. One need not think of outright idolatry.

Man shall renew himself, which is externally symbolized by washing oneself and putting on clean or more festive garments.

Verse 4. Jacob hides these things by burying them. Putting them underground removes them from sight as the dead.

> *5And as they journeyed, a terror from God fell upon the cities that were around them, so that they did not pursue the sons of Jacob. 6And Jacob came to Luz (that is, Bethel), which is in the land of Canaan, he and all the people who were with him, 7and there he built an altar, and called the place El-bethel (God is in Bethel) because there God had revealed himself to him when he fled from his brother. 8And Deborah, Rebekah's nurse, died, and she was buried under an oak below Bethel; so he called its name Allon-bacuth (Oak of Weeping).*

Jacob's residence can be moved to Bethel undisturbed in spite of the enmity which their bloody deed against Shechem must have provoked among the surrounding cities (compare Ex. 34,24). *A terror from God fell upon the cities.* The pilgrims appeared to them like higher beings (compare 9,2) whom they did not dare pursue.

Verse 6. For the Canaanites the name always remained Luz in spite of 28,19.

Verse 8. This episode is told, to mention the giving of another name near Bethel.

> *9God appeared to Jacob again, when he had come from Paddan-aram, and blessed him. 10And God said to him, "Your name is Jacob; but no longer shall your name be called Jacob, but Israel shall be your name". So he called his name Israel. 11And God said to him, "I am God Almighty; be fruitful and multiply; a nation and a company of nations shall come from you, and kings shall spring from your loins. 12The land which I gave to Abraham and*

*Isaac I will give to you, and I will give the land to your descend-
ants after you." ¹³Then God went up from him in the place where
he had spoken to him.*

After Jacob has appeared as pilgrim before God, the new name Israel
and the blessing connected with it is definitely confirmed by God.
Again refers to 28,12ff.

Verse 10. This is the giving of the new name which the angel of
32,28f. had only heralded. Your name shall no longer be Jacob. A
second name, when not merely a different pronunciation of the old one
as Abraham for Abram and Sarah for Sarai, does not supersede the old
name. It, on the contrary, affords the opportunity to alternate names as
is henceforth done; the use of one or the other is always intentional.

Verse 11. *Be fruitful and multiply* is a promise, a challenge, a blessing, a comfort, and a joyful affirmation of life. It presupposes a nation
which enjoys the present and is conscious of a mission; the same
expression is used for all mankind at the creation and after the flood
(1,27;9,1). It does not refer to Jacob personally, who has only one more
son, namely Benjamin, but to his sons and descendants. The *nation* is
Israel, and the *company of nations* are its tribes (Redak).

Verse 12. A nation requires a land.

Verse 13. *God went up from him* a sign that the apparition had been
real, and not only a dream (Ramban).

*¹⁴And Jacob set up a pillar in the place where he had spoken with
him, a pillar of stone; and he poured out an outpouring on it and
poured oil on it. ¹⁵So Jacob called the name of the place where
God had spoken with him, Bethel.*

This pillar differs from that of 28,22, but shall correspond to it. He
dedicates it by pouring oil and probably wine on it.

*¹⁶Then they journeyed from Bethel; and when they were still some
distance from Ephrath, Rachel travailed, and she had hard labor.
¹⁷And when she was in her hard labor, the midwife said to her,
"Fear not; for now you will have another son." ¹⁸And as her soul
was departing, for she died, she called his name Ben-oni (Son of
My Sorrow); but his father called his name Benjamin (Son of My*

Right Hand). ¹⁹*So Rachel died and she was buried on the way to Ephrath, that is Bethlehem,* ²⁰*and Jacob set up a pillar upon her grave; it is the pillar of Rachel's tomb which is there to this day.*

A tomb aside from that of Deborah is in the neighborhood namely that of Rachel. The story gives the reason for Rachel not being buried in the family tomb at Hebron.

Verse 17. The midwife tried to encourage her by telling her that it is a son.

Verse 18. *Son of my right hand.* This is the lucky side.

Verse 19. The tomb of Rachel is in the south in the land of Judah where such a tomb is still today pointed out according to Jewish, Christian, and Moslem tradition.

The emphasis upon Rachel's death on the journey carries another specific intention; Jacob was consequently not able to introduce his beloved Rachel to his old father.

²¹*Israel journeyed on, and pitched his tent beyond the tower of Eder.* ²²*While Israel dwelt in that land Reuben went and lay with Bilhah his father's concubine; and Israel heard of it.*

Tower of Eder which is, tower of the herd; such towers are mentioned several times in the Bible.

Verse 22. Scripture glosses over this incident as briefly as possible and tries to excuse Reuben by calling Bilhah a concubine, not a wife, of Jacob. The affair reminds of Absalom's rebellion (II Sam. 16,20 ff). According to I Chr. 5.1 Reuben lost his rank as first-born, and his claim to rule by this deed. In the order of birth he remains Jacob's first-born (verse 23). *Jacob heard of it* shall explain 49,4.

Now the sons of Jacob were twelve. ²³*The sons of Leah: Reuben, Jacob's first-born, Simeon, Levi, Judah, Issachar, and Zebulun.* ²⁴*The sons of Rachel: Joseph and Benjamin.* ²⁵*And the sons of Bilhah Rachel's maid; Dan and Naphtali.* ²⁶*And the sons of Zilpah, Leah's maid: Gad and Asher. These were the sons of Jacob who were born to him in Paddan-aram.*

The sons are called *the sons of Jacob* although he had just been given the name Israel. His birthname was and remained Jacob which was decisive for the listing of the descendants.

> ²⁷*And Jacob came to his father Isaac at Mamre, or Kiriath-arba, that is, Hebron, where Abraham and Isaac had sojourned.* ²⁸*Now the days of Isaac were a hundred and eighty years.* ²⁹*And Isaac breathed his last; and he died and was gathered to his people, old and full of days; and his sons Esau and Jacob buried him.*

Isaac must have gone there from Beer-sheba, in order to be buried in the family tomb.

Verse 29. Here Esau is mentioned first as he was the first-born of the same mother. Thus the brothers who were so different meet at last at the father's grave. That is the complete reconciliation.

Chapter 36

The Descendants Of Esau

These are the descendants of Esau, that is Edom. ²Esau had taken his wives from the daughters of Canaan: Adah the daughter of Elon the Hittite, and Oholibamah the daughter of Anah, the daughter of Zibeon the Hivite, ³and Basemath, Ishmael's daughter, the sister of Nebaioth. ⁴And Adah bore to Esau Eliphaz; Basemath bore Reuel; ⁵and Oholibamah bore Jeush, Jalam, and Korah. These are the sons of Esau who were born to him in the land of Cannan.

Esau like Jacob has two names; he had received his second name, Edom (red) because of his greed for the "red" pot of lentils; while Jacob had received his after the wrestling with the angel. This paragraph tells of Esau fathering a family in the land of Canaan which he later moved to the mountains of Seir. Esau took his wives from the daughters of Canaan in conscious opposition to the views of his father's house.

Verse 2. The names of Esau's wives mentioned here differ from those in 26,34 and 28,19. Perhaps the only interpretation possible without resorting to the assumption of different authors for these passages would be that the names of these wives had at some time been changed, Basemath to Adah and Mahalath to Basemath. Esau marries them under their old names received from their parents; now when the descendants are reported they are called by their new names. Yet Judith the daughter of Be-eri the Hittite (26,34) must be different from Oholibamah. If Esau had four wives why is the first, Judith, omitted here?

It is also strange that the second wife, Oholibamah, is called the daughter of two different men, Anah and Zibeon. Rashi thought that she was a child of Zibeon from incestuous intercourse with the wife of his own son Anah.

⁶Then Esau took his wives, his sons, his daughters, and all the members of his household, his cattle, all his beasts, and all his property which he had acquired in the land of Canaan; and he went into a land away from his brother Jacob. [7]For their possessions were too great for them to dwell together; the land of their sojournings could not support them because of their cattle. [8]So Esau dwelt in the hill country of Seir; Esau, that is Edom.

Esau leaves Canaan with his entire household and all his possessions. The name of the country Edom or Seir to which he departs is intentionally not mentioned, till he arrives there (verse 8). Now Esau definitely abandons the land of the fathers which God had promised to the descendants (17,8;Ex. 6,4), which Isaac had wished for Jacob (28,4), and in which Jacob desired to stay (37,1).

[9]These are the descendants of Esau the father of the Edomites in the hill country of Seir. [10]These are the names of Esau's sons: Eliphaz the son of Adah the wife of Esau, Reuel the son of Basemath the wife of Esau. [11]The sons of Eliphaz were Teman, Omar, Zepho, Gatam, and Kenaz. [12]Timna was a concubine of Eliphaz, Esau's son; she bore Amalek to Eliphaz. These are the sons of Adah, Esau's wife. [13]These are the sons of Reuel: Nahath, Zerah, Shammah, and Mizzah. These are the sons of Basemath, Esau's wife. [14]These are the sons of Oholibamah the daughter of Anah, the daughter of Zibeon, Esau's wife: she bore to Esau Jeush, Jalam, and Korah. [15]These are the chiefs of the sons of Esau. The sons of Eliphaz the first-born of Esau: chief Teman, chief Omar, chief Zepho, chief Kenaz. [16]Chief Korah, chief Gatam, chief Amalek. These are the chiefs of Eliphaz in the land of Edom; they are the sons of Adah. [17]These are the sons of Reuel, Esau's son: chief Nahath, chief Zerah, chief Shammah, chief Mizzah; these are the chiefs of Reuel in the land of Edom; they are the sons of Basemath, Esau's wife. [18]These are the sons of Oholibamah, Esau's wife: chief Jeush, chief Jalam, chief Korah; these are the chiefs of Oholibamah the daughter of Anah, Esau's wife. [19]These are the sons of Esau and these are their chiefs; that is Edom.

Verse 11. Teman; his region is often mentioned in the Bible as famous for wisdom (Jer. 49,7). One name, Korah (verse 16), has been omitted from these 7 grandsons, attributed to Adah, Esau's wife (verse 12).

Verse 12. Eliphaz had married a daughter of Seir as concubine. The father Esau had married a granddaughter of Seir. Esau had taken a wife of the younger, while his son of the older generation. The father of Timna's husband is the husband of her niece. Her son was Amalek. Amalek is the most hated enemy of Israel because of his treacherous conduct during the exodus from Egypt (Ex. 17,14; Deut. 25,17 ff.); this intends to explain the baseness of Amalek by his low birth; he was the son of a concubine.

Verse 15. The Hebrew word translated as "chief" perhaps rather means "tribe", originally a group of a thousand. This would then be an enumeration of the tribes of Edom, corresponding to the tribes of Israel.

Now follows the family of Seir because of its relationship by marriage to Esau's house. The two women Timna and Oholibamah are important; the first is a daughter, the second a granddaughter of Seir.

> ²⁰*These are the sons of Seir the Horite, the inhabitants of the land: Lotan, Shobal, Zibeon, Anah.* ²¹*Dishon, Ezer, and Dishan; these are the chiefs of the Horites, the sons of Seir in the land of Edom.* ²²*The sons of Lotan were Hori and Heman; and Lotan's sister was Timna.* ²³*These are the sons of Shobal: Alvan, Manahath, Ebal, Shepho, and Onam.* ²⁴*These are the sons of Zibeon: Aiah and Anah; he is the Anah who found the jemim in the wilderness, as he pastured the asses for Zibeon his father.* ²⁵*These are the children of Anah: Dishon and Oholibamah the daughter of Anah.* ²⁶*These are the sons of Dishon: Hemdan, Eshban, Ithran, and Cheran.* ²⁷*These are the sons of Ezer: Bilhan, Zaavan, and Akan.* ²⁸*These are the sons of Dishan: Uz and Aran.* ²⁹*These are the chiefs of the Horites: chief Lotan, chief Shobal, chief Zibeon, chief Anah,* ³⁰*chief Dishon, chief Ezer, and chief Dishan; these are the chiefs of the Horites, according to their chiefs in the land of Seir.*

Inhabitants of the land occupying it, without or contrary to allotment by God. Our passage is in accord with Deut. 2,12.20; by divine ordinance the inhabitants of Canaan had to make room for Jacob which is Israel, so those of Seir for Esau which is Edom. Esau too received a land as compensation for the region of the north which he had yielded to his brother in fulfillment of the promise to the ancestor Abraham (15,18ff). Seir has seven sons according to verses 20-21.

Verse 22. Now follow the descendants of the seven.

Verse 24. *Anah found the jemim* Most Jewish interpreters explained this difficult word as "mules" and claimed that Anah discovered their breeding. Others explain the word as "hot springs." The purpose of the remark can only be to distinguish this Anah, son of Zibeon, from the Anah of verse 25 who is Seir's son (verse 20).

Altogether the seven sons plus seventeen grandsons are twenty-four.

Similarity in names and confusion in family relationships are intended to characterize the family of Horites into which Esau marries.

> [31]These are the kings who reigned in the land of Edom, before a king reigned for the Israelites. [32]Bela the son of Beor reigned in Edom, the name of his city being Dinhabah. [33]Bela died and Jobab the son of Zerah of Bozrah reigned in his stead. [34]Jobab died, and Husham of the land of the Temanites reigned in his stead. [35]Husham died, and Hadad the son of Bedad, who defeated Midian in the country of Moab, reigned in his stead, the name of his city being Avith. [36]Hadad died, and Samlah of Masrekah reigned in his stead. [37]Samlah died, and Shaul of Rehoboth on the Euphrates reigned in his stead. [38]Shaul died, and Baal-hanan the son of Achbor reigned in his stead. [39]Baal-hanan the son of Achbor died, and Hadar reigned in his stead, the name of his city being Pau; his wife's name was Mehetabel, the daughter of Matred, daughter of Mezahab.
>
> [40]These are the names of the chiefs of Esau, according to their families and their dwelling places, by their names: chief Timna, chief Alvah, chief Jetheth, [41]chief Oholibamah, chief Elah, chief Pinon, [42]chief Kenaz, chief Teman, chief Mibzar, [43]chief Magdiel, and chief Iram; these are the chiefs of Edom, according to their dwelling places in the land of their possession; that is Esau, the father of Edom.

Here follow the names of eight kings of Edom. Even in the Middle Ages a Jewish scholar claimed that this paragraph was written at the time of king Jehoshaphat. The defenders of Mosaic authorship of the Pentateuch interpret the first king in Israel (verse 21) as either God, which is the Mosaic theocracy, or Moses himself (according to Deut. 33,5). Prevailing opinion today holds this first king ruling over Israel to be Saul; or it is interpreted "before a king of Israel ruled over Edom", which would be David. This is wrong in any case.

The book of Genesis is intended as an introduction to the history of Israel under Moses; therefore it does not look beyond his time. It may perhaps speak of kingship as a promise (17,6.16;35,11); later kingship may be prophesied as in the speeches of Balaam, yet the naming of a number of post-Mosaic Edomite kings is from its point of view as impossible as an enumeration of Israelite kings. Rather, just as the genealogy of Esau is supposed to lead to Amalek who attacked Israel during the exodus, and to the chiefs of Edom who trembled after Israel's passage through the Red Sea (Ex. 15,15), so the kings of Edom are mentioned to lead to the last one with whom Moses negotiated in vain (Num. 20,14) for free passage through his land. The Israelite reader of the report in Numbers would wonder: Edom, Jacob's brother, already had a king at a time when kings were merely promised to Israel? Here is the answer, this was already the eighth king.

Verse 31 may well be understood: these eight kings have already reigned in Edom although there is yet no king in Israel. *Before* need not mean that the second event follows immediately; it may mean that it will happen later. In other words the first event may, but need not, have occurred long before (see 13,10 and other passages).

None of these kings is the son of his predecessor as in the house of David; an elective kingship may be assumed. Each king is from a different locality, mentioned by name, to characterize all these kings as non-Edomites, in contrast to Deut. 17,15. The basic reason for listing these kings is to stress that they were not descendants of Esau, not the kings promised to Abraham and Sarah for their descendants (17,6.16). Those shall come from Jacob.

Verse 35. *Who defeated Midian in the country of Moab.* This report also looks toward the time of Moses. In Num. 22,4 the king of Moab is an ally of Midian. Our passage says that this was not always so; earlier Edom had aided Moab against Midian. The former enemies were united only against Israel.

Verse 39. The mother of this king Hadar again (as Oholibamah), has two fathers. Here too the meaning could be that she had a legitimate and an illegitimate father. Her doubtful birth would reflect on the king himself. The last mentioned Edomite woman was a bastard like the first. This king is supposed still to live at the time of writing; therefore not "he died".

Verse 40. The chiefs of Esau's sons in the land of Edom had been enumerated in verses 15ff; those of the sons of Seir the Horite are separately listed in verses 21-29. After the Horites have been absorbed in Esau and an Edomite kingdom is in existence, only chiefs of Esau who are chiefs of Edom exist. Timna and Oholibamah, the two women of the family of Seir also have chiefs. As no other chiefs of Seir are mentioned, the Horites lived on in the new nation only through women who were married to men of Esau's family.

The Intention Of The Chapter

Before the Bible turns to the last topic of the book of Genesis, the sons of Jacob becoming the sons of Israel, it takes leave from the other son of Isaac. He did not become the heir of the promises and the third patriarch because of his descendants. He married Canaanite women and not only settled in another land, but was absorbed among a foreign people. The moral conceptions of this people about marriage and family were the very opposite of those of Israel (Lev. 18). Esau walked in the ways of Canaan and Egypt. He had three wives, one was the daughter of a Hittite and native Canaanite, one of an emigrant Canaanite, the third of granddaughter of the Egyptian maidservant Hagar. The wives taken by Esau and his first-born, Eliphaz, were partly born under immoral circumstances. There was a tangle of abominable intercourse, worse than in the Greek house of the Labdakides. Not their faith, but their morality was repulsive to Israel. Their line of descendancy is a caricature. Esau which is Edom had kings before Jacob, which is Israel; but they were not those promised by God from the seed of Abraham and Sarah.

Chapters 37-50

Jacob's Descendants

The story of Joseph has been praised as a treasure of world literature. Mohammed called it the most beautiful of all stories. Even Voltaire had to confess that it is one of the most precious documents which has been handed down to our own ages from antiquity. Neither Egypt nor Babylon can offer anything even remotely comparable. The matchless story of the lost son moves old and young alike. As a literary work it is artistic perfection. It has unity in spite of considerable length, natural motivation of the characters, freshness of color, simplicity and charm of language. Yet matter and form are only ways of expressing certain national, religious, and ethical ideas. The soul of the story in its depth, purity, and beauty have still not been completely recognized.

The narrative is divided into the following parts: 1) Joseph's sale to Egypt, (Judah's family), Joseph in prison (chapters 37-40); 2) Joseph's elevation, the brothers before him (chapters 41-44, 17); 3) Joseph makes himself known, the transfer of the family, Joseph's activities in Egypt (chapters 44,18-47,27); 4) Jacob's death (chapters 47,28-50).

Chapter 37

Joseph Sold to Egypt.

Jacob dwelt in the land of his father's sojournings, in the land of Canaan. ²These are the descendants of Jacob: Joseph, being seventeen years old, was shepherding the flock, at the side of his brothers, as an aid at the side of the sons of Bilhah and at the side of the sons of Zilpah, his father's wives; but Joseph brought the gossip about them which was evil to his father. ³Yet Israel loved Joseph more than all his sons; because he was a son of old age for him, and he made him a long robe with sleeves. ⁴But his brothers, when they saw that their father loved him more than all his brothers, hated him and could not stand his peaceful greeting.

Jacob dwelt wanted to dwell there in peace (Midrash, Rashi); no one loves Canaan as his "fatherland" as much as Jacob (30,25) who had to live abroad for the longest time. Yet that land had been the scene of the story long enough; it shall be moved to Egypt. Otherwise, this family, now in its third generation, might take root in Canaan, in which they shall only sojourn at this time. Jacob would not have left of his own free will. A contrast to Esau (36,6 ff.) is also intended (Rashbam, ibn Ezra, Ramban).

Verse 2. *These are the descendants of Jacob* is not followed by his name as in 6,9;11,10. *Joseph* gives substance to the story of Jacob's descendants. Literally taken, the descendants of Jacob are the seventy souls of 46,27.

Shepherding the flock at the side of his brothers. He was not an equal of his brothers; Joseph cared for the sheep, but due to his youth only as an aid. It is also a contrast to verse 12; henceforth they shepherded the flock without him. *As an aid* is usually translated "as a lad", but it indicates the assisting and confiding attachment which a young man shall find in his elders rather than age. He is a subordinate helper similar to the position of Joshua to Moses or of Gehazi to Elisha. Joseph's youth also justified his assignment to the sons of the maidservants. Bilhah, the maid of his mother Rachel is mentioned first which may mean that she had been like a second mother to him. He grew up with her sons, Dan and Naphtali, to whom Gad and Asher, the sons of the other maid, Zilpah, attached themselves. Or Bilhah is mentioned first because her sons were older than those of Zilpah.

The gossip about them which was evil vicious words spoken about the sons of Bilhah and Zilpah by others. It would be evil gossip about Joseph to assume with some translators that this generous youth could invent malicious words. Leah's sons, however, are quite capable of such action.

Sons of a principal wife, they spoke slightingly about the sons of the maidservants. The Midrash claims that they called them "slaves".

The wives of his father Joseph resented their conduct as an insult to the father, so he complained about it to Jacob. Joseph's action was well-meant, but unwise, as it did not change Leah's sons. Hatred, however, was generated only by the father's preferment of Joseph over all his sons.

Verse 3. Joseph was out of favor with his brothers, but his father compensated him with still greater love. *Israel* this name is intentionally used; it indicates the ideal unity of the family. The father's love divided the brothers, but also brought them together again. His greater love for Joseph is not mentioned as a reproach, as Joseph *was for him a son of old age*. Not born in his old age as were all his sons (ibn Ezra), but a son which old age loves and needs, full of understanding, especially close, and similar in his thinking to the old father (Onkelos, Ramban).

A long robe. The term occurs again in II Sam 13,18 ff. "thus were the virgin daughters of the king clad of old, with sleeves." The translation "many-colored" robe originated in the Septuagint, but has no linguistic basis. The word indicates a long robe, with sleeves reaching down to the wrists. Long robes are worn by people who need not work. Jacob with fatherly love saw the future master in Rachel's first-born son. Showing this openly was a mistake.

Verse 4. *Their father.* They must have said, 'Is he not our father too? Are we not Joseph's brothers?' Out of respect, however, they do not turn against the father. *Could not stand his peaceful greeting.* They were incapable of returning his greeting (Luzzato, Abrabanel), could not say shalom to him. "Could not speak peaceably with him" would have been expressed differently in Hebrew.

⁵Now Joseph had a dream and he told it to his brothers and they only hated him the more. ⁶He said to them. "Please, hear this dream which I have dreamed. ⁷Behold, we were binding sheaves in the field, and lo, my sheaf arose and stood upright; and behold, your sheaves gathered around it, and bowed down to my sheaf." ⁸His brothers said to him, "Are you indeed to be king over us? Or are you indeed going to rule us?" So they hated him yet more for his dreams and for his words.

Joseph's story contains six dreams in three parallel pairs—two of Joseph, two of the butler and baker, and two of Pharaoh. Each pair brought Joseph nearer to greatness. A distinction should be made between dreams *in* which and dreams *through* which God speaks. In the first category God appears and speaks either making a request or, more frequently, prohibiting or warning. These dreams need no interpretation, as everyone understands their language. They are not "dreams", but divine speeches, addressed to a sleeping person. All the dreams of the Joseph story consist in images and incidents. They too "speak", but several interpretations are possible. The dreamer therefore desires an explanation, preferably by an expert interpreter. Dreams in which God appears demand action from man, while the second type foretells future events. Those are Israel's method to express God's communication with man. These testify to the general human belief that fate may indirectly suggest the future to man. The differences between Joseph's dreams and those of the patriarchs correspond to their respective places in the history of Biblical religion. Nearness to God decreases. He still speaks with Abraham, Isaac, and Jacob in person, but no longer with Joseph. The dreams are also a literary device to achieve progress in the story.

Verse 6. *Please.* Joseph would have liked to allay their hostility.

Verse 7. *Binding sheaves in the field.* This is probably an allusion that grain will make Joseph a ruler (Ramban, Redak, Abrabanel). The meaning of the dream could not be misunderstood, especially in connection with the princely robe, and was perhaps even provoked by it. It humiliated the brothers.

Verse 8. Their excited answer like Joseph's account is rythmical.
For his dreams and for his words. They hated him not only for his, perhaps pretended (Abrabanel) dreams, but also for his manner of

telling them. Hatred mentioned three times is deep rooted and
sufficient motive for murderous intent (Deut. 4,42; 19,4).

> *⁹Then he dreamed yet another dream, and told it to his brothers
> and said, "Behold, I have dreamed yet a dream; behold, the sun,
> the moon, and eleven stars were bowing down to me." ¹⁰He told it
> to his father and to his brothers. Then his father rebuked him and
> said to him, "What is this dream that you have dreamed? Shall I
> and your mother and your brothers indeed come to bow ourselves
> to the ground before you?" ¹¹His brothers were jealous of him; but
> his father kept the matter in mind.*

The first dream draws upon the earth, the second upon the sky. As
usual the dream itself represents the impossible, even as sun, moon,
and stars never appear together. Nor is it accurate as Joseph's mother
was no longer alive.

Verse 10. As the father appears in the dream, Joseph must tell it to
him and his brothers. The father alone replied in the presence of the
brothers to let them hear the rebuke (Ramban). He reproached Joseph,
"What is this dream?" Reprehensible thoughts must have inspired it.

To bow ourselves to the ground a strongly emotional overstatement
of verse 9. The maddening element of both dreams is the word "bow
down", the rule of the youngest son over the whole family. These
dreams had an entirely different meaning for Joseph, the noblest of
brothers, as shown in 42,9.

Verse 11. Jealousy is not the same as hatred, but means a loss of one's
composure in the face of another person's unmerited good luck and
airing this feeling in words. Hatred can be silent.

The father rebuked Joseph, but his inner attitude was different. While
the brothers take it personally, Jacob began to think about the objective
content of the matter. Does it have substance? Thus he is later (45,28)
able to believe that Joseph is alive and has attained greatness
(Rashbam).

> ¹²Now, his brothers went to pasture their father's flock near She-
> chem. ¹³And Israel said to Joseph, "Are not your brothers pastur-
> ing the flock at Shechem? Come, I will send you to them." And he
> said to him, "Here I am." ¹⁴So he said to him, "Go now see after
> the peace of your brothers, and after the peace of the flocks; and

bring me back a report." So he sent him from the valley of Hebron,
and he came to Shechem.

Joseph must be conveyed to Egypt; he was brought there through the
guilt of his brothers who wanted to do away with him. As the father
had to be deceived they had to separate Joseph from him. The previous
scenes have led to a break; the brothers no longer wanted to live with
the hated one; as the father sustained him, they went away.

Verse 13. The father sent Joseph after them to reestablish peace.
Israel indicates that the sons should be united. Cautiously he tested
him: What would you think if I send you to them to Shechem? I know
that is asking a great deal of you. Yet Joseph the good son and concilia-
tory brother, answered without hesitation like Abraham, "Here I am".
His journey too will be sacrificial.

Verse 14. What shall Joseph do? Seemingly, he shall inquire after the
well-being of the brothers; however, this can only be a pretext. The
father wants to reconcile them after they have departed in anger. The
sending of Joseph as messenger of peace should afford them gratification. Peace, peace is the watchword of Israel. Indeed Joseph will find
them united, but among themselves and against him.
And bring me back a report. He will not return. It is the manner of
tragedy that people unsuspectingly speak without knowing the future
meaning of their words.
From the valley of Hebron. There Abraham was buried in the valley
like Moses (Deut. 34,6). Jacob took Joseph to the ancestor's grave; from
there he sent him to seek peace with his brothers. Before they parted he
must have spoken of the past and the future of the family.

> ¹⁵*And a man found him wandering in the field; and the man*
> *asked him, "What are you seeking?"* ¹⁶*"I am seeking my*
> *brothers," he said, "tell me, please, where they are pasturing the*
> *flock."* ¹⁷*And the man said, "They have gone on from here, for I*
> *heard say, 'Let us go to Dothan.'"* *So Joseph went after his broth-*
> *ers and found them in Dothan.*

Had Joseph gone against his will, he might now have turned home
and said, "I did not find them in Shechem." However, he did not want
to come back without result (Rashbam) as he too was anxious "for the
peace of the brothers". He shall meet them; God's intentions are
fulfilled under all circumstances; if one way does not work, he creates

another. Joseph followed the divine hint obediently (Ramban). The *man*, even if not expressly called so, was a messenger of God who *found* Joseph.

Verse 16. Joseph naturally told more details: 'I am a son of Jacob. My brothers are supposed to pasture here etc.' Yet the Bible has him speak with moving ambiguity, *I am seeking my brothers!* A sentence which reflects the soul of Joseph and of the whole story.

Verse 17. *I heard say* some people who must have been your brothers.

> *18They saw him afar off, and before he came near to them they conspired against him to put him to death. 19They said to one another, "Behold, Mister Dreamer is coming. Come now, let us kill him and throw him into one of the pits, and we will say that a wild beast has devoured him. We shall see what will become of his dreams!" 21When Reuben heard it, he wanted to rescue him out of their hands, saying, "We will not take a life." 22Further Reuben said to them, "Shed no blood, cast him into the nearest pit which is in the desert, but lay no hand upon him."—that he might rescue him out of their hands, to restore him to his father.*

Verse 19. *Mister Dreamer*, mockingly as if it were a profession.

Verse 20. They wanted to throw the body into a pit that it might not be found and their lie seem credible. This also prepares for Reuben's suggestion. *We shall see what becomes of his dreams.* A contemptuous defiance of God who has sent the dreams. They believed in their truth, but also that they could undo them. Their speech commences and closes with the hated dreams.

Verse 21. Reuben the oldest brother intervened. *Let us not take a life* emphatically, as a life cannot be restored. First Reuben established that he and they, all of "us" could and would not commit a murder. That was unimaginable!

Verse 22. *Shed no blood* again expresses horror of murder; *Lay no hand on him* characterizes even the beginning of it as a despicable action of violence. Reuben spared no effort to prevent that. *To restore him to his father* Only he, the oldest son, thought of the father, but he lacked courage to oppose his brothers completely. His well meant suggestion was as imprudent as his offer in 42,37. *Into one of the pits which is in the desert* remote from people; his cries for help will go unheard. This detail is necessary so that Reuben may rescue Joseph without the brothers noticing it.

> ²³*So when Joseph came to his brothers, they stripped Joseph of his robe, the long robe with sleeves that he wore.* ²⁴*And they took him and cast him into the pit. The pit was empty, there was no water in it.*

He was to be humiliated before they rid themselves of him. This prepares for verses 31 and 33.

Verse 24. They would not have cast him into a full well as they no longer intended murder (Rashbam, Ramban).

> ²⁵*Then they sat down to eat; and looking up they saw, behold, a caravan of Ishmaelites coming from Gilead, with their camels bearing gum, balm, and myrrh, on their way to carry it down to Egypt.* ²⁶*Then Judah said to his brothers, "What profit is it if we kill our brother and conceal his blood?* ²⁷*Come, let us sell him to the Ishmaelites, and let not our hand be upon him, for he is our brother, our own flesh." And his brothers heard it.*

After the heavy and painful work they sat down to eat; in this way time is gained for the events at the pit, (compare II Kings 9,34).
Ishmaelites is not the name of a people, but the appelation of an occupation: raiser, keeper, or driver of camels; similarly Canaanite means merchant and later Aramean or Edomite means heathen. Egypt was the destination of such caravans, which gave Judah an idea.

Verse 26. Reuben's words had impressed Judah; his appeal is not to emotion, but to reason. Leaving Joseph in the pit also means to kill him (V. 20).

Verse 27. *Let not our hand be upon him* is a concession to Reuben.
And his brothers heard it, not that they agreed as most commentators think; in Hebrew this would at least have required heard "him", "his words", or "his voice". Merely *Heard it* need not be followed by action, but rather indicates that they heard it with misgivings (see verse 21;35,22; Num. 16,4). The brothers heard it, but before they could decide, the following had occurred.

²⁸*Then Midianite people, traders, passed by; and they drew Joseph up and lifted him out of the pit, and sold Joseph to the Ishmaelites for twenty pieces of silver; and they took Joseph to Egypt.*

The misunderstanding of this passage has been fatal for the entire Joseph story. Since ancient times it has been assumed according to 40,15; 45,4 f.—that the brothers sold Joseph. Rashbam, (see also Sefer Hayashar, Hiskuni and other Jewish commentators) saw that it was done by Midianites. They were traders who passed through the land as buyers, not like the Ishmaelites merchants in foreign commerce (see also Seforno). The Midianites passed the cistern and *they drew up Joseph* as they were probably attracted by his cries; finally they—there is no other subject between—*sold Joseph to the Ishmaelites* and these Ishmaelites, provided with camels and prepared for such trading trips, *took Joseph to Egypt.* This is the incontestable statement of the text. For 40,15; 45,4 see the commentary there. Here we stand at the fatal turning point of Israel's history; its central event is the exodus from Egypt, and through Joseph, who finally draws the whole family after him, Israel enters Egypt.

²⁹*When Reuben returned to the pit—behold, no Joseph in the pit—he rent his clothes.* ³⁰*And he returned to his brothers and said, "The lad is gone; and I, where shall I go?"*

Reuben will use the time, while the brothers eat, to rescue Joseph. The words *no Joseph in the pit* picture his consternation. *He rent his* clothes like a mourner. Were we to assume that the brothers had sold Joseph, this attitude of Reuben would be incomprehensible.

Verse 30. How can I appear before our father? Reuben strongly felt his responsibility as the oldest son.

³¹*Then they took Joseph's robe, slaughtered a goat, and dipped the robe in the blood;* ³²*and they sent the long robe with sleeves, and had it brought to their father, and had it said, "This we have found; see now whether it is your son's robe or not."*

The Hebrew word conceals the sender. Jacob shall not know that the robe came from them and not even that Joseph had arrived at his destination. Naturally, they acted so as not to betray themselves. The speech has been put into the mouth of the supposed finders by the brothers in order to draw the desired conclusion from Jacob.

> *33He recognized it, and said, "The robe of my son! A wild beast has devoured him! Joseph is without doubt torn to pieces!"* *34Then Jacob rent his garments, and put sackcloth upon his loins, and mourned for his son many days. 35All his sons and all his daughters rose up to comfort him; but he refused to be comforted, and said, "No, I shall go down to Sheol to my son, mourning." Thus his father wept for him.*

The father's exclamations are of great psychological truth and shocking effect. The first is not even a complete sentence as if language failed him. He could only repeat the words of the others. The next shows his mind at work and draw the worst conclusion. These are exactly the words of the sons in verse 20. Their calculation has indeed succeeded. With the third exclamation the unhappy man collapsed under the heartrending thought that his beloved Joseph had been torn to pieces by wild beasts.

Torn to pieces from the language of shepherds; this favorite son had been his pet lamb. His last word is the beloved name.

Verse 34. Jacob now observed the customs of mourning for the dead. *Many days*, not limiting himself to the usual period.

Verse 35. *And all his daughters.* Daughters-in-law are called daughters (compare Ruth 1,11f). Here began repentance and inner change of the sons. Jacob will not discard the signs of mourning until his own death.

> *36Meanwhile, the Midianites had sold him to Egypt for Potiphar, a courtier of Pharaoh, the captain of the guard.*

Joseph was not dead. *To Egypt* namely to the Ishmaelites who were on their way to Egypt and actually delivered him there (39,1). The position of his master prepares for Joseph's future closeness to Pharaoh.

Chapter 38

Judah and Tamar

It happened at that time that Judah went down from his brothers and spread out near a respected Adullamite, whose name was Hirah. ²There Judah saw the daughter of a respected Canaanite whose name was Shua; he married her and went in to her, ³and she conceived and bore a son, and he called his name Er. ⁴Again she conceived and bore a son, and she called his name Onan. ⁵Yet again she bore a son, and she called his name Shelah. And it was in Chezib when she bore him.

Judah went down from Hebron which is in the mountains. He was also the first of his brothers to lower himself by seeking intercourse with Canaanites.

Verse 3. The name of the first son was given by the father, who expected him to continue his family name, Judah.

Verse 5. Judah's sons, as well as all his brothers, with the exception of Joseph, were born in Canaan.

⁶And Judah took a wife for Er his firstborn, and her name was Tamar. ⁷But Er, Judah's firstborn, was wicked in the sight of the Lord; and the Lord slew him. ⁸Then Judah said to Onan. "Go in to your brother's wife, and perform the duty of a brother-in-law to her, and raise up offspring for your brother." ⁹But Onan knew that the offspring would not be his; so when he went in to his brother's wife he spilled it on the ground, lest he should give offspring to his brother. ¹⁰And what he did was displeasing in the sight of the Lord, and he slew him also.

Tamar means "palm tree".

Verse 7. Er's offense which displeased God, is not mentioned but a similar death to that of Onan suggests a similar sin. According to the

Midrash Er did not want to beget children so as not to mar the beauty of his wife by pregnancy.

Verse 8. Judah requests Onan to perform the levirate as it is found in later law (Deut. 25,5 ff).

The name levirate comes from the Latin word for brother-in-law. This custom demanded that if a man had died without male descendants, his brother should marry the widow. Its purpose was to maintain the deceased brother's name and to build a family for him. Marrying the brother's wife under any other circumstances was prohibited (Lev. 18,16; 20,21). Only in this case the surviving brother should set aside inhibitions of custom and law. Our story represents Judah as founder of the levirate institution.

Verse 9. Onan obeys his father, but selfishly voids his intentions during the sexual intercourse. This is told quite realistically, and gave its name to a well-known vice.

Verse 10. God caused Onan to die, which indicates that Judah's request had been pleasing to God.

> [11]Then Judah said to Tamar his daughter-in-law, "Remain a widow in your father's house, till Shelah my son grows up"—for he feared that he would die, like his brothers. So Tamar went and dwelt in her father's house.

Now the duty would revert to Shelah, the third brother. Tamar was called Judah's daughter-in-law, even after the death of her husband; correspondingly Judah remained her father-in-law verses 13 and 25. As in Hebrew both terms indicate the protection of the young wife by the house of her in-laws, it was uncharitable of Judah still to recognize her as his daughter-in-law and as the betrothed of Shelah, and nevertheless to send her to her father's house. He told her to wait for Shelah, but kept his true reason to himself—Shela should not die, like his brothers.

> [12]In the course of considerable time the wife of Judah, Shua's daughter died; and when Judah was comforted, he went up to Timnah to his sheep-shearers, he and his friend Hirah the Adullamite. [13]And when Tamar was told, "Your father-in-law is going up to Timnah to shear his sheep," [14]she put off her widow's garments and put on a veil, wrapping herself up, and set at the entrance to the crossroads, which is on the road to Timnah; for

she saw that Shelah was grown up and she had not been given to him in marriage.

Judah was comforted. The mourning period was over and he returned to the joys of living.

Verse 14. The widower Judah has comforted himself, so Tamar still remaining a widow in her parents' house decided to terminate her widowhood. She veiled herself so as not to be recognized by Judah (Rashi and others). *At the entrance to the crossroads* visible to everyone (Rashi).

> ¹⁵*When Judah saw her, he thought her to be a harlot, for she had covered her face.* ¹⁶*He went over to her at the road side, and said, "Come, let me go in to you," for he did not know that she was his daughter-in-law. She said, "What will you give me, that you may come in to me?"* ¹⁷*He answered, "I will send you a kid from the flock." And she said, "Will you give me a pledge, till you send it?"* ¹⁸*He said, "What pledge shall I give you?" She replied, "Your signet, and your cord, and your staff that is in your hand." So he gave them to her, and went in to her, and she conceived by him.* ¹⁹*Then she arose and went away, and taking off her veil she put on the garments of her widowhood.*

Judah has trapped himself.

Verse 17. Signets were in general use for the signing of contracts. A number of them have been found in Israel. A cord may have been carried as a mark of a man's dignity; the signet was usually tied to it. Staffs were also worn with insignia on them. All these are objects of an individual character by which the owner could be recognized beyond any doubt.

> ²⁰*When Judah sent the kid by his friend the Adullamite to receive the pledge from the woman's hand, he could not find her.* ²¹*And he asked the men of the place, "Where is the cult prostitute who was at the crossroads by the wayside?" And they said, "No cult prostitute was here."* ²²*So he returned to Judah, and said, "I have not found her; and also the men of the place said, 'No cult prostitute was here.'"* ²³*And Judah replied, "Let her keep the things, lest we be laughed at; you see, I sent this kid, and you could not find her."*

Verse 21. Hirah called her a *cult prostitute* in the manner of the Canaanites to whom he is speaking, perhaps also out of consideration for Judah and from a feeling of decency. Women who prostituted themselves in the service of a religious cult were found frequently in antiquity.

Verse 23. In spite of their value, we will pursue this matter no further; for it would be embarassing (Rashi): 'I hope she will not show them to strangers who would think it contemptible for me to have given them to a harlot. In any case I have tried to keep my promise.'

> *24About three months later Judah was told, "Tamar your daughter-in-law has played the harlot; and moreover she is with child by harlotry." And Judah said, "Bring her out, and let her be burned." 25As she was being brought out, she sent to her father-in-law to let him know, "By the man to whom these belong, I am with child." And she said, "Recognize, I pray you, whose these are, the signet and the cord and the staff." 26Then Judah acknowledged them and said, "She is more righteous than I, inasmuch as I did not give her to my son, Shelah." And he did not lie with her again.*

The penalty of being burned alive in the later law applies (Lev. 21,9) to the daughter of a priest who has played the harlot while in the house of her father as well as to immorality with mother and daughter (Lev. 20,14). Adultery is punished by ordinary execution (Lev. 20,10), in case of a betrothed girl by stoning to death (Deut. 22,23f). Rashbam assumes an older law, Ramban claims Judah is represented as a ruler and judges on his own authority.

Luzzato thinks that Judah applies the severest punishment because the sons of Jacob (chapter 34) were especially strict regarding their family honor.

Verse 25. These are not the words of Tamar's messenger, but only interpretation of the intent of her message. The message itself is presented in the next sentence.

Verse 26. She is more right and better than I; I had done wrong, and she has done right. *And he did not lie with her again.* Tamar's pregnancy was providential intention now fulfilled which Judah recognized.

> *27When the time of her delivery came, behold, there were twins in her womb. 28And when she was in labor, one put out a hand; and*

> the midwife took and bound on his hand a scarlet thread, saying, "This came out first." ²⁹But as he drew back his hand, behold, his brother came out; and she said, "What a breach you have made for yourself! A breach over you!" Therefore he called his name Perez (Breach). ³⁰Afterward his brother came out with the scarlet thread upon his hand; and his name was called Zerah.

Verse 29. One gave precedence to the other, different from Jacob and Esau. The one who really came out first is the first-born. The midwife angrily reproached him and prophesied that he will suffer for it in the future.

Meaning and Purpose of Chapter 38

Tamar has been described as a woman who wants a child at any price, disregards custom and law, even commits incest, and risks life and honor for her purpose. Actually this story, often regarded as objectionable, is the crown of the book of Genesis and Tamar one of the most admirable women.

The purpose of the chapter can be recognized by its conclusion. It leads to Perez the ancestor of David and the Judaean royal dynasty. The book of Ruth which closes with the name of David expressly mentions Tamar and Perez (Ruth 4,12) and knows no higher blessing for Ruth at her wedding than her house may be like that of Tamar. And rightly so!

One point regarding the institution of the levirate, here introduced by Judah, is usually overlooked; will the woman agree to it? The levirate implies that a woman who marries must under certain circumstances be ready to become the wife of one of her husband's brothers. It is not merely the one man, but the whole family and clan to which she joins herself. Neither the brother nor she can be forced to the levirate according to Talmud and Shulhan Aruh (Eben Haezer 165). Her willingness would show loyalty not only to her deceased husband, but to the whole family which she would maintain. Should the brother refuse she is right in publicly disgracing him for his lack of piety by the ceremony described in Deut. 25,5ff (Halitzah).

In our case Judah thinks of the levirate only after the death of Er. Tamar could have refused and regarded herself as a widow, no longer bound to his family. In spite of her bad experience with the first brother, she silently places herself at the disposal of the second. He dies too, after having treated her despicably, yet she does not repudiate this family, but waits for the third brother. When he is withheld from her, she induces her father-in-law to cohabitation.

Her motive cannot have been the wish for a child at any price; she could have had one by marrying another man. She, however, is aware of the exalted mission which became hers by marrying into Judah's family. The laconic way of Scripture must be supplemented. Without doubt Judah informed Tamar about his family, their mission, and the divine promises when he gave her to his oldest son. After Reuben (35,22) and Simeon and Levi (chapter 34) had been rejected, Judah as the next had reason to think that the promise "Kings shall spring from you." (35,11; 17,16) referred to him. Tamar has understood that she would be the mother of these kings. She wants to live solely for this mission. When, after the refusal of the last son she turns to the father, she merely acts as Judah did by the levirate. The intention is the same and the expression "incest" is out of place. The wife of my son is no more closely related to me than the wife of my brother.

The Biblical prohibitions against marriages between close relatives have moral reasons not biological or mystical ones. There are three women—mother, sister, and daughter—who must not be married because of an initially different moral relationship. This relationship must not conflict with the intimacy of marriage. In addition husband and wife are one flesh from which the prohibitions of the father's, the brother's, and the son's wife are derived; their wives are in this way the same as mother, sister, and daughter. All other prohibited relations can be derived from this. Horror of incest is not cause, but effect of the prohibition.

Biblical thinking knows considerations which under certain circumstances are of higher standing than any law, for instance the preservation of life and the duties which serve this purpose. Tamar had learned this from Judah and his levirate, but he had stopped half way. She is unshakably steadfast in her loyalty and binds him without his knowledge by signet, cord, and staff. The symbolism is evident. Tamar is the worthy successor to the wives of the patriarchs. All of them had lived only in the thought of the promised future—Sarah 16,2; 21,10ff.; Rebekah 25,22; 27,46; Leah and Rachel 30,1 ff.

Tamar stands even higher as she was originally a stranger. Her descent is not mentioned, only her name. This is intentional in contrast to Judah's wife. Undoubtedly Tamar too was the daughter of a Canaanite, because Judah lived among Canaanites and had taken a wife for himself from them. Calling her Tamar, and not "the daughter of a Canaanite man", points to her as an individual of special worth. Her merit consists in her responsiveness to the exalted mission of ancestress of the Messiah. Nobility of mind is more than nobility of family. Tamar represents the triumph of the spirit over "blood", and the attraction of Israel's national-religious ideas and of its faith. Another example is Jethro (Ex. 18).

We now understand that Judah's wife (verse 2) is called the daughter of a Canaanite. Her father Shua was a genuine Canaanite with a Canaanite bent of mind, and his daughter and her sons were similar. They have no understanding for Israel's mission. Er does not want to beget children, and Onan will beget none for someone else. That is part of the Canaanite-Egyptian perversity (Lev 18,2). A genuine son of Abraham begets children for his people and for eternity. Those men are killed by God who desires life and ordains events in such a way that Judah himself begets the ancestor of the kings. The woman is of foreign blood, but she is not only his equal, but even superior to him in moral purity and consistency. Ruth is the worthy successor of Tamar. She too is of foreign origin, from Moab; and Moab himself had been born in incest (19,37). Yet again a noble mind triumphs over "blood". Ruth speaks that which Tamar thought, "Where you go I will go; your people shall be my people, and your God my God" (Ruth 1,16). After joining a house in Israel, Ruth will remain loyal unto death, and even offer herself covertly to a remote relative of her deceased husband.

This chapter is vital for the book of Genesis which tells the origins of Israel. However, Israel's story culminates in kingship. The tribe from which the king would come had to be indicated, even more so his ancestors. Chapters 34, 36, and 38 refer to each other. Each one of them is concerned with mixed marriage. A daughter of Jacob marries a Canaanite—she is lost; Jacob's brother marries Canaanite women—he is absorbed into the foreign people to such a degree that Esau and Edom become identical; a noble stranger marries into Israel and becomes the ancestress of Israel's most glorious family.

Ranke stated that artistic considerations necessitate the insertion of this chapter into the Joseph story. Following chapter 37 a delay is needed; the plot shall not be unravelled too swiftly. Chapter 38 permits a pause while Joseph's fate matures and while the father still mourns at home. This, however, would not sufficiently explain the use of this particular story for the delay. The Midrash says: Before bondage begins, the redeemer is born. Joseph's coming to Egypt begins Israel's bondage. On the other hand, Perez is the ancestor of the Messianic king. The hero of the following story is Joseph, but salvation will come from Judah.

Chapter 39

Joseph And Potiphar's Wife

After Joseph had been brought to Egypt, it is necessary to provide an
occasion for meeting Pharaoh; for only he can raise him to a rank which
will enable him to bring his family and to provide for them.

> *Joseph had been taken down to Egypt, and Potiphar, a courtier of*
> *Pharaoh, the captain of the guard, an Egyptian bought him from*
> *the Ishmaelites who had brought him down.*

Potiphar's titles are listed as each of the following stories show how
Joseph wins the hearts of the high and mighty everywhere, finally the
heart of the king himself. Potiphar, an Egyptian noble, was representative of Egypt in his thought and religion. This affords the correct
perspective to the unbecoming conduct of Potiphar's wife as well as his
own honorable behavior. While she, in adulterous sexuality, pursued
the handsome youth, he, an Egyptian, recognized Joseph's moral qualities or at least their usefulness. Now we may understand the position of
chapter 38. Chapter 39 supplements it; the sexual manners of the land
of Egypt and those of the land of Canaan are placed side by side (Lev.
18,3). In a spirit of justice the good aspects or noble personalities of
these foreign peoples are gladly acknowledged (there Tamar, here
Potiphar).

> ²*The Lord was with Joseph, and he became a lucky man; so he*
> *was in the house of his master, the Egyptian.* ³*His master saw that*
> *the Lord was with him, and that the Lord caused all that he did to*
> *prosper in his hands.* ⁴*So Joseph found favor in his sight and*
> *attended him; he made him overseer of his house and put him in*
> *charge of all that he had.* ⁵*And it came to pass from the time that*
> *he made him overseer of his house and all that he had, the Lord*
> *blessed the Egyptian's house for Joseph's sake; the blessing of the*
> *Lord was on all that he possessed, in house and field.* ⁶*So he left*
> *all that he had in Joseph's charge; and having him he had no*

*concern for anything but the food which he ate. Now Joseph was
handsome and good-looking.*

Verse 2. Joseph lived as a slave in a strange country, but he was
neither alone nor forsaken as God was with him. God stands by those
who are with Him. Joseph did not fail in any task as might otherwise
have been feared; on the contrary he succeeded in everything. He
became *a lucky man* as the people called him.

Verse 3. Potiphar observed his work and tried to discover the source
of his constant success. The cause could only lie in that quality which
distinguished him from the other slaves, his religion, his God. It is to
Potiphar's credit that, even though an Egyptian, he understood and
acknowledged this. A later Pharaoh will say, "Who is the Lord? I do not
know him." (Ex. 5,2).

Verse 4. Joseph had won his master's personal favor. He was no
longer one of many servants; therefore the name Joseph is mentioned
again. He appointed him as his personal attendant and granted him
far-reaching authority.

Verse 5. Joseph now had an independent position and the success
became immediately apparent. There was a blessing on everything; it
grew and multiplied.

Verse 6. prepares for Joseph's words in verses 8 and 9. He *had no
concern but the food which he ate.* According to Bereshith Rabbah (see
Rashi) this is an inoffensive expression for Potiphar's wife. Ibn Ezrah
and others say: Joseph was not allowed to touch his master's bread, as
(43,32) Egyptians and Hebrews must not eat together. Rashbam
explains that he cared for nothing if only the meal was on the table. In
this way he would be like his colleagues (chapter 40) and his master
Pharaoh who dream only of food. Ramban thinks he discovered that
Joseph asked for nothing but his food. His only fault was being handsome.

> ⁷*And it came to pass after these things, that his master's wife cast
> her eyes upon Joseph, and said, "Lie with me."* ⁸*But he refused
> and said to his master's wife, "Lo, having me my master has no
> concern over anything in the house, and he has put everything
> that he possesses in my hand:* ⁹*He is not greater in this house than
> I am; nor has he kept back anything from me except you, because*

you are his wife; how then can I do this great wickedness, and sin against God?"

Lewdly and shamelessly she stated what she wanted from him.

Verse 9. Joseph spoke of marriage like a civilized man. A wife is not an object and possession which can be shared with strangers as among some nations. Considerately he says "my master", not "your husband". The fear of God consists in respecting that which another man has reserved for himself. He did not speak of her sin in appealing to him, as he respected his master's wife in her. In view of her passion it would have been in vain.

> ¹⁰*Yet it happened, as she spoke to Joseph day after day, and he would not listen to her, to lie with her or to be with her, ¹¹that he entered one day into the house to do his work and none of the men of the house were in the house. ¹²She caught him by his garment, saying "Lie with me." But he left his garment in her hand, and fled and went out.*

Verse 10. After the woman has been denied, she pretends not to have meant it that way. She harrasses him, at least to be with her.

Verse 11. *One day.* Rashi claims on a special day, perhaps the festival of the inundation of the Nile when everyone was away; she had excused herself by illness and remained at home.

> ¹³*And when she saw that he had left his garment in her hand, and had fled out of the house, ¹⁴she called to the men of her household and said to them, "See, one has brought us a Hebrew man to have his play with us; he came to lie with me and I cried out with a loud voice; ¹⁵and when he heard that I lifted up my voice and cried, he left his garment with me and fled and went out." ¹⁶Then she laid up his garment by her until his master came home.*

She saw that fleeing without the garment would attract attention, so she altered the facts. The Bible ridicules her attempt to find witnesses after the event. Here and later she emphasized that she had cried out which according to the law in Deut. 22,24-27, would prove that she had resisted the rape.

Verse 14. According to verse 11 no one would have been able to hear it; she only called the people of the household together afterwards in an attempt to persuade them that she had shouted. *See, one has brought us a Hebrew man*, not her husband (Rashi, Ibn Ezrah). She would not speak so contemptuously of him before his people; but "one" refers to the slave-dealer. She appealed to the envy and the racial prejudice of the Egyptians, putting herself on the level of the servants and making her case theirs.

Verse 16. She waits until "his master", not "her husband", came home as she wanted to complain about a slave, putting the garment by her as if she would change nothing at the scene of the crime.

> *17And she told him the same story, saying, "The Hebrew servant, whom you have brought us, came to have his play with me; 18but as soon as I lifted up my voice and cried, he left his garment with me, and fled out of the house." 19When his master heard the words of his wife which she spoke to him, saying, "This is the way your servant treated me," he became angry. 20Joseph's master took him and put him into the prison where the king's prisoners were confined. So he was there in the prison.*

She implied that it was entirely his fault.

Verse 19. She said *your servant*, whom you favored. He forgot what he owes to you and me. *He became angry* not against Joseph which would have had to be stated expressly, but against his wife (Abrabanel, Seforno). He had always found Joseph reliable. It could not have been the first time that she had cast her eyes on a handsome youth. Her so-called proof was not convincing; her profusion of words must have aroused suspicion; and finally she even reproached him. Had he believed her, Joseph would have had to be sentenced to death or to another grave penalty. Yet the master considered his wife and house and saving face; therefore he put Joseph into prison.

> *21But the Lord was with Joseph and got him kindness and gave him favor in the sight of the keeper of the prison. 22The keeper of the prison committed to Joseph's care all the prisoners who were in the prison; and whatever was done there, he was the doer of it. 23The keeper of the prison paid no heed to anything that was in his care, because the Lord was with him; and whatever he did, the Lord made prosper.*

There too God is with Joseph. The loveable qualities of his personality made him popular; this attraction is as an irrational power ascribed to God. Kindness means affection; favor, all kinds of privileges.

Verse 22. The tasks in which the prisoners did not always succeed, he completed satisfactorily.

Verse 23. This master also ascribed Joseph's lucky character to his God, perhaps only in a superstitious way. God is with his own under all circumstances, and Joseph proved his worth in prison just as under happy conditions. Socrates was given an opportunity to escape from jail, but refused. Joseph may even have had the keys, but he too remained faithfully there.

Chapter 40

Joseph Interprets Dreams In Prison

It happened after these events that the butler of the king of Egypt and the baker offended their lord the king of Egypt. ²And Pharaoh was angry with his two courtiers, the chief butler and the chief baker, ³and he put them in custody in the house of the captain of the guard, in the prison, the place where Joseph was confined. ⁴The captain of the guard charged Joseph with them, and he waited on them; they continued in custody for some time.

Butler and baker represent eating and drinking. The butler is mentioned first because he presented his cup to the king and waited on him more directly than the baker. He is also the main personage in the following narrative. They went to prison as they had "offended" Pharaoh—Joseph because he did not want to offend God. The nature of their offense is not mentioned, but it is natural to suspect that they failed in their respective offices.

Verse 3. *The captain of the guard*, the former master of Joseph, reappears; this does not contradict "the keeper of the prison" in 39.22. Potiphar as captain of the guard was also charged with the prison which even seems to have been located in his house; the keeper functioned under him. This agrees with our explanation of 39.20. Potiphar imprisoned Joseph not as punishment, but to guard and protect him from further pursuit by his wife. He simply gave Joseph another position in which he could continue to use his proven qualities as a reliable servant. Nevertheless, this was a restriction of his movements, a confinement and Joseph could complain (v. 14 ff).

⁵And in one and the same night they both dreamed—the butler and the baker of the king of Egypt who were confined in the prison—each his own dream and each according to its interpretation. ⁶When Joseph came to them in the morning and saw them, they were troubled. ⁷So he asked Pharaoh's courtiers who were in

*custody with him in his masters house, "Why are your faces
downcast today?" ⁸They said to him, "We have had dreams, and
there is no one to interpret them." And Joseph said to them, "Do
not interpretations belong to God? Tell them to me, please."*

Rashbam, Ibn Ezra, Ramban thought that each dream was such that it
could and did correspond to later interpretation; they were true
dreams. The meaning is rather that they did not dream all kinds of
things in confusion, but only those matters which were later told to
Joseph and interpreted by him.

Verse 7. Joseph treated them with respect. They were his compan-
ions in misfortune. 'Perhaps I have been remiss in my service?'
(Abrabanel).

Verse 8. This is typical of Egypt. If at liberty, they would have sought
a professional interpreter of dreams. *Do not interpretations belong to
God?*—the deity who sends dreams also possesses interpretations; perhaps I, inspired by God, can clarify them for you and you will need no
interpreters. God is the source of morality for Joseph (39,9), and here
the source of knowledge. Still better is the explanation of Ibn Ezra and
Ramban: 'You need not worry that I shall be guided by fear of
consequences or other considerations in my interpretation'. Modestly
he declined credit as in 41,16 (compare with Deut. 1,17).

*⁹So the chief butler told his dream to Joseph, and said to him, "In
my dream, behold, there was a vine before me, ¹⁰and on the vine
there were three branches; and as soon as it budded, its blossoms
shot forth, and the clusters ripened into grapes. ¹¹Pharaoh's cup
was in my hand; and I took the grapes, pressed them into
Pharaoh's cup, and placed the cup into Pharaoh's hand."*

Verse 11. Everything happened quickly, almost simultaneously. In
contrast to the speed of verse 10 stands the cautious deliberateness of
the actions in this verse. The threefold use of "Pharaoh" indicates the
devotion of this servant and is an important hint for the interpretation.

*¹²Then Joseph said to him, "This is its interpretation: the three
branches are three days; still three days, and Pharaoh will lift up
your head and restore you to your office; and you shall place
Pharaoh's cup in his hand as formerly, when you were his butler.
¹⁴But remember me, when it is well with you, and do me a*

kindness, I pray you: Make mention of me to Pharaoh, and so get me out of this house. *15For I am indeed stolen out of the land of the Hebrews; and here also I have done nothing that they should put me into the dungeon."*

Really only one element in the dream needed interpretation, that is, translation from the symbolic language of dreams—the number three. Everything else is an image of reality. Joseph recognized this immediately. Numbers indicate periods of time. Here, because of the speed of the development, they point to the unit of time nearest at hand, so the three branches are three days. It is still more likely (Bechor Shor, Ibn Ezra and others) that Joseph knew Pharaoh's birthday was three days off (V.20); on such a day Pharaoh would give signs of his grace. For this reason the courtiers worried about their fate, and had their dreams shortly before this day.

Verse 13. Joseph interpreted in favor of the butler, saying to himself that a man dreams as he acts. The butler must have been a conscientious man who presented only pure wine which his hands had pressed from the grapes to his master. *Pharaoh will lift up your head*, he will speak to you so that you can lift up your head.

Verse 14. I say this with such confidence that I already add a request for myself (Rashbam). It is the prophetic manner to state a prophecy as quite certain and to strengthen the confidence in its truth by already suggesting practical steps for later (for instance Ex. 11,2).

Verse 15. Your intervention will not be for a guilty or worthless man (Bechor Shor). Here Joseph opens his heart for the first time. The expression once more proves that not the brothers, but the Midianite traders had drawn Joseph from the pit and sold him. *I am indeed stolen* not sold for pay. *The land of the Hebrews* is the land where the Hebrews lived (Ramban). *I have done nothing that they should put me into the dungeon.* His account was more detailed; this is a condensation. He told how he had been stolen out of a pit into which he had been cast. Something similar had happened to him here too. The Hebrew uses the same word for pit and dungeon.

16When the chief baker saw that his interpretation was favorable, he said to Joseph, "I also had a dream: behold there were three cake baskets on my head, 17and in the uppermost basket there

were all sorts of baked food for Pharaoh, but the birds were eating
it out of the basket on my head."

The chief baker is characterized unfavorably by believing Joseph will
always interpret auspiciously. *Cake baskets,* better (Rashi and others)
wicker baskets so that the birds could reach the food. The dream itself
did not show the man in a favorable light. He dreamt superficially and
acted without caution. The baked food was ready without his labor; he
mentioned Pharaoh only once, and did not see him or wait on him in
person.

> *18And Joseph answered, "This is its interpretation: the three bas-*
> *kets are three days; 19still three days, and Pharaoh will lift up*
> *your head—from you!—and hang you on a tree; and the birds will*
> *eat your flesh from you."*

There will be a lifting of head for him too, but unfortunately in
another sense. Probably this play on words is an imitation of the
language of Egyptian dream interpreters.

> *20It happened on the third day, which was Pharaoh's birthday,*
> *that he made a feast for all his servants, and lifted up the head of*
> *the chief butler and the head of the chief baker among his*
> *servants. 21He restored the chief butler to his butlership, and he*
> *placed the cup in Pharaoh's hand; 22but he hanged the chief*
> *baker, as Joseph had interpreted to them. 23Yet the chief butler*
> *did not remember Joseph, but forgot him.*

Verse 23. "To remember" is not merely "not to forget", but to make a
mental note in order to act correspondingly at the proper time. This
right time would have been the next birthday of Pharaoh. Yet he let it
pass as he had forgotten Joseph, or rather had never intended to remember him. Ingratitude is an Egyptian fault (Ex. 1,8). God, however,
remembered Joseph and arranged matters so that Joseph must be
remembered.

Chapter 41

Joseph's Elevation

It happened at the end of two whole years, that Pharaoh dreamed that he was standing by the Nile, ²and behold, there came up out of the Nile seven cows sleek and fat, and they fed in the reed grass. ³And behold, seven other cows, gaunt and thin, came up out of the Nile after them and stood by the other cows on the bank of the Nile. ⁴And the gaunt and thin cows ate up the seven sleek and fat cows. And Pharaoh awoke.

Pharaoh had this dream during the night before his next birthday, a very appropriate time for a ruler solicitous of his country.

Verse 3. *They stood by the other cows,* indicating that the fat and lean years should directly succeed each other (Ramban).

⁵And he fell asleep and dreamed a second time; and behold seven ears of grain, plump and good, were growing on one stalk. ⁶And behold, after them sprouted seven ears, thin and blighted by the east wind. ⁷And the thin ears swallowed up the seven plump and full ears. And Pharaoh awoke, and behold, it was a dream.

Seven ears on one stalk are a sign of abundance (Rashbam). The east wind is dry and hot.

⁸And it was in the morning, when his spirit was troubled, that he sent and called for all the magicians of Egypt and all its wise men; and Pharaoh told them his dream, but there was none who could interpret them to Pharaoh. ⁹Then the chief butler said to Pharaoh, "I remember my offenses today. ¹⁰When Pharaoh was angry with his servants, and put me and the chief baker in custody in the house of the captain of the guard, ¹¹we dreamed on the same night, I and he, each having a dream with its own meaning. ¹²A young Hebrew was there with us, a servant of the captain of the guard, and when we told him, he interpreted out dreams to us, giving an interpretation to each man according to his dream. ¹³And as he interpreted to us so it came to pass; I was restored to my office and he was hanged."

Pharaoh's spirit was restless and uncertain about the meaning of the dream. He could hardly wait till morning. Magicians are a specifically Egyptian profession also mentioned in the exodus story. Pharaoh calls all of them and all the wise men in order to be quite certain; this makes Joseph's triumph even greater. *Pharaoh told them his dream,* singular as he was certain that it was only one. *But there was none who could interpret them.* They mistakenly saw two different dreams in them. Rashi, Rashbam say that they gave interpretations, but none which could satisfy Pharaoh.

Verse 9. *I remember my offenses today.* No one likes to do so, but it cannot be avoided if I am to tell something suitable to this matter. This is the chief butler's deserved punishment. He had not mentioned Joseph's innocence, so he must now mention his own offenses. He speaks of them in the plural in deferential exaggeration (Delitzsch). It would be honorable if this plural form were to indicate that he included having forgotten Joseph among his offenses (Bereshith Rabbah and others).

¹⁴Then Pharaoh sent and called Joseph, and they brought him hastily out of the dungeon; and when he had shaved himself and changed his clothes, he came before Pharaoh. ¹⁵And Pharaoh said to Joseph, "I have had a dream, and there is no one who can interpret it; and I have heard it said of you that when you hear a dream you can interpret it." ¹⁶Joseph answered Pharaoh, "It is not in me; God may give Pharaoh a favorable answer."

God's help comes in an unexpected way. Suddenly the despised Hebrew slave stands in the splendor of the court before Pharaoh's throne!

Verse 15. *When you hear a dream.* Pharaoh means, "you understand the language of dreams", because dreams are a language too (Ehrlich).

Verse 16. Joseph gains sympathy through his first word. His answer is respectful and obliging, yet even before the king he points to a higher power.

17Then Pharaoh said to Joseph, "Behold, in my dream I was standing on the bank of the Nile; 18and behold, seven cows, fat and sleek, came up out of the Nile and fed in the reed grass; 19and behold, seven other cows came up after them, poor and very gaunt and thin, such as I have never seen in all the land of Egypt for gauntness. 20And the thin and gaunt cows ate up the first seven fat cows, 21but when they had eaten them no one would have known that they had eaten them, for they were still as gaunt as at the beginning. Then I awoke. 22I also saw in my dream seven ears growing on one stalk, full and good; 23and seven ears, withered, thin, and blighted by the east wind, sprouted after them, 24and the thin ears swallowed up the seven good ears. I told it to the magicians, but there was no one who could explain it to me."

The repetition of the dreams by Pharaoh is not superfluous. All depends on the impression which the account makes on the person who has the answer. This account is colored by Pharaoh's later terror and perplexity felt upon awakening.

Verse 19. The description is more personal and drastic. The good and fat cows had made no special impression on Pharaoh. The others were all the more terrible and what happened afterwards was incomprehensible.

Verse 21. This verse is new and emphasizes the point which troubles Pharaoh.

25Then Joseph said to Pharaoh, "The dream of Pharaoh is one; God has revealed to Pharaoh what he is about to do. 26The seven good cows are seven years, and the seven ears are seven years; the dream is one. 27The seven lean and gaunt cows that came up after them are seven years, and the seven empty ears blighted by the east wind; there will be seven years of famine. 28It is as I told Pharaoh, God has shown to Pharaoh what he is about to do. 29Behold, there will come seven years of great plenty throughout all the land of Egypt, 30but after them will arise seven years of famine, and all the plenty will be forgotten in the land of Egypt; the famine will consume the land, 31and the plenty will be unknown in the land by reason of that famine which will follow, for it will be very grievous. 32And the doubling of Pharaoh's dream means that the thing is fixed by God, and God will shortly bring it to pass.

Three elements determine the interpretation: the two visions are only one dream; the numbers are periods of time, namely years; and the disappearance of the full in the empty without a trace means famine after abundance. All self-explanatory details are omitted—the cows rising out of the river is obviously due to the fact that all fertility comes from the Nile; the gaunt cows do not feed on grass, as none remains; cows refer to plowing (Ramban, Abrabanel), ears to harvesting. The wisdom of Joseph consists in distinguishing the important from the unimportant. The dream is one. This observation must be put at the beginning; otherwise everything would be spoiled. Pharaoh had already prepared for this by not telling that he went back to sleep (verse 22).

God has revealed to Pharaoh what he is about to do and this dream, Joseph continues, is indeed very important. It is a matter of state and a recognition of the royal office that God has specifically sent it to Pharaoh. There is no need for interpreters as God has spoken to Pharaoh clearly; one must only translate the divine language correctly.

Verse 30. *Seven years of famine will arise* as if they had thus far been kept down against their will. The good years will soon be completely forgotten. This is the reason that the lean cows and ears did not look as if they had swallowed the fat ones. The famine will finish the country unless previous precautions are taken.

Verse 31. This verse is not superfluous; if man is tormented by hunger he completely forgets that he ever was satisfied earlier. It is not ingratitude, but the rumbling of an empty stomach.

Verse 32. One point remains to be interpreted; it is skillfully placed at the end, making the subsequent advice more urgent.

The doubling of the dream in the same night means that it will come with certainty and speed. This is a statement interesting for the understanding of Biblical style. Repetition and parallelism mean definiteness and emphasis.

> *33Now therefore let Pharaoh select a man discreet and wise, and set him over the land of Egypt. 34Let Pharaoh proceed to appoint overseers over the land, and take the fifth part of the produce of the land of Egypt during the seven plenteous years. 35And let them gather all the food of these good years that are coming, and lay up grain under the authority of Pharaoh for food in the cities, and let them keep it. 36That food shall be a reserve for the land*

*against the seven years of famine which are to befall the land of
Egypt, so that the land may not perish through the famine."*

Joseph is not forward with this suggestion, but (Ramban) it belongs
to the interpretation, namely of the fact that the lean eats the fat, and in
spite of this just stays alive. We should transfer some abundance to the
time of starvation.

Verse 34. *The fifth part* is a double tithe.

Verse 35. *In the cities* as centers for the surrounding region, not only
in the capital. The grain is to be kept with care.

*³⁷This proposal seemed good to Pharaoh and to all his servants.
³⁸And Pharaoh said to his servants, "Can we find such a man as
this, in whom is the spirit of God!" ³⁹So Pharaoh said to Joseph,
"Since God has shown you all this, there is none so discreet and
wise as you are; ⁴⁰you shall be over my house, and all my people
shall be provided at your command; only as regards the throne
will I be greater than you."*

Pharaoh and his servants, the high officers, like the captain of the
guard and the chief butler, are delighted, the magicians and wise men
of Egypt possibly less so.

Verse 39. The interpretation seems so evident to Pharaoh that it is
unnecessary to wait till it happens. The nature of the matter demands
immediate action.

Verse 40. Joseph now has the same position with Pharaoh and for the
whole kingdom as originally in the house of his first master (39,9),
which had served as preparation for him.

*⁴¹And Pharaoh said to Joseph, "Behold, I am setting you over all
the land of Egypt." ⁴²Then Pharaoh took his signet ring from his
hand and put it on Joseph's hand, and dressed him in garments of
fine linen, and put the chain of gold about his neck; ⁴³and he
made him ride in the two-seated chariot which he had; and they
cried before him, "Abrech!" Thus he was set over all the land of
Egypt. ⁴⁴Pharaoh said to Joseph, "I am Pharaoh, and without your
consent no man shall lift up hand or foot in all the land of Egypt."
⁴⁵And Pharaoh called Joseph's name Zaphenath-paneah; and he*

gave him in marriage Asenath, the daughter of Potiphera priest of On. So Joseph went out over the land of Egypt. ⁴⁶Joseph was thirty years old when he stood before Pharaoh king of Egypt. And Joseph went out from the presence of Pharaoh, and went through all the land of Egypt.

Now Pharaoh speaks and acts officially.

Verse 42. All this agrees with ancient Egyptian customs (Yahuda) and finds illustrations in Egyptian inscriptions and pictorial monuments.

Verse 43. Many commentators think of a chariot for the officer second to the king as I Sam. 23,17. More plausibly a special two-seated chariot for Pharaoh existed. It is a sign of honor and friendship to let someone sit at his side in the royal chariot and to ride with him through the streets in this way. A person was thus publicly distinguished as Pharaoh's closest confidant. *Abrech!* is bow the knee! (Bechor Schor, Ibn Ezra and others).

Verse 44. *I am Pharaoh.* I speak as Pharaoh, with authority, as "I am the Lord" (Ex. 6,2 and often).
No one may act without your consent. It is the language of an absolute ruler.

Verse 45. Many attempts have been made to explain the names. They are, of course, Egyptian. Potiphera is not identical with Potiphar (37,36). One was captain of the guard and a courtier, the other is a priest of On, which is the old priestly city of Heliopolis, famous for its Temple of the Sun. The priests were the noblest class and the priest of On one of the first men of the kingdom. Thus Joseph becomes closely connected with the aristocracy of the country. The new name is one reason that the brothers will not hear Joseph mentioned when they come to Egypt. *So Joseph went out over the land of Egypt* like the sun (19,23). He truly became addressed as king, my god, my sun (le roi soleil) similarly in the documents of Boghazköy, for the king of the Hittites.

Verse 46. *When he stood before Pharaoh* to receive his authority, as a prophet before God (I Kings 17,1). He now travelled through the whole country to take the steps he had advised.

> ⁴⁷During the seven plenteous years the earth brought forth abun-
> dantly; ⁴⁸and he gathered up all the food of seven years which
> were in the land of Egypt, and stored up food in the cities; he
> stored up in every city the food from the fields around it. ⁴⁹Joseph
> stored up grain in great abundance, like the sand of the sea, until
> one ceased to measure it; for it could not be measured.

Verse 48. Ramban imagines that all food was already controlled and rationed in the seven plenteous years in order to prevent waste.

Of seven years which were in the land of Egypt the product of seven years.

> ⁵⁰Before the year of famine came, Joseph had two sons, whom
> Asenath, the daughter of Potiphera priest of On, bore to him.
> ⁵¹Joseph called the name of the first-born Manasseh, "For", he
> said, "God has 'made me forget' all my hardship and all my
> father's house." The name of the second he called Ephraim, "For
> God has 'made me fruitful' in the land of my affliction."

The Talmud (Taanith 11a) says that one must not beget children during a famine.

Verse 51. *My father's house.* The sad thoughts connected with it (Delitzsch); he had not forgotten his family.

Verse 52. Egypt had been a land of affliction for Joseph until now, as it would later be for Israel. Joseph uses the word God as motivation for both names, in keeping with his religious disposition, in gratitude.

> ⁵³The seven years of plenty that prevailed in the land of Egypt
> came to an end; ⁵⁴and the seven years of famine began to come, as
> Joseph had said. There was famine in all lands; but in all the land
> of Egypt there was bread. ⁵⁵When all the land of Egypt was
> famished, the people cried to Pharaoh for the bread; and Pharaoh
> said to all of Egypt, "Go to Joseph; what he says to you, do." ⁵⁶So
> when the famine had spread over the whole face of the land,
> Joseph opened all in which was something, and sold to Egypt, for
> the famine was severe in the land of Egypt. ⁵⁷All the earth came to
> Egypt to Joseph to buy grain, because the famine was severe over
> all the earth.

Verse 55. Nothing grew and the storehouses were still closed. The people cry for *the* bread; they knew it was there; they demand the opening of the storehouses of Pharaoh. He refers them to Joseph who shall determine time and manner of selling, a preparation for 47,13ff.

Verse 56. Joseph waits until the emergency is obvious and general. Everyone shall feel the famine. *Then he opened all in which there was something* the store-houses.

Verse 57. *All the earth* means the surrounding countries. According to historical records such general famine in Egypt and adjacent countries had been frequent.

The Meaning Of This Story.

What is the wisdom of Joseph's interpretation of Pharaoh's dream? Was it so great and not available to the wise men of Egypt?

The interpretation consists in one lucky idea: seven means seven years; therefore seven good and afterwards seven bad years. This idea is not new with Joseph; in prison he had interpreted numbers similarly; there, however, they represented days. As a child of Canaan, as a descendant of Isaac and Abraham who had lived through such periods he also knew of famine.

The mere finding of this interpretation cannot have been decisive for Joseph's elevation. It seems plausible, but who could know whether it would come true. One would have to wait and see. Pharaoh had liked the interpretation because it touched the core of his worries as a ruler. He must have been further pleased by the conclusion drawn by Joseph and his advice which are inseparable from the interpretation. Nothing is wiser than to prepare for times of future scarcity in days of abundance. Joseph's wisdom consists first in his ability to read the soul of another person, to elucidate his vague thoughts and anxieties and then to give practical advice.

The decisive element is the form which Joseph gives his interpretation and to which the commentators have given no attention. He uses the word *God;* Joseph began, "God may give Pharaoh a favorable answer", not I. He goes from the prison to the throne of the king, and this is his first word. This speech is as pious as it is frank. He who is aware of God, is humble and fearless at the same time. Even a king is nothing compared to God. We are not told of Pharaoh's reaction to this; then after reporting his dreams, Joseph begins his interpretation with God (verse 25) and ends with God (verse 28); he emphasizes this once more by twice using "God" in verse 32. God is the first and the last subject in Joseph's speech before he passes on to practical matters which are the business of man; regarding this he wisely does not mention God. Joseph speaks of God four times, and Pharaoh who had not used the word God previously, understands the subtle lesson which the Hebrew slave teaches him and says to his servants, "Can we find such a man as this in whom is the spirit of God?" He turns to Joseph and says, "Since God has shown you all this, there is none so discreet and wise as you are." God and his own father are the central thoughts of Joseph.

Egyptian wisdom has been known to surround itself with an aura which impressed the whole ancient world. Even the Greeks, Herodotus and Plato, regarded Egypt with unlimited respect. Its intellectuals had not failed to construct a philosophy expressing the belief that all things in heaven and on earth are interrelated; the smallest and the greatest influence each other; nothing is unimportant. Thus small things may be omens of future events. Dreams are shadows of the future, hints given by the deity with or without intention. For this reason the wise men of Egypt could not possibly give Pharaoh's dreams the same interpretation as Joseph. They were experts in omens and dreams, but such as these lie beyond their horizon. The philosophy of paganism is a product of surrounding nature, especially in Egypt of the changelessness of nature. The all determining factor was the miraculous Nile; its regular and beneficial inundations each year seemed unalterable like laws of nature. Yet these dreams told of years of plenty followed by years of scarcity. The Egyptians more than any other people could delude themselves to believe that good years will last forever. Pharaoh's wise men could conceive of the failure of the Nile as little as that the sky would collapse. If it had happened occasionally in the past, it was forgotten after one generation. Furthermore the lean cows and ears meant years of famine. The wise men of Egypt, of this house of bondage, did not dare tell the king that under his reign bad years would occur.

The greatness of Joseph's interpretation and the superiority of his wisdom is his courage in telling the truth even before a king. He would have liked to give Pharaoh a favorable interpretation, but he cannot do so as it depends on God. He reminds Pharaoh that there is an irrational element and that good fortune is inconstant. He interprets not so much Pharaoh's dreams as his duties. Israel's wisdom originates in the belief in an almighty God, creator and ruler of the world who makes times change and it wants to teach men what they shall do. God tells this to Pharaoh through dreams as a concession to the Egyptian way of thinking which would otherwise not have responded to the advice. At the same time the dreams promote God's beneficial design. Joseph would not have attained power without them, nor would Israel have come to Egypt.

Pharaoh is worthy of the divine language of the dream as Joseph wins him over by his speech. Pharaoh too is wise, as he shows by having such dreams, being troubled by them, and by telling them in a manner which leads half way to the right interpretation. With sure judgement he accepts Joseph's interpretation as the only correct one; he is receptive to the religious idea and takes a lesson from a "semitic slave" and enthusiastically agrees to Joseph's advice. Common sense comes to the fore in this Egyptian ruler in spite of all official "wisdom". How different from the Pharaoh of Moses!

The Joseph story is intended to create a counterpart to the other Pharaoh. It is to the credit of the Bible to have drawn the figure of this Egyptian ruler so that he and Joseph are worthy of each other, a harmony which is not the least charm of the story. Joseph is wise, as is Pharaoh; his servants who show themselves pleased by Joseph's words are wise, so is the narrator; only the "wise men of Egypt" are unwise.

Joseph's wisdom has defeated that of the Egyptians because it was founded in God; it was wisdom coming from God and leading to him, and is fundamentally identical with fear of God. It is a happy combination of deep insight, knowledge of the human heart, sympathy with human destiny, and practical sense. It presents the genuinely Jewish combination of brains and heart.

Wisdom was highly cherished in all antiquity, including ancient Israel. The Bible is full of its praise; some of its books are largely devoted to it. Yet it is no accident that the word "wise" first appears in this chapter. The Jewish way had its first opportunity to measure its strength against foreign wisdom in Joseph. This story is the oldest example of an often treated popular topic; an intellectual contest before a ruler or a large audience. The mental tournaments of nations are the tournaments of their wisdom. Joseph has won and shows the nature of true eternal wisdom. The wise men of Egypt must have hurried off as they literally must later before the other Pharaoh (Ex. 9,11). That is the quiet humor of this popular story.

Chapter 42

The Brothers' First Journey to Egypt.
> *When Jacob learned that there was grain in Egypt, Jacob said to his sons, "Why do you look at one another?" ²And he said, "Behold, I have heard that there is grain in Egypt; go down and buy grain for us there, that we may live, and not die." ³So ten of Joseph's brothers went down to buy grain from Egypt. ⁴But Jacob did not send Benjamin, Joseph's brother, with his brothers, for he feared that harm might befall him.*

Jacob has not been mentioned for four chapters; so he is reintroduced by twice using his name as subject of the sentence. *Why do you look at one another?* You look at one another seemingly content as if we lack nothing (Rashi and others); or you look as if undecided upon who shall take the initiative (Seforno). Certainly they felt the famine and had considered a journey to Egypt, but they do not know how to broach the subject to the father; will he let them go or may it not remind him of the sad plight of Joseph?

Verse 3. *Joseph's brothers,* called thus in preparation for meeting him. All of them must go in order to demonstrate the quantity of food needed as all of them have families (verse 19).

> *⁵Thus the sons of Israel came to buy among the others who came, for the famine was in the land of Canaan. ⁶Now Joseph was governor over the land; it was he who sold to all the people of the land. And Joseph's brothers came and bowed themselves before him with their faces to the ground. ⁷Joseph saw his brothers and knew them, but he treated them like strangers and spoke roughly to them. "Where do you come from?" he said to them. They said, "From the land of Canaan to buy food." ⁸Thus Joseph knew his brothers, but they did not know him.*

Sons of Israel expresses their change since chapter 37. Although they come like other people, they enter Egypt as the moral unit of "sons of

Israel" even this first time. They will later move there, and be redeemed from there as "sons of Israel". Israel, this time unwittingly, sent them to Joseph as he had sent him to them (37, 13).

Verse 6. Joseph as governor has foreigners brought before himself. He had expected the brothers and had given corresponding orders.

Verse 7. Now Joseph must decide how to act towards them. He could have revealed his identity immediately, reproached them for their actions, and shown how he had nevertheless advanced in the world. He is too generous to desire or enjoy their humiliation and his triumph. He could now have stretched out his hand for reconciliation. He was too wise for this; it would not have been true reconciliation, had the brothers remained unchanged.

Joseph had last seen them filled with hatred and resolved to do away with a brother; it had brought untold grief on their father. Joseph's noble soul was not aggrieved for the evil done him, but for their base mentality which might commit similar acts. The father stands in the center of his thoughts. Would they, given the opportunity, again afflict him? His whole conduct is aimed at discovering this. He shows no desire for revenge. His heart overflows with love, but he must control himself and pretend to be a stranger. In doing so he unwittingly executes a divine judgment which consists not so much in punishment as in trials, designed to awaken the guilty conscience, to make repentance apparent, to effect a change in the evildoer. These trials are felt as punishment only, until the inner change and the final end reveals them as acts of God's love and educational wisdom.

> [9]And Joseph remembered the dreams which he had dreamed for them; and he said to them, "You are spies, you have come to see the weakness of the land." [10]They said to him, "No, my lord, but to buy food have your servants come. [11]We are all sons of one man, we are honest men, your servants are not spies." [12]He said to them, "No, it is the weakness of the land that you have come to see." [13]And they said, "We, your servants, are twelve brothers, the' sons of one man in the land of Canaan; and behold, the youngest is this day with our father, and one is no more." [14]But Joseph said to them, "If I said to you, you are spies, [15]by this you shall be tested; by the life of Pharaoh, you shall not go from this place unless your youngest brother comes here. [16]Send one of you, and let him bring your brother, while you remain in prison, that your words may be tested, whether there is truth in you; or else, by the

life of Pharaoh, surely you are spies." [17]*And he put them altogether under guard for three days.*

Verse 9. This does not mean that Joseph was satisfied in seeing his dreams fulfilled, when the brothers bowed themselves before him. They honor him so as does everyone else; it would have been a triumph for him only if they had known he was Joseph. The explanation lies in the words Joseph remembered dreams which he had dreamed for them; these words reveal the true meaning of his dreams and what Joseph had thought when he told them to his father and brothers.

The usual translation is "dreams he had dreamed *of* them", but the Hebrew clearly says "he had dreamed *for* them". When the sheaves of the brothers had gathered around his sheaf and bowed to it, its meaning for him had not been that he would once rule over them or be able to tyrannize them (which really does not happen later at all), but that he would care for them, protect them, keep them alive, like an ideal ruler, and they would thank him for it. In the second dream he had not thought that sun, moon, and stars and the whole universe, would pay homage to him. He thought that it would be his good luck to bring honor and splendor on parents and brothers; they would gratefully acknowledge it by bowing to him. He would be the center of his family by giving them light and life.

At this moment he thinks of these benevolent dreams of childhood. He considers how he may completely fulfill them and gather not only the already present brothers but the entire family around himself as distributor of blessings.

This can bring true satisfaction only if they have changed to become truly his brothers; he must speak roughly to them in in order to test them. This test shall also bring the last, still absent, brother and the father to him. All of this is wonderfully accomplished by the events and through Joseph's wisdom and love.

You have come to see the weakness of the land, its secret places (Ibn Ezra). Ancient Egypt's distrust of travellers is well known. The frontiers toward Syria were strongly fortified and strictly guarded; all who came and went were noted and the authorities were kept informed about them (Erman).

Verse 11. No father would risk all his sons at once on such a dangerous mission.

We are all sons of one man The Midrash says that their words imply an unintentional truth as they may also include Joseph. He must have felt this ambiguity.

Verse 13. You see only ten before you, as *the youngest is today with his father.* This awakens sad memories in Joseph: so once was I! It also comforts him to know that the father has a substitute for him!

And one is no more. They cannot know that the man whom they address may hereby judge that they are honest and speak the truth.

Verse 14. Joseph cannot prove that they are spies; they shall prove their innocence by verifying the facts they have related about themselves.

Verse 15. As an Egyptian and in his official capacity, Joseph takes an oath by the life of the ruler.

Verse 17. He puts them together so they can decide whom to send.

> ¹⁸*On the third day Joseph said to them, "Do this and you will live, for I fear God:* ¹⁹*if you are honest men, let one of your brothers remain confined in the prison house, and let the rest go and carry grain for the famine of your households,* ²⁰*and bring your youngest brother to me; so your words will be verified, and you will not die." And they did so.*

Reggio thinks that Joseph changed his mind as they had answered him (as in 44, 22) 'we cannot do so; the father would not let him go for fear of not seeing him again; it would be his death.' Rather all of them remain.

I fear God I not only give orders and threaten, but also acknowledge certain considerations, fear sin (39,9) and do not want to endanger your father's life.

> ²¹*Then they said to one another, "In truth we are guilty concerning our brother, in that we saw the distress of his soul, when he besought us and we would not listen, therefore is this distress come upon us."* ²²*And Reuben answered them, "Did I not tell you not to sin against the lad? But you would not listen. So now there comes a reckoning for his blood."* ²³*They did not know that Joseph understood them, for an interpreter was between them.* ²⁴*Then he turned away from them and wept; and he returned to them and spoke to them. And he took Simeon from them and bound him before their eyes.*

The same situation which once occurred with Joseph is reproduced as they return to the father with one brother missing; they shall even ask him to give up the second Joseph. That is retribution! Since the father's mourning, twenty years earlier, their action has constantly tormented them; in all their thoughts Joseph is "the" brother. This is what they deserve. Joseph's entreaties were not mentioned in 37,23f. It is a special refinement of the narration to place it here where emotions matter.

Verse 22. At that time someone had warned them; this same Reuben now reminds them how he had tried to excuse *the lad* by his youth and to deter them by his defenselessness. *There comes a reckoning for his blood*. Reuben need not think that Joseph is dead, as he cannot prove that. Yet "to bring distress to a soul", to be deaf to a supplication is like shedding blood (compare Lev 19,16). This stranger fears God and is considerate of our old father, what a contrast to our action.

Joseph's request is neither excessive, nor dangerous. They might have been content. They accept his suggestion immediately in verse 20. They will bring the youngest brother and stand justified. Yet, they possess that deeper vision (Ex 14,30; 31) which sees moral causes behind the physical ones. This change has been brought about by the father's grief and the fear of afflicting him again.

Verse 23. It is a nice idea of the Midrash to state that this interpreter might have been Joseph's oldest son Manasseh and that Joseph spoke his mother tongue at home with his children although they had been born in Egypt.

Verse 24. Joseph is deeply moved by this proof of their change, given unwittingly in his presence, but is is not yet complete so he must restrain himself before them. He turns away and weeps, over the sorrow of his youth which they recall to his mind, their former hatred, and their present repentance, the distress of their souls which he cannot yet relieve, and certainly over his lonely father. His remarks to them are reported in verse 34.

He bound Simeon before their eyes. Bereshith Rabbah claims: only before their eyes; afterwards he released him and fed him.

> ²⁵And Joseph gave orders to fill their bags with grain, and to replace every man's money in his sack, and to give them provisions for the journey. This was done for them. ²⁶Then they loaded their asses with their grain, and departed. ²⁷And as one

opened his sack to give his ass provender at the lodging place, he saw his money in the mouth of his sack; ²⁸and he said to his brothers, "My money has been put back; here it is in the mouth of my sack!" At this their hearts failed them and they turned trembling to one another, saying, "What is this that God has done to us?"

As soon as Joseph is in touch with his family he feels the obligation to provide for them (45,5-11). Yet he cannot tell this to them.

Verse 28. The reason for this scene at the lodging place, although all will later empty their sacks before the father and find the money, is given in their phrase, *"What is this that God has done to us?"* Following verse 21, this is the second step in their growing consciousness of guilt. They now speak of God as the certain cause of this visitation. They suspect that God wants to destroy them (43,18) and cannot imagine that this is a deed of love of their brother. They should pronounce this confession of guilt only among themselves, (as verse 21f) not before the father.

²⁹*When they came to Jacob their father in the land of Canaan, they told him all that had befallen them, saying, ³⁰"The man, the lord of the land, spoke roughly to us, and took us to be spies of the land. ³¹But we said to him, 'We are honest men, we are not spies; ³²we are twelve brothers, sons of our father; one is no more, and the youngest is this day with our father in the land of Canaan.' ³³Then the man, the lord of the land, said to us, 'By this I shall know that you are honest men: leave one of your brothers with me, and take grain for the hunger of your households, and go your way. ³⁴Bring your youngest brother to me; then I shall know that you are not spies but honest men, and I will deliver to you your brother, and you shall trade in the land.' " ³⁵So they emptied their sacks, behold, every man's bundle of money was in his sack; and when they and their father saw their bundles of money, they were terrified.*

Verse 30. The report only presents the facts important for Jacob.

Verse 34. *And you shall trade in the land.* This seems to be an addition, invented by the brothers. Yet this must have been the content of Joseph's speech in verse 24, and Joseph had not said it for their sake, but so they could reassure the father.

Verse 35. *Bundles of money.* Each man's money tied together, obviously by intention.

> ₃₆And Jacob their father said to them, "You have bereaved me of my children: Joseph is no more, and Simeon is no more, and now you would take Benjamin; all this has come upon me." ³⁷Then Reuben said to his father, "Slay my two sons if I do not bring him back to you; put him in my hand, and I will bring him back to you." ³⁸But he said, "My son shall not go down with you, for his brother is dead, and he only is left. If harm should befall him on the journey that you are to make, you would bring down my gray hairs with sorrow to Sheol."

Reuben, the oldest, answers because he feels himself responsible for Benjamin as once for Joseph, and he deeply sympathizes with the father (37,22). His suggestion is of course unacceptable. The father would lose two grandsons in addition; is a child an object for which one can pay double compensation? His words shall give the strongest expression to his promise: I would rather lose two sons. . . !But how can he with such certainty promise that he will return Benjamin? Does he have the power to do so when they are in Egypt?

Verse 38. Jacob shakes his head. Now in his sorrow he no longer shrinks from the word *dead.* Of his mother only one son remains. He calls Benjamin "his son", not "your brother", and Joseph "his brother"; this is bitter for the others, as if he only had these two. The chapter closes on this sorrowful, somber note (as 37,35). Benjamin is a second Joseph. Judah remains silent. He may have told the brothers (Redak to 43,1) to leave the father alone; later hunger will cause him to yield.

Chapter 43

The Second Journey of The Brothers

The famine was severe in the land. ²And when they had eaten the grain which they had brought from Egypt, their father said to them, "Go again, buy us a little food." ³But Judah said to him, "The man solemnly warned us, saying, 'You shall not see my face, unless your brother is with you.' ⁴If you will send our brother with us, we will go down and buy you food; ⁵but if you will not send him, we will not go down, for the man said to us, 'You shall not see my face, unless your brother is with you.'"

Again Judah (as in 37,26 ff.) speaks the decisive word after a futile suggestion from Reuben. Judah states that the man made a formal demand, taking an oath (42,15 f.) and threatening them with death (42,18; 20). Joseph had taken an oath only for its effect on his father's decision.

⁶Israel said, "Why did you treat me so ill as to tell the man that you had another brother?" ⁷They replied, "The man questioned us about ourselves and our kindred, saying, 'Is your father still alive? Have you another brother?' What we told him was in answer to these questions; could we in any way know that he would say, 'Bring your brother down'?" ⁸Judah said to Israel his father, "Send the lad with me, and we will arise and go, that we may live and not die, both we and you and also our families. ⁹I will be surety for him; of my hand you shall require him. If I do not bring him back to you and set him before you, then let me bear the blame for ever; ¹⁰for if we had not delayed, we would now have returned twice."

Jacob no longer refuses; he will clearly agree, but he wants at least to vent his feelings once more.

Verse 7. This verse and 44,19 show the contents of conversation in 42,7 ff., even if it had to be formulated differently there.

Verse 8. Judah's offer is all the more admirable as it is so late. He knows that the father will anyhow agree, but he deeply sympathizes with him and wants to sweeten the decision even if it is already made. He pledges himself, not as usually said to carry his point, but out of tender love for the father who shall have no moment of anxiety during their absence—as far as he is capable of it. He can only promise that Benjamin will be under his protection on the trip, but not what will happen to him in Egypt, nor whether he will be allowed to return.

Verse 9. *Then let me bear the blame for ever* for shame I shall not dare to let myself be seen before you.

Verse 10. 'We have already lost much time.' Judah tries to hide his agitation by this mild reproach.

> *¹¹Then their father Israel said unto them, "If it must be so, then do this: take some of the choice fruits of the land in your bags, and carry down to the man a present, a little balm and a little honey, gum, myrrh, pistachio nuts and almonds. ¹²Take double the money with you; namely the money that was returned in the mouths of your sacks carry back with you; perhaps it was an oversight. ¹³Take also your brother, and arise, go again to the man; ¹⁴may God Almighty grant you mercy before the man, that he may release to you your other brother and Benjamin. As for me, If I am bereaved of my children, I am bereaved."*

These words do not refer to Judah's offer, but to the danger of starvation and the man's threat of which Jacob had not known previously; for this reason it had not yet been mentioned in 42,34. *Do this* Jacob knows from experience (32,20) that a mighty man's anger can be pacified by a present.

Take some of the choice fruits of the land The Hebrew has a special expression for qualities of a land which are praised in song (Targum, Rashi and others). The realist sees the superiority of a land in its products, already in the Egyptian Sinuhe story.

A little balm etc. The quantity is not important as with greedy Esau (32,14 ff.). This shall merely be courtesy. Jacob speaks to his sons as they shall speak before the man.

Verse 13 Last comes the hardest matter for Jacob: *Take also your brother. If I am bereaved, I am bereaved* This cry of despair expresses irrevocable fate and consequently the impotence of man. There is a fine contrast between this emotional speech and the calm tone of the following narration (Gunkel).

> ¹⁵So the men took this present, and they took double the money with them, and Benjamin; and they arose and went down to Egypt, to stand before Joseph. ¹⁶When Joseph saw Benjamin with them, he said to the steward of his house, "Bring the men into the house and slaughter an animal and prepare, for the men are to dine with me at noon."

Uneventful journeys are always reported briefly (for instance 24,10;37,28;42,5). Joseph recognizes Benjamin immediately; it could be no one else. Now he must consider a satisfaction owed to the brothers for the accusation of being spies. An opportunity must also be created for the "theft" of the cup. Both purposes will be achieved if the brothers are brought to his house, to eat and drink with him. The steward must have had Joseph's full confidence and must have known the secret. Joseph would not have him deal so with the money and the cup without giving a truthful explanation. Joseph had himself been a steward and had enjoyed and deserved the fullest trust. He must have chosen a worthy man; the relationship can be imagined like that of Abraham and his servant (15,2; 24,2).

> ¹⁷The man did as Joseph had told him, and brought the men to Joseph's house. ¹⁸And the men were afraid because they were brought to Joseph's house, and they said, "It is because of the money, which was replaced in our sacks the first time, that we are brought in, so that occasion may be sought against us and they fall upon us, to take us as slaves and our asses." ¹⁹So they went up to the steward of Joseph's house and spoke to him at the door of the house, ²⁰and said, "O, my lord, we came down the first time to buy food; ²¹and when we came to the lodging place we opened our sacks, and behold, there was every man's money in the mouth of his sack, our money in full weight; so we have again brought it with us, ²² and we have brought other money down in our hand to buy food. We do not know who put our money in our sacks." ²³He replied, "Rest assured, do not be afraid; your God and the God of your father must have put treasure in your sacks for you; I have received your money." Then he brought Simeon out to them.

Verse 18. They are afraid that they will be held as slaves;—a suspicion which turns out to be justified. *And our asses* Maimonides (More

III,40) uses them as an example of people who are more concerned for
their possessions than for themselves. They probably also thought of
the grain which they will now be unable to bring home; it is a terrible
situation if they think of the father. Worse is still to come (chapter 44).

Verse 19. *At the door.* Before they had entered; later it might be too
late.

Verse 23. The steward reassures them: you have nothing to fear.
I have received you money which literally taken is true.
He brought Simeon out to them This is done only now which shows
the great care of the narrator. As soon as Joseph saw Benjamin with the
brothers, he had to release Simeon. Were this reported in verse 16, the
episode of verses 18 ff. and the fear of the brothers would have been
senseless. Now it proves that all is well.

> ²⁴And when the man had brought the men into Joseph's house,
> and given them water, and they had washed their feet, and when
> their asses had been given provender, ²⁵they prepared the present
> for Joseph's coming at noon, for they had heard that they should
> eat bread there.

Even their beloved asses are well cared for. *They had heard:* they
were aware of proper behavior; this was the occasion to offer their
presents.

> ²⁶When Joseph came to the house, they brought into the house to
> him the present which they had with them, and bowed down to
> him to the ground. ²⁷And he inquired about their welfare, and
> said, "Is your father well, the old man of whom you spoke? Is he
> still alive?" ²⁸They said, "Your servant our father is well, he is
> still alive." And they bent and bowed respectfully. ²⁹And he lifted
> up his eyes and saw his brother Benjamin, his mother's son, and
> said, "Is this your youngest brother of whom you spoke to me?"
> And he said, "God be gracious to you, my son!" ³⁰Then Joseph
> made haste, for his heart was moved toward his brother, and he
> was about to weep. And he entered his chamber and wept there.
> ³¹Then he washed his face and came out; and controlling himself,
> he said, "Let food be served."

Having greeted the brothers Joseph first asks for the father whose old
age they have reported. To us this betrays his anxiety and his secret
hope soon to be able to embrace him.

Verse 28. They bow to him in gratitude for his interest (Rashi); perhaps better: they bow to God who has preserved the father's life, like our "thank God".

Verse 29. The great lord "sees" someone only when he wants to take notice of him. *The son of his mother* which is the strongest tie between them, although Joseph had hardly known her and Benjamin not at all; he is his full brother, like him motherless, who has taken his place with the father, the only one who is completely innocent. The first word Joseph addresses to him is God.

> *32They served him by himself, and them by themselves, and the Egyptians who ate with him by themselves, for the Egyptians might not eat with the Hebrews; for that is an abomination to Egypt. 33And they sat before him, the first-born according to his birthright and the youngest according to his youth; and the men looked at one another in amazement. 34Portions were taken to them from Joseph's table, but Benjamin's portion was five times as much as any of theirs. So they drank and were merry with him.*

Joseph is served separately due to his rank (Biur and others).

The Egyptians might not eat bread with the Hebrews The antipathy of the ancient Egyptians towards everything foreign was proverbial. Herodotus mentions it as well.

An abomination for Egypt. This phrase ascribes the law to the religious and cultural constitution of the land and the people. This description of the meal shall show Joseph in his full splendor as ruler and also the high honor which he conferred upon his brothers. This party is already a fulfillment of the dreams in chapter 37 (see 42,9).

Verse 33. They sat down according to age by themselves or upon Joseph's invitation. Their amazement is more about the whole ceremony of verse 32 f. which impresses them and had been arranged for this purpose.

Verse 34. Joseph has them served portions from his table as a courtesy according to old custom. Benjamin's preferment is also a test to see whether they will envy him as they had envied Joseph (Seforno).

They drank and were merry with him. It became an animated party. At the same time this makes the disappearance of the cup possible.

Chapter 44

The Return Of The Brothers.
> Then he commanded the steward of his house, "Fill the men's
> sacks with food, as much as they can carry, and put each man's
> money in the mouth of his sack, ²and put my cup, the silver cup,
> in the mouth of the sack of the youngest, with his money for the
> grain." And he did as Joseph told him.

Joseph gives them an abundant supply of food for the journey as it is
the custom with guests who are about to leave for a long trip. The
steward may then reproach them even more. (verse 4)

Verse 2. The hiding of the cup in Benjamin's sack is an effective
elaboration of the episode of the money which was put in the sacks of
the brothers the first time. It had been their own money, but this is a
cup from Joseph's house; it will be missed, sought, and found with the
youngest brother. He will appear to be a manifest thief who can be
retained as a slave.

> ³As soon as the morning was light, the men were sent away with
> their asses. ⁴When they had gone but a short distance from the
> city, Joseph said to his steward, "Up, follow after the men; and
> when you overtake them, say to them, 'Why have you returned
> evil for good ⁵Is it not from this that my lord drinks, and he will
> see a bad omen in it. You have done wrong in so doing.'" ⁶When
> he overtook them, he spoke to them these words. ⁷They said to
> him, "Why does my lord speak such words as these? Far be it
> from your servants that they should do such a thing. ⁸Behold, the
> money which we found in the mouth of our sacks, we brought
> back to you from the land of Canaan; how then should we steal
> silver or gold from your lord's house? ⁹With whomever of your
> servants it be found, let him die, and we also will be my lord's
> slaves." ¹⁰He said, "Let it be as you say, but so: he with whom it is
> found shall be my slave, and the rest of you shall be free."

Verse 4. They had left the city which seems proof that they wanted to depart with the cup. Joseph does not indicate the words, but the manner in which the steward shall speak.

Verse 5. The steward still maintains appearances. He does not directly accuse them of "stealing" his lord's cup, nor even by a milder expression. He begins as if a direct accusation were not necessary: 'So, that is your gratitude!' He pretends, omitting the word "cup", that they must, of course, know to what he refers; he closes: 'You have done wrong, people like you, in your position! This cup has affectionate value for my lord. He is accustomed to drink from it.' Not as many commentators claim, "he uses it for divination". This would not fit to Joseph's religious character. Rather *he will see a bad omen in it* (Redak and other Jewish commentators). Even today an enlightened person feels badly upon losing an object of affectionate value, as his wedding ring.

Verse 7. They in their indignation use the harsh words, 'we are supposed to have stolen '

Verse 8. Have we not demonstrated that we do not care for money?

Verse 9. Certain of their innocence they offer to accept a higher punishment than any law would demand. They unanimously declare themselves responsible for each other.

Verse 10. The steward agrees, but not to their exaggeration. As Joseph later (verse 17) decides similarly, he must have given this instruction to his steward. The real intention of the steward is to obtain their agreement that the matter shall be judged only according to *with whom it is found*. There shall be no discussion of how it happened, how the cup came into Benjamin's luggage.

> [11]Then every man quickly lowered his sack to the ground, and every man opened his sack. [12]And he searched, beginning with the eldest and ending with the youngest; and the cup was found in Benjamin's sack. [13]Then they rent their clothes, and every man loaded his ass, and they returned to the city.

Eager to prove their innocence they do not want to move another step or turn back; the search shall take place here and now; they even help the accuser by unloading their sacks and opening them.

Verse 12. He starts with the eldest so that their confidence of vindication may grow; their terror is all the more sudden.

Verse 13. They rent their clothes as once the father, who is now always on their mind, for Joseph (37,34).

> ¹⁴*When Judah and his brothers came to Joseph's house, he was still there; and they fell before him to the ground.* ¹⁵*Joseph said to them, "What deed is this that you have done? Do you not know that such a man as I would take it as a bad omen?"* ¹⁶*And Judah said, "What shall we say to my lord? What shall we speak? Or how can we clear ourselves? God has found out the guilt of your servants; behold, we are my lord's slaves, both we and he also in whose hand the cup has been found."* ¹⁷*But he said, "Far be it from me that I should do so. Only the man in whose hand the cup was found shall be my slave; but as for you go up in peace to your father."*

At this moment Judah is placed at the head of the brothers. He is the leader in the following sentences, so we are prepared for verses 16 and 18ff.

Joseph was still there He had not yet gone about his business. Silently and with resignation, they throw themselves to the ground, an example of oriental dignity in the face of misfortune.

Verse 15. *A man as I* cannot take such a thing lightly. His question makes it possible for Judah to speak.

Verse 16. They might have asked several things. Is it conclusive evidence of someone's theft, if the object is found with him? Can it not have been placed there maliciously? Are there witnesses to the theft? What of their words to the steward? When and how shall the theft by Benjamin have been possible? Yet they forego any argument. Not only because it would be futile before the powerful man, but they immediately understand this misfortune, even if the present charge is false, as punishment for another deed.

God has found the guilt of your servants. They know their guilt well; it is the crime which they had committed against their brother. After 42,22 and 28 this phrase is the third step in recognition of their sin, the confession that they are guilty and deserve punishment. According to a higher moral order an exact relationship exists between their distress and their crime. They acknowledge that the men who act against them are only tools of higher justice. God is the true judge. Their public profession of this and acceptance of the verdict is their repentance and greatness.

He has found out They were unable to hide anything. It is something quite different than the cup that had been hidden and found; someone else, namely God, has found it. They are now resolved not to separate one from another in the emergency. Judah may make this heroic declaration in the name of all of them.

Even with this generous offer, their trial is not yet completed. Shared misfortune is only half a misfortune; a judge cannot accept a sacrifice; nor does Joseph know whether they would even be willing to buy the freedom of the youngest by their own slavery. Only then would he be certain of their complete inner change. Then they would be wholly his brothers and fit for reconciliation. Therefore he speaks as a man who cannot agree to the punishment of innocent people.

Verse 17. These words give Judah the occasion for his long speech.

Judah's Speech

This speech has always made an overwhelming impression on every feeling heart. Its effect first lies in the exciting tenseness of the moment. The fate of people who have gained our sympathy is at stake. We know the result, yet we tremble. This is highest art. The next factor are the persons who act in this drama. Judah shows himself for the first time in all his greatness. His speech brings good arguments, is prudent, controlled, and yet filled with emotion; it is respectful, yet firm and daring, even with a clear undertone of reproach. He petitions, but does not humiliate himself. Undoubtedly Judah recognized a trick in the matter of the cup, even if he could not know the purpose. He forgoes any attempt to clear the intrigue as the judge is a party to it. He offers himself as slave; his pledge and his love to the father compel this self-sacrifice. As only one shall remain as slave, let it be me in order that the father may see the youngest again. Judah does not even know that he appeals to the lost brother whom he, Judah, once wanted to sell as slave to Egypt. It is a brother to whom he speaks of the father and with whom he wrestles for a brother. Judah and Joseph represent contrasts in character, but common love of the father will unite and reconcile them.

The effect of the speech also lies in the suffering persons. There at home is the gray head of a much tried father close to the grave, weeping for one favorite son, and anxious for the other; here before us is the youth, full of fear of this severe man. The simplest devices of language effect all this.

Judah's statement seems to vary in some points from the former conversations. However nothing he reports of their first interrogation can be at variance with truth as it is Joseph before whom he repeats it. He passes over everything which cannot contribute to the desired effect and might uselessly irritate the powerful man. He has two arguments: 1) Following his former attitude, Joseph cannot in fairness hold their youngest brother and 2) he, Judah, cannot return without him to the father. Regarding formal variations, it is the method of the author to vary the report of the same events according to the situation, so that the complete facts must be combined from the different accounts. This is a psychologically motivated rule of style. The narrator has reserved all circumstances and words liable to have the greatest effect for this point. He omitted or softened them in former reports.

> [18]Then Judah went up to him and said, "Oh my lord, let your servant, I pray you, speak a word in my lord's ears, and let not your anger burn against your servant: for you are like Pharaoh himself. [19]My lord asked his servants saying, 'Have you a father, or a brother?' [20]And we said to my lord, 'We have a father, an old man, and a young brother, the child of his old age; and his brother is dead and he alone is left of his mother's children; and his father loves him.' [21]Then you said to your servants, 'Bring him down to me that I set my eyes upon him.' [22]We said to my lord 'The lad cannot leave his father, for if he should leave his father, he would die.' [23]Then you said to your servants, 'Unless your youngest brother comes down with you, you shall see my face no more.' [24]And it happened, when we went back to your servant my father and told him the words of my lord, [25]and when our father said, 'Go again, buy us a little food,' [26]we said, 'We cannot go down, for we cannot see the man's face unless our youngest brother is with us.' [27]Then your servant my father said to us, 'You know that my wife bore me two sons; [28]one left me and I said, surely he had been torn to pieces; and I have never seen him since. [29]If you take this one also from me and harm befalls him, you will bring down my gray hairs in sorrow to Sheol.' [30]Now, therefore, when I come to your servant my father, and the lad is not with us, then, as his life is bound up in the lad's life, [31]it will happen, when he sees that the lad is not with us, he will die; and your servants will bring down the gray hairs of your servant our father with sorrow to Sheol. [32]For your servant became surety for the lad to my father.

> saying, 'If I do not bring him back to you, then I shall bear the
> blame in the sight of my father for ever.' ³³Now therefore, let your
> servant, I pray you, remain instead of the lad as a slave to my
> lord; and let the lad go back with his brothers. ³⁴For how can I go
> back to my father if the lad is not with me? I fear to see the evil
> that would come upon my father."

Then Judah went up to him, according to Ramban, in order to make a
suggestion, namely verse 33; both verses refer to each other through the
phrase "I pray you". Seforno states that Judah refers to Joseph's own
words in verse 17, "You want to do no wrong"; let me prove that you
would, if you insist on your verdict.

For you are like Pharaoh himself One cannot argue with a king.
Perhaps this is also a slightly ironical allusion to verse 15 "such a man
as I."

Verse 19. Even the first word is an accusation. Your questioning
started the whole confusion. Yet the charge of espionage is not
mentioned; hereby Judah lets it be understood that it was certainly only
a pretext. What concern of his was it if they had a brother or a father?
Were other customers thus questioned? We, however, answered you
truthfully.

Verse 20. *His father loves him.* After the preceding this indicates that
originally the older brother had been the beloved son.
And his brother is dead Someone who has disappeared is also now
declared dead.

Verse 21. *I may set my eyes upon him* This cannot merely mean
"see" him (Rashbam and others), but 'I will treat him well'; nothing
evil shall happen to him; perhaps moved by hearing that he was the
favorite of his father (Abrabanel). Following such a promise it would be
improper for a great lord to retain Benjamin as a slave, even if he had
stolen the cup. Joseph must have said to them: 'Do not fear that I have
evil intentions regarding your brother. I merely want to be convinced of
your truthfulness. Bring him down; I shall keep an eye on him.'

Verse 22. Who would die? Ibn Ezra and many commentators think
the father; Rashi, Ramban claim—the lad.

Verse 27. Judah's report of the father's reply in verses 27-29 agrees
neither with 43,6, nor 42,36-38. Nevertheless Judah is right in his

account. Naturally they had heard the father mourn Joseph's disappearance during these more than twenty years many times and in various
forms; it is the art of Scripture to let Judah quote his most moving cries
of grief here. They will stir Joseph deeply and also betray that their
unforgettable impression had been the true cause of the inner change of
Judah and his brothers. Jacob's dirge begins with the memory of his
happy love in younger days and ends by speaking of the nearby grave
after sorrowful old age. Life now wants to take from him the last of the
people whom he loved most.

Verse 28. *I have never seen him since.* Jacob seems not to exclude the
possibility of seeing him again. He regarded it possible that Joseph still
lived. His sons must have confessed to him that the bloody coat had
been a deception and that they too did not know what had become of
the brother. As they are so deeply repentant, it seems unlikely that they
had not confessed the truth lest the father remain without any hope.
Perhaps this was the comfort of 37,35. Now we understand that the
brothers had at the time not brought the coat themselves, but sent it to
the father through others. They needed to retract no lie as they had
pronounced none. Nor had they claimed that Joseph had been torn to
pieces by a wild beast; they had even tried to dissuade the father from it
when they saw the effect. Therefore they waver between "he is no
more" (42,13;32;36) and "he is dead" (42,38). The brothers as well as
the father believed Joseph dead as he did not return; yet at times they
did not exclude the possibility that he might still live.

Verse 33. *Now therefore.* This finally introduces the suggestion
which is the purpose of the whole speech.

Verse 34. Even if I had not pledged myself formally, I could not
return to my unhappy father without the lad. Judah's pledge expressed
that he would never have the heart to do so. Here at the end Judah no
longer says "your servant" or "my lord". Formalities are dropped and
only the heart speaks. He closes, as Joseph in verse 17, with the word
"father", the idea which dominates the whole story.

Chapter 45

Joseph Makes Himself Known

Then Joseph could not control himself before all those who stood by him; and he cried. "Make every one go out from me." So no one stayed with him when Joseph made himself known to his brothers. ²And he wept aloud, so that the Egyptians heard it, and the household of Pharaoh heard it. And Joseph said to his brothers, "I am Joseph; is my father still alive?" But his brothers could not answer him, for they shrank away from his presence.

Undoubtedly Joseph would have revealed his identity, even if they had been satisfied to leave Benjamin behind. He would not have let his father mourn for ever. He would have invited him to come, even if it meant giving up the brothers, but he had always been confident of regaining all of them. The hour has come. Now they shield Benjamin, the other son of the same mother, a second Joseph; their speaker is willing to sacrifice himself and to become a slave in his place out of love toward the father. Thus all of them have become his true brothers, and reconciled, he can embrace them. He had not sought reparation or apologies, still less retaliation and vengeance, but certainty that tried and chastened, they would practice love toward another brother; they would love him whom the father loved.

With tears irresistibly welling up he can no longer observe court etiquette; he can only cry, *Make every one go out from me*. Thus once more they stand opposite each other without witnesses. He does not want to shame his brothers before people (Rashi and others). The brothers would feel dismayed and how would they appear in the eyes of strangers when Joseph says to them, "I am Joseph whom you have sold etc." He wants them to enjoy respect and honor in Egypt. Even the strongest emotion does not deprive Joseph of delicacy of feeling.

Verse 2. Joseph's voice is muffled by tears while giving the order. The Egyptians and the courtiers understand and leave respectfully. Joseph had wept when he heard Reuben's speech (42,24), when he welcomed

302

Benjamin (43,30), and now he weeps after Judah's speech—every time
he regains a brother (the same in verses 14,15 with Benjamin and all his
brothers). He further weeps at the reunion with his father (46,29) and
over his father's dead body (50,17). He has tears only for his father and
his brothers, never for his own misery.

Verse 3. *I am Joseph; is my father still alive?* This is the most
important of all questions for him. Truly, the brothers had repeatedly
said that the father was still alive, but they did not know to whom they
had spoken. Is it really true? Now, I ask as his son, for I am Joseph. The
father for whom I asked, is my father. Their first feeling must be shame
and fear of retribution.

> *⁴So Joseph said to his brothers, "Come near to me, I pray you."
> And they came near. And he said, "I am your brother Joseph
> whom you sold into Egypt. ⁵And now do not be distressed, or
> angry with yourselves, because you sold me here; for God sent me
> ahead of you to preserve life. ⁶For the famine has been in the land
> already the second year: and there are still five years in which
> there will be neither plowing nor harvest. ⁷And God sent me
> ahead of you to preserve you on earth and to keep you alive, for a
> great deliverance. ⁸So it was not you who sent me here, but God;
> and he has made me a father to Pharaoh, and lord of all his house
> and ruler over all the land of Egypt. ⁹Make haste and go up to my
> father and say to him, 'Thus says your son Joseph, God has made
> me lord of all Egypt; come down to me, do not tarry; ¹⁰you shall
> dwell in the land of Goshen, and you shall be near to me, you and
> your children and your children's children, and your flock, your
> herds, and all that you have; ¹¹and there I will provide for you; for
> there are yet five years of famine to come; lest you and your
> household, and all that you have, come to poverty.' ¹²And now
> your eyes see, and the eyes of my brother Benjamin see, that it is
> my mouth that speaks to you. ¹³You must tell my father of all my
> splendor in Egypt, and of all that you have seen. Make haste and
> bring my father down here." ¹⁴Then he fell upon his brother
> Benjamin's neck and wept; and Benjamin wept upon his neck.
> ¹⁵And he kissed all his brothers, and wept upon them; and after
> that his brothers talked with him.*

Come near to me. All etiquette must be dropped. This verse seems to
contradict our explanation of 37,28 that not the brothers, but Midianites without their knowledge had drawn Joseph out of the pit and sold

him to Ishmaelites who brought him to Egypt where Potiphar bought him. It only seems a contradiction. First of all Joseph would not want to express an accusation at this moment, immediately retracted in a second sentence. He reads their soul: they think he can now punish them, but events were connected in an entirely different way: I came here to Egypt in order to rescue you in the famine, and that can only have been God's doing. Therefore God has sent me here (verse 8), not you.

Joseph cannot begin with this contrast in verse 4. They could not have understood him had he said: I am Joseph whom you have 'sent' here. He needs a contrast to the word, "God sent me". For this reason he must use a harsher word, more befitting their shame and fear; as he was actually "sold", he chooses this word "sold" which he can also connect with "here, to Egypt". For this context it is not so important who sold Joseph or to whom he was sold, but where he came by this sale, to Egypt. The words of Joseph abbreviate the events. This is permissible as they anyhow were the indirect cause of his having been sold by casting him in the pit. The effect and result is, as often, ascribed to its indirect originator.

It should further be noted that the Hebrew word "sell" also means "to abandon," "to cast out" without thought of a business transaction and of money. God "sells" Israel into the power of their enemies (Deut. 32,30,Judg.2,14;3,8;4,2;10,7; I Sam.12,9; Is.50,1).

Verse 5. *And now* you have rather reason for satisfaction and rejoicing. *God sent me ahead of you to keep you alive.* A very tender phrase to help them over their embarassment, almost jokingly; I was only your quartermaster, sent in advance.

Verse 8. Therefore I could say and I do not budge from it. . . .; now Joseph can substitute "sent" for "sold". He must still explain how he will be able to provide for them. God has also given him power. You are not guilty, and I can claim no credit. Everything came from God.

A father to Pharaoh and lord of all his house. Father means moral authority, often used for priest (Judg 17,10) and prophet (II Kings 5,13). Joseph cannot be king next to or above Pharaoh. He is also not merely the first of his servants, but the lord of all his house; the relation to the king is thus pictured as intimate and authoritative at the same time. The king remains king, yet subordinates himself to another man.

Verse 9. *Thus says your son.* Joseph wants these words repeated exactly, first the word "God". Hereby the father will already recognize his son Joseph. The father too shall not tarry; Joseph can hardly wait for the reunion.

Verse 10. Jacob shall not come for a visit with Joseph in the capital, but for permanent settlement in a region of his own. Goshen is, as generally assumed, the Wadi Tumilat, a region in Lower Egypt to the East of the Nile. The main reason for the invitation is to have the father and his whole house close to him.

Verse 12. Joseph wants to stress in one sentence that they have seen and heard him. *Benjamin* because he was not there when I was sold (Bechor Shor).

Verse 13. *Make haste* that he may have this joy soon (Seforno). Joseph's speech is in its way equal to that of Judah. Judah and Joseph represent two supplementary ideals, pride and benevolence which combined form the Israelite ideal of character.

Verse 15. The brothers do not weep, but are ashamed (Redak).
This is the real turning point of the story; brotherly hatred has died away, and those tears seal a new union which makes the twelve sons of Jacob into true brothers, "sons of Israel".

> ¹⁶*When the report was heard in Pharaoh's house, "Joseph's broth-ers have come," it pleased Pharaoh and his servants well. ¹⁷And Pharaoh said to Joseph, "Say to your brothers, 'Do this: load your beasts and go back to the land of Canaan; ¹⁸and take your father and your households, and come to me, and I will give you the best of the land of Egypt, and you shall eat the fat of the land.' And you are ordered, 'Do this, take wagons from the land of Egypt for your little ones and for your wives, and carry your father, and come. ²⁰Give no thoughts to your goods, for the best of all the land of Egypt is yours.' "*

Ramban: It pleased Pharaoh and his servants; for it had been disgraceful for them to have a foreigner, a slave released from prison, attain royal rank; therefore they were all happy when his distinguished brothers came to him. It is a handsome testimony for Joseph and his popularity, but also for Pharaoh and his servants, that they cordially share in his joy; they must also have considered it as serving the interest of the country (compare 41,37). Seforno: Pharaoh thought that

Joseph would care for the country with still greater devotion, if he and his family could regard Egypt as their home.

Verse 17. This confirms that Joseph could depend upon the approval of the king for his invitation (verse 9). Pharaoh is very gracious, not merely in the contents of his speech, but it seems to us that he expresses himself decidedly in Hebrew style. He selects good and even choice Hebrew words.

Verse 18. *The fat of the land* is the best of its produce. Pharaoh thinks mainly of food while Joseph in verses 7 ff. had thought further.

Verse 19. It befits a king not only to pay the travel expenses for invited guests, but also to order a splendid and honorable reception. They shall *take wagons from the land of Egypt* from official transportation. This order marks the strangers as guests of the king. Splendid wagons for the children and women, but the father will be carried like the ark of the covenant (Num.7,9). The king understands the soul of his servant and knows that he causes him the greatest pleasure by publicly honoring his father. Thus the king becomes an instrument in the divine plan for reuniting the whole family. The house of Israel is brought to Egypt by the invitation of a Pharaoh.

> ²¹*The sons of Israel did so; and Joseph gave them wagons, according to the command of Pharaoh, and gave them provisions for the journey.* ²²*To each and all of them he gave festal garments; but to Benjamin he gave hundred shekels of silver and five festal garments.* ²³*To his father he sent in like manner ten asses loaded with the good things of Egypt, and ten she-asses loaded with grain, bread, and provision for his father on the journey.* ²⁴*Then he sent his brothers away, and as they departed, he said to them, "Do not quarrel on the way."*

These provisions for the journey are again a nice detail. The great king cannot care for such minutiae, but Joseph thinks like a mother when her sons depart. Food was scarce and nothing could be bought on the way.

Verse 22. Why *festal garments?* Had it not been a garment of Joseph which had excited their hatred? Now he treats them to such a distinction and, so to say, raises them to equal rank with himself. It is a present to mark the reconciliation.

Verse 24. Do not reproach each other when you discuss the events (Rashi, ibn Ezra), by asking whose guilt was greater or smaller.

> ²⁵So they went up out of Egypt and came to the land of Canaan to their father Jacob. ²⁶And they told him, "Joseph is still alive, and he is ruler over all the land of Egypt." And his heart fainted, for he did not believe them. ²⁷But, when they told him all the words of Joseph, which he had said to them, and when he saw the wagons which Joseph had sent to carry him, the spirit of their father Jacob revived; ²⁸and Israel said, "It is enough; Joseph my son is still alive; I will go and see him before I die."

Verse 26. *His heart fainted* Rashi explains that his mind turned it away incredulously; he did not pay attention to what he had heard.

Verse 27. Only his Joseph could speak thus; these words agree with his character. With a glance at the wagons which are ready to fetch him, he declares that he wants to leave immediately.

Verse 28. *And Israel said.* The difference between Jacob and Israel cannot be overlooked here. It is inconceivable that Scripture lets one name immediately follow the other without specific intention. Even up to now the name Israel had been used only when speaking of the unity of the brothers (37,3;13. 43,6;8;11 etc.). At the terrible news of Joseph's disappearance, the father had again become "Jacob" and had rent his clothes as such (37,34); the good news that he is still alive revives Jacob to his former life and makes him once more "Israel". Israel is the name for the father of the brothers who had been reconciled and united by Joseph. The change of Jacob to Israel is not only the destiny of the father, but also of the children.

Chapter 46

The Departure

This journey is the leave-taking of the whole clan from a land which had been their home for three or four generations. Nothing remains behind except graves. They have the promise that they will later possess the land forever, but only through remote descendants. They are going to Egypt as invited guests, to their own son and brother who is highly respected there. Yet it is a foreign country with strange customs and laws. Jacob knows the difficulties of living in foreign lands. Though he looks forward to it, he may well worry. He will find his Joseph there, but it is more important whether he will have his God there too. He receives wonderful comfort. The God of his ancestors appears to him as he is about to cross the border and gives him a parting blessing; he is the God who holds sway and protects beyond any border. As God of the fathers he never forsakes their children: Be not afraid, as you go down to Egypt; I will go with you; I will always accompany you.

> So Israel took his journey with all that he had, and came to Beer-sheba, and offered sacrifices to the God of his father Isaac. ²And God spoke to Israel in visions of the night, and said, "Jacob, Jacob." And he said, "Here am I." ³Then he said, "I am God, the God of your father; do not be afraid to go down to Egypt; for I will make of you a great nation there. ⁴I will go down with you to Egypt, and I will also bring you up again; and Joseph's hand shall close your eyes." ⁵Then Jacob set out from Beer-sheba; and the sons of Israel carried Jacob their father, and their little ones, and their wives, in the wagons which Pharaoh had sent to carry him. ⁶They also took their cattle and their goods, which they had gained in the land of Canaan, and thus they came to Egypt, Jacob and all his offspring with him, ⁷his sons, and his sons' sons with him, his daughters, and his sons' daughters; all his offspring he brought with him to Egypt.

Beer-sheba is the birth place of Jacob's father Isaac; here Abraham had planted a tree to symbolize taking root in the country (21,33) ; Abraham had returned to Beer-sheba from the mountain of Moriah (22,19); from there Jacob had departed for Haran. Jacob must truly part from the fatherland. He turns to the God of his father Isaac with sacrifices. The father has died, but the son remains in communion with him now, in the future, and even in a foreign land through God who had guided him and had been worshipped by him. By this sacrifice he professes the God whose guidance did not end with the father's death, nor stops at national borders.

Verse 2. There is already comfort in pronouncing Jacob's name with fatherly love.

Verse 3. *The God of your father.* In this connection it does not mean the physical father only, but the ancestors and includes Abraham, because the consolation of a future return shall be given Jacob; this will be a return into a land which had been promised to the fathers. This central thought of the story of the patriarchs explains the solemnity of the revelation.

Jacob was worried about the promise he had received (28,13f.; 35,11 f.). Will the family not be lost in Egypt or at least endure hardships? The answer is, *"I will make of you a great nation there."* This already alludes to the contrast between the seventy souls and the numerous future people. There are reasons for which they shall and can grow into a people in Egypt. Seforno states that there they must live segregated (43,32), whereas in Canaan they are in danger of absorption through intermarriages.

Verse 4. In God's unlimited love he shares everything with his faithful ones—a foreign country, imprisonment (39,9;21), and exile, and in so doing removes the sting of all suffering. Regarding his own person, Jacob receives the assurance, *Joseph's hand shall close your eyes.* Rashbam and others however translate, "Joseph will take care of your affairs." You will have an old age without worries.

Verse 5. Beer-sheba had been the last way station from which the journey now continues without further interruption. The whole family is put in wagons of state. All the splendor was really for the father. He is called Jacob, but the sons are now *the sons of Israel,* fully united to bring him in joy to Joseph.

Verse 7. The whole family enters Egypt; none of them remain in Canaan. Therefore a list of all "the sons of Israel" is now given.

[8]*Now these are the names of the sons of Israel, who came into Egypt. Jacob and his sons. Reuben, Jacob's firstborn,* [9]*and the sons of Reuben: Hanoch, and Pallu, and Hezron, and Carmi.* [10]*And the sons of Simeon: Jemuel, and Jamin, and Ohad, and Jachin, and Zohar, and Shaul, the son of a Canaanite woman.* [11]*And the sons of Levi: Gershon, Kohath, and Merari.* [12]*And the sons of Judah: Er, and Onan, and Shelah, and Perez, and Zerah; but Er and Onan died in the land of Canaan; and the sons of Perez were Hezron and Hamul.* [13]*And the sons of Issachar: Tola, and Puvah, and Job, and Shimron.* [14]*And the sons of Zebulon: Sered, and Elon, and Jahleel.* [15]*These were the sons of Leah, whom she bore to Jacob in Paddan-aram, together with his daughter Dinah; altogether his sons and daughters thirty-three persons.* [16]*And the sons of Gad: Ziphion, and Haggi, Shuni, and Ezbon, Eri, and Arodi, and Areli.* [17]*And the sons of Asher: Imnah, and Ishvah, and Ishvi, and Beriah, and Serah their sister. And the sons of Beriah: Heber and Malchiel.* [18]*These are the sons of Zilpah, whom Laban gave to Leah his daughter; and these she bore to Jacob—sixteen persons.* [19]*The sons of Rachel, Jacob's wife: Joseph and Benjamin.* [20]*And to Joseph in the land of Egypt were born Manasseh and Ephraim, whom Asenath, the daughter of Potiphera the priest of On, bore to him.* [21]*And the sons of Benjamin: Bela, and Becher, and Ashbel, Gera, and Naaman, Ehi, and Rosh, Muppim, and Huppim, and Ard.* [22]*These are the sons of Rachel who were born to Jacob—fourteen persons in all.* [23]*And the sons of Dan: Hushim.* [24]*And the sons of Naphtali: Jahzeel, and Guni, and Jezer, and Shillem.* [25]*These are the sons of Bilhah, whom Laban gave to Rachel his daughter, and these she bore to Jacob—seven persons in in all.* [26]*All the persons belonging to Jacob who came into Egypt, who were his own offspring, not including Jacob's sons' wives, were sixty-six persons in all;* [27]*and the sons of Joseph, who were born to him in Egypt, were two persons; all the persons of the house of Jacob, that had come into Egypt, were seventy.*

The number seventy seems to have been traditional for the house of Jacob (Ex. 1,5; Deut. 10,22). As Jacob himself had to be counted among those *who had come to Egypt of the house of Jacob*, he is here included in the number seventy. We have an analogy to this way of counting a person with the seventy and yet also setting him off against the seventy.

Abimelech is one of the seventy sons of Gideon (Judg. 8,30), but kills his brothers, "seventy men upon one stone"; and one of them, Jotham was even left alive (Judg. 9,5). In other words seventy is an approximate number. The two wives together have twice as many sons as their two maidservants and each one has twice as many descendants as her maidservant.

Verse 12. The death of Er and Onan in Canaan is mentioned to tell that they alone did not come to Egypt and therefore are not to be counted among the seventy persons.

Verse 15. Rashbam and other Jewish commentators count Jacob as the thirty-third person here.

Verse 19. Rachel was Jacob's favorite "wife".

Jacob's Reunion With Joseph

²⁸He sent Judah before him to Joseph to show the way before him to Goshen; and they came into the land of Goshen. ²⁹Then Joseph made ready his chariot and went up to meet Israel his father in Goshen: and he presented himself to him, and fell on his neck, and wept on his neck a good while. ³⁰Israel said to Joseph, "Now let me die, since I have seen your face and know that you are still alive."

Jacob's message to Joseph can only state that he is on his way and will soon arrive; Joseph shall set out for the meeting. Then Judah, returning from Joseph, must inform Jacob that Joseph is coming. The second *before him* therefore refers to Joseph. Thus entirely in the spirit of the whole story, Judah is the intermediary between the father and the beloved son. He who once separated them, now unites them. The Hebrew word here translated by *he presented himself*, is elsewhere the formal term for divine appearances. His Joseph, wept over as lost and dead for twenty-two years, and now approaching with a large entourage—is for Jacob like an apparition from a higher world! An overwhelming sight, intentionally prepared by Joseph for the happiness of his father.

Verse 30. *Now* with his wishes fulfilled (Delitzsch) he may die. No joy can any more be worthwhile when compared to this experience.

31Joseph said to his brothers and to his father's household, "I will go up and tell Pharaoh, and will say to him, 'My brothers and my father's household, who were in the land of Canaan, have come to me; 32and the men are shepherds; for they have been owners of cattle; and they have brought their flocks, and their herds, and all that they have.' 33When Pharaoh calls you, and says, 'What is your occupation?' 34you shall say, 'Your servants have been owners of cattle from our youth even until now, both we and our fathers,' in order that you may dwell in the land of Goshen; for every shepherd is an abomination to Egypt."

Joseph instructs his brothers and his father's household, not the father himself who need not bother with anything (see to verse 4). A king must be dealt with in the right way. Joseph will first go in for an official audience; he will tell Pharaoh that his brothers have come. He will then suggest a place to settle them, explaining that they are shepherds with herds (Ramban).

Verse 33. Pharaoh can be expected to call for you. Then it will be your task to emphasize my words: We were always shepherds *from our youth even until now, both we and our fathers.* If you do so, Pharaoh will not try to dissuade you and will naturally think of Goshen. According to his plan, his brothers should live there, (45,10) separated from the Egyptians.

Verse 34. For *every shepherd is an abomination to Egypt.* This need not indicate any moral disparagement, but a person who always handles cattle smells like them, and people keep him at a distance without any contempt.

Chapter 47

The Meeting With Pharaoh

So Joseph went in and told Pharaoh, My father and my brothers, with their flocks and herds and all that they possess, have come from the land of Canaan; they are now in the land of Goshen." ²And from among his brothers he took five men, and presented them to Pharaoh.

Joseph's words point to the petition he intends to make; it will be a matter of caring for the flocks as well as for the people. *They are now in the land of Goshen* clearly states how appropiate it would be to leave them there. Consistently and diplomatically Joseph holds to his original purpose (45,10;46,34).

Verse 2. As Joseph brings his father with whom the eleven brothers are twelve persons, Joseph presents exactly half of the men.

³Pharaoh said to his brothers, "What is your occupation?" And they said to Pharaoh, "Your servants are shepherds, as our fathers were." ⁴They said to Pharaoh, "We have come to sojourn in the land; for there is no pasture for your servants' flocks; for the famine is severe in the land of Canaan; and now, we pray you, let your servants dwell in the land of Goshen." ⁵Then Pharaoh said to Joseph, "Your father and your brothers have come to you—the land of Egypt is before you; settle your father and your brothers in the best of the land; let them dwell in the land of Goshen; and if you know any able-bodied men among them, put them in charge of my cattle."

The brothers had understood Joseph's words in 46,34, the importance of representing themselves as shepherds.

Verse 4. Before speaking the decisive word, they make an expectant pause; perhaps Pharaoh will think of it by himself (Abrabanel). As

Pharaoh does not reply, they must start again and state their position.
We have come to sojourn in the land; by these words they define
themselves as strangers in Egypt, now and in the future reserving the
right to a later exodus. They are conscious of their national destiny
which prohibits their absorption in Egypt.

Verse 5. *Pharaoh said to Joseph.* He does not address his answer
directly to them. His gracious approval has the character of an order
given to the responsible minister; this is all the more so as the favor
concerns this minister personally. *Your father and your brothers have
come to you* is very courteous as the emphasis is on "to you" (Ramban).
You must certainly be very happy to have your family with you now,
and I am glad to favor them, which means you.

Verse 6. *The land of Egypt is before you.* You make the choice. If a
king gives a present, he must not be stingy.

Settle them in the best of the land. Your petition was not necessary; I
would go even further, but if they desire the land of Goshen I approve
it. He will even elevate them in their position as shepherds. Joseph
shall appoint those of them who are known to him as able to be
Pharaoh's chief shepherds. It is all the more disgraceful of the later
Pharaoh to enslave their descendants. This Pharaoh is a king according
to the heart of the narrator; he is without prejudice, generous, wise and
kind.

> ⁷*Then Joseph brought in Jacob his father, and set him before
> Pharaoh, and Jacob blessed Pharaoh. ⁸And Pharaoh said to Jacob,
> "How many are the days of the years of your life?" ⁹And Jacob
> said to Pharaoh, "The days of the years of my sojourning are a
> hundred and thirty years; few and evil have been the days of the
> years of my life, and they have not attained to the days of the
> years of the life of my fathers in the days of their sojourning."
> ¹⁰And Jacob blessed Pharaoh, and went out from the presence of
> Pharaoh.*

Jacob's part differs from that of the brothers. He is not a petitioner and
stands before the king in dignity as an old man; Joseph is proud of his
father. This is the reason for the special presentation. Jacob who probably never saw a king before knows what is proper; he *blesses Pharaoh,*
expresses good wishes for his welfare (Ramban). The Talmud (Ber.
58 a) has formulated a special prayer (berakha) for appearances before a
king, "Praised be he who has given of his splendor to human beings."

As Jacob's blessing probably contained a wish for the king's long life (II Sam.16,16 and likewise Egyptian and Babylonian texts) this offered an appropriate opening for Pharaoh's question in verse 8.

Jacob's answer shows that he understood two implications in Pharaoh's question (Knobel-Dillmann). It is natural to ask an old man for his age and in this way make him tell of his life experiences. On the other hand the question must refer to the special situation. Pharaoh would say: it is commendable that you in your advanced age—for is it not so that you are very old and have experienced much?—have made the journey to our country; I wish that your life may have a long and happy evening here.

Verse 9. Jacob answers: You ask how many the years of my life are? It depends on what is understood by "life". If you ask how long I am alive, the answer is 130 years. He calls them not merely years, but *the years of my sojourning.* This expresses not only the somber thought that man is a sojourner on earth (compare Psalm 119,54 and 39,13), but also clearly alludes to the words of his sons in verse 4, "We have come to sojourn in the land." Jacob covertly indicates that he too regards himself only as a sojourner in Egypt. The word "life" however has another suggestive meaning, particularly in the Hebrew, happy, higher, true life. In this sense, Jacob continues, the years of my life were few and evil, not attaining in value to the years of my fathers in spite of their sojournings. It cannot be objected that he may become older than his ancestors; he merely compares his happy years with their happy ones.

Verse 10. Jacob departs with another blessing from Pharaoh who has addressed him so graciously.

> [11]*Then Joseph settled his father and his brothers, and gave them a possession in the land of Egypt, in the best of the land, in the land of Ram'eses, as Pharaoh had commanded.* [12]*And Joseph provided his father, his brothers, and all his father's household with food. according to the number of their dependents.*

Admission of Semitic shepherds to Egypt is mentioned several times on Egyptian monuments. There have been different attempts to identify Ram'eses.

Verse 12. *According to the number of their dependents.* This stresses Joseph's correct and conscientious attitude; his family too received just enough to survive.

Joseph In Office

¹³Now there was no food in all the earth; for the famine was very severe, so that the land of Egypt and the land of Canaan languished by reason of the famine. ¹⁴And Joseph gathered up all the money that was found in the land of Egypt and in the land of Canaan, for the grain which they bought; and Joseph brought the money into Pharaoh's house.

Verse 14. The food had to be bought, so all the money of these countries finally comes to Joseph who as a faithful servant of the state pays it into the king's treasury. In Egypt the king is the state.

¹⁵And when the money was all spent in the land of Egypt and in the land of Canaan, all the Egyptians came to Joseph and said, "Give us food; why should we die before your eyes? For our money is gone." And Joseph answered, "Give your cattle, and I will give you food in exchange for your cattle, if your money is gone." ¹⁷So they brought their cattle to Joseph; and Joseph gave them food in exchange for the horses, the flocks of sheep, the flocks of cattle, and the asses; and he supplied them with food in exchange for all their cattle that year.

In the end the people have spent all their money. No more buyers can come from Canaan. The Egyptians as natives insist on being fed. There are riots and a clamor—shall we die before your eyes?

Verse 16. *If your money is gone* which he cannot quite believe, as people hide their money in such times. Or, if there is no more money, other ways of payment exist. It has been asked what could Joseph do with all these animals? He could have left them with the people who were no longer the owners. The Hebrew expression pictures Joseph as shepherd and father of these immature people. They are not much better now than their own cattle.

¹⁸And when that year was ended, they came to him the following year, and said to him, "We will not hide from my lord that our money and the herds of cattle are all at an end and are my lord's; there is nothing left in the sight of my lord but our bodies and our lands. ¹⁹Why should we die before your eyes, both we and our lands? Buy us and our land for food, and we with our lands will be slaves to Pharaoh; and give us seed, that we may live and not die, and that the land may not be desolate." ²⁰So Joseph bought

all the land of Egypt for Pharaoh; for all the Egyptians sold their fields, because the famine was severe upon them. The land became Pharaoh's ; ²¹and as for the people, he resettled them city by city from one end of Egypt to the other. ²²Only the land of the priests he did not buy; for the priests had a fixed allowance from Pharaoh and lived on the allowance which Pharaoh gave them; therefore they did not sell their land. ²³Then Joseph said to the people, "Behold, I have this day bought you and your land for the Pharaoh. Here is seed for you, and you shall sow the land. ²⁴And at the harvests you shall give a fifth to Pharaoh, and four fifths shall be your own, as seed for the fields and as food for yourselves and your households, and as food for your little ones." ²⁵And they said, "You have saved our lives; may it please my lord, we will be slaves to Pharaoh." ²⁶So Joseph made it a statute concerning the land of Egypt, and it stands to this day, that Pharaoh should have the fifth, the land of the priests alone did not become Pharaoh's.

This year too came to an end. The people say *"We will not hide from my lord anything"*. It is not as you suspect (verse 16) that we yet have money (Redak, Biur). The money and the herds still exist, but they now all belong to "my lord".

Verse 19. This appeals to Joseph's moral responsibility. Man and soil belong together; the one cannot "live" without the other. The soil's food is the seed; growth and production its life and procreation. Joseph shall buy both together and both shall be enslaved to Pharaoh.

Verse 21. Joseph can and will not accept their offer of self-enslavement, but as they alienated themselves from the soil, he makes the change effective by relocating the people town by town. The former owner is transferred to different soil. There is no reason to accept the version of the Septuagint "and as to the people Joseph made slaves of them". See the explanation at the end of this chapter.

Verse 22. The priests received a food allowance from Pharaoh, a salary in form of food; consequently they had no need to buy food and to sell their soil.

Verse 23. After the purchase of the land and the relocation of the people, Joseph gives them seed, expressly stating the relationship between Pharaoh, the soil, and its cultivators. Pharaoh is now the owner; he must supply the seed, but can also determine the distribution of the products as in verse 24 *"You shall give a fifth to Pharaoh, and four fifths shall be your own."*

Verse 25. They express their thanks to Joseph and ask him, repeating their offer of verse 19, to inform Pharaoh of their sentiments.

This arrangement of agrarian conditions in Egypt, here ascribed to Joseph, is largely confirmed by Egyptian sources and by the statements of Greek writers. In the New Kingdom "real property belonged partly to the government partly to the priests and was cultivated for both by serfs." (Erman). It also seems to agree with the known facts that the tenants had to deliver 20% of the production. It can therefore not be doubted that the Bible was familiar with conditions in Egypt.

There remains the question of the purpose of this detailed description of Egyptian conditions embodied in the story of Jacob's family. A judgement about Joseph's activities cannot be separated from this. They have often been used for attacks on the Old Testament and have been called "despotism without ethical considerations" or "financial speculation" and even worse than that by modern anti-Semites. The following points must be considered:

1) Incontestably Joseph saves the Egyptians from starvation according to this story. Ex. 1,8 could not have been written if this would not have been regarded as meritorious and obliging Egypt to eternal gratitude to Joseph.

2) It is just that the people pay for the food as long as they possess money. Actually, they only repay that which they had received when Joseph bought their surplus. The herds as movable property are merely another form of money.

3) Indignation because of the people and land of Egypt falling into dependency is misplaced. Joseph does not demand it, but the Egyptians offer it. This is the true intention of the whole story. The book of Genesis is intended, as we must emphasize again and again, as an introduction to Exodus. There the main topic will be Israel leaving Egypt, "the house of bondage". How did this country become a house of bondage? Through the servile attitude of this people for whom bread is more important than liberty. They are not so much attached to their soil that they would rather die than surrender it. In servility they positively thrust their enslavement upon Pharaoh as thanks for the expected food. This Joseph, the former slave, will not accept! Instead he buys the soil, but the people are only relocated. He avoids even the word "slaves" in his reply. The tax of 20% on the produce is moderate compared with agrarian conditions in other countries of antiquity.

4) The Torah indicates its own judgement by sharply contrasting the

Egyptian attitude with Israel's feelings. Israel regarded nothing as more precious than liberty and could not imagine slavery of one Israelite to another. Even the establishment of kingship was only reluctantly conceded. The house of Ahab perished because he deprived a commoner of his inherited vineyard. The Israelite author could have only contempt, scorn, or pity for the servile spirit of the Egyptian people. They were like their cattle, without property or liberty, content if they were fed and willing to be transferred to another feeding place (verse 17). They were like immature children who cannot care for themselves and, on their own application, are declared incapable of managing their affairs in order to be supported by the state.

5) The Torah has shown with unmistakable sarcasm that it disapproved of Egyptian conditions. The priests have the privilege of being fed by the king, and yet have land of their own and keep it. An Israelite reader would ask, why do priests who are supported by society need land? Ours have none. "God is their portion"; all land is God's and the "owners" are only his tenants. In Egypt the king is God through the servile attitude of the people.

Jacob's Last Will

> ²⁷*Thus Israel dwelt in the land of Egypt, in the land of Goshen; and they gained possession in it, and were fruitful and multiplied exceedingly.* ²⁸*And Jacob lived seventeen years in the land of Egypt; so the days of Jacob, the years of his life, were a hundred and forty-seven years.*

Scripture now returns to the house of Jacob. These years of harmonious living together of the whole family—therefore the name Israel—under the protection of the powerful brother are the happiest years in Jacob's life.

Verse 28. Here the name "Jacob" is used because of the genealogical character of the verse. The father lives exactly as many years with his son in Egypt as the son had lived in the house of the father in Canaan (37,2); for both it is a repetition which compensates for their suffering.

> ²⁹*And when the time drew near that Israel must die, he called his son Joseph and said to him, "If now I have found favor in your sight, put your hand under my thigh, and promise to deal kindly and faithfully with me. Do not bury me in Egypt, ³⁰but when I sleep with my fathers, carry me out of Egypt and bury me in their burying place." He answered, "I will do as you have said." ³¹And*

he said, "Swear to me"; and he swore to him. Then Israel bowed himself upon the head of his bed.

Declining vigor shows Jacob that he will soon die (Ramban). He *called his son*, because it is a son's duty to bury his father (25,9; 35,29); *Joseph* because only he has the power to do this. Midrash, Rashi: you have brought me here and you must carry me back. A person's requests for the disposition of his body after death, must be asked as a favor—*If now I have found favor in your sight*—and the execution of his wishes by the survivor is a kindness; he must depend on his faithfulness. The motive for Jacob's wish cannot be an antipathy against Egypt or its paganism, because for centuries afterwards Israelites will be buried in Egypt. Not to be buried in Egypt is only the introduction to his wish to be buried elsewhere, namely in the grave of his fathers.

Verse 30. Jacob wants to be buried in Canaan, because it is his home and the common grave of the three patriarchs Abraham, Isaac, and Jacob will tie the people of Israel to the Promised Land.

Verse 31. Joseph shall swear, Jacob does not distrust him, but in order that Joseph might be able to refer to this oath before Pharaoh (Ramban) as Joseph does in 50,5 f. Jacob *bows himself*, perhaps a gesture of thanksgiving to God. Now I can die without worry.

Chapter 48

Jacob And His Grandsons Ephraim And Manasseh.
> After these events it was said to Joseph. "Behold, your father is ill," so he took with him his two sons, Manasseh and Ephraim. ²And it was told to Jacob, "Your son Joseph is coming to you"; then Israel summoned his strength, and sat up in bed.

This is an introduction to both chapter 48 and chapter 49. The whole story of the patriarchs finds its climax in Jacob's blessings, his death, and burial. *It was said to Joseph* by a messenger as in 47,29.

Verse 2. Joseph's coming is reported to Jacob, so that he can prepare himself. *Israel* wants to see Joseph and his grandchildren at this hour as patriarch of the people. *He summoned his strength* so as not to alarm Joseph.

> ³Jacob said to Joseph, "God Almighty appeared to me at Luz in the land of Canaan and blessed me, ⁴and said to me, 'Behold, I will make you fruitful, and multiply you, and I will make you a company of peoples, and will give this land to your descendants after you for an everlasting possession.' ⁵And now your two sons, who were born to you in the land of Egypt, before I came to you to Egypt, shall be mine; Ephraim and Manasseh shall be mine, as Reuben and Simeon are. ⁶And the offspring born to you after them shall be yours; they shall be called by the name of their brothers in their inheritance. ⁷Regarding me, when I came from Padan, Rachel to my sorrow died in the land of Canaan on the way, when there was still some distance to go to Ephrath; and I buried her on the way to Ephrath, that is Bethlehem."

Jacob said This name is used because Ephraim and Manasseh shall subsequently be enrolled among the "sons of Jacob".

Verse 4. *I will make you fruitful and multiply you.* This is a contrast to 47,27; in Egypt too Israel was fruitful, multiplied, and acquired possessions, but as a grant from men, therefore only temporarily. Jacob wants to speak of the growth of the people and its acquisition of land as promised by God.

It will not be merely a crowd of individuals, but *a company of peoples* a national organism in which each subdivision has its own tribal life and all together form a religio-political body, founded upon physical relationship. The land in which they shall live will be Canaan; this possession will be everlasting. The meaning of Jacob's words is that they are certainly prospering here in Egypt, but have a higher destiny, promised by God which can be fulfilled only in Canaan; therefore they cannot stay here for ever. This also sets Jacob's request for burial in Canaan into the right light. The people of Israel shall go back and the return of the patriarch Israel is a model for it. Jacob is not mislead by their present prosperity.

Verse 5. I regard you and your two sons as if I had brought you with me to Egypt like all the others. Here he already puts Ephraim before Manasseh: he is resolved to establish this precedence (Luzzato) whereas for Joseph (verse 1) and, provisionally, for the Bible their sequence is naturally according to age. *They shall be mine as Reuben and Simeon are;* his two eldest sons whom he mentions here in spite of the severe judgement later in 49,3 ff.

Verse 6. *Offspring born to you* after my coming to you; this could mean that Joseph had other children in these seventeen years (Rashbam and others) or is only hypothetical "which you will or might still have" (Onkelos, Septuagint and many others). No other sons of Joseph are mentioned anywhere. It refers to the distribution of the Promised Land. If Joseph should still have descendants after Ephraim and Manasseh, they will not directly participate in the distribution of the land like these two, but only indirectly under the name Joseph; as Joseph becomes divided into Ephraim and Manasseh, under the names of these. Ephraim and Manasseh, although only grandsons, are elevated to the rank of tribes.

Like the tribes of Reuben etc. each one of them will receive a tribal territory, named after him, and will provide its tribal prince for all occasions. Correspondingly the distribution of the land is made in Num. 26. Joseph and his two sons shall be elevated although they had not actually come to Egypt with Jacob. Ephraim and Manasseh have a twofold position, by birth and as persons they are grandsons of Jacob, but for the later organization of the people Jacob equates them with his sons and elevates them to the rank of tribal chiefs. Thus Joseph also rises in rank and is given a twofold position; he is a son of Jacob, but as father of tribal chiefs he enters into equality with Jacob himself; this is the purpose of the arrangement. Jacob immediately before his death gives his beloved son the highest honor and sign of love; he places him on a level with himself. He becomes, so to say, the fourth patriarch of the people of Israel; there will be a "house of Joseph" as there is a "house of Israel". Joseph receives a dignity from his father which will have its root in his own people and will be more lasting than that given him by Pharaoh. Jacob's motive is his love for him.

Verse 7. Finally Jacob speaks of Rachel's death and her burial. The purpose of reporting this here must be related to the context in verses 3–6 and 8–22. If Abraham, Isaac, and Jacob (with their wives, except Rachel,) are buried in the same place, this means that only they are the three patriarchs. The common place of burial is testimony and symbol for the unity of the whole people which is descended from these first parents. On earth it corresponds to the One God in heaven, the God who guided them and whom they worshipped. No one else was ever buried in the cave of Machpelah. Now Jacob had, in verses 5 and 6, equalized Ephraim and Manasseh with his own sons, and thus Joseph with himself. He had established a "house of Joseph" within Israel, with Joseph as its patriarch. These two brothers and tribes have yet another father to revere than the others. This is also the reason for which Joseph has himself conveyed to Canaan. All Israel has a unifying point in the grave not only of the patriarchs, but also of their wives; the house of Joseph shall have a grave of an ancestor in the Promised Land, that of their grandmother Rachel. In her, in her grave, they shall be united.

Regarding me in a tone of resignation like 43,14. All his sons, including Joseph, have been restored to Jacob; he has even, in a way, gained two new sons. Yet one beloved person is gone for ever, the mother of Joseph, the father of these boys. Jacob in his deep sentiment has never forgotten the wife of his first love; he cannot but remember her in his last hours. In these final chapters he mentions the names of all his dear ones: Abraham, Isaac, Sarah and Rebekah, his other wife Leah, all his sons, his grandsons Ephraim and Manasseh; Rachel could not be omitted. He is about to bless his grandsons; he begins with the lamentation, Why could Rachel not live to see this! She cannot bless you as a living person; she will do it from her grave. The Bible has reserved Jacob's words of mourning for this hour when he himself is close to death.

In the land of Canaan emphasizes that the grave of the ancestor which shall become sacred to the Joseph tribes is located in the land of their future settlement.

On the way recalls the terror of that hour.

> ⁸*Now Israel looked upon Joseph's sons, and he said, "Who are these?" ⁹Joseph said to his father, "They are my sons, whom God has given me here." And he said, "Bring them to me, I pray you, that I may bless them."*

Who are these? does not mean that Jacob saw them only now or that he did not know them. He has mentioned their names in verse 5; nor can it be assumed that Joseph had never brought them to him in these seventeen years. This is rather an introduction to his blessing: *he looked upon them.* So far they had respectfully stayed in the background. Now Jacob wants to draw them near. By doing this in the form of a question he gives Joseph an opportunity to use the word "God" in his reply.

Verse 9. Children are a gift of God's favor. *Bring them to me* taking them tenderly by the hand (Hos. 11,3). I will bless them, so that God who has given them may be with them in the future too. Before Jacob blesses them he will have them close to his eyes, kiss, embrace them, and so to say grasp his good fortune in his hands.

> ¹⁰*Now the eyes of Israel were heavy with old age, so that he could not see. So Joseph brought them near to him; and he kissed them and embraced them. ¹¹And Israel said to Joseph, "I had not thought to see your face; and lo, God has let me see your children also." ¹²Then Joseph removed them from his knees, and he bowed himself to his face to the earth.*

Heavy refers to the eyelids which often droop with an old man, as if they were heavier than previously; in reality his power to hold his eyes open and to fix them on an object has become weaker. The scene is patterned after chapter 27. Jacob who cannot have forgotten the blessing by his father takes it as his model.

Verse 11. This moment awakens memories in Jacob which are bitter and sweet at the same time; once he had been able thus to caress his favorite son Joseph, but he was forced to let him go from his arms—forever, as he had believed. Now he may embrace the children of the son whom he had given up as lost. This moment forces him to exclaim: what a change through God's guidance! I would not have dared to believe that I would see you again, but God has let me see more than any human imagination could expect.

God has let me see your children; this is the best compensation for his blindness in verse 10. His eye is dim with age, but God makes him capable of seeing a happiness which even the keenest foresight could not have perceived.

Verse 12. *Then Joseph removed them from his knees.* The children had been snuggling against his knees at the side of the bed as Rembrandt has painted it so beautifully in his famous picture. Joseph *bowed himself to his face to the earth.* As son and as father he cannot remain unmoved by Jacob's tenderness; so he thanks God, turning to the face of Jacob whom he also thanks by this for his intention to bless the children. This gesture of solemn emotion would have been weakened if the boys stood between them. At the same time he uses the interruption to bring the boys into the position which seems correct to him.

> ¹³*And Joseph took them both, Ephraim in his right hand toward Israel's left hand, and Manasseh in his left hand toward Israel's right hand, and brought them near him.* ¹⁴*And Israel stretched out his right hand and laid it upon the head of Ephraim, who was the younger, and his left hand upon the head of Manasseh, intentionally crossing his hands, for Manasseh was the first-born.* ¹⁵*And he blessed Joseph, and said, "The God before whom my fathers Abraham and Isaac walked, the God who has led me all my life long to this day,* ¹⁶*the angel who has redeemed me from all evil, bless the lads; and in them let my name be perpetuated, and the name of my fathers Abraham and Isaac; and let them grow into a multitude in the midst of the earth."*

One blesses a person by laying one's hand on his head or keeping the hand over it; hereby one points to him, concentrates on him, and takes him under protection. The right hand is preferred for this as the stronger one. Therefore this hand is due to the older child if both children are blessed at the same time. Joseph has the children stand accordingly.

Verse 14. *Israel stretched out his right hand and laid it upon the head of Ephraim who was the younger,* well considering his action. See verse 19 for the reason.

Verse 15. To bless Ephraim and Manasseh means to bless "Joseph" a
he had been divided into these two tribes. Jacob turns 1) to *the Go*
before whom my fathers walked; in whose sight and under whos
protection they were privileged to live. 2) to *the God who has led me o*
my life long. The piety of his fathers had been an active, conscious fait
in God. Jacob, looking back on his whole life in humble confessior
now recognizes that he had always been guarded by a faithfu
shepherd; this is an excellent metaphor in the mouth of the exemplar
shepherd Jacob (Dillmann).

Verse 16. Jacob's personal experiences cannot be exhausted in on
sentence; so he starts to speak of them once more. He had just calle
himself a lamb of God. but it must not be assumed that his life was s
smooth.

The angel who has redeemed me from all evil. He recognizes tha
there was a protective angel at his side in all his miseries (28,12;32,2
May the lads like Abraham, Isaac, and myself stand under God's protec
tion and (Seforno) be regarded by Him as worthy of it. May they b
called true descendants of those worshipers of God and testify to it b
quoting these names of the ancestors as I have now done.

> *17Joseph had seen that his father laid his right hand upon th
> head of Ephraim, and it displeased him; and he took his father
> hand, to remove it from Ephraim's head to Manasseh's heac
> 18And Joseph said to his father, "Not so, my father; for this one a
> the first-born; put your right hand upon his head." 19But his fathe
> refused, and said, "I know, my son, I know; he also shall become
> people, and he also shall be great; nevertheless his younger brotl
> er shall be greater than he, and his descendants shall become
> full nation." 20So he blessed them that day, saying, "By you Israc
> will pronounce blessings, saying, 'God make you as Ephraim an
> as Manasseh;' " and thus he put Ephraim before Manasseh.*

This displeased Joseph; it was repugnant to his feelings. Manasseh i
the first-born and the right hand is due to him. He cannot have believe
it an error on the part of Jacob as the crossing of the hands must hav
been intentional. Rather he believes (Rashbam and others) that Jaco
did not understand that Joseph had placed the two boys convenientl
for him, Manasseh to Joseph's left, that is to Jacob's right. Joseph woul
not have opposed his father's outspoken will, certainly not by coercior
even if in a delicate way. His grasping of Jacob's hand expresses: yo

seem to assume that I naturally have my first-born in my right hand and he therefore stands to your left; this is why you cross your hands.

Verse 18. I wanted to make it convenient for you so that you would not have to cross your hands. He softens his action by addressing him "my father".

Verse 19. Jacob shakes his head: *I know, my son, I know.* The repetition with "my son" softens his refusal.

Verse 20. The real blessing is verse 15f. Verse 20 shall be its enhancement and final confirmation. To pacify Joseph further, he gives a blessing common to both. In future Israel every father in our people will, when he pronounces a blessing, speak like me, your father Israel. Can there be a higher blessing for you?

Previously verse 19 had enlarged the blessing of verse 15 into a prophecy. It can be further enhanced by their becoming the model of blessing for others—Joseph for every father in Israel, Ephraim and Manasseh for all sons. The highest blessing that can be wished upon a person, is that he may be like someone who is generally recognized as a blessed man. The happiest father is one who can serve as model for all fathers and that is Joseph. By blessing the sons in the father and the father in the sons the natural relation of father and sons is preserved; the difficulty of the sons in this chapter standing for tribes and yet being individuals is overcome. Jacob wants to say that every family in Israel shall desire your good fortune of the grandfather blessing the grandsons led to him by his son and so blessing both generations simultaneously (see the whole Psalm 128).

As Jacob pronounces a prophecy, the preferment of the younger son is not personal favoritism and arbitrariness. This also justifies—after the event, the action of Jacob's mother (see 25,23;27,5ff.). That which had been tricked out of the father by fraud, Jacob now proclaims openly and with forethought.

> ²¹Then Israel said to Joseph, "Behold, I am about to die, but God will be with you, and will bring you again to the land of your fathers. ²²I give to you one shoulder above your brothers which I took from the hand of the Amorite with my sword and with my bow."

Israel said The new beginning indicates that this is something special, but it must stand in some inner relationship to the elevation of Ephraim and Manasseh.

Verse 22. There is much controversy about this verse. What is a "shoulder"? Were the last part of the sentence taken literally, it would show Jacob in a light totally contrary to his character in the story so far. We know him, in contrast to Esau, as a peaceful man, preferrably dwelling in his tent, a shepherd and worried father of a family who is afraid of hostile encounters and abhors deeds of violence as those of his sons against Shechem. Now on his death bed he is supposed to have boasted of warlike deeds and conquest of land by sword and bow! This is hard to believe. Only an interpretation, not contrary to the character of Jacob and consistent with the context, can be correct. Jacob can also not dispose of the Promised Land. That will be the task of Moses and his successor.

The passage must refer to the only piece of land in Canaan which could be disposed by Jacob, the field near Shechem which he had bought according to 33,19 and where later (Josh.24,32) Joseph was buried. This "shoulder" of land is here given to Joseph as a burial place. The phrase in verse 21 "I am about to die" is always followed by dispositions for a funeral. Jacob has already spoken about his own in 47,29f. He cannot say to Joseph: when you die; what father would? He hints at it and desires to say: When God brings our people to the land of our fathers and you like me want to be buried in the Promised Land, here is a burial place for you.

The passage is connected with 50,24. Jacob has bought this field for a hundred pieces of money (33,19) and this he calls "with my sword and my bow", a witty reference to the "weapons of violence" of Simeon and Levi in 49,5. Compare also Psalm 44,4ff. I, Jacob says, made a conquest by peaceful "weapons" (silver bullets).

This chapter clearly shows how the book of Genesis refers to the later history of the tribes and patterns the history of the fathers accordingly. The later ascendancy of the tribe of Ephraim is represented in the book of Genesis as a blessing of the patriarch Jacob.   •

Chapter 49

Jacob's Last Words

It would be inappropriate to call this chapter "Jacob's Blessing"; the blessing appears only in Verse 28, and the pronouncements over the first three sons are the opposite of a blessing. Jacob rather gathers his twelve sons around his deathbed to tell them, what he thinks of them and what will befall their descendants at a later time. He begins with the six sons of Leah and ends with the two sons of Rachel; between stand the four sons of the maid servants. Judah and Joseph are the central figures; ten of twenty-three verses deal with them. This corresponds to the preceding stories in which Joseph and Judah played the main parts. The sons are addressed, but turn almost imperceptibly into their tribes. The language is highly poetical, archaic, and often obscure.

> Then Jacob called his sons, and said, "Gather yourselves together that I may tell you what shall befall you in latter days. ²Assemble and hear, O sons of Jacob, and listen to Israel your father.

The name "Jacob" is used as they are to be addressed as "sons of Jacob". The following is an expression of Jacob's personal opinion, not a prophetical revelation inspired by God. Aside from the exclamation in verse 18, God and religion are not mentioned. We can only expect that which Jacob, looking into the future with the keen vision of a dying man and knowing the character of his sons, could hope or fear for them.

In latter days literally "at the end of days", does not mean the end of all history, but the remote future.

Verse 2. now *Israel* is used, possessing a unifying meaning and moral weight. The beginning *hear* is characteristic of the speech of the leader, prophet and teacher. All Scripture is a "Hear O Israel!" The first to pronounce it is the father Israel himself.

> ³*Reuben, you are my first-born, my might and the first fruit of my manhood, pre-eminent in dignity, and pre-eminent in power. ⁴Unstable as water, you shall not have pre-eminence because you went up to your father's bed; then you defiled it—he went up to my couch!*

The mere statement that Reuben is the first-born would be superfluous. Jacob intends to say that he must start with him when he intends to address his sons one after the other. You are the first-born; what a promise might that have been! This idea is now interpreted, being the first-born is nothing accidental and indifferent. You are the first fruit of my marriage, begotten in the vigor of my life and my love. It might have meant pre-eminence, but Reuben has lost his pre-eminence because he defiled his father's wife Bilhah (35,22). This rejection of Reuben agrees with all which is reported about him and his tribe. His position as oldest son and tribe was never contested, but he proved himself incapable of leadership. The tribe produced no remarkable man, no judge, no king, no prophet. His rejection is motivated by lack of respect for the father. A bad son could command no obedience from his brothers. A man who could not control himself was not fit to control others.

> ⁵*Simeon and Levi are brothers; weapons of violence are common to them. ⁶O my soul, come not into their council; o my honor, be not joined to their company; for in their anger they have slain men, and in their wantonness they drove off oxen. ⁷Cursed be their anger, for it is fierce; and their wrath, for it is cruel! I will divide them in Jacob and scatter them in Israel.*

They are called "brothers" with superior irony—these inseparable ones! this motivates that he takes them together in one pronouncement and prepares for their condemnation.

Weapons of violence are common to them. The Hebrew words are difficult and admit various translations and interpretations.

Verse 6. I do not want to be associated with them because of their violence. The second half of the verse refers to the story of chapter 34.

Verse 7. Their passions, not their persons are cursed. The punishment must correspond to the deed. Therefore *I will divide them;* Rashi and others interpret that they shall be separated from each other and in the future have no more possibility for common enterprises.

8Judah, you: your brothers shall pay homage to you; your hand shall be on the neck of your enemies; your father's sons shall bow down before you. 9Judah is a real lion; from the prey, my son, you have gone up. He stooped down, he crouched as a lion, and as a lioness; who dares rouse him up? 10The scepter shall not depart from Judah, nor the ruler's staff from between his feet, until he comes to Shilo; and to him shall be the homage of the peoples. 11Binding his foal to the vine and his ass's colt to the choice vine, he washes his garments in wine and his cloth in the blood of grapes; his eyes shall be redder than wine, and his teeth whiter than milk.

In Hebrew the first sentence is a pun on the name Judah. "Your name is rightly Judah (praise); your brothers will praise you." They pay homage to you as leader and ruler after the three older brothers have been rejected.

Verse 9. The lion resting his body on his paws is a great sight; it is as if Jacob would say: look at him, this powerful man! The lion is an image of the ruler who takes to his throne after victory.

Verse 10. Leaves the image and speaks directly of Judah. From of old the words have been interpreted as a prophecy of David's kingship from the house of Judah.

Until he comes to Shilo These Hebrew words are the most controversial passage of the whole book of Genesis. They have been interpreted in many ways. The old translations (Septuagint, Onkelos etc) translate "until he comes to whom it (the rule) belongs", meaning the Messiah. Christian orthodoxy saw in this a prophecy fulfilled in Jesus, whereas some rabbis in the Talmud referred the verse to Hillel who was supposed to be descended from David.

We believe that this pronouncement promises reconciliation of the tribes after the split into the northern kingdom (Ephraim) and the southern kingdom (Judah) which occurred after the death of Solomon. A solution doing justice to both sides would be a kingship from Judah, proclaimed on the territory of Ephraim, at Shilo, the old sacred place of pilgrimages of all tribes (Judg. 21,19; I Sam. 1,3 etc), the center of Israel in the time before David. It is all the more fitting as Shilo was very close to Shechem (Judg. 21,19) where other great national events took place (Josh. 24; I Kings 12,1). There homage and obedience by the peoples (i.e. tribes 28,3;48,4) will come to Judah. It is the same idea as Is. 11,13

"Ephraim shall not be jealous of Judah, and Judah shall not harrass
Ephraim."

Such an interpretation frees the passage of all Messianic content and
is in agreement with the spirit of the whole Joseph story which emphasizes the reconciliation of hostile brothers. Without this interpretation
of the passage the final words of Jacob would lack the idea which we
expect first in the last address of a father to his assembled sons—an
admonition to unity.

Verse 11. This verse describes the action of this king from Judah on
his arrival in Shilo, at his festive entry for his coronation. He is like the
king of Zion and Jerusalem, of whom Zech. 9,9 says that he enters
riding on an ass's colt. The ass is the riding animal for noblemen (Judg.
5,10) and princes (Judg. 10,4;12,14). The extravagant expressions
depict the intoxicated joy over his victorious appearance; they may
even describe a wine harvest festival in its three phases of picking,
pressing, and drinking.

He washes his garments in wine and his cloth in the blood of grapes.
A poetical phrase as in treading the wine press the clothes become
stained with wine (Rashbam and others). The phrase "blood of grapes"
is also poetical.

Verse 12. This verse describes the beauty of the ruler who like the
beloved of Song of Songs 5,10 is white and red (compare Lam. 4,7).

The position ascribed here to Judah corresponds to his role in history. The star of Judah shone forth in the person of David and the scepter
did not cease from Judah as long as there was an Israelite state. With the
exception of Levi his tribal name is the only one surviving and passing
on to all descendants of Jacob. All of them finally became "Jews".

> *13Zebulun shall dwell at the shore of the sea; he shall become a
> haven for ships, and his border shall be near Sidon.*

Sidon is the great Phoenician sea and trade city. This characterizes
Zebulun as a tribe engaged in trade and gaining wealth by its closeness
to the sea and to the trading center of Sidon.

> *14Issachar is a strong-boned ass, crouching between the sheep-
> folds; 15He saw that a resting place was good, and that the land
> was pleasant; so he bowed his shoulder to bear, and became a
> toiling laborer.*

He is strong, but lazy; loafing pleases him. The words are ironical, imitating the speech of the lazy one. Issachar knows nothing better than to stay and to rest, particularly if the native land is so pleasant. He is the opposite of Zebulun, the versatile brother who looks out over the sea.

Verse 15. It results in his becoming a slave who must do forced labor like a prisoner of war, a thing most contemptible in the eyes of an Israelite.

> *16Dan judges his people, as one the tribes of Israel. 17Dan shall be a serpent in the way, a viper by the path, that bites the horse's heels, so that his rider falls backward. 18I wait for thy salvation, O Lord.*

Again a pun, on the name Dan (i.e. judge). He fights for the protection of all Israel. By providing justice Dan makes the community *his people,* as if the tribes of Israel were one (compare Judg. 20,11).

Verse 17. The comparison with a serpent is related to the preceding. One of the messengers of God's justice besides sword, famine, plague, and wild beasts is also the serpent (Num. 21,6; Deut. 32,24; Amos 9,3). Or the lion (Judah) and the serpent (Dan) supplement each other as two opposite ways of fighting, with violence and with slyness. The viper or cerastes is regarded as extremely dangerous.

Verse 18. The place and purpose of these words is hard to understand. Following verse 9 it is the only time that Jacob again speaks in the first person singular and pronounces the name of God. No satisfactory explanation has been found.

> *19Raider raid Gad, but he raids at their heels.*

This verse contains four Hebrew puns on the name Gad (raid). It would say that enemies raid Gad in vain; rather may he or will he raid them; he will gain the upper hand over them.

> *20Asher's food is rich and he yields royal ointments.*

Not "dainties" as usual translated, but ointments (Rashbam), the very best oil such as kings demand or give each other as present, for instance in the letters of El-Amarna.

²¹Naphtali is a hind let loose, that bears comely fawns.

Onkelos, Rashi and others translated the last part of the verse "who gives off beautiful words" as an allusion to the song of Deborah in Judg. 5; she had Barak from the tribe of Naphtali at her side. The comparison with a hind is interpreted as hinting either at the swift heroes of this tribe (Psalm 18,34) or at the speedily ripening fruits of the plain of Genasar which belonged to the tribe of Naphtali. An entirely different translation (Skinner) compares Naphtali with "a slender terebinth tree which produces fine branches."

> *²²Beautiful is Joseph, more beautiful than ever seen; the girls climb up the walls for him. ²³The archers fiercely attacked him, shot at him, and harassed him sorely; ²⁴Yet his bow remained in vigor; his arms and hands were made strong by the hands of the Mighty One of Jacob (from there!—the shepherd, Rock of Israel), ²⁵by the God of your father who may help you, by God Almighty who may bless you with blessings of heaven from above, with blessings of the deep that couches beneath, with blessings of the breasts and of the womb. ²⁶The blessings of your father are mighty beyond the blessings of my progenitors to the bounties of the everlasting hills; may they be on the head of Joseph, and on the brow of the prince among his brothers.*

This pronouncement about the most beloved son competes in length and lofty diction with that of Judah, but is full of obscurities.

Verse 22. Other translators find a comparison of Joseph with a many-branched fruit tree whose branches climb over the wall in the verse. It, however, alludes to 39,6 and the adventure with the wife of Potiphar.

Verse 23. The "arrows" are hostile and slanderous speeches; the tongue is often compared with bow or arrow (see Jer. 9,2.7); words can wound and kill. It is doubtful whether the persecution of Joseph by his brothers or by the wife of Potiphar is meant. The latter is preferrable as (Redak) it would have been indelicate on the part of Jacob to remind the sons of their conflict.

Verse 24. The translation is not certain, but the sentence must refer to the triumphs and successes of Joseph in Egypt, his wisdom and virtue.
  By the hands of the Mighty One of Jacob. Joseph's vigor in overcoming his opponents came from God. As God showed himself helpful and

as a savior to the father, so he aided the son whose religion and strength came from remembering the father and his God. *From there!* pointing to the sky where the shepherd is found. But shepherd and rock are disparate figures of speech.

Verse 25. Now Jacob turns in direct speech to Joseph. *God Almighty* is the God of the patriarchs. *Blessings of heaven from above* are dew and rain. *Blessings of the deep that couches beneath* mean wells that spring from the deep. *Blessings of the breasts and of the womb* The breasts of the mothers shall give abundant milk and their wombs give birth again and again, the opposite of the curse in Hos. 9,14.

Verse 26. *The blessings of your father.* The blessings pronounced over your father (27,28f. etc) were already a climax; now Jacob wants to see them transferred to Joseph.

Verse 27. Joseph is called *the prince among his brothers* (Septuagint and Jewish commentators). This refers to his elevation in Egypt and is a beautiful climax to this pronouncement abundant in blessings for the favorite son. It begins with the tribulations he had to suffer and closes with his present glory.

The relationship to the brothers is described only with Judah (verse 8) and Joseph; they pay homage to Judah for his deeds in war, to Joseph for his royal solicitude. Both supplement each other. The pronouncement over Judah is full of a martial spirit, that over Joseph of blessing and peace. Judah is the peak of power, Joseph of happiness.

> 27*Benjamin is a ravenous wolf, in the morning devouring the prey, and at even dividing the spoil."*

Benjamin is (43,8f.;44,18ff.) the protege of Judah; so the same character is ascribed to him. Judah is a lion, Benjamin a wolf, the smaller beast of prey.

> 28*All these are the twelve tribes of Israel; and this is what their father said about them; and he blessed them, blessing each with the blessing suitable to him. 29Then he charged them, and said to them, "I am to be gathered to my people; bury me with my fathers in the cave that is in the field of Ephron the Hittite, 30in the cave that is in the field Machpelah, to the east of Mamre, in the land of Canaan which Abraham bought with the field from Ephron the Hittite to possess a burying place. 31There they buried Abraham*

*and Sarah his wife; there they buried Isaac and Rebekah his wife;
and there I buried Leah—the field and the cave that is in it were
purchased from the Hittites.''* [33]*When Jacob finished charging his
sons, he drew up his feet into the bed, and breathed his last, and
was gathered to his people.*

He blessed his sons does not refer to the preceeding pronouncements
as these were not always blessings (Reuben, Simeon-Levi). However,
Jacob having spoken so far as ancestor of the tribes, now blesses his
sons as a dying father, *each with the blessing suitable to him* with
varying words of blessing which the Bible does not deem necessary to
report.

Verse 29. This is Jacob's last will. This charge to all the sons to bury
him with his fathers does not contradict the charge to Joseph in 47,29f.
Joseph shall obtain the permission, but it is the duty of all sons to bury
their father.

Verse 31. Every generation has fulfilled this duty of love; so must
you!

Verse 33. Now he has said all which had to be arranged. It is a
magnificent conception to present the whole future people in such a
scene. The ancestors of the twelve tribes stand at the deathbed of the
patriarch in order to hear the last words of the old father; he holds a
mirror up to them and in the face of death the future is unveiled to him.
The ideal unity of the nation could not be presented more impressively;
it is also expressed with unique energy and absoluteness by the fact
that Israel, the ancestor's name, is at the same time the name of the
nation and the sons are also tribes. This is the fitting end for the book of
Genesis and the best transition to the book of Exodus. The author has
held himself to the situation without committing any flagrant anachro-
nism.

Chapter 50

Jacob's Funeral. End Of The Book

Then Joseph fell on his father's face, and wept over him and kissed him. ²And Joseph commanded his servants, the physicians, to enbalm his father. So the physicians enbalmed Israel; ³forty days were required for it, for so many are required for enbalming. And the Egyptians wept for him seventy days.

Joseph As the father had loved him above all his brothers, so had he loved the father. He *kissed him,* as if he could not believe that he was dead; it is a leave-taking; so Elisha kisses his father and mother good-by before following Elijah (I Kings 19,20).

Verse 2. Joseph had everything required by Egyptian custom done to his father. It may be assumed that the enbalming refers to the mummification of the corpse which is known in all details from the reports of ancient Greek writers and through archaeology.

Israel The physicians were aware that they were dealing with a godly man.

Verse 3. *Seventy days* of formal mourning after the enbalming must also have been Egyptian custom.

⁴When the days of weeping for him were past, Joseph spoke to the household of Pharaoh, saying, "If now I have found favor in your eyes, speak, I pray you, in the ears of Pharaoh, saying, ⁵My father made me swear, saying, 'I am about to die: in my tomb which I hewed out for myself in the land of Canaan, there you shall bury me.' Now therefore I will go up, I pray you, and bury my father; then I will return." ⁶Pharaoh answered, "Go up, and bury your father, as he made you swear."

Joseph spoke to the household of Pharaoh to the people who were always around the king as no one was allowed to appear before the king

337

without having been called (46,33). Permission of the king was required for leaving the country, but Joseph was as certain of it as of the settling of his family (45,10;46,34).

Verse 5. Compare with 47,31. Joseph quotes only those points which will impress Pharaoh from the speech of his father. The grave has already been prepared and waits for Jacob's body. Perhaps this refers also to the Egyptian practice of building their tombs before death.

I will return You need not worry that I might not return as later the Pharaoh of Moses fears (Ex. 5,3ff.;10,24).

Verse 6. Pharaoh answered his people so that they might tell Joseph.

> ⁷*So Joseph went up to bury his father; and with him went up all the servants of Pharaoh, the elders of his household, and all the elders of the land of Egypt,* ⁸*as well as all the household of Joseph, his brothers, and his father's household; only their children, their flocks, and their herds they left in the land of Goshen.* ⁹*And there went up with him both chariots and horsemen; it was a very great company.* ¹⁰*When they came to the threshing floor of thorns, which is beyond the Jordan, they lamented there with a very great and sorrowful lamentation; and he made a mourning for his father seven days.* ¹¹*When the inhabitants of the land, the Canaanites, saw the mourning on the threshing floor of thorns, they said, "This is a grievous mourning to the Egyptians." Therefore its place was named Abel-mizraim (mourning of Egypt); it is beyond the Jordan.*

The transfer of the corpse is done with the greatest honors due only to a high dignitary; the same were probably later given to Joseph. The Bible does not report them with him, but with Jacob to show how much Joseph honored his father. The story of Joseph is a hymn of filial love from beginning to end.

Verse 8. The mourning family follows behind the dignified and splendid cortege. Brothers who once were hostile walk in harmony behind the father's coffin, like Ishmael and Isaac (25,9), Esau and Jacob (35,29). Death brings reconciliation.

Verse 10. *Beyond the Jordan.* This is east of the river, not yet on Canaanite soil; it is said from the viewpoint of the Canaanites.

Here, at the departure from Egypt, another mourning ceremony is performed, "a lamentation" which consisted in loud, bitter, and ryth-mical exclamations praising the deeds and qualities of the deceased. People rent their clothes and girded themselves in sackcloth. The ceremony is described as *very great and sorrowful*. The Hebrew is economical with superlatives, but compare the "great" feast 21,8 at the weaning of the first son; the author may have thought of that event as contrast to the death of the last patriarch. The mourning is extended to seven days in order to do special honor to the father and to impress the inhabitants of the land.

Verse 11. This verse testifies to the deep impression made by this extraordinary procedure. The fact that the Canaanites will remember it will be important later. The name Abel-mizraim plays on the Hebrew words for "meadow" and for "mourning". The Israelites shall be able to say in future times, "Even Egypt honored our ancestor by a great mourning." The procession had not taken the shortest route from Egypt, but the longer way around the Dead Sea; this is also in honor of the deceased; it is the way later taken by Moses and Joshua with Joseph's coffin. Jacob is the forerunner and pathfinder for the later people of Israel.

> ¹²Then his sons did to him as he had commanded them; ¹³for his sons carried him to the land of Canaan, and buried him in the cave of the field of Machpelah, to the east of Mamre, which Abraham bought with the field from Ephron the Hittite, to possess as a burying place. ¹⁴After he had buried his father, Joseph returned to Egypt with his brothers and all who had gone up with him to bury his father.

From the moment when the coffin is lifted and carried to the grave no more distinction is made between Joseph and his brothers. All of them are Jacob's *sons*.

Verse 13. The burial in the family grave is an affair of the family. It is the return of the patriarch to the *land of Canaan* and sets the pattern for the later entrance of Israel into the Promised Land. The arrangements of the ceremonies in Egypt had been left to Joseph.

Verse 14. Joseph returns to Egypt with his brothers after they have fulfilled the father's last will (47,30;49,29).

> ¹⁵When Joseph's brothers saw that their father was dead, they said, "It may be that Joseph will hate us and pay us back for all

*the evil which we did to him." 16So they sent a message to Joseph,
saying, "Your father gave this command before he died, 17'Say to
Joseph, Forgive, I pray you, the transgression of your brothers and
their sin, because they did evil to you.' And now, we pray you,
forgive the transgression of the servants of the God of your
father." Joseph wept when they spoke to him.*

Now they became fully aware of the meaning of the father's death.
They fear that Joseph might act according to popular morality and
retaliate; as they have done to him, he will do to them. Consideration
for the father might have restrained his revenge as long as the father
was alive. Now they are completely in his power.

Verse 16. They can only appeal to his mercy, and in their anxiety do
not dare to approach him directly, but act through messengers as Jacob
had done with his brother Esau (32,4). Their stammering fear is
expressed by the repetition of the same words over and over again,
forgive, and transgression. They are anxious that none of their words is
lost, for in their opinion life and death depend upon that, again similar
to Jacob, before Esau (32,4 ff.21). They believe to possess a strong
argument in the father's last will. He is supposed to have commanded
them before his death to ask Joseph's forgiveness. Although such a
command had not been reported, it is not a white lie of the brothers.
The father must often have thought about the relationship of Joseph
and his brothers after his death. Although he was certain that Joseph
was not like Esau: "When the days of mourning for my father are over, I
will kill my brother (27,41)", Jacob wished that Joseph pronounce his
forgiveness and that they shall ask him for it. This will be complete
repentance and final reconciliation. The brothers say *your father*, not
our father, feeling unworthy in their contrition. They admit that only
Joseph was a true son and that the father had been right in "loving
Joseph more than any of his children".

Verse 17. Jacob had them perform this scene of reconciliation not
while he was still alive; it might have been felt as forced upon them. It
shall be a message from the grave. When after my death the brothers are
afraid of Joseph's vengeance and ask his forgiveness, it will be I who
speaks to him. Thus Jacob had certainly spoken to the people around
him more than once before his death.

*And now, forgive the transgression of the servants of the God of your
father* They do not say "of your brothers", or "of the servants of
your—or even of—our father". By these words they take the last step to

the height on which only the truly repentant stand. The father who spoke thus is dead, but the God to whom he prayed, who had spoken through him, whose servants we declare ourselves to be, lives for ever. By these words the brothers become "sons of Israel" in the true sense. It is not the mortal father, but his God in whom the reconciliation shall be completed and in whom the brothers remain brothers beyond the death of the father.

Joseph wept when they spoke to him. He weeps because they believe a go-between necessary, because they are afraid of him, because they think him capable of such attitude, because he hears the father's voice. His youth which had been poisoned by their hatred rises up before him, and it is they who in their self-humiliation remind him of it. These his last tears are really their tears.

> 18His brothers also came and fell down before him, and said, "Behold, we are your servants." 19But Joseph said to them "Fear not, for am I in the place of God? 20As for you, you meant evil against me; but God meant it for good, to bring it about that many people should be kept alive as they are today. 21So do not fear; I will provide for you and your little ones." Thus he reassured them and comforted them.

We are your servants They try to anticipate the dreaded retaliation by offering it themselves. It is appropriate to pay homage to a distinguished brother, but to be his servant is deepest humiliation (compare 9,25). Their action which had brought Joseph into Egyptian bondage, is completely atoned.

Verse 19. *Am I in the place of God?* You speak to me as if I were. He may punish or revenge, but I could not do it, even if I wanted it as I am only a man. Yet you also misunderstand God.

Verse 20. *You meant evil against me, but God meant it for good.* This sentence is the moral quintessence of the story of Joseph and the culmination of Biblical ethics. Retaliation and punishment are superseded by faith in divine guidance which leads not to death, but means life. Their request for pardon is not answered by Joseph with 'I forgive you'. God's guidance does not even permit that to him, as God had not let them commit the deed. God had taken from the one the opportunity to offend, and from the other the gratification of forgiving. Certainly, there was evil against me, but you only *meant* it, and through God's "meaning" it has been turned into good. His "meaning" is doing. You should not fear me, but together we should thank God.

God has done so *to bring it about that many people should be kept alive*, not only you, but all of Egypt. God is the power that gives (30,2) and sustains life.

Verse 21. Joseph will treat his brothers after the father's death as during his lifetime; yet he does not want to be regarded as their generous benefactor. He says that he could not act differently because he is only God's instrument for the preservation of human life.

He reassured them, should a sting of self-accusation still remain in their minds, giving them plausible words and arguments.

The scene accomplishes the aim not only of the Joseph story, but of the entire tale of the patriarchs in establishing the ideal unity of the sons of Israel. The first book of the Bible tells the people of Israel who were its fathers. Yet, descent is only the body for the spirit which shall animate the true Israel. The spirit is not produced by mere descent, it is generated by a struggle between the human and the divine. The suffering in Egypt and the liberation from bondage will come to a people which is not only of the same blood, but united through their fathers in the God of the Fathers. Thus they can stand the suffering and deserve the liberation.

Abraham had two sons, but they had been incompatible. Isaac had two sons, but they had parted for ever. In Jacob's twelve sons the future seemed secured. Yet in their great number was implied the danger of disunity. Indeed, discord arose; they hated and persecuted the best son. However, at the end, complete reconciliation is achieved, not by a third party which mediates between them, but by their inner change. The hated son had waited for it and acknowledges it in brotherly love. The power which leads to reconciliation is the thought of their common father, alive and dead, and of the eternal God in whom the generations meet.

The plan of the entire book appears in its great outline. God, recognized in the story of creation as creator, guiding power, and judge of the universe, was the God of Abraham, Isaac, and Jacob, of Israel's patriarchs, and the sons of the last of them became true "sons of Israel". The great personal factors in the subsequent national history are God and Israel.

²²*Joseph dwelt in Egypt, he and his father's house; and Joseph lived a hundred and ten years.* ²³*And Joseph saw Ephraim's*

*children of the third generation; the children also of Machir the
son of Manasseh were born upon Joseph's knees.*

Verse 23. Joseph still sees descendants from his children. Ephraim is
mentioned first according to 48,5. From Manasseh he saw even great-
great-grandsons. He could take them on his lap. We see, as it were, the
picture of the fortunate old man. Yet the deeper intention of this report
is that they have still seen the ancestor Joseph. The last rays of the
setting sun had been shining upon them. They have sat on his lap; he
had drawn them to him and still participated in their education, and so
given them something of himself. The sons of Machir are contemporaries of Moses (Num. 26,29ff.), the fourth generation (15,16) which reen-
ters Canaan. As children they had seen Joseph, the pride and glory of
their people in Egypt; they shall live to see the redemption and the
Promised Land.

> [24]And Joseph said to his brothers, "I am about to die; but God will
> remember you, and bring you up out of this land to the land
> which he swore to Abraham, to Isaac, and to Jacob." [25]Then
> Joseph took an oath of the sons of Israel, saying, "God will
> remember you, and you shall carry up my bones from here." [26]So
> Joseph died, being a hundred and ten years old; and they
> enbalmed him, and he was put in a coffin in Egypt.

In these last words of Joseph the names Abraham, Isaac, and Jacob
stand side by side for the first time, as those who had received the
promise of the land. The story of the patriarchs is completed. Joseph
knows that the descendants will undergo suffering, but he leaves them
the assurance that God will remember them. *God will remember you*
will be the watchwords of redemption, and Moses will bring them from
the God of Abraham, Isaac, and Jacob (Ex. 3,16) and through them will
he be recognized as sent by God. (Ex. 4,31).

Verse 25. This oath which Joseph takes from "the sons of Israel" is
later executed by Moses (Ex. 13,19). The last words of Joseph, the truest
son of Israel, are worthy of his whole life. All honor and splendor of
Egypt have not changed him. Until death and beyond he remains a son
of Jacob and of his people. He wants to return to the land from which he
had come, to rest in its native soil, and thus to live on in the midst of his
people.

Verse 26. His coffin—the Hebrew says ark—waits in Egypt for the redemption and the home-coming of Israel into the Promised Land. This will be the theme of the following books which will have another ark, that of the Law in their center.

Abbreviations

The Books of the Hebrew Bible.

Gen	Genesis	Nahum	Nahum
Ex	Exodus	Hab	Habakkuk
Lev	Leviticus	Zeph	Zephaniah
Num	Numbers	Hag	Haggai
Deut	Deuteronomy	Zech	Zechariah
Josh	Joshua	Mal	Malachi
Judg	Judges	Psalms	Psalms
1 Sam	1 Samuel	Prov	Proverbs
2 Sam	2 Samuel	Job	Job
1 Kings	1 Kings	Song	Song of Solomon
2 Kings	2 Kings	Ruth	Ruth
Is	Isaiah	Lam	Lamentations
Jer	Jeremiah	Eccles	Ecclesiastes
Ezek	Ezekiel	Esther	Esther
Hos	Hosea	Dan	Daniel
Joel	Joel	Ezra	Ezra
Amos	Amos	Neh	Nehemiah
Obad	Obadiah	1 Chron	1 Chronicles
Jon	Jonah	2 Chron	2 Chronicles
Mic	Micah		

Of the books of the New Testament the following are quoted: Acts = *Acts of the Apostles;* Romans = *The Epistle of Paul to the Romans;* Hebrews = *The Epistle of Paul to the Hebrews.*

Books and Terms

(only those quoted in this abridged edition)

ABOT

"Fathers", a chapter of the Talmud, containing sayings of early rabbis, mostly ethical; printed in every Jewish prayer book.

ABRABANEL

Rabbi Isaac Abrabanel, Jewish scholar and statesman, born in Lisbon, Portugal, 1437, died in Venice, Italy, 1508. Hebrew commentary often printed.

B.C.E. and C.E.

Jewish way of speaking of the Christian Era: B.C.E. instead of B.C.; C.E. instead of A.D.

BECHOR SHOR

Joseph Bechor Shor lived at Orleans, France, in the 12th century; his Hebrew commentary on Genesis edited by Jellinek, Leipzig 1856.

BERESHIT RABBA

A homiletic Midrash to the book of Genesis in Hebrew and Aramaic, compiled from the 4th to the 6th century.

BIUR

Hebrew commentary by Solomon Dubno, born at Dubno, Russia, in 1738, died at Amsterdam, Netherlands, in 1813. Co-operated with Moses Mendelsohn.

BOGAZKÖY

A Turkish village with ruins of the city of Hattusa, capital of the Hittite empire between 1800 and 1200 B.C.E. Numerous ancient texts were found in the excavations.

DELITZSCH

Franz Delitzsch, Protestant German scholar. Neuer Commentar ueber die Genesis 1887.

DILLMANN

A. Dillmann, Protestant German scholar; Die Genesis, 6th edition 1892; an adaptation of an older commentary by Knobel.

EBEN HAEZER

The part of the Shulhan Aruh dealing with Jewish family law.

EL-AMARNA LETTERS

Discovered in 1887 at Tell el-Amarna in Middle Egypt; more than 370 letters now in museums; they came from the royal archives of Amen-hotep III and his son. Many writen by Canaanite scribes in Palestine, all in Babylonian language and characters. Some may be found in English translation in Ancient Near Eastern Texts relating to the Old Testament edited by James B. Pritchard, Princeton 1950.

EHRLICH

Arnold B. Ehrlich, Jewish scholar, born at Wlodawa, Poland, in 1848, died in New York 1919. Mikro Kipheshuto 1899-1901; Rand-glossen zur Hebraeischen Bibel 1908-1914.

ERMAN

A. Erman, German Egyptologist; Aegypten und Aegyptisches Leben im Altertum 1885.

GUNKEL

H. Gunkel, Protestant German scholar; Genesis uebersetzt und erkla-ert 1901; 4th edition 1917.

HAGGADA
Jewish legends and stories of early times, often imaginatively inter-
preting the Scriptures.
HAMMURABI
King of Babylon; ruled 1726-1686 B.C.E.; his law code has been
found; can be studied in Ancient Near Eastern Texts relating to the
Old Testament edited by James B. Pritchard, Princeton 1950.
HERODOTUS
Greek historian 484-425 B.C.E.
HIGHER CRITICISM
The use of historical methods in the study of the Bible, often claim-
ing that Bible books were written by authors different from those to
whom tradition ascribes them. Assumes, regarding Genesis, a num-
ber of authors writing at different times and from different points of
view; they are designated as J,E,P etc.
HISKUNI
Hiskiya ben Manoah, lived in the 13th century. Hebrew commentary
often printed.
IBN EZRA
Abraham ibn Ezra, Bible commentator and poet, born at Toledo,
Spain, in 1092, died probably in Rome, Italy, 1167. Hebrew commen-
tary often printed.
ISAAC ARAMA
Isaac ben Moses Arama, born in Spain about 1420, died in Naples,
Italy, 1492. His Hebrew commentary to the Pentateuch Akedat Yitz-
hak often printed.
JOSEPHUS
Flavius Josephus, Jewish historian 37-93 C.E.
KNOBEL
Protestant German scholar (see Dillmann).
LUZZATO
Samuel David Luzzato, born at Trieste, Italy, in 1800, died at Padua,
Italy, in 1865. Hebrew commentaries Hamishtadel, Vienna 1849,
and in connection with his Italian translation of the Pentateuch
Padua 1871 ff.
MAIMONIDES
Rabbi Moses ben Maimon, Jewish philosopher and scholar, born at
Cordova, Spain, in 1135, died at Fostat, Egypt, in 1204. His greatest
philosophical work was the More Nebuhim (Guide to the Perplexed);
many editions.
MIDRASH
Jewish interpretation of the Bible originating from approximately
500 B.C.E. to 900 C.E.; the term indicates the method of these inter-

pretations as well as the books in which they were collected, e.g. Bereshit Rabba.

ONKELOS

Ancient translator of the Pentateuch into Aramaic; little is known about his time and life, but the work is often printed.

PHILO

Jewish Hellenistic philosopher, 20 B.C.E. to 54 C.E.

PLUTARCH

Greek biographer and moralist 46-120 C.E.

PROCKSCH

O. Procksch, Protestant German scholar; Die Genesis uebersetzt und erklaert 1913.

RABBI AKIBA

Early Palestinian rabbi who died about 135 C.E. as martyr; systematizer of Jewish law.

RANKE

German scholar: Untersuchungen ueber den Pentateuch 1834-40

RAMBAN

Also called Nahmanides; Rabbi Moses ben Nahman, born at Gerona, Spain, in 1195, died at Acre, Israel, in 1270; Hebrew commentary often printed.

RASHBAM

Rabbi Samuel ben Meir, interpreter of Bible and Talmud, born at Rameru, France as grandson of Rashi in 1085, died there about 1158. Hebrew commentary on Genesis often printed.

RASHI

Rabbi Solomon ben Isaac, the most popular Jewish Bible and Talmud interpreter, born at Troyes, France, in 1040, died there in 1105. Hebrew commentaries often printed.

REDAK

Rabbi David Kimhi, a Jewish scholar born at Narbonne, France, about 1160, died there in 1235. Hebrew commentary on Genesis edited by Ginzburg, Petersburg 1842.

REGGIO

Isaac Samuel Reggio, born at Gorizia, Italy, in 1784, died there in 1855.; wrote a Hebrew commentary in connection with his translation of the Bible into Italian.

SANHEDRIN

Supreme Jewish council during the centuries preceding the destruction of Jerusalem in 70 C.E.

SEFER HAYASHAR

A midrash, probably compiled in the 12th century.

SEFORNO
Obadiah ben Jacob Seforno, born at Cesena, Italy, about 1475, died at Bologna, Italy, about 1550. Hebrew commentary often printed.

SENECA
Lucius Annaeus Seneca, Roman Stoic philosopher 4 B.C.E. to 65 C.E.

SEPTUAGINT
The Greek version of the Hebrew Bible, about 270 B.C.E.

SHULHAN ARUH
Jewish code of religious law by Joseph Caro, born in Spain 1488, died at Safed, Israel, in 1575.

SINUHE STORY
Si-Nuhe, an Egyptian official living in the 20th century B.C.E., wrote an account of his voluntary exile in Asia. The tale has survived in many manuscripts. English edition in Ancient Near Eastern Texts relating to the Old Testament edited by James B. Pritchard, Princeton 1950.

SIRAH
An apocryphical book, originally in Hebrew, perhaps written about 190 B.C.E.

SKINNER
J. Skinner, Protestant English scholar. A Critical and Exegetical Commentary on Genesis 1910–1912; 2nd edition 1930.

SPIRA
Juda Loeb Spira lived about 1800 in Russia. His Hebrew commentary is named Ha-rehassim Lebika.

SULZBERGER
Jewish scholar, wrote Am Ha-aretz, Philadelphia 1909.

TALMUD
The voluminous collection of Jewish law and tradition in Hebrew and Aramaic made between 200 and 500 C.E.; quoted according to name of individual books and page, e.g. Taanit 11a.

TARGUM
Ancient translation or paraphrase of the Hebrew Bible into Aramaic.

TORA
Hebrew name for the Pentateuch or Five Books of Moses.

TUCH
Fr. Tuch, Protestant German Bible scholar; Kommentar ueber die Genesis 1838; 2nd edition by A. Arnold and A. Merx 1858.

YAHUDA
Abraham S. Yahuda; Jewish scholar, born in Jerusalem 1877. Die Sprache des Pentateuch in ihren Beziehungen zum Aegyptischen 1929; English translation 1933.

Bibliography of

Benno Jacob

1890

1. *Das Buch Esther bei den LXX.* Wilhelm Keller. Giessen, 1890. (Separatabdruck aus der *Zeitschrift für die alttestamentliche Wissenschaft.* 1890.) 62 pp.

2. *Dr. Manuel Joel.* Gedächtnis-Rede. gehalten bei der Trauerfeier im jüdisch-theologischen Seminar am 16 November 1890. Breslau, 1890. Verlag von Wilhelm Jacobson und Co. 17 pp.

1893

3. *Dritter Jahresbericht über den Religionsunterricht der Synagogengemeinde zu Göttingen.* Ostern, 1893–1894. 16 pp.

1894

4. *Vierter Jahresbericht über den Religionsunterricht der Synagogengemeinde zu Göttingen.* Ostern, 1894–1895. 18 pp.

1895

5. *Fünfter Jahresbericht über den Religionsunterricht der Synagogengemeinde zu Göttingen.* Ostern, 1895–1896. 18 pp.

1896

6. "Beiträge zu einer Einleitung in die Psalmen." *Zeitschrift für die alttestamentliche Wissenschaft.* January 16, 1896–1900. pp. 129–181.

7. *Sechster Jahresbericht über den Religionsunterricht der Synagogengemeinde zu Göttingen.* Ostern, 1896–1897. 18 pp.

1898

8. *Siebenter Jahresbericht über den Religionsunterricht der Synagogengemeinde zu Göttingen.* Ostern, 1897–1898. 24 pp.

9. Zu Bacher's Bemerkungen. *Zeitschrift für die alttestamentliche Wissenschaft.* 1898. pp. 351–352.

10. *Unsere Bibel in Wissenschaft und Unterricht.* Vortrag gehalten in der

wissenschaftlichen Vereinigung jüdischer Schulmänner zu Berlin. Berlin, 1898. Druck Rudolf Mosse. 23 pp.

11. *Ein Mann nach dem Herzen Gottes.* Dr. Jakob Stein Seminardirektor a. D., gestorben February 6, 1898. Rede gehalten an seinem Grabe. Göttingen. 8 pp.

12. "Miscellen zu Exegese, Grammatik und Lexikon." Remarks to Is 7.25, Ez 4.10f, I Chr 9.25 (12.22 u.a.) Ps 58.9, 102.8, 111.10, Ex 9.14f Zecher ladovor. *Zeitschrift für die alttestamentliche Wissenschaft.* January 18 II, February, 1898. pp. 287–304.

13. *Achter Jahresbericht über den Religionsunterricht der Synagogengemeinde zu Göttingen.* Ostern, 1898–1899. 8 pp.

1899

14. *Yolad und Holid Erzeuger und Erzieher.* Eine bibelexegetische Untersuchung meiner lieben Helene gewidmet zur Geburt und Beschneidung unseres Erstgeborenen—Jacob Ernst Yaakov Eliyohu. Göttingen, September 24, October 1, 1899. 20 Tishri–27 Tishri 5660. 33 pp.

15. *Neunter Jahresbericht über den Religionsunterricht der Synagogengemeinde zu Göttingen.* Ostern, 1899–1900. 24 pp.

1900

16. "A Study in Biblical Exegesis." *Jewish Quarterly Review.* (Old Series) 1900. Vol. 12. pp. 434–451.

1901

17. *Predigten, Betrachtungen und ausgewählte Gebete von Dr. Benjamin Rippner.* (Aus seinem Nachlass zu einem Andachtsbuch für Synagoge und das Israelitische Haus zusammengestellt von Benno Jacob.) Berlin, 1901. M. Zulzer und Co. XV picture. 671 pp.

18. "Christlich-Palästinisches." *Zeitschrift der Deutsch-Morgenländischen Gesellschaft.* 1901.

1902

19. "Das hebräische Sprachgut im Christlich-Palästinischen." *Zeitschrift für die Wissenschaft für das alte Testament.* 1902.

1903

20. Mit Wilhelm Ebstein. *Die Medizin im Alten Testament.* Stuttgart, Verlag von Ferdinand Enke, 1901. iv. 184. *Die Medizin im Neuen Testament und im Talmud.* Stuttgart, Verlag von Ferdinand Enke, 1903. vii. 338 pp.

21. "'Im Namen Gottes' Eine sprachliche und religionsgeschichliche Untersuchung über Schem und Onoma im alten und neuen Testament." *Vierteljahrsschrift für Bibelkunde. Talmudische und Patristische Studien.* June, 1903. Vol. 1. Heft 1. Berlin. Verlag S. Calvary. pp. 128–148.

22.   "Im Namen . . ." Review of Heitmüller W., *Im Namen Jesu' Monatsschrift für jüdische Geschichte und Wissenschaft*. Göttingen, 1903. pp. 162–184.

23.   *'Im Namen Gottes.' Eine sprachliche und religionsgeschichtliche Untersuchung zum Alten und Neuen Testament*. Berlin. Verlag von S. Calvary und Co. 1903. iii 176 pp.
     Reviewed in *Deutsche Literaturzeitung*, No. 39, October 1, 1904. pp 2338–2344, by W. Brandt, Amsterdam. *Der Israelit. Central Organ für das orthodoxe Judenthum*, No. 8, December 29, 1904. (Literarische Beilage zu No. 103, 104.) pp. 2235–2236, by J. Holzer. *Literarisches Zentralblatt für Deutschland*, No. 47, Vol. 55, November 19, 1904. pp. 1570–1571, by SK. *Theologische Rundschau*, 1905, Heft 6. pp. 250–253, by Nowack. Also *Allgemeine Zeitung des Judentums*, Vol. 69, No. 8, February 24, 1905. pp. 90–93, by Hermann Vogelstein. Also *Revue Juive*, p. 291, by Mayer Lambert.

1904

24.   *Grabrede bei der Beerdigung unserer lieben Franziska Katz*. October 22, 1903. Göttingen, 1904. 8 pp.

1905

25.   *Grabreden bei der Beerdigung unserer geliebten Eltern* (Theodor Benfey und Juliet Benfey). Göttingen, 1905. 15 pp.

26.   *Der Pentateuch. Exegetisch-Kritische Forschungen*. Leipzig. Verlag von Veit und Co. 1905. Zwei Tafeln viii. 412 pp.

27.   "Berichtigungen zu Mandelkerns grosser Konkordanz." *Zeitschrift für die alttestamentliche Wissenschaft*. Vol. 25. pp. 343–345.

1906

28.   *Entgegnungen auf Prof. Königs Besprechung von Jacob 'Der Pentateuch.'* Sonderabdruck aus *Theologische Studien und Kritiken*. January, 1906. Heft 3. Gotha. pp. 481–484.

29.   "Genesis." *The Jewish Encyclopedia*. New York. Vol. 5. 1906. pp. 599–610.

30.   "Exodus." II. Critical View. *The Jewish Encyclopedia*. New York. Vol. 5, 1906. pp. 303–305.

31.   "Deuteronomy." II. Critical View. *Jewish Encyclopedia*. New York. Vol. 4. 1906. pp. 543–546.

32.   *Festpredigt* gehalten am 1 März 1906 zur Feier des fünfzigjährigen Bestehens der israelitischen Waisen-Erziehungsanstalt zu Paderborn. pp. 1–10.

1907

33.   *Die Wissenschaft des Judentums. Ihr Einfluss auf die Emanzipation der Juden*. Berlin. 1907.

34.   "Eine neue Wendung in der Pentateuchkritik. Eine Erwiderung." (Reply to review of his own *Der Pentateuch* as reviewed by Eduard König.)

Zeitschrift für evangelischen Religionsunterricht. Berlin. January 18, 1907. Heft 6. pp. 301–308.

1908

35. "Besprechung von F. Coblenz Jüdische Religion. Ein Lehrbuch." *Monatsheft fur Geschichte und Wissenshaft des Judenthums.* Vol. 52. Heft 7/8. Quelle und Meyer. 1908. pp. 497–508.

36. *Eine endgültige Abfertigung.* Herr Dr. Coblenz in Bielefeld. Verfasser der 'Jüdischen Religion.' Dortmund. pp. 11. (appeared about 1909. Reply to answer of Coblenz to critical book review published in Monatsschrift für Geschichte und Wissenschaft des Judentums 1908. Heft 7/8)

37. "Juedische Religion." *Ost und West. Illustrierte Monatsschrift für das Gesamte Judentum.* Heft 11. VIII Jahrgang. November, 1908. (Reprint of Review of book by F. Coblenz Jüdische Religion. Leipzig. 1908.) pp. 652–661.

38. "Miscellen zu Exegese, Grammatik und Lexikon." *Zeitschrift für die Wissenschaft des alten Testamentes.* 1908.

1909

39. *Die Abzählungen in den Gesetzen der Bücher Leviticus und Numeri.* Frankfurt a.M. Verlag von J. Kauffman 1909. 35 pp.

1910

40. "Zur Stellung des Rabbiners. Eine Antwort." (Response to a reply to his article by same name in this journal. Critique published by Felix Makower.) *Allgemeine Zeitung des Judentums.* February 10, 1910.

1912

41. "Erklärung einiger Hiobstellen." *Zeitschrift für Wissenschaft des alten Testamentes.* 1912.

42. *Die Thora Moses. I Das Buch.* Volksschrift über die jüdische Religion. I Jahrgang, 3. und 4. Doppelheft. Frankfurt a.M. J. Kauffman. 1912/1913. 100 pp.

43. "Liebermann von Sonnenberg." (about personal experiences with this anti-Semite in Göttingen and surrounding towns.) *Mitteilungen des Verbandes der jüdischen Jugendvereine Deutschlands.* Nummer 3. 2, Jahr 3. Berlin. February 1912. pp. 6–9.

1914

44. "Bibelwissenschaft." Reviews of Johannes Doeller. *Compendium hermeneuticae biblicae.* 1914. Bernhard Mairhofer. *Sev. Luegs Biblische Realkonkordanz.* Mainz. 1913. Paul Kaegi. *Die Bibel Eine moderne Bearbeitung und Nachdichtung.* München. 1914. Daniel Volter. *Der Ursprung von Passah und Mazzoth, neu untersucht.* Leiden. 1914. *Bibliographischer Vierteljahrsbericht für die jüdische Literatur.* Vol. 1, Number 1. Leipzig.

June 1, 1914. Wilhelm Caspari. *Die israelitischen Propheten.* Leipzig. June 1, 1914.

46. "Segen. Eine Betrachtung." *Freie Jüdische Lehrerstimme.* Number 1, Vol. 3. Wien. March, 1914. pp. 1–3.

1915

47. "Der Herr der Heerscharen. Aus den Kriegsbetrachtungen." (Sonderabdruck aus der *Zeitschrift des Centralvereins deutscher Staatsbürger jüdischen Glaubens 'Im deutschen Reich'.*)

1916

48. *Quellenscheidung und Exegese im Pentateuch.* Leipzig. 1916. Verlag von M. W. Kauffman. 108 pp.

1919

49. *Isidor Goldschmidt. Rede gehalten an seinem Grabe.* Dortmund. 1919.

1920

50. "Professor Droogstoppel. 'Im deutschen Reich'. *Zeitschrift des Centralvereins deutscher Staatsbürger jüdischen Glaubens.* (Review of Friederich Delitzsch 'Die grosse Täuschung. Kritische Betrachtungen zu den alttestamentlichen Berichten über Israels Eindringen in Kanaan, die Gottesoffenbarung am Sinai und die Wirksamkeit der Propheten.' Berlin. 1920.) Berlin. No. 6, 7, 8. Vol. 26. July–August, 1920. pp. 181–190; 222–233.

51. *Krieg, Revolution und Judentum.* Rede gehalten im Zentralverein deutscher Staatsbürger jüdischen Glaubens. Berlin. 1920. Philo Verlag (Neue, durch Nachtrag vermehrte Ausgabe. 36.–55. Tausend.) 32 pp.

52. *Die Juden und das Berliner Tageblatt.* Ein Briefwechsel. Seulen-Verlag. Berlin, 1920. 20 pp.

1922

53. "Gott und Pharao." *Monatsschrift für die Geschichte und Wissenschaft des Judenthums.* 1922. pp. 118–126; 202–211; 266–290.

54. "Moses am Dornbusch. Die beiden Hauptbeweisstellen im Pentateuch, Ex. 3 und 6, aufs Neue exegetisch geprüft." *Monatsschrift für die Geschichte und Wissenschaft des Judenthums.* Vol. 66. 1922. pp. 1–33; 116–138; 180–200.

1923

55. "The Decalogue. 'Ten words'." *Jewish Quarterly Review.* Vol. 14, Number 2. October, 1923. pp. 141–187.

1925

56. *Installation Der Orden B'nai Briss.* Mitteilungen der Grossloge für Deutschland VIII. Berlin. December, 1925. Number 12. (Rede) pp. 230–233.

1926

57. "Einführung in das I. Buch Moses. Die Schöpfung." *Der Morgen.* 1926. Vol. 1, Number 1. pp. 35–54.

58. "Einführung in das I. Buch Moses. Das Paradies." *Der Morgen.* 1926. Vol. 1, Number 2. pp. 195–208.

59. "Einführung in das I. Buch Moses. Kain." *Der Morgen.* 1926. Vol. 1, Number 3. pp. 348–357.

60. "Einführung in das I. Buch Moses. Übermenschen und Sinflut. Völkertafel und Turmbau." *Der Morgen.* 1926. Vol. 1, Number 4. pp. 463–479.

61. "Einführung in das I. Buch Moses. Die Erzväter." *Der Morgen.* 1926. Vol. 1, Number 6. pp. 671–680.

1927

62. "Einführung in das I. Buch Moses. Die Erzväter (zweiter Teil)." *Der Morgen.* 1927. Vol. 2, Number 1. pp. 97–104.

63. "Einführung in das I. Buch Moses. Abraham." *Der Morgen.* 1927. Vol. 2, Number 3. pp. 281–290.

64. "Einführung in das I. Buch Moses. Abraham." *Der Morgen.* 1927. Vol. 2, Number 5. pp. 507–513.

65. "Einführung in das I. Buch Moses. Abraham." *Der Morgen.* 1927. Vol. 2, Number 6. pp. 564–576.

1928

66. "Belloc. Eine Replik." *Allgemeine Rundschau.* Vol. 25, Number 6. February 11, 1928. p. 90. (Reply to answer of review of Hilaire Belloc's 'Die Juden' by Rudolf Obermeier.) Verlagsort München.

67. "Antisemitismus. Einleitung. I. Im Altertum. III Von der Franzoesischen Revolution bis zur Gegenwart. Antisemitische internationale Kongresse." *Encyclopaedia Judaica.* Berlin. 1928. Vol. 2. pp. 955–972; 1007–1045; 1099–1101.

68. "Zum Antisemitismus im Altertum." *Monatsschrift für höhere Schulen.* Sonderabdruck. Berlin. Weidmannsche Buchhandlung. 1928. pp. 127–131.

1929

69. *Auge um Auge. Eine Untersuchung zum Alten und Neuen Testament.* Berlin. Philo Verlag. 1929. 144 pp.

70. "Die Zehngebote. Betr̨ chtung zum Wochenfest." *Nachrichtenblatt der Synagogen Gemeinde des Kreises Saarbrücken. 1929. Vol. 2, Number 5. p. 1.*

1930

71. *Die Biblische Sintfluterzählung. Ihre Literarische Einheit.* (Vortrag gehalten auf dem Internationalen Orientalistenkongress zu Oxford am 30, August 1928.) Berlin. 1930. Philo Verlag. 13 pp.
72. "Mischehen." *Der Morgen.* 1930. Vol. II, Heft 3. pp. 257–278.
73. "Zeremonial—und Sittengesetz." *Gemeindeblatt der Jüdischen Gemeinde zu Berlin.* 20 Jahrgang Nr. 12. December, 1930. pp. 545–551.

1931

74. "Verbindlichkeit des Zeremonialgesetzes? Entgegnung." *Jüdisch-liberale Zeitung.* 1931. 1, Beilage. Vol. II, Number 26/27. p. 4.

1933

75. "Den bibliska syndaflodsberattelsen och des litterara enhet." Foredrag pa internationelle orientalistkongressen i Oxford 1928. (*Bibliskt Manadshafte* 1933. Number 4. April. pp. 130–134; pp. 158–160. May. Number 5.)
76. *Helene Jacob geb. Stein. Worte des Gedenkens, gesprochen am Jahrestage.* Hamburg. May 10, 1933. (April 4, 1872–May 19, 1932.) 11 pp.

1934

77. *Das Erste Buch der Tora Genesis. übersetzt und erklärt.* Schocken Verlag. Berlin. 1934. 1055 pp.

1935

78. "Buchbesprechung Jüdische Religionslehre." *Jüdische Literatur.* February 21, 1935. Number 8. p. 18.

1938

79. "Israel in Agypten. Rückblick auf Exodus 1–15." *Jahrbuch fur Jüdische Geschichte und Literatur.* Band 31, 1938. Berlin. pp. 84–98.
80. Editor, Das Judentum der Gegenwart. *Encyclopaedia Judaica.* 1929–1938. Verlag Eschkol. Berlin.

1942

81. "The Childhood and Youth of Moses, the Messenger of God." Essays in honour of the Very Rev. Dr. J. H. Hertz, Chief Rabbi of the United Hebrew Congregations of the British Empire. London, Edward Goldston. 1942. pp 245–260.

1946

82. "Aus der Rede zur Fahnenweihe der Rheno-Bavaria." (Auszug aus den KC Blattern 1920.) KC Blätter Festschrift. October 23, 1946. New York. 50 Jahre KC. 60 Jahre Viadrina. pp. 19–20.

1961

83. "From B. Jacob's Commentary on Genesis." The Angels visit with Abraham: Genesis 18.1–33; Jacob and the Angel: Genesis 32.25–31; Judah and Tamar: Genesis 38.1–30. (Translated with introduction by Ernest I. Jacob.) *Conservative Judaism.* Summer, 1961. pp. 3–21.

1962

84. "Krieg, Revolution und Judentum." *Aus Geschichte und Leben der Juden in Westfalen.* Eine Sammelschrift. Ner Tamid Verlag. Frankfurt a Main. 1962. pp. 93–109. (With picture of author and copy of p. 891 of Genesis commentary.)

1964

85. "The Decalogue. The First Three Commandments." (Translated by Walter Jacob with introduction by A. Joshua Heschel.) *Judaism.* Spring, 1964. Vol. 13, Number 2. pp.

1971

86. "Hear, O Israel." (Translated by Ernest I. Jacob and Walter Jacob) *Jewish Spectator.* April 1971. pp. 5-7.

Undated Publications

87. Jacob Bernays. Unsere Mitarbeiter an der deutschen Wissenschaft." *Israelitisches Wochenblatt.* p. 446.

88. "Ein Wort an unsere Akademiker." *Monatsschrift für Liberales Judentum.* Separatabdruck. Dortmund. 16 pp.

89. "Der erste deutsche Jude. Moses Mendelssohn." p. 461.

90. "Amen, Eine Betrachtung." Separatabdruck aus *Freie Jüdische Lehrerstimme.* II Jahrgang. Number 7. p. 5.

91. *Das hebräische Sprachgut im Christlich-Palästinischen.* 30 pp.

92. "Die Stimme des Lehrers." Separatabdruck aus *Freie Jüdische Lehrerstimme.* Vol. II, Number 1. p. 8. with notes at end.

93. *Die Söhrie Moses.* 4 pp.

Life And Work of Benno Jacob

1. Frederick T. Haneman. "Benno Jacob." *Jewish Encyclopedia.* New York. 1904. Vol. 7. p. 30.

2. Max Wiener. "Benno Jacob." *Jüdisches Lexikon*. Berlin. 1922. Vol. 3. p. 107.

3. Jakob Klatzkin. "Benno Jacob." *Encyclopedia Judaica*. Berlin. 1931. Vol. 8. p. 738.

4. Ludwig Holländer. "Zum 70. Geburtstag von Rabbiner Dr. Benno Jacob." (Viadrina) pp. 3-5. "Benno Jacob's Kampf mit Liebermann von Sonnenberg." *K.C. Blätter Zeitschrift des Kartell Convents der Verbindung Deutscher Studenten jüdischen Glaubens*. January, 1933. Vol. 23, No. 1. Berlin. pp. 3-7.

5. "Benno Jacob." *Universal Jewish Encyclopedia*. New York. 1942, Vol. 6, p. 13.

6. Ernest I. Jacob. "Benno Jacob." *Bulletin Congregation Habonim*. May, 1945. Vol. 5, Number 7. pp. 4-6.

7. M. Eschelbacher. "Zur Erinnerung an Benno Jacob." *Mitteilungsblatt für die jüdischen Gemeinden in Westfalen*. October/November, 1959. Number 3. p. 4.

8. Ernest I. Jacob. "The Torah Scholarship of B. Jacob." *Conservative Judaism*. Summer. 1961. pp. 3-21.

9. Ernest I. Jacob. "Life and Work of B. Jacob." *Paul Lazarus Gedenkbuch*. Beiträge zur Würdigung der letzten Rabbinergeneration in Deutschland. Jerusalem. 1961. pp. 93-100.

10. M. Eschelbacher. "Benno Jacob 1862-1945." *Association of Jewish Refugees Information*. London. September, 1962. Vol. 17, Number 9. p. 8.

11. F. Goldschmidt. "A Vigorous Fighter." *Association of Jewish Refugees Information*. London. September, 1962. Vol. 17, Number 9. p. 8.

12. Max Eschelbacher. "Benno Jacob (1862-1945)" *Tradition und Erneuerung*. Zeitschrift der Vereinigung für Religiös-Liberales Judentum in der Schweiz. December, 1962. Number 14. pp. 210-215.

13. Ernest I. Jacob. "Benno Jacob als Rabbiner in Dortmund." *Aus Geschichte und Leben der Juden in Westfalen*. Eine Sammelschrift. Ner TamidVerlag. Frankfurt a.M. 1962. pp. 89-92.

14. Kurt Wilhelm. "Benno Jacob, A Militant Rabbi." *Year Book VIII*. Leo Baeck Institute. New York. 1962. pp. 75-94.

15. Jacob Rotschild. "Benno Jacob". *Encyclopedia Judaica*. Vol 9, Jerusalem. 1971. pp. 1206 f.

66287

BS
1235
.J27213
1974

Jacob, Benno.
        The first book
    of the Bible:
    Genesis

L3

DATE DUE

NOV 1 3 2006	

GAYLORD   PRINTED IN U.S.A.